for the 21st Century Mind

Richard Dolan Press
Rochester, New York 14619
USA

Copyright ©2014 by Richard M. Dolan
All rights reserved. No part of this book may be used or reproduced in any manner whatsoever without written permission except in the case of brief quotations embodied in critical articles or reviews.

Richard Dolan Press and logo are registered trademarks of Richard Dolan Press.

Library of Congress Cataloging-in-Publication Data

Dolan, Richard Michael
    UFOs for the 21st Century Mind: A Fresh Guide to an Ancient
  Mystery / by Richard M. Dolan
  486 p. cm.
  Includes bibliography and index.
  ISBN 978-1495291609
  1. Unidentified Flying Objects
  2. History.
  I. Dolan, Richard M. II. Title

First published in the United States by Richard Dolan Press

First Printing: January 2014

Cover concept and illustration by Michelle Montany
Cover design by Mark Brabant (http://hoveringobject.com)
Back cover photo of author © by Michelle Montany

All photographs and illustrations in this book were reproduced with the kind permission of their owners, or else are in the public domain.

Manufactured in the United States of America.

UFOs

for the 21st Century Mind

A Fresh Guide to an Ancient Mystery

Richard M. Dolan

Richard Dolan Press

Also by Richard M. Dolan

UFOs and the National Security State: Chronology of a Cover-Up, 1941-1973. Hampton Roads Publishing, 2002.

UFOs and the National Security State: The Cover-Up Exposed, 1973-1991. Keyhole Publishing Company, 2009.

A.D. After Disclosure: When the Government Finally Reveals the Truth About Alien Contact (with Bryce Zabel), New Page Books, a Division of Career Press, Inc. 2012.

To the countless UFO researchers of the past who made this research possible, and to the truth seekers of today and tomorrow.

Contents

Acknowledgments. xii

Foreword by George Noory. xiv

Introduction. 1

Chapter 1. What Are UFOs?. 7
    What are UFOs? 8
    Getting Technical 9
    And Yet 13
    What Can UFOs Be? 15
    UFOs and the Problem of Science 17
    Who Decides What is Proof?. 20
    Implications: What if They are Real? 21
    Political Implications. 23
    Economic Implications.. 26
    Religious Implications 27
    Scientific Implications 29
    Cultural Implications 30
    Global Implications. 32

Chapter 2. Theories of Ancient Visitation. 33
    Our Journey to Understand the Past. 33
    Ancient Images. 35
    A Lost Civilization?. 38
    Pyramids. 40
    Other Structures, Inexplicable and Explicable. .. 43
    Flying Trinkets. 46
    Ancient Writings: Vimanas 48
    Ancient Writings: Egypt. 51
    Ancient Writings: The Bible. 54
    Ancient Astronauts. 55
    The Annunaki.. 56
    More Ancient Stories.. 62
    Charles Fort. 67
    Summary. 69

Chapter 3. Into Modernity: Airships, Foo Fighters,
    and Flying Saucers, 1896 to 1969. 71
    The Airships. 71
    After the Airships. 76
    World War Two.. 80
    Ghost Rockets. 86

    1947. 87
    Belgian Congo Mines. 91
    1952 and Washington, DC. 92
    Aerial Encounters and Air Space Violations 93
    Encounters with Beings 94
    Abductions. 99
    Operation Dominic: UFO Crash in the Pacific. 101
    The Crescendo of the 1960s. 106
    Minot AFB. 111
    Malmstrom AFB. 112
    Shag Harbor. 114
    Mutilations and More. 115

Chapter 4. UFO Secrecy and Those Who Fought It. 118
    The Early Cover-Up. 119
    1947: The Dam Breaks. 123
    1948: Estimating the Situation. 128
    The Case of James Forrestal. 133
    Unknown Objects Over Sensitive Airspace. 135
    The Crisis of 1952. 137
    Challenging the Air Force. 145
    More Sightings and A New Crisis. 149
    The Condon Committee. 154
    The End of an Era. 158

Chapter 5. Digging Deeper—The Breakaway
    Civilization. 162
    UFO Crash: Roswell. 165
    UFO Crash: Aztec. 170
    UFO Crash: Kingman. 172
    UFO Crash: Brazil. 174
    UFO Crash: Las Vegas. 175
    UFO Crash: Kecksburg. 176
    UFO Crash: Bolivia. 179
    Other Crashes. 180
    Stringfield's Leaks. 181
    Going Deeper Still: The Sarbacher-Walker Saga. 184
    Bodies, Technology, and Area 51. 186
    German Technology. 195
    The Requirements of Secrecy. 202
    The Breakaway Civilization. 204
    Paying For It All. 207

Chapter 6. High Strangeness—UFOs from
    1970 to 1990. 211
    The Delphos UFO of 1971. 211
    The Wave of 1973: Two Interesting Cases. 214

High Strangeness in Spain.. 216
The Strange Year of 1975 217
Intruder Alert... 218
A Sphere over the Canaries........................... 222
Incident over Tehran. 223
Around the World During the Late 1970s........... 224
Enter the 1980s.. 228
The Hudson Valley Sightings........................... 232
Around the World and in Space. 235
Gulf Breeze... 239
Area 51... 241
Soviet UFOs.. 242
Triangles over Belgium. 246
Summary... 247

Chapter 7. UFOs, 1991 to the Present................... 249
The Beginning of the Video Era..................... 250
UFOs that Weren't. 253
The Tether Incident... 255
Terror in the Air... 258
Encounters with "Them"................................... 261
The Khoury Incident... 262
The Kelly Cahill Case... 264
Schoolchildren in Zimbabwe......................... 265
An Entity in Varginha, Brazil........................... 267
The Washington Elk Case................................ 268
Who Are These Beings?...................................... 270
The Spectacular Yukon Sighting..................... 271
The Phoenix Lights... 273
Triangles. 276
UFOs in the 21st Century.................................. 280
UFO Over O'Hare Airport................................. 284
And Over Stephenville, Texas. 285
Northern Canadian Military Encounter.............. 286
The Turkish UFO Videos. 289
How Deep Does This Go?................................. 290

Chapter 8. Contact and Abduction...................... 291
Where the Rubber Meets the Road. 291
Contact vs. Abduction... 292
Alien Abductions: Birth of an Idea................. 294
The Hill Abduction Case..................................... 295
The Herb Schirmer Abduction........................... 299
The Charles Moody Abduction. 300
Fire In the Sky: Travis Walton........................... 302
The Andreasson Affair... 305
Enter Budd Hopkins... 307

 Into the Darkness. 308
 Alien Implants. 311
 John Mack. 315
 The Other Side of Contact. 318
 Adamski and the 1950s. 321
 Telepathic Contact: The Affa Case. 324
 Towards Assessing the Claims. 327

Chapter 9. The Growth of Ufology. 330
 From the Ashes of the Condon Committee. 330
 American Ufology: The Big Four. 331
 Scientific Ufology. 334
 Intelligence Community Penetration. 335
 Entering the Weird. 338
 Psychosocial Explanations. 340
 FOIA and the Crash Retrieval Syndrome. 341
 The Intelligence Empire Strikes Back: The
   Early 1980s. 342
 The Eve of the Internet and the State of Ufology. 344
 The First Bulletin Boards. 345
 Out Come the Leaks. 346
 Bob Lazar and Area 51. 348
 Rumors of Disclosure Around 1990. 349
 The Web and the First Wave of Research. 350
 21st Century: Explosion 351
 YouTube and Facebook. 352
 The Decline of Professional Journalism. 353
 Whistleblowers, Real and Alleged. 355
 Increase of Sightings. 356
 The Need for Proper Investigations. 358
 The Modern Armchair Researcher. 360
 The Philosophical Divide. 366
 Ufology's Future. 369
 Ufology: Getting Personal. 370

Chapter 10. Who Are They? What Do They Want? 373
 The Problem of Human Perception. 373
 So. Who. Are. They?. 375
 The Grays. 377
 Human-Looking Aliens. 384
 Other Types of Beings. 391
 Channeled Beings. 393
 New Age Aliens. 394
 A Word on Crop Circles. 399
 Getting to the Bottom Line. 401

**Chapter 11. Weird Science: Propulsion, Energy,
   Spacetime, and Consciousness.** **403**
   The Radical Science of UFOs. 403
   Propulsion. 406
   Electrogravitics. 408
   Energy. 413
   Spacetime. 417
   Miguel Alcubierre. 418
   Dimensions and Strings. 420
   Time. 424
   Entanglement, Consciousness, and the "Others". 427
   Living with Uncertainty. 428
   Consciousness. 429
   Entanglement. 432
   Connecting to Ufology. 434

Chapter 12. Into the Future, Into Ourselves. **436**
   Humanity's Trajectory. 436
   What Can Cause Disclosure?. 440
   What Happens After Disclosure?. 442
   Energy. 445
   A Cultural Revolution. 449
   Science and the Scientists. 454
   Computing and Technology. 456
   Geopolitics. 458
   The Future. 464
   The Long View. 465
   Humanity's Destiny. 467

Conclusion. **470**

Index. **473**

About the Author. **485**

Acknowledgments

Writing this book has been an adventure for me, and there have been a number of people who have helped me with their encouragement, insights, research support, and manuscript review.

I would like to thank my friend Kelly Weary, who in 2011 invited me to prepare an *Introduction to Ufology* course for the online International Metaphysical University. The twelve lectures I created for that program formed the foundation for this book, and Kelly was there throughout the creation of that lecture series, providing encouragement and much helpful conversation throughout.

Mike Clelland, Race Hobbes, Chase Kloetzke, Sam Maranto, Peter Robbins, and Jennifer Stein. They are all my trusted friends, confidants, and professional colleagues. In addition to the many stimulating conversations I have had with each of them about all matters ufological, they were careful readers of this manuscript, whether in full or part, often providing helpful ideas for inclusion in this book.

The late James Allen. During the summer of 2013, James and I had several long conversations about the science of UFO propulsion and related matters. During that time, in addition to the valuable research tips he provided, we developed a genuine friendship. His unexpected death later that year was heartbreaking to me, and I shall miss him.

My Rochester friends, Jason Mombert and Chuck Harrison, who listened to me so often discussing the progress of this book, and who provided much needed companionship during a tumultuous year.

Dr. Hal Puthoff, of the Institute for Advanced Study at Austin, who read this manuscript carefully and, as always, provided me with invaluable commentary.

George Noory, host of *Coast to Coast AM*, who graciously offered to write the Foreword to this book, and for which I will always be thankful. I also appreciate the support of George's producer, my good friend Tom Danheiser.

I was very fortunate to have a number of careful editors and proofreaders of this book. Foremost among these were Holly Kennedy, Anne Meisingset, Dr. Joe Buchman, and Debra Dalock. It is impossible to overstate how much I owe these people. Each of them looked over my manuscript carefully, each of them provided unique insights, commentary, suggestions, and corrections. In particular, I owe a special thanks to Joe and Debbie, who during the final stages of the manuscript attended their task with a near fanatical attention to detail and an unerring eye for the interests of the reader. Their impeccable proofreading, fact-checking, and consultation made this a measurably better book.

Finally, my friend, Michelle Montany. More than anyone else, she was there for me during this entire project. Her dedicated friendship, to say nothing of her insightful commentary, were of greater help to me than any author has a right to expect. On top of all that, she conceived of this book's cover illustration, and then painstakingly created it. It's the best cover I could have imagined. No—better than I could have imagined. Thank you, Michelle. I doubt I can ever express to you the full extent of my gratitude.

Beyond these people, there are countless others who have given me their friendship and advice. I can never list all of them, there are simply too many. I want all of them to know, however, that they have my undying thanks.

Despite the substantial help and support I have received from such wonderful friends, all limitations, oversights, and errors of this book are my responsibility alone.

Richard M. Dolan
Rochester, New York
January 2014

Foreword
by George Noory

I will never forget the excitement I felt as a boy when reading a book given to me by my mother: *We Are Not Alone*, by Walter Sullivan, the great science writer for the *New York Times*. What an eye-opening book it was for me to learn Sullivan's theories about how the universe was teeming with life, about how humanity was probably just one tiny part of the vast ocean of activity that filled our cosmos. Not long after that, I read an article in *Look* magazine about the famous UFO abductees, Betty and Barney Hill. After that, I was hooked. All I wanted to do was go into broadcasting and interview experts on these fascinating subjects and learn everything I could possibly learn about the great mysteries of our world.

So there has never been a question in my mind that UFOs are real, that they mean something important, and that their existence means that other intelligent beings are interested in humanity and this beautiful planet we live on. Throughout the many paths of my life, I never lost that interest, that curiosity. I kept it during my years as Executive Producer at WJBK-TV in Detroit, and also during my years in the U.S. Naval Reserve. In 1996, I began hosting the late night program, *Nighthawk,* on KTRS radio in St. Louis, and was able to fulfill my dream of talking to knowledgeable people about ideas and possibilities that exist at the outer edges of our reality.

Since then, as host of *Coast to Coast AM*, I have been incredibly fortunate to be part of a growing family of over 500 affiliates around the world that brings the best of the best from so many subjects to millions of listeners every night. Having the opportunity to talk to such amazing guests has been an education for me. We discuss and analyze just about everything that matters in our world today, whether it's current events, consumer rights, economics, new technologies, cutting-edge physics, mysteries in space, spirituality, prophecies, consciousness, conspiracies, or the New World Order.

And of course, UFOs, a subject that continues to fascinate me. However, in a field that is so complex and mysterious, it's easy to feel like you are lost in a maze. In the first place, there are simply so many aspects to it. Not only are there thousands upon thousands of UFO sightings of the past, but more baffling sightings happen every day. Then there are claims of alien abduction and even implants, without a doubt one of the most intriguing parts of the phenomenon. Beyond this, there are countless scientific questions connected to the subject, whether you are interested in antigravity, or space travel, or multiple dimensions, or time travel. It's all riveting, but there is simply so much to digest.

But UFOs can be challenging for another reason. That's because there is a lot of bad information out there mixed in with the good research. You know there is something very important going on, but you can't always feel confident that you are getting reliable information.

That is one reason I have always appreciated Richard Dolan. I first met Richard in 2001 when he was my guest on KTRS. Right away, I could see that he was someone who was destined to make an impression in the field of UFO research. Over the years, he has been a frequent guest of mine on *Coast to Coast AM*, a true no-nonsense researcher and author who probes the government's relationship to UFOs: what it knows, what it's hiding. He always comes to the table with engaging conversation and thoughtful insights on UFOs, cover-ups, and the important matter of Disclosure—that is, if or when the government reveals the truth about UFOs. The thing that comes through time and again about Richard is that he does his homework and is one of the most committed people I know in the field. I consider him a bulldog in search of the truth, someone who won't stop until he reaches his destination.

In our interviews, we have discussed the themes of his previous books, his two volumes of history, *UFOs and the National Security State*, probably the most comprehensive and reliable guides to the modern history of UFOs. That is how we all got to know him. Then he did something quite different: he peered into the future by writing *A.D. After Disclosure*, looking ahead at a world in which UFO secrecy were to end. So many questions come to mind. Can Disclosure ever really happen? How might it change our world? What happens to our politics, economy, and society? Will we ever have genuine contact with extraterrestrials? Richard took on these questions and helped to open up an entire new area of study for the rest of us.

Now he has done something new once again with this book, *UFOs for the 21st Century Mind.* In a field that can be so confusing, so complex, he has taken his many years of thinking about UFOs and written a completely fresh overview of the entire subject. While I read this book, it became obvious to me that something like this has been long overdue.

Many of the topics in here are ones I've discussed with him previously: the history, the politics, the cover-up, Disclosure. All of these are handled with the insight, depth of research, and passion for truth that I have come to expect from him. Even so, much in here is new, including several incredible UFO sightings that have never appeared anywhere else, along with a deep analysis of just how the UFO cover-up has damaged the civil liberties of people around the world.

But what jumps out about this book is that it is covers so much more even than this, everything from ancient aliens, to abduction, to channeling, and thoughts on who or what these other beings might be. There is also a lot of fresh thinking about just what UFOs are. After all, how do we separate genuine UFO encounters from sightings of modern drones and other off-the-shelf technologies used by ordinary people?

One of the most fascinating parts of this book are the many ways that UFOs challenge our scientific paradigms. From something as simple as propulsion technology (how do these objects travel the way they do?) to space-time, to dimensions, entanglement, and consciousness—all of these are handled clearly and evenly by Richard, doing justice to difficult subjects in a way that is simply riveting.

This is an ambitious work that truly ties the many different aspects of the UFO subject together. It's rare to find something like this, especially considering the care and thoroughness that went into it.

We are at a time in history when each and every one of us has got to stand up and fight for truth the best way we can. Because if we don't, those people who have their own agenda on this planet are going to win. We need reliable information that makes sense of our world, that energizes us to keep going and fight on the side of the angels. We will need courage and persistence, but with truth on our side, I believe we will win in the end.

George Noory
Los Angeles, California
January 2014

Introduction

As long as we have had eyes, we have observed inexplicable wonders in the skies, in the oceans, and all around us. Finally, during the last few generations, we have sat up and noticed. Now we face the most impenetrable of mysteries.

It is not merely that unidentified flying objects have been traversing our world. Nor that they do things that are supposed to be impossible. Nor that they look unlike any known aircraft, or that they seem to violate the principles of aerodynamics. All of this has been and is true, and all of it is certainly a problem. But the problem goes deeper.

After all these years, we still don't know who precisely is operating these objects. We may have ideas, but in fact we don't know. More puzzling still is the logic of their behavior. Why buzz our aircraft? Why play cat and mouse games? Why the bizarre (apparent) interactions with people around the world? We are dealing with an unknown phenomenon that behaves inexplicably, and apparently does not want to reveal itself to us.

It is easy for a person to go through life without thinking about any of this. We have other priorities, and the official powers of our society dismiss the topic. Even most of the anti-establishment, alternative researchers know this topic is a third rail: touch it at your peril. It's not from a lack of curiosity. I've spoken with many of these researchers. Most of them are fascinated by UFOs but fear the ridicule. You can only fight so many battles—why wear yet another albatross that only makes your life more difficult? It is hard enough to research things like government spying, financial corruption, 9/11 conspiracies, chemtrails, or many other important subjects that require our attention.

For my part, I have spent the last twenty years researching UFOs.

In that time, I have found that this phenomenon intersects with many of the above subjects. In fact, I would go further and say that a proper study of UFOs is a revolutionary experience. It shatters old belief systems and forces us to look at our world in a completely new way. Everything is affected: history, politics, economics, science, religion, culture, and our ultimate vision of who and what we are as human beings.

Yet, looking back on the history of UFO research, it turns out that surprisingly little work has been done to describe the big picture. There have been many good books written, for sure. Many have focused on key sightings that have defied our understanding. Others have discussed military and government policy on UFOs. Several have focused on abductions and other forms of contact with these other beings. Others still have described different scientific aspects of the phenomenon. There are also a smaller number of books that deal with the challenges of investigating UFOs, certainly an important topic. Only the smallest handful have ever tried to be anything like a comprehensive guide, and none have really pulled it off. Talk about a gaping hole in the field.

Even worse, much of the earlier thinking on the subject feels antiquated. Up until roughly the end of the Cold War, that is around 1990 or so, the field was still something of an old boys club. A lot of good work was done but, in general, less was known or appreciated about the phenomenon itself. Archival research was rudimentary, as was overall historical knowledge. There was scant familiarity with worldwide sightings, little appreciation of abductions until nearly 1980, and a number of sciences connected to UFOs were a complete mystery—propulsion technology being one obvious example of many.

Cultural beliefs of earlier decades didn't help, either. Political insights were naive, with a strong dose of old-fashioned patriotism and trust in government, and a belief that government secrets could not be kept for very long. Scientific attitudes were equally conservative. The dominant approach was "nuts and bolts" ufology, rather like Victorian materialism that denied (or ignored) the truly strange sciences of quantum mechanics, entanglement, and non-locality, all of which now seem relevant to UFOs.

Since the 1990s, however, the field has exploded. Many more people from around the world are now engaged in it, with a greater diversity of beliefs and philosophies. Ufology is now a wide-open ball game, replete with generational divides, cultural wars, new ideas, new arguments, and little agreement as to priorities. This trend strengthened after 9/11, an event that radicalized many people around the world into permanent suspicion against global political elites, and certainly against the U.S. national security state.

The people are different, the attitudes are different, and so is our technology, which has buried us in data. Prior to the 1990s, simply getting access to good UFO reports was a problem that nearly every researcher faced. Today, we can sift through more than ten thousand raw reports that are filed online every year in North America alone. Added to this overabundance are hundreds of new UFO videos posted each year to YouTube. And then there are thousands more stories and rumors that come our way via social networking sites like Facebook and Twitter. In other words, ufology is splintered and overwhelmed.

What we need is an up-to-date assessment of where we are in this incredible field. That is why I wrote this book. This is a comprehensive overview of the UFO phenomenon for people of the 21st century.

It offers up-to-date information and analysis relating to the full history of UFOs, from ancient times to our own era. This alone is an incredibly rich aspect of the phenomenon, and the sheer quantity of good reports is astonishing. Trying to make sense of it all leads us to wonder if humanity has been someone's pet project for quite some time. However, it also appears that activity has been heating up considerably for the past several decades. Does this mean we are on the brink of something big?

There is much more than history for us to consider, however. There are important political issues, such as the relationship of the U.S. government and military/intelligence community to UFOs. That is, the cover-up. In analyzing this, we find that UFOs pose a serious problem to that community, one that its members may not be handling as well as they would like. It also strongly appears that at least some of the UFOs people are seeing are made by *us* as opposed to *them*. Moreover, we find that the suppression of open, public information about UFOs has created serious distortions in our political culture and our economics. A key factor here has been the creation of an expansive national security apparatus and black-budget society, a portion of which was created to hide the UFO reality. This apparatus has taken over much of what remains of traditional republican institutions around the world, certainly within the United States.

But there is more to a full understanding of UFOs than history and politics. The subject raises important philosophical and investigative issues, including how ordinary objects and events might fool us, and how they differ from "true UFOs." Moreover, in an age of Google, Facebook, and Youtube, when information practically overwhelms us, we might want to know how to separate fact from fiction, and legitimate issues from fear-mongering or fantasy-peddling.

Then there are issues pertaining to science and technology. To the extent that these objects are craft, how do they operate? How might interstellar travel be possible? How is it that these beings often seem to have a mind-to-mind communication with us? What does that mean about human consciousness? What can a study of UFOs teach us about physics, dimensions, and the structure of our reality?

Nor must we forget the beings behind the phenomenon, whoever and whatever they are. In understanding UFOs, it is crucial that we assess the history and claims of contact, that we try to understand the nature of that contact, and perhaps puzzle out just who and what we are dealing with. There is a great deal of information from individuals who appear to have had interactions with some of these beings, as incredible as that may sound.

Finally, to understand the UFO phenomenon with a fresh perspective, we ought to try peering into the future. That includes what has become a pervasive topic in the field: whether or not there will be, or can be, any kind of true "Disclosure" of the UFO reality. That is, an official recognition, one that includes government and all the associated institutions that dominate our world. Because this can only be speculative by its very nature, we need to be careful in forming our judgments. Yet, the matter is important enough that it demands our attention, since we are fools if we assume that tomorrow will be the same as today. Our civilization is rapidly changing, and with it our once-solid beliefs of what is possible and what is not. It seems likely that *Disclosure*, whether by design, accident, or necessity, will be the ultimate revolutionary experience.

Any subject that provokes so many profound ideas and can take us to so many amazing destinations is worthy of our time and consideration. But we should not expect easy answers. I first entered the field of ufology after having studied history for many years, in particular U.S. diplomacy and modern Europe. When I initially became intrigued by UFOs during the early 1990s, I thought I might be able to take a detour of a few months to find out once and for all if there was anything to it. I discovered that there was indeed something to it, and I have spent the last twenty years exploring a field that has never once released its grip on me. Several times, it has prompted me to reevaluate the world and my place in it.

Recall in *The Matrix*, when Morpheus offers Neo the choice of a red pill or blue pill. The blue pill allows him to return to his ordinary conventional world, while the red pill offers him truth. If only it were so easy: one simple red pill and all is revealed. In reality, we must take red pills on a regular basis, since the illusions of our world are in many layers. We realize something new, something important, and that gives us clarity for a little while. Soon we notice other oddities and discrepancies, and we realize we need to go further. And so it goes.

Ufology offers a perfect example of such complexity. I started out years ago with one simple question. It was not *are UFOs real?* or *are aliens real?* I wanted to know something even more basic: *were UFOs ever important to the U.S. national security community?* One simple question with one simple answer (yes). However, that simple answer led to countless more questions. I still do not have all the answers I am looking for, and probably never will. But that is no reason for despair, for this is a subject in which it can truly be said that the journey is the reward.

I now invite you to take that journey with me.

Chapter 1
What Are UFOs?

In the twenty years I have studied UFOs, I have been smacked around, kicked down, and wrestled to the ground by some of the most amazing and perplexing mysteries you can imagine. That's been satisfying enough, but what has made it even better is knowing that so many people like to look down their noses at this topic. After all, UFOs are supposed to be something for fanciful minds. Of course, that certainly isn't the case, but that feeling of studying something almost, shall we say *forbidden,* makes this subject fascinating and naughty at the same time. What can be better than that?

Make no mistake, it is a bizarre phenomenon. It is worth remembering that most reports of UFOs are explainable in prosaic terms. Still, it is also true that, no matter how hard even the best analysts try, certain reports defy an easy explanation. Some of these things appear to be somebody's technology, doing things that are supposed to be impossible. To whom they belong is one of the magic questions.

But first I think it will be helpful to examine what constitutes *evidence* and *proof* when we talk about UFOs. This is trickier than you might think. What exactly would constitute proof that UFOs are real and, in some way, alien?

Assuming there is reasonable evidence to support the belief that some UFOs are indeed "alien," or something "not us" (which is my position), we can contemplate another tricky issue. That is, *who* and *what* they are, or, more realistically, who and what they might be. There are several interesting possibilities.

Then, I would like to open a discussion that will recur throughout this book. This concerns the many potential implications of the UFO phenomenon itself, especially as they relate to our global cultures and social organization. After all, what would happen to world politics if the President of the United States were to state officially that UFOs are real? How would such knowledge affect our economics, religion, spiritual beliefs, science, and culture? What would happen if there were ever open contact between us and ... *them*?

The UFO phenomenon is not simply a fun, diversionary topic. It is not something to dabble with during moments of boredom. It is mind-bending and reality-shattering.

What are UFOs?

Wherever you travel, no matter the country or culture, you would be hard-pressed to find someone who has not heard of UFOs. The term is recognized around the world. It is, in fact, a worldwide brand.

There is a good reason for this. All you need to do is ask around a bit, and you will find many people with their own UFO story. Often it is their own personal sighting, and sometimes multiple sightings. Sometimes it concerns a dramatic story told to them by a family member, often with no one else in the room. Every now and then, a military retiree, perhaps a father, mother, uncle, or grandparent will whisper such an account. Those stories, too, are out there, many of them.

Consider the following scenario.

You are outside on a large front lawn after a nice dinner, relaxing with five of your friends, all adults and professionals. It is around 7 p.m., toward the end of a beautiful spring day. The sky is still light, and you are all enjoying the picturesque scene. Then, to everyone's great surprise, an enormous, round craft approaches from the horizon. It is moving slowly, perhaps thirty or forty miles per hour. White lights are visible at its outer edges and it is rotating slowly in a counter-clockwise direction. What is truly astonishing, however, is the object's immense size. Your best estimate is that it is perhaps one thousand feet wide, more than three football fields. Unfortunately, the sunlight makes it hard to notice most of the details of this gargantuan object. Then, as it appears over you, it stops. Perhaps it noticed you, you wonder.

Chapter 1: What Are UFOs?

From here, your experience becomes even more incredible, more impossible. You watch, dumbfounded, as this giant in the sky splits into four smaller, wedge-shaped, craft. You wonder, how can this be? Then, almost instantaneously, the four objects zoom away to the North, South, East, and West. Almost as baffling is the silence, because throughout this amazing encounter, no one has heard a sound coming from this aerial display. The event is so shocking to you and your friends that, for many years after, none of you ever speak about it, not even among yourselves.

This event occurred in the town of Hydes, Maryland, on May 15, 1976. Not until 1999, however—twenty three years later—was it was reported anywhere, in this case to the National UFO Reporting Center, on the Web.

This type of sighting is extraordinary, inexplicable, and utterly commonplace. UFO reports include many examples of craft that are silent, divide into smaller segments, and zip away noiselessly at amazing speeds. These seemingly impossible reports come not only from ordinary people, but also from military personnel, and like those from the military, silence is usually the rule for civilians when it comes to UFO reports. Military personnel have their secrecy protocols, of course, but trauma and fear of ridicule usually serve well enough to keep most people quiet.

However you try to interpret the phenomenon, every indication points to the number of UFO witnesses reaching not into the thousands, but well into the millions. Whether you consider UFOs to be nonsense or of great importance, people are seeing things that are affecting them deeply. Because there are no institutional structures for them to report or discuss what they see, they often keep silent, and try to forget or only secretly cherish one of the most incredible experiences of their lives.

Getting Technical

When we think of UFOs the natural instinct is to connect them with extraterrestrials. That is, beings from another part of the universe who have come here to Earth. There are some good reasons for this, which we will explore in a short while. But, if you want to get technical (and who *doesn't* want to get technical) all UFO means is "unidentified flying object."

That could be just about anything.

Some people are surprised to learn that about ninety percent of all UFO reports can be and have been explained. The former Harvard astronomer, Donald Menzel, once compiled a *List of Things Mistaken for UFOs*, and it is quite thorough.[1] Menzel claimed to believe that no UFO was ever an alien craft, and in fact was the world's leading debunker during the 1950s and 1960s. While he certainly had his biases, his list remains relevant, as long as we do some updating for our own era.

Menzel divided the causes of UFO sightings into different categories: Material Objects, Immaterial Objects, Astronomical, Physiological, Psychological, Photographic Records, Radar, Hoaxes, and various combinations of these. Within each category he made further distinctions. Among "Material Objects," for instance, he included meteors, re-entering satellites, rocket launchings, blimps, balloons, aircraft and aircraft lights, clouds, contrails, military test craft or experiments, magnesium flares, migrating birds, paper and debris, kites, leaves, insect swarms, fireworks, dust devils, elevated streetlights, window reflections, or lights from cars, beacons, and lighthouses.

These were just a few of them. Certainly, some of the items are far-fetched. We are entitled to wonder how many people would be dumb enough to mistake an insect swarm for a UFO. Still, it does happen that people can be fooled by many things. It can happen to anyone, and it could happen to you.

Today, there are other items we can add to Menzel's List of Material Objects. Most important, it seems, are the many, increasingly sophisticated, objects that people are putting into the air. Starting with the military contribution, more and more craft of great sophistication are flying about, a few of which (such as Northrop Grumman's X-47 drone), look like a classic flying saucer when seen from certain

---

[1] Menzel's list is available at The Center for UFO Studies, www.cufon.org/cufon/ifo_list.htm

perspectives. Some drones have an ability to hover for very long periods of time, and many do not look anything like ordinary aircraft. But it is not just the military technology that causes false UFO reports. Ordinary people are better able than ever to set aloft objects that may look like UFOs, but are anything from candle-lit Chinese lanterns to remotely-controlled craft with LED lights or other video effects attached to them. Appearances can be deceiving, although there are still no known cases of human created craft that can instantly accelerate from a hovering position, especially without a sound. So, if you witness something like that, you might want to make a note of it.

The U.S. Navy's X-47B, built by Northrop Grumman, a pilotless drone with the size and performance of many piloted fighter aircraft.

For Menzel material objects were only one cause of UFO reports, but other causes were non-material. These included atmospheric phenomena such as the aurora borealis, noctilucent clouds (that is, very high clouds that sometimes shine brightly at twilight) and other phenomena such as sundogs, moondogs, paraselene (a reflection of ice crystals in clouds under the moonlight), reflections from fog and mist, and more.

Then there are astronomical causes. The Planet Venus may be the cliché go-to explanation for UFO debunkers, but it became one for a reason: it is quite bright and has fooled people for years into thinking they were seeing an unknown craft. Besides Venus, there are other astronomical causes of UFO sightings: artificial satellites, comets, Jupiter and Mars (which can be quite bright in the night sky at times) and, incredibly, the Moon.

Stars have deceived people. Earth's atmosphere can play tricks with our eyes. When slow-moving clouds enter the mix, it can seem as though a star is changing color and darting around the sky. I saw this effect myself, rather dramatically. Beneath a clear and dark desert sky, I noticed a light that seemed to be jumping to different points. Only when I positioned a video recorder on the roof of my car (to prevent camera shake), did I see that it was not moving in the least. A subsequent check with astronomy software proved that it had been a bright star.

As that example shows, sometimes we are deceived not so much by the objects themselves as by our own senses. Our bodies are instruments, and instruments can make mistakes. It happens to everyone—we see things that simply are not there. For this, too, Menzel compiled a list (which he clearly enjoyed doing). For example, he realized that any bright source, such as the Sun, the Moon, street lights, headlights, the flash of a camera, or many other things, creates an "after-image." If you are not thinking consciously of it, such after-images can fool you into thinking you are seeing strange lights in the sky. Other problems can simply come from poor eyesight, reflections from eyeglasses, and so on.

And not simply the eyes. Our very minds can create the illusion of something being there that is not. This can simply be a matter of poor or incomplete observation, preconceived ideas about the object itself, or a genuine psychological disturbance. To be sure, mistakes of the human mind have caused their share of UFO reports.

Technology can also lie. We are inundated with photographs of UFOs that are not UFOs. Even in Menzel's day, pictures could lie, whether from internal camera reflections to defects during the photo development process to crude fakery. Today, we have PhotoShop, AfterEffects, and many other software packages for image and video editing. Indeed, it is still possible for experts to analyze digital evidence for authenticity, but it can be very difficult, and meanwhile we are drowning in a flood of such evidence and claims. Photos and videos must therefore be of limited value as evidence. No matter how genuine they may be, the hundreds of UFO photographs and videos that appear each year will not be considered strong evidence without something else to support them. For starters, something like corroborating witness testimony, with multiple witnesses being much better than one.

Then we have radar, which is certainly a reliable and important tool for managing air traffic. Even so, radar instrumentation can be subject to illusions and effects, such as anomalous refraction, scattering, ghost images, multiple reflections, and more. Granted, the professionals in the field are usually familiar enough with these effects that they do not pose great problems, but radar is not infallible.

Finally, let us not forget that there are always people who enjoy a good prank. When it comes to any alleged UFO sighting, we must always consider the possibility of a hoax. It has happened many times.

And Yet ...

Still, when we review the thousands upon thousands of UFO reports that have been filed, we begin to see something. After running them through the best filters we can, after considering all prosaic explanations, there have always been a certain number that remain truly inexplicable.

Different sources have given different figures for the percentage of the truly inexplicable. Some have argued five percent or even lower; others have gone higher than twenty percent. Generally speaking, ten percent appears to be the most typical, and is probably the most realistic. We should remember that some databases, such as the old Project Blue Book, run by the U.S. Air Force during the 1950s and 1960s, at times used questionable and even dishonest methods to "solve" some of their cases. The Air Force was more concerned with solving UFO cases politically than in any scientific sense. UFOs had to be put to sleep, at least as far as the public was concerned. This meant that any explanation, including the most ridiculous, could be used to explain otherwise inexplicable cases. As a result, Blue Book's final percentage of unsolved cases (six percent), is almost certainly underestimated.

For the past few decades, the largest database of investigated UFO reports is probably that of the Mutual UFO Network. MUFON's database includes many thousands of reports, and the organization generally arrives at an unsolved percentage of roughly ten percent.[2]

There has always been a remainder, a residue, of UFO cases, that are of such detail, backed by credible witnesses and instrumentation, that there seems to be no reasonable explanation for them. These are the true UFOs, the heart of the mystery.

This is where the real debate takes place. How do we interpret these cases? Some investigators have concluded: "it's real and someone is here." Others remain confident that there are explanations for these cases that may prove to be scientifically interesting, but which are not evidence of alien visitation. But even this only takes us into the shallow waters. From here, matters get trickier still.

Most UFO skeptics do concede that there are some reports of extraordinary aerial objects that we might call UFOs, but that is no reason to assume these are alien. There are, after all, many deeply secret black budget technologies and projects, and not all of them even American. Especially today, in a world that now has a few drones that look like flying saucers, it might seem that any so-called UFO is probably something manufactured on Earth.

---

[2] It is worth mentioning that MUFON's investigations have typically been restricted by lack of resources (such as money), which are needed to do the job well. At a minimum, gas money alone for investigators can become an issue, at least over time, considering that distances to a sighting location may be more than one hundred miles from where the investigator lives. In the context of current gas prices and typical automotive gas mileage, that can easily exceed $30, not considering any other factors. But of course, there are usually other factors which compound the problem. There is usually a need for equipment of some sort or another, whether these be relatively inexpensive camcorders to conduct interviews, instruments to read electromagnetic signatures or radiation, cameras for night vision or infrared, and more. And let us not forget time. While most investigators do not get paid for their work, their time is not free. People always have other things they can do with their lives, and the fact that they do not get paid to conduct investigations inevitably means that there are fewer investigations than there could be otherwise. Investigating a UFO report is seldom easy, and usually takes time. And time is money.

Of course, when we talk about UFOs—true UFOs[3]—we think of aliens. The real question is, are there true UFOs? Are we, the inhabitants of Planet Earth, being visited by beings that are from some other place?

Rather than trying to answer that question definitively, let us ease into it. As we shall see, there is much to consider, both pro and con.

Having thought about this problem for twenty years, my personal suggestion is that, whatever position you the reader may have, be prepared to modify it. There is much more of interest about UFOs than simply answering the question, "do they really exist, or not?" The depth and nuance of the phenomenon is beyond that of most other fields of study.

What Can UFOs Be?

One way to start would be to ask, what *might* UFOs be? The answer turns out to be: many things.

During the 1960s a remarkable student of this subject, a scientist and writer named Ivan Sanderson, explored that very question, and even developed a six-page outline of the possibilities.[4] Thus, UFOs could be inanimate or animate. If inanimate, they might be natural or artificial, each possibility with several subsets. If animate, they could also be natural or artificial. If natural, they might be solid (like meteorites), non-solid (gaseous, as in clouds), or non-material (energy packets, as in bolides). If artificial, they could be self-contained items (such as artificial satellites), transports (like freighters), manned devices (like airplanes), auxiliary devices (like space probes), or missiles (like bullets and ICBMs).

But Sanderson was nothing if not imaginative. UFOs might also be alive, he postulated. After all, why not? If so, just as with inanimate objects, they might be natural or artificial. Natural animate objects could include life-forms indigenous to space, or indigenous to atmospheres, or to solid bodies. Artificial life forms could be natural

---

3 Or 'trufos,' as Naval Optical Physicist Dr. Bruce Maccabee has sometimes put it.
4 Sanderson, Ivan T. *Uninvited Visitors: A biologist looks at UFOs.* Cowles, 1967.

life forms that were domesticated or altered, genetically created life-forms, or biochemically created life-forms.

Sanderson pointed out that natural UFOs (he called them Unexplained Aerial Objects, or UAOs) are of little interest to our investigation. Natural phenomena (such as meteors, unusual clouds, ball lightning, temperature inversions, mirages, or swamp gas) may be interesting scientifically, but not especially to those of us looking for true UFOs.

The second category of inanimate objects, however—those classified as artificial—are much more interesting, and closer to our idea of true UFOs. The very idea of unknown objects being manufactured means that some life-form was involved in creating them. We know that some of these unknown objects over the years have been manufactured by our own black-budget programs using technologies that were well ahead of those available in the commercial world. But could some UFOs be manufactured technology made by *Others*? In Sanderson's view, the answer was obvious: of course!

But Sanderson went beyond these conventional notions. More intriguing still are UFOs that may be animate. That is, alive. We normally do not think of UFOs like that, but the idea has arisen from time to time over the years. Sanderson, a biologist by training, gave it serious consideration. "Life, and especially intelligent life," he wrote, "is, to the mechanistic world, an oddity; in some ways an anachronism, and in many ways a pest." For him it was obvious that the universe, with a potentially infinite level of complexity and variety, could easily produce life forms that would stagger our imaginations.

So, yes, he argued, it was entirely possible that UFOs were living, intelligent life forms, or (to put it another way) intelligent machines, both organic and inorganic. That is, with blood or with circuits. Sanderson was nothing if not ahead of his time. Consider this passage he wrote in the mid-1960s:

> The very idea of an animated machine or of a mechanical animal is impossible to conceive by the average person. When the average person is asked to contemplate 'life,' he immediately thinks of an animal .... The variety of life-forms found even on this, our own, tiny, insignificant planet

is so great that mere contemplation of some of them is almost more than a biologist can stand. What forms life could take elsewhere is quite beyond the grasp of our materialist outlook, because their variety is probably infinite.

Sanderson is engaging because he opens our minds to possibilities we might normally discount, not because of logic, but simply because most of us had not yet thought of them.

UFOs and the Problem of Science

Considering the possibilities is fascinating, but UFOs are a hard nut to crack. We naturally want that magic bullet we call *proof* to resolve, beyond any doubt, that they are real and to learn what they are.

Proof is the eternal ufological quest. But what is it? What would constitute proof?

This is a harder problem than most people think. If you saw a large, spherical object descend silently, hover, and instantly accelerate to the edge of the horizon within a second or two, you would probably be convinced that, yes, you just saw a real UFO. But how would you convince others of this fact? How could you prove it?

Consider some tricky issues regarding UFOs and the scientific method.

In the first place, a genuine scientific investigation demands repeatability, either of observation or result. There are also certain assumptions connected with the scientific method. One is that the scientist has some form of control over the phenomenon under study, and that it will perform in some way that is consistent or can be predicted.

However, what if UFOs were under the control of another intelligence, one more advanced than our own? If there were a superior intelligence operating on Earth, we might wonder whether science, as we practice it, can be of much help. What proof of *them* would appear, except as they might desire?

That is challenging enough. But suppose also that we are dealing with an important national security issue? Naturally, I will be returning to this idea later in this book, but for now let us suppose that this is so.

In that case, this vexing scientific problem would further be hampered by secrecy protocols, censorship, and even disinformation from agencies charged with protecting what would arguably be the most important secret in the world.

Those would be formidable obstacles, but there are others. Consider how science is conducted today. It is easy for us to slip into outdated ideas about science. Many of us stay stuck to the ideals we learned in our youth. Meanwhile, reality races ahead.

Science, we were taught in school, is the bastion and foundation of intellectual freedom in the world. It is an independent search for truth, and the destroyer of social and religious myths.

But how independent is science, really? In whose interest is it practiced today? This is no idle question, for gone are the days of scientists following their intellectual passions in a search for truth. One of the pioneers in environmental science, James Lovelock, put it this way:

> Nearly all scientists are employed by some large organization, such as a governmental department, a university, or a multinational company. Only rarely are they free to express their science as a personal view. They may think that they are free, but in reality they are, nearly all of them, employees; they have traded freedom of thought for good working conditions, a steady income, tenure, and a pension.[5]

The observation is so obvious, and yet we sometimes forget it too easily. In fairness, science is an expensive business. To do it well, you need money, which means sponsorship. And when someone else is paying the bills, they make the rules. Few are the scientists who receive a blank check to do their work. And who writes the checks? In most nations, it is usually either private industry or a government defense agency. Certainly this is so in the U.S., where, since the Second World War, the military has been the largest sponsor of scientific research.

But if the military and intelligence communities have had a strong interest in the UFO phenomenon, and deeply classified the subject, we would certainly have a situation in which government public funds for

---

5 Lovelock, James, *The Ages of Gaia: A Biography of Our Living Earth*, Norton, 1995, p. xvii.

UFO research would be absent, but in which black budget, classified dollars would flow more freely. This, of course, has been the claim among several researchers, including myself.[6] If there is no public funding for scientific research on UFOs, then few if any scientists will give it any consideration. They would have nothing to gain and everything to lose for their efforts. The result is widespread ignorance by most scientists of even the basics of the UFO phenomenon. Those who study outside the black world generally use their own personal funds and do so privately and quietly.

Overlapping the world of science are the colleges and universities, where the situation is the same. From a UFO researcher's perspective, it would be great if research could be conducted in the universities. Unfortunately, the subject is almost wholly off-limits there. Like the world of science, the academic world is an intellectual bureaucracy with an established hierarchy. A young graduate student with an interest in UFOs can not safely explore it within that environment except, perhaps, as a debunker. Even finding a qualified research supervisor would be daunting, since a cycle of ignorance has been long established. As a result, most of the contributions to our understanding of UFOs have come from outside the academic and scientific communities, at least within the United States.

Let us strip away our illusions. At every level, from the bottom up, intellectual freedom is a chimera in our world of so-called education. A century ago, Bertrand Russell commented on public schools as conformity factories ("What's the difference between a bright, inquisitive five-year-old, and a dull, stupid nineteen-year-old? Fourteen years of the British educational system.") Today, American educator John Taylor Gatto speaks eloquently about this problem.

> I've noticed a fascinating phenomenon in my thirty years of teaching: schools and schooling are increasingly irrelevant to the great enterprises of the planet. No one believes anymore that scientists are trained in science classes or politicians in civics classes or poets in English classes. The truth

---

6 See Dolan, Richard M. "Science, Secrecy, and Ufology," December 26, 2000, richarddolanpress.com, and "A Breakaway Civilization: What It is, and What It Means for Us," April 2011 www.afterdisclosure.com/2011/04/breakaway.html

is that schools don't really teach anything except how to obey orders.[7]

All of which is to say: do not expect breakthroughs in UFO studies to come from the formal educational system. Having said that, I have sometimes wondered, if UFOs *were* to be studied within higher education, how would it even be done? Where? There is no simple answer. Certainly the Department of History is one logical place. Clearly, however, there is more to the study of UFOs than history. Analysis of UFO data can take one into far ranging areas, from the liberal arts into the hardest of hard sciences. It would be interesting to speculate how ufology would be structured within a university setting: would it be considered a subset of one of the established fields of study, or would it receive its own department and funding?

Taking all this into account, we can get a sense of how difficult it could be to establish a formal scientific study of the UFO phenomenon, something that would be more than a low-budget effort by interested amateurs.

Yet, even considering the stark limitations imposed by having essentially no money to work with, ufologists have obtained reasonable proof for the reality of a genuine phenomenon: of an intelligent *something* that has been operating in the skies, oceans, and lower orbit of our world. Something that is not supposed to exist, but does. In other words, although we may find ourselves outmatched by what seems to be a superior intelligence, our scientific tools have enabled us to 'capture' it, so to speak. More on this later.

Who Decides What is Proof?

There is another matter to be considered regarding science and UFOs: who decides what is proof? The problem seems like a scientific one, but upon closer analysis we see it is almost entirely political.

Clearly, it is of great importance. Even on topics less controversial than UFOs, the court of science can be slow-moving, confusing, messy, and unsatisfying. Egos and arguments pervade. Consider the

---

7 Gatto, John Taylor. *Dumbing Us Down: The Hidden Curriculum of Compulsory Schooling.* New Society Publishers (2002), p. 21.

Chapter 1: What Are UFOs?

arguments over such politically charged issues as climate change or genetically modified foods. Scientists line up on either side of a huge divide, hurling conflicting data and accusations at the other side. Meanwhile, people look on and wonder how to make up their own minds, and whether public policies relating to these issues are in their interest.

Regarding UFOs, the combination of its bizarre complexity and the national security obfuscation enveloping it have made the problem knottier still. In the first place, officially speaking, there is no true UFO phenomenon, the biggest hurdle to an intelligent, open debate. But still, we feel instinctively, there must be a final arbiter, a judge to lay the gavel down and *decide*. In the past, one such arbiter was the so-called Condon Committee, an Air Force sponsored scientific study based out of the University of Colorado, which in early 1969 released its conclusion that UFOs were not a problem worthy of further scientific effort. Except that as we study the workings of that committee, we find it was an intensely political situation, and one in which the conclusion was foregone from the beginning, all for political reasons.[8]

In an era in which the scientific establishment has worked so closely for so long with the military and intelligence community, in which government funding dominates every important research decision, in which the heads of key scientific government organizations have close personal relationships with the heads of political and military institutions, how can the political be extracted from the scientific? The answer is: it cannot.

Implications: What if They are Real?

If UFOs are real, in the sense that they are (a) truly unexplained, (b) the product of some form of non-human intelligence, and (c) the product of an advanced, technological, non-human intelligence that does not come from "here," then clearly we are talking about something with tremendous implications for our civilization. Implications that become practically endless. Implications that become, in a word,

---

[8] Years later, the best analysis of this still remains Saunders, David R. and Harkins, R. Roger, *UFOs? Yes! Where the Condon Committee Went Wrong*. Signet, 1968.

revolutionary.

In the first place, let us ask, *who are they and what do they want?* So much depends on the answer to this. Unfortunately, even after all these years, there is no clear agreement among serious researchers.

There appear to be beings we have come to call "Grays." Short in stature with very large heads, black wrap-around eyes, thin bodies and ears, and tiny noses and mouths. They have become ubiquitous in our culture, replacing "little green men" as the dominant form of alien in the popular mind.

But the Grays are more than a pop culture meme. Decades of study have led many researchers to conclude that these beings abduct humans in the dead of night and perform various procedures on them. These procedures, as often recounted by alleged abductees, seem to be geared toward some sort of breeding and genetic manipulation program. In other words, the Grays may be creating a race that is some sort of hybrid between human and Gray. If we ever prove openly that the Grays and these activities are real, the public reaction would be overwhelming.

There have also been reports and claims of encounters with beings decidedly less attractive even than the Grays. These are of beings described as reptilian and even insect-like. If such claims are to be believed, some of these creatures may not be especially pleasant, and some may be hostile. If they are real, and if they too are responsible for some of the UFO phenomenon, a worldwide panic could easily follow. What might these beings want? Are they truly visitors, or have they been here for a long while?

There is also the possibility that some of these beings are human, or at least look like us. No doubt this would be easier to cope with psychologically, in particular since many of them are described rather like Scandinavian supermodels. Of course, learning that a race of super-intelligent Nordic supermodels are here on Earth, perhaps even secretly ruling the world, might give the rest of us a serious inferiority complex.

Over the years, I have formed the opinion that all of these types and more might well be real. Of course, until I meet and touch one myself, I can never be certain. Yet, it may simply come down to bioengineering. Skeptical scientists have emphasized the improbability of aliens from another world looking humanoid, reptoid, or insectoid. After all, those life forms evolved here on Earth. Shouldn't we expect life elsewhere to be a bit more unusual?

The answer to this is *yes*, but with a qualifier. The qualifier is that any life able to reach our world, and wanting somehow to interact with it, would face the basic problem of biological hostility. Not so much from humanity, although we might be an annoyance. Rather, the problem would come from Earth's microbes, gravity, atmosphere, solar radiation, and so on. We evolved on Earth; presumably, they did not. Yet, if they want to interact with Earth in some direct way, how better than via genetic manipulation of native life forms? Or even breeding and enhancing their own humans, possibly over thousands of years?

There are other possibilities of what these other beings might be. None are easy to know for certain, probably even in a future world in which the UFO secret is out. After all, what about the managers of the UFO secret? In all likelihood, they find elements of this phenomenon just as puzzling as the rest of us. Are we dealing with beings that are somehow interdimensional, whatever that really means? Or time travelers? A lost human civilization that somehow broke away from the rest of humanity millennia ago?

Knowing who they are will be very important, but in essence everything will come down to how we judge their intentions. Are they benevolent, benign, or hostile? And how will we know these intentions? Will they be open and honest or deceptive? Will humanity even be able to know or agree?

Political Implications

No matter who or what is behind the UFO phenomenon, it carries important implications. We can start with politics.

If we were to learn, officially speaking, that UFOs are "real," then the powers-that-be had better hope they convince the world that there has never been any recent past important interaction with them.

Certainly no retrievals of crashed UFOs. That alone would prove there has been a deep cover-up, one filled with layer upon layer of lies.

Yet, even without a revelation that we acquired any of their technology, the disclosure of this reality would be a political nightmare to handle. Could it be that there has been a longstanding knowledge of this phenomenon, but no real interaction? No communication? No retrieval of technology or bodies? In theory, it is certainly possible, although, as I will argue later in this book, it seems much more likely that real alien craft have been recovered. And the claim has been made repeatedly that there is also communication going on, between us and them. Indeed, I encountered one such claim myself from a source that I consider credible.

For the moment, simply ask yourself: what if the crash of a real alien craft near Roswell in 1947, or something like it, happened? What if an alien craft was recovered by the U.S. military. If you were the President at the time and were briefed on this, what would you do?

President Harry Truman with Secretary of Defense James Forrestal in 1948. If Roswell "happened," these two men would have been well aware.

You might think the world ought to know about something so important and profound. But then you might think again. Certainly, your advisors would remind you of the dangers of disclosing this fact.

Chapter 1: What Are UFOs?

How severe might be the public panic? Who are these other beings? Do we have anything to worry about? What can we learn from the technology we have recovered, and how do we keep it from our enemies?

Other questions would arise almost immediately: how to create operations to listen for and decipher alien communications, to retrieve future downed vehicles, to accommodate any live or dead beings. It would be quickly obvious that all of these would require the utmost secrecy, at least for a while.

Even Congress could not be told, or else the secret obviously would not last long. But keeping Congress in the dark would require the creation of otherwise illegal secret appropriations. In other words, black budgets. If UFOs *are real,* they would have been a key foundation of America's black budget. It would be absolutely necessary to do an end-run around the Constitution (which tasks Congress, not the Executive Branch, with both appropriating and then reviewing all government expenditures) in order to fund a program that would deal with the presence of *Others* on Planet Earth.

Once such a secret system is in place, it would inevitably grow. It would become necessary to manage key institutions to keep them compliant. You would need to start with the academic, scientific, journalistic, and political institutions, developing relationships with key members of those groups who would then serve as watchdogs, keeping the rest of the pack in line whenever someone strayed too far into the UFO topic. Any and all tools would be necessary, starting with ridicule and censure, continuing on to the loss of one's career, or worse.

If UFOs are real, and especially if they have been recovered, then this type of development would be likely. Through the years and decades and generations, such a long-lasting cover-up would create a strong discrepancy between what we might call *official truth* and the *actual truth*. All societies have such a discrepancy to one degree or another. But year after year of UFO denial would contribute to a discrepancy of massive size. After all, when the most awe-inspiring and dramatic fact of one's lifetime becomes off-limits to genuine political or scientific discussion, when secret budgets are set aside to deal with that reality, then what we have is a loss of the foundation of our freedoms and failure of the democratic system.

With the foregoing in mind, ask yourself: what would be the political upshot if UFO secrecy were to end? We will return to this theme in much greater detail later in this book.

Economic Implications

The economic ramifications of the UFO phenomenon are just as dramatic as the political. We might start by asking how much money may have gone into the UFO secret. After all, whether the policy is justified or not, whether it is right or wrong, there is every likelihood that it has cost taxpayers a pretty penny, all without their knowledge or consent. Also relevant is whether anyone has been illegally profiting from this secret. We can assume that somewhere the answer is yes.

Let us wind back the clock to the beginning of the cover-up. Some part of our military has just recovered technology that did not come from our civilization or our world. Obviously, this technology needs to be studied. Therefore, at some point, it needs to be passed on to those groups within private industry that are best suited to study and hopefully replicate it. It should go without saying that all of this needs to be under tightly controlled conditions.

In which case, we may ask, how long before some clever scientist or team develops new ideas based on what has been studied? Is it possible that secret UFO technology has spurred advances in solid state electronics, fiber optics, high tensile fibers, integrated circuits, and other technologies? Is it possible that acquired UFOs have contributed to the development of human technology and economic growth since the 1940s and 1950s? In theory, it appears to be quite possible, assuming of course that UFOs are real and we have acquired some of their technology.

There is another economic factor to consider relating to UFOs. Whatever fuel these objects use to move from Point A to Point B, it is certainly not petroleum. Anything that can hover silently, then accelerate instantly at ultra-high speed is clearly using something better than oil as its main source of energy. Certainly, ordinary people would appreciate having access to this incredible source of energy, especially if it burned cleanly. If such an amazing fuel and technology became public knowledge, it would quickly replace oil, coal and natural gas as the world's main sources of energy.

This would seem to be a wonderful thing. Replacing oil is one of humanity's most coveted dreams. By now, everyone understands that the long-term future of our species, and our world, cannot include oil as our main source of energy. It pollutes horribly and harms life on Earth. A better, cleaner, more abundant source of energy would surely be more desirable, except from the point of view of those people who own the oil industry, some of the most powerful people in the world. For generations, they have monetized oil. What if the source of energy behind UFOs is impossible to centralize, and therefore harder to exploit for money?

Aside from that, oil is the foundation of our world. Even under the most ideal conditions, transitioning out of an oil-dominated world would have a volatile effect on the global stock market and economic system. After all, most of the value of any consumer product is determined by the amount of energy that went into making and transporting it. Generally, that means oil.

Therefore, if we say nothing else, we can conclude that the UFO phenomenon poses a threat to the established economic order: specifically to those wealthiest people and groups that own the greatest shares in the petroleum industry, and in general to the financial markets that would be shaken by the end of the oil era.

Religious Implications

What would the admission of a UFO reality do to religion? Would it mean anything at all?

The answer is *yes*, it would certainly mean something. Of course, the world has many different religions, so everything would depend on which one we mean. Still, to the extent that any religion deals with the creation of the world, the creation of mankind, and to the extent to which people today continue to believe in versions of those accounts, the UFO phenomenon has profound implications. This will be especially evident after we review the history of ancient UFOs, or "ancient aliens," in the next chapter. Because, if it appears that *they* have been with us for a long time, many people will inevitably wonder if they were the gods of ancient times, or even God himself?

It doesn't take an excess of imagination to see things in this way when reviewing the Hebrew Scriptures, for instance. Time and again, the God of the Israelites directly intervened to save the day, and had a very personal relationship with Moses. Other parts of that collection are also suggestive of aliens and their technology. The vision of Ezekiel comes to mind, in which the prophet beheld a wondrous apparition of angels in a flaming chariot in the sky. When you consider the ideas of the various ancient alien theorists, we naturally ask whether beings from elsewhere became our so-called gods and were instrumental in creating human religions. For practicing Christians, probably the most sensitive question would be: was Christ an extraterrestrial? What would it mean if he had been?

Even if aliens were to announce themselves tomorrow and make such a claim, people would still have to decide whether or not to believe them. They could be lying, after all. Ultimately, arriving at sound answers to such matters, and understanding our long-term relationship to these other beings, may turn out to be impossible.

Regarding those people and groups that presumably maintain secrecy over UFOs, they would surely be concerned with how religious believers would respond to the news that UFOs and aliens are real. Religions are unlikely to collapse in the aftermath of Disclosure, as is sometimes supposed. Deeply religious people are unlikely simply to abandon their lifelong convictions. Instead, we might expect them to interpret the new reality through their religious perspective. An evangelical Christian will interpret an alien presence very differently than a Buddhist or Wiccan or New Age believer.

Of course, the end of UFO secrecy would certainly initiate powerful long-term changes in the world's major religions. While such change may not come from those who are of adult age when Disclosure occurs, it will come from their children and grandchildren, who will look at the world very differently. Undoubtedly, this will include a new spirituality.

Scientific Implications

Beyond the new technologies that may quietly have come from the successful analysis of recovered UFOs, it is possible that even more fundamental scientific breakthroughs have been made, all within the clandestine world charged with studying them.

Returning to the matter of petroleum, and the certainty that UFOs do not use it, we are faced with a new reality that portends awesome possibilities for the future of our energy paradigm. Scientists have long speculated about an energy holy grail, that is, something along the lines of free energy. Is this what powers UFOs? If so, what would it be?

Scientists today have several candidates, including controlled nuclear fusion, cold fusion, and the exotic but real Zero Point Energy (ZPE). These are energy sources that, if tapped, would transform our world overnight. What is the likelihood that one or more of these sources of energy are understood by scientists who are studying UFOs within the classified world?

Consider other fields, like computing, biotechnology, materials science, or even more arcane subjects such as theoretical physics. It may well be that in all of these fields, and others, breakthroughs have been made within the classified world. After all, if we consider that classified science is sometimes decades ahead of public science, how much further ahead would a classified program be, considering that it had access to technology that was eons ahead of our own? The open literature on artificial intelligence, nanotechnology, and quantum computing already discusses near future technologies in ways that seem magical. Is it possible that elements of the classified scientific community have already achieved some of those breakthroughs?

The scientific implications of UFOs hardly end here. As we shall see in the chapters describing many fascinating UFO cases, there are reasons to believe that these objects, or the beings inside them, somehow manipulate space-time reality. In other words, UFOs represent more than merely incredible technology, but a radically new understanding of space and time itself. Imagine what our world would be like if humanity learned how to master space and time. Could we travel, Star Trek-like, through the universe at warp speed? Could we somehow travel through time or into other dimensions or reality?

There are many important questions nagging at our scientific community today. Are any of them better understood within the classified world in ways that have not yet reached the public realm? Keeping scientific secrets of this magnitude is not impossible and, as I will argue later in this book, has happened for a long time. In our world today, there are important unresolved questions concerning such subjects as the origin of life, genetic manipulation, disease, biological evolution, memory, consciousness, gravity, and other fundamentals about the universe itself. As astonishing as this may at first seem, a true understanding of the UFO phenomenon almost certainly has something to teach us about each of these questions.

Cultural Implications

UFOs and ETs have had an enormous impact on our popular culture. Many of the highest grossing movies of all time have dealt explicitly with space travel and extraterrestrials. Disney paid George Lucas $4 billion dollars for the rights to the Star Wars franchise. But their influence via television has probably been even greater. Can anyone truly calculate the effect of the *Star Trek* franchise on world culture? It is a fair guess that when people around the world envision the future of the human race, many will think along the lines laid down by that pioneering television show: interstellar travel, meeting with alien races, becoming members of some sort of galactic federation, and continuing on the great journey of discovery. Of course, one might respond that most of these movies and television shows were not truly related to UFOs, which is true in a narrow sense. Yet, the UFO phenomenon was without question the major spark behind many, if not most, of them. Whenever the U.S.S. *Enterprise* separates its "saucer section" from the rest of the vessel, we can thank UFOs for the inspiration.

Apart from popular entertainment, however, UFOs have had other influences on our culture, mostly as a result of the cover-up. Most of these influences have been negative. For if we assume that UFOs are real, and there has been a cover-up, then it would be a cover-up that has permeated our society at nearly every level. It would mean that a major truth in our world has been suppressed, which in turn has damaged the willingness and ability of many people to investigate and see truth when it does appear. After all, if someone is used to taking the word of the established authorities on a particular subject, even when the facts do not agree, it can cause a disconnect or discrepancy between what one thinks reality is, and what it really is.

The cover-up, however, may have produced one silver lining. We like to think of our species as able to handle the open acknowledgment of UFOs and other beings, but what if we really cannot, at least not without a serious crisis? This might especially be the case if we were to learn that there is some unpleasantness to the presence of these *Others*. If that is so, then we might conclude that the cover-up has preserved human culture to some extent, rather than allowing it to disintegrate within panic. I do not personally subscribe to this belief, but it is worth consideration.

As substantial as the cultural impact of UFOs has been on our world so far, it is likely to be dwarfed by the end of the secrecy that envelops it. This has been something I have reflected on for some time. What I see is something no less than a replay of the 1960s, a decade when anything and everything seemed possible, when people developed a powerful distrust of their government, when they explored an array of alternative realities. This time, however, such a transformation will occur within the social and technological frameworks of the 21st century. A wild ride indeed. Because the major fact, sitting front row and center, will be the challenge, whether benign, benevolent or hostile, posed by the reality of highly advanced other beings here among us on Planet Earth.

Global Implications

When we try to look further ahead into the post-Disclosure world, which is the theme of this book's final chapter, we arrive at the likelihood of political revolution. Whether or not this ultimately will be something positive for mankind is not something I would care to predict. If prior revolutions are our guide, the post-Disclosure Revolution will probably usher in developments both beneficial and malign. Clearly, though, a major alteration of human politics will be necessary on a global scale. This will be not merely in order to cope with these other beings, whoever they are and whatever they want, but also to deal with the new technologies that undoubtedly will arise in the aftermath. Quite probably, too, from the demands laid down by the people themselves for a new and, it is to be hoped, more open and transparent political system. Disclosure may be the signal to lay down an open form of global fascism, but it does not have to be that way.

In the very long run, after Disclosure, humanity and our home Planet Earth will look very different than they do today. After all, we are already on an incredible trajectory. The disclosure of an extraterrestrial reality would only hasten the best of that. For better or for worse, ending the Big Secret will put us on the fast track.

Chapter 2
Theories of Ancient Visitation

We have had the ability to write and record our history for just over 6,000 years. Only in the last two hundred have we even tried to understand our ancient past with anything approaching sophistication. A mere two centuries ago, the sciences of geology and archeology were in their infancy. One hundred and fifty years ago, we were just beginning our excavations of early human habitations, just as Charles Darwin shocked the world with a theory that life was part of a dynamic, ever-changing survival of the fittest process which he termed evolution. Even a century ago, our knowledge of ancient cultures was negligible compared with what we know today. Our knowledge of our deep past has come to us very recently. We still have large holes in that knowledge and I suspect that, inside one of these holes, reside the ancient gods.

Our Journey to Understand the Past

We have spiritual beliefs today, but not like the ancients. Thousands of years ago, people confronted forces well beyond their control and understanding: hence the gods. During ancient times, it was universally held that human civilization was a gift of the gods. Whether in Egypt, Mesopotamia, Israel, Greece, Scandinavia, Britain, India, China, Africa, the Americas or elsewhere, most people believed the gods brought them the tools of civilization—agriculture, writing, medicine—everything worth having. When the monotheistic religions became dominant, the gods became a God, but the beat continued.

Then, starting around the 15th century, a revolution in thought swept first through Europe, and then worldwide. From Copernicus, whose astronomy placed the Sun and not the Earth at the center of our solar system, to Galileo and his experiments with gravity (and his discovery of Jupiter's moons), to Isaac Newton who presented the laws of physics, to the idea of Earth no longer as thousands of years old, but millions and then billions, to the concepts of Darwinian evolution, genetics, relativity, and quantum mechanics. Step by step, each of these developments, and many others, broke down the old paradigm of belief in the gods or God.

The new idea which took form was powerful, and it continues to dominate our civilization today: that everything can be understood rationally, scientifically. The ancient beliefs came to be seen as quaint relics of an ignorant time. Now, despite some gaps here and there, mankind has things pretty well understood, or so we tell ourselves. We see the natural world as powerful, but within our intellectual grasp. The same applies to our understanding of the past. We see it as wholly natural, human-based, sensible. Gods need not apply.

Yet, within that comfortable worldview, puzzles remain. One is the incredibly rapid pace of human evolution. We understand the Earth to be roughly 4.5 billion years old. Complex life started around 600 million years ago. The dinosaurs existed from around 230 million years ago to 65 million years ago, and it is fairly easy to track their development over those 165 million years. Considering the fairly limited changes over such a long period of time, evolution was an excruciatingly slow process.

That is the norm: slow change over millions of years. Consider the shark, so perfectly adapted to its environment that it has barely changed over millions of years. Or the horse, whose evolution is so beautifully depicted in New York City's Museum of Natural History. Over a period of 60 million years, the horse evolved from a small, cat-sized creature with ordinary feet that lived in a dense forest, to the large majestic creature of the open plains, now with hooves that are perfectly adapted to its new environment. Or the whale. Once a land creature that lived at the water's edge, it took millions upon millions of years to evolve into the largest mammal ever seen, breathing air but swimming to the depths of the oceans.

Chapter 2: Theories of Ancient Visitation

Now consider *homo sapiens*. By comparison, we have evolved in no time at all. Only four million years ago the distant ancestors of humanity, *australopithecus afarensis*, walked the plains of eastern Africa. They looked more like chimpanzees than human beings. A mere one million years ago *homo erectus* appeared. This was a radical departure from *australopithecus*. *Erectus* certainly looked and acted more like us, but he was not a recognizable human being.

In fact, according to standard evolutionary theory, it took less than one million years to evolve from something *not us* into something recognizable as us. To be more precise, the current estimate is that our species is a mere 200,000 years old, perhaps a little bit older. Such amazing evolutionary speed finds no parallel anywhere else on Earth. A natural question is, *why so fast*? Certainly, there may be a credible naturalistic explanation, but it is not unreasonable to wonder.

Was our rapid evolution caused by a kind of positive feedback loop stemming from our increasingly complex brains, behaviors, and discoveries, in which one development led to another, then to another, and so on?

Or did we receive evolutionary help, tweaked by some more advanced species? And is that the source of our belief in the gods?

Ancient Images

Let us take a closer look at these possible gods. We may start by asking whether ancient UFO stories can shed any light on the matter.

How long have people seen UFOs? If we are being visited, when did it begin? If the gods of ancient times were real, were they extraterrestrial, or did they come from some other dimension, time or reality?

These are difficult questions, perhaps impossible to answer, but the first of them is at least within our grasp. For it surely does appear that people have been recording UFOs throughout the course of our history.

The earliest bits of evidence may well be in European cave paintings, which represent some of the earliest examples of human art in existence. In particular, the French cave of Pech Merle portrays several objects that bear more than a passing resemblance to flying saucers moving among the local wildlife. The painting is roughly 19,000 or 20,000 years old. Interpreting such images is always a tricky business, but some ancient human artist did indeed depict *something* that looks like a hat-shaped UFO flying above the animals.

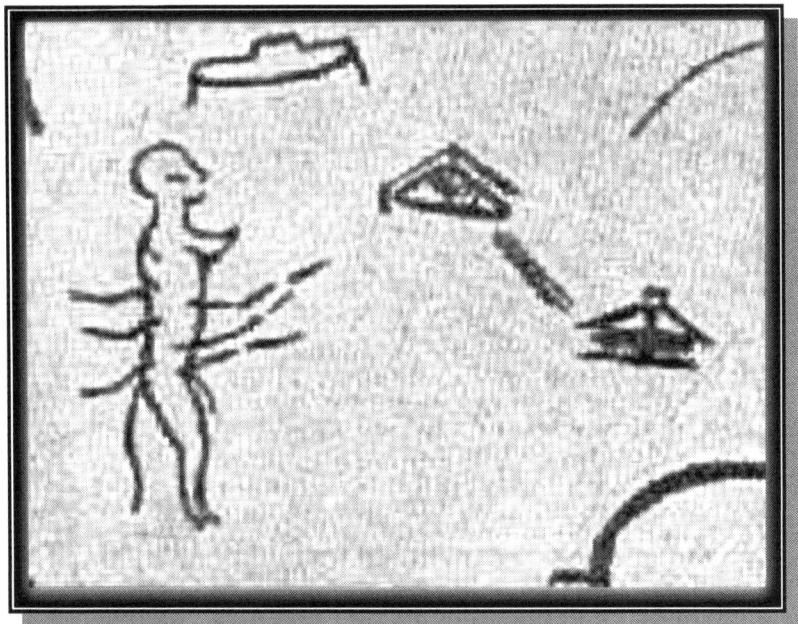

Cave art from Pech Merle depicting odd structures.

There are several hat-shaped images in these caves. The image above is sometimes called "the banner." But, of course, how would cave dwelling humans have a banner? Below the object is a person who appears to have many lines going through him, perhaps spears. In all likelihood, we will never know the full meaning of this image. Is the banner an early drawing of an alien craft?[9]

Some of the most eerily compelling pieces of suggestive ancient artwork are the cave paintings of Kimberley, Australia. These were created 5,000 years ago by the native aborigines, and they depict entities which they called the Wandjina, or sky beings. In the aboriginal tradition, these beings were part of the beginning of creation and had great powers over nature. One of them even became the Milky Way. When looking at the haunting images of the Wandjina, it is easy

---

9 Clottes, Jean. *Cave Art*, Phaidon Press, 2008

Chapter 2: Theories of Ancient Visitation

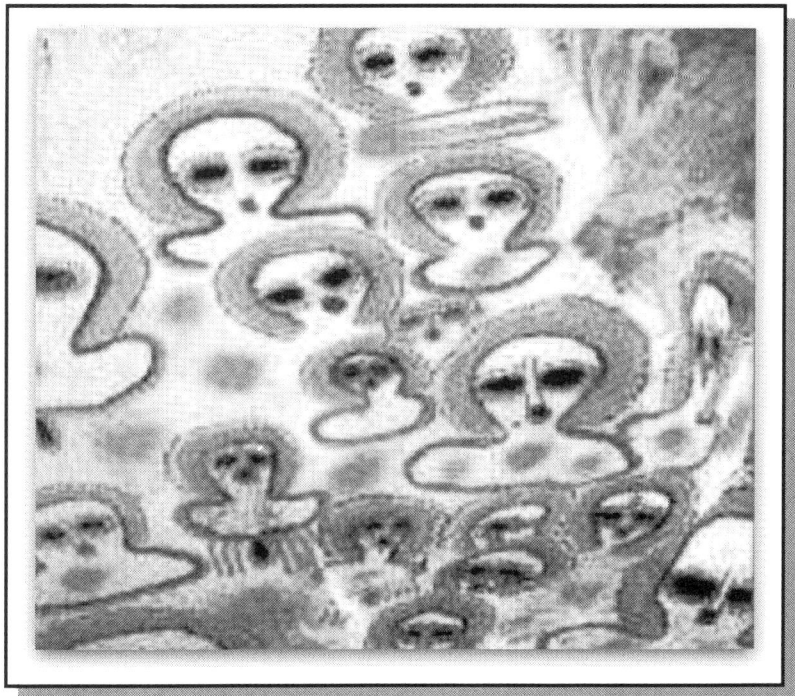

Aboriginal rock paintings in Kimberley, Australia, roughly 5,000 years old.

to think of gray aliens: oversized heads, no hair, large black eyes, no ears, no mouth, and pure white skin. Until the modern era of UFOs and depictions of ET beings, scholars had no point of reference for the Wandjina, no way to understand why these native Australians would create God beings so radically different in appearance from themselves.

There are many such ancient paintings on rocks and in caves around the world that depict what look like ET beings. In the northern Italian region of Lombardy, there is a rock painting dating to the Copper age, between 5,000 and 7,000 years ago. It depicts apparent priests or God figures. Each of them has what appears to be a halo, except that these halos look rather more like helmets, with straight lines extending out from them.

There are also interesting petroglyphs in North America, the most spectacular being in Utah. These are also quite ancient, around 3,000 years old. One of them, in Utah's Barrier Canyon, depicts a number of tall beings without arms, standing ominously. One of these, larger than the rest, looks very much like the images from Kimberley, Australia. There are similarly suggestive beings painted on rocks in Utah's Sego Canyon.

Unfortunately, these ancient people lacked written languages to more precisely describe what they were depicting. Certainly, these ancient artists may have been trying to paint something other than extraterrestrials. But they do appear to have been depicting powerful beings of some sort. Scholars vaguely interpret some of these as being "priest" figures. Perhaps. Regardless, the images are arresting. At the very least, they are suggestive that ancient peoples perceived beings that were powerful and godlike and different from themselves. From where did such an idea arise?

A Lost Civilization?

Even within the relatively short period of the last ten thousand to twenty thousand years, there may well be enough gaps in our knowledge to have included a lost, highly advanced, human civilization. Sometimes mixed in with the idea of a lost civilization is the thesis of ancient astronauts, that is, extraterrestrials. Mainstream scholars have long dismissed such ideas as heresy or even lunacy. Yet, the case for something like a lost civilization, although not as strong as proponents argue, is also not as weak as the mainstream arguments depict. Proponents point to a number of seemingly inexplicable oddities to support the idea of an advanced, lost civilization.

Some arguments are stronger than others. One that fails to persuade centers around the Piri Reis map, said to be a copy of a map from the Library at Constantinople, which was pillaged and looted in 1204 during the infamous Fourth Crusade. As argued by several researchers, most notably Graham Hancock in his bestseller, *Fingerprints of the Gods*, the map appears to depict the coastline of Antarctica centuries before its discovery by European explorers in 1820. Not only this, but it has been argued that it depicts Antarctica's natural coastline as it actually appears beneath the massive layers of ice. When Hancock published his book in 1995, contemporary science argued that the ice sheet covering Antarctica was at least 14 million years old (a number that has since been revised to 34 million years). Therefore, if we accept the map as an accurate depiction of the unencumbered Antarctic coast, it would mean that the continent was ice-free during the much more recent past. Hancock put the figure at not more than around 10,500 B.C.E. The theory he drew upon to explain the sudden climatic shift was derived from Charles Hapgood, an American college professor who developed a theory of Earth Crustal Displacement. Hapgood's idea was that the earth's crust, which is essentially like a thin layer of skin, can suddenly slip and create new locations for the poles. The weight of polar ice, he suggested, was one of the causes for these shifts.

The idea has no identifiable support among professional geologists, who favor the concept of plate tectonics as a way to explain the movement of land masses (which, they maintain, occurs much more slowly). In addition, there have been many core samples taken of Antarctic ice, the oldest of which is believed to be 530,000 years old.[10] Other core samples have shown a fully developed ice cap during the entire period between 40,000 to 6,000 years ago, that is, during the development of the earliest human settlements. In addition, scholars who have examined the Piri Reis map point out many inaccuracies on the map itself, no matter how one interprets it. Of course, one might always ask why any extreme southern continent would be on a map so old, a perfectly reasonable question. The answer is that such a continent (called *Terra Australis*) had been widely speculated to exist for several reasons. One was from the idea that something was needed to "balance" the land masses in the north, another from the observed presence of icebergs in the more extreme southern areas.[11] With such strong refutations coming from contemporary research and scholarship, there seems to be no room for a lost civilization in the history of Antarctica.

But this is not to refute the idea of either a lost civilization or a long-standing extraterrestrial presence in our world. There are enough

---

10 "Antarctic Ice Core over 500,000 Years Old Extracted," March 14, 2002. www.ens-newswire.com/ens/mar2002/2002-03-14-04.html
11 Fitzpatrick-Matthews, Keith. "Hancock's Antarctica: the continent that 'dare not speak its name.'" www.badarchaeology.com/?page_id=560

mysteries from our distant past to make reasonable minds wonder.

Pyramids

In addition to rock and cave paintings, there are archeological structures left behind by the ancients, some of which still defy our common sense. Foremost among these must be the Great Pyramid of Giza. Professional Egyptologists dismiss claims that the Great Pyramid is anything other than a pharaoh's tomb, built by human labor and ingenuity. And yet, studying the astonishing engineering, massive size, and mathematical perfection of that structure, we are forced to ask, how is it possible that such professionals could form opinions that fly in the face of the obvious?

It is not simply the fact that 2.3 million blocks of stone were used to build a pyramid that covers more than 13 acres of land. After all, a few modern engineers have claimed that they, too, could create such a massive structure, given enough time and money. But it is the precision of the pyramid that is so astonishing. It is easy to forget that it originally had an outer casing of white limestone blocks, perfectly polished and fitted. For thousands of years, the structure looked like a brilliant, white, gleaming beacon, unlike any other structure in existence. It required an earthquake to shake the limestone blocks loose, after which the local inhabitants removed most of them to build the city of Cairo. A few of those blocks remain today. They average a massive sixteen tons each, yet the fine joints are no thicker than a piece of paper.

The overall precision of this structure is breathtaking. This enormous object, 750 feet long at each base, is situated precisely along the four cardinal points: North, South, East, West. The ratio of its circumference to its original height equals the value of *pi*: 3.14, something not supposed to have been known for more than another millennium. Also, the geographical position of the great pyramid may well be the most significant of any structure in the world. Students have pointed out that it is positioned nearly exactly at the latitude and longitude lines that contain more land and less sea than any others on Earth. Thus, it can truly be said that the Great Pyramid is at the geographical center of the Earth. From this fact alone, it would seem that the builders of the Great Pyramid knew a great deal about the geography of our planet.

The Great Pyramid contains so many more incredible facts, but it is enough here to state that a detailed study of it yields even more questions. Yet, for whatever odd reasons, professional Egyptologists continually ignore them. One thing is clear: prior to the 20th Century, there was no other human civilization that could have even considered replicating it. This opens the question of whether there has been much greater knowledge somewhere on Planet Earth, knowledge that has been lost, either originating from extraterrestrials or from a lost advanced human civilization. Either way, it is a genuine mystery.

The mystery does not end there. Everyone knows something about other pyramids in Egypt and Central America. However, in recent years, we have come to recognize the existence of ancient pyramids throughout the world. The number of them is staggering. Central America alone is said to have more than one thousand pyramids, most of which have never been properly investigated. China is now understood to have many ancient pyramids, over three hundred so far. A massive pyramid in Bosnia is currently being investigated. For many years, it had not been recognized as such, but simply as a geometrical-looking large hill that had been terraformed by earlier inhabitants. However, since 2005, investigators have described it as a massive pyramidal construction with its own tunnel complex. Similar debates have been occurring regarding pyramid structures in Italy, Slovenia, Australia, Indonesia, the U.S. state of Ohio, and elsewhere.[12]

It is fascinating and exciting to ponder the likelihood of a relationship among all these structures, assuming we can definitively agree that they are in fact actual pyramids. We do not yet appear to be at that point, but of course the research is just beginning. Yet, there are theories trying to tie them together. Most intriguing is that the ancient pyramids and other megalithic sites are laid out in a grid, not according

---

12 A very good website offering information on this mystery is world-pyramids.com. There is an active Facebook page associated with it, as well:
https://www.facebook.com/WorldPyramids

to our current understanding of a grid, but one in which the patterns are based upon natural Earth energies. Further claims are that these ancient structures were positioned in a kind of web that tapped into a source of inexhaustible energy.[13] The claim certainly feels outlandish, and is supported by nothing that a professional scientist would consider valid evidence. Yet, we do seem to have ancient pyramids dotting our planet, and it is reasonable to wonder if there is a connection. If there is, what can it be?

Before moving on from the pyramids, we can touch on the debate over the Sphinx, situated with the three great pyramids at Giza. It became an issue during the early 1990s, when Robert M. Schoch, Ph.D., a geologist and associate professor of Natural Science at Boston University, noted that the Sphinx displayed erosion patterns that were not consistent with the patterns caused by wind and sand, but rather by water. However, there had not been significant rainfall in that area for many thousands of years. Moreover, he pointed out that during most of the recorded history of the Sphinx, it had been buried under sand, often up the neck. In such a state, it would be exposed to no weather elements at all. So how did the erosion take place? Based on what is known of weather patterns in northern Egypt through the millennia, Schoch dated the monument to between 7,000 and 5,000 BCE, long before the dawn of Egyptian civilization, during a period when the northern Sahara was not a desert, and received much more rainfall. Additional work by John Anthony West, who analyzed the archeo-astronomical aspects of the Sphinx, supported Schoch and pushed the date even further back. Thus, the fundamental chronology of ancient civilization had been challenged.

The academic world dismissed this argument as nothing more than crackpot ravings. Several geologists disputed Schoch's analysis, claiming that the erosion patterns are indeed those of wind and sand. Moreover, as Egyptologists argued, building the Sphinx in 7,000 BCE or earlier was impossible. Even as late as 3,000 BCE, people were living essentially in mud huts; they could hardly have created a monument

---

13 Asserted, for instance, by David Hatcher Childress in *Anti-Gravity and the World Grid* (Lost Science (Adventures Unlimited Press, 1987).

Chapter 2: Theories of Ancient Visitation

on the order of the Sphinx several millennia prior.

Then came one of the most important archeological discoveries of all time: Gobekli Tepe. This is a remote location at the top of a mountain ridge in southeastern Turkey which includes massive stones that have been definitively dated to no less than 9,000 BCE. The site is elaborate and includes beautifully carved stonework that staggered experts who had long maintained that such sophistication was impossible for people at such an early stage of development. Its construction predates all the important developments of what we associate with civilization: pottery, metallurgy, the invention of writing and the wheel, even agriculture and animal husbandry. It implies organization of an advanced order that was not supposed to be possible. Human society, after all, was still at a hunter-gatherer stage, not farming, not in large communities, and definitely not supposed to create something like *this*. Gobekli Tepe shows that there was a much more sophisticated presence on Earth around 10,000 BCE than experts had ever thought possible. This is not speculation, but unarguable fact.

If Gobekli Tepe could exist at that early date, then why not the Sphinx? Indeed, why not the Great Pyramid, and why not some of the other pyramids dotting the globe? The only problem with accepting such a conclusion is that it would force us to revise long-held beliefs on the development of human civilization. It would mean that there was a much more advanced human civilization at that early date, a civilization which somehow disappeared or went into remission. May we call this a lost civilization?

Before we get lost in this theory, as intriguing as it sounds, we should remind ourselves that there are no other signs of advanced civilization from much before 4,000 BCE. In other words, no wheel, nor any evidence of written language. Yet, clearly, we can at least acknowledge that scholars have greatly underestimated the activity on Planet Earth circa 7,000-11,000 BCE. Something very interesting was going on.

Other Structures, Inexplicable and Explicable

There are other impressive ancient sites that cause us to wonder.

Most of these have only been studied in relatively recent years, and we still have much to learn. Realistically, most of them are probably not evidence of either ancient astronauts or lost civilizations.

One which has received much recent attention, primarily because of the television show, *Ancient Aliens*, is Pumapunku, located near the town of Tiwanaku on the high Bolivian plains in the Andes. The Incas once believed this area was where the world was created. Small wonder, considering the magnificent stonework found there. The site is a terraced earthen mound with many megalithic blocks. Most unusual are the large number of precision small holes and other shapes that have been drilled or cut into them.

An example of the precision stonework at Pumapunko.

Even so, there is much disagreement over the crucial matter of when the site was built, as well as whether or not ancient peoples were capable of the kind of precision exhibited there. Proponents of an ancient astronaut theory sometimes have claimed the site to be 12,000 to 17,000 years old, far earlier than any known advanced human civilization. It has been claimed that the stones there are predominantly granite, andesite, and diorite, all exceptionally hard. From the perspective of mainstream scholarship, however, there is no real controversy. First, the dating of the site, based on extensive analysis of relevant organic samples, place its age at roughly 500 CE. The reason given for the much earlier dating appears to have been a misinterpretation of a piece of sculpted artwork, which some believed to be a type of elephant. If so, this surely would be interesting, since elephants only existed in the Americas' distant past. Most scholars believe that the image is of two stylized condors.

Regarding the stonework itself, it is unquestionably impressive. However, the huge stone structures are not of granite, but sandstone, which is decidedly easier to work. Even so, scholars concede they do not know how the heavy lifting and beautiful masonry were accomplished. That is not to say they believe the local inhabitants were incapable of doing it. Brian Dunning, writing in his *Skeptoid* blog, pointed out that there are other equally impressive examples of stonemasonry around the ancient world, including the Parthenon, Persepolis, and more. He concluded, "it is unnecessary to invoke aliens to explain the structures.[14]"

Perhaps the real question is whether or not the stonework shows signs of machining, as this has been the claim. Indeed, many of the large pieces are identical and made with incredible precision. It is not enough for mainstream scholars simply to throw up their hands and exclaim "we don't know," regarding stonework that looks as though it was machined. But was it really? That is the question and we do not have a firm answer.

There are other examples of ancient stonework that have probably received an overly-enthusiastic reception from ancient astronaut theorists. One would be the hundreds of large stone spheres found in Central America, mostly Costa Rica but also Guatemala and Vera Cruz. They are perfectly shaped, or very nearly so, and as large as eight feet in diameter. There are no comparable examples of such large stone

---

14 Dunning, Brian. "The Mystery of Pumapunku," *Skeptoid* #20, April 20, 2010, skeptoid.com/episodes/4202

balls found anywhere else. The people who allegedly shaped them are not known to have had anything more than crude tools, and would have had to transport them from fairly distant sources.

Still, many researchers do not believe these to be evidence of extraterrestrials or anything else equally unconventional. John W. Hoopes, for example, argues that the balls were probably made in a manner similar to that of many ancient polished stone axes and statues. One would begin with a roundish boulder, then work it into a spherical shape through a combination of controlled fracturing, pecking, grinding, rapid temperature changes, more pecking and hammering, then polishing. All of this can be done without metal tools or advanced machinery. Certainly, the quality of workmanship is exceptional, but not obviously beyond the ingenuity and skill of ancient people.[15]

Still, there are ancient ruins that boggle the mind. One must be the colossal stones cut at Baalbek, Lebanon. Most of the ruins there are Roman, but the site also contains enormous megaliths which are believed to be 2,000 years older than the Roman ruins. They do not fit with any known culture. The cutting and fitting of these stones, some weighing more than 1,500 tons, was done with perfection, despite being the largest cut stones in the world (some 68 x 14 x 14 feet). To this day, there is no reasonable explanation of who cut and prepared these stones, or was able to transport them roughly fifty miles from their origin, or place them on top of each other so perfectly, so early in the history of our civilization.[16]

Flying Trinkets

Aside from huge structures, there are other artifacts and depictions that are curious, including a few of what seem to be ancient flying craft. While such evidence is not directly suggestive of extraterrestrial influence, it remains interesting enough for us to wonder about what

---

15 Hoopes, John. "Debunking the 'Mystery' of the Stone Balls." www.world-mysteries.com/sar_12.htm
16 Quasar, Gian J. "Baalbek, A Colossal Enigma." www.bibliotecapleyades.net/esp_baalbek_1.htm

Chapter 2: Theories of Ancient Visitation

is missing in our knowledge of the ancient world.

One of these was an object found in 1898, in a tomb at Saqqara, Egypt, and was dated to around 200 BC. It has the head of a bird, but otherwise looks like a glider or airplane. However, because it was found before there were any airplanes, it was described as a "wooden bird model" and stored in the basement of the Cairo Museum. A number of years later, people began to realize its importance, so the Egyptian government created a special committee of scientists to study it. Then they labeled it as (drumroll, please) a model airplane! It has the same proportions of a what is known as a "pusher glider," with curved wings that slope downward slightly, giving the plane maximum lift without detracting from speed.

We might wonder, then, how someone more than 2,000 years ago devised a model of a flying device with such advanced features, requiring such knowledge of aerodynamics. Was this simply a lucky fluke?

The most famous model of an ancient flying craft comes from South America. It is a beautiful pre-Columbian gold trinket more than 1,000 years old. To anyone with common sense, it looks like a delta wing aircraft. Archaeologists, however, call it a "zoomorphic object," meaning that it is animal-shaped. But what animal could this represent? It does not resemble a bat, nor an insect, nor any other kind of flying creature one can imagine. It looks like an aircraft.

Much study and investigation have been done on this little trinket. Suffice to say that it flies, as was demonstrated on an episode of *Ancient Aliens*. A replica model of it was built, with the simple addition of a propeller. It flew perfectly. Another lucky fluke?

With all ancient artifacts and ruins, as with everything else in life, we should refrain from jumping to conclusions, constantly seek out all sides to a question, and do our best to form reasonable hypotheses (which must always be amenable to revision, following new information). Otherwise, we spend our lives doing nothing more than filling in the blanks of what we think we already know. Having offered this disclaimer, we must conclude that there are archeological mysteries

UFOs for the 21st Century Mind

A Pre-Columbian artifact. A replica of it (with an added propeller) flew.

which not only beg explanation, but which lead us toward a radical revision of our ancient past.

Ancient Writings: Vimanas

Archeology can tell us a great deal, but reading ancient writings is still more satisfying. Sure enough, there are a number of ancient writings that are believed to be suggestive of UFOs and extraterrestrial encounters. Let us start with some ancient writings that have received recent attention: the vimanas.

Much has been written about vimanas, especially on the web. One can easily become lost amid the sites, although it soon becomes evident that most of them simply copy each others' statements. It is obvious that precious few sites that discuss vimanas have any original research.

The word *vimana* is Sanskrit, and has had many meanings over the years: the palace of an emperor or a god, a temple, a chariot, or a vehicle. Today, it means aircraft. In Sanskrit literature, vimanas are mentioned in the poetic epics known as the Vedas. There are number of Vedas, including the *Rig Veda*, which does not mention vimanas, but does have a passage dealing with golden colored birds that fly up to heaven. This has sometimes been (very loosely) translated to imply

Chapter 2: Theories of Ancient Visitation

a vessel that jumps into space.

However, vimanas are mentioned in the *Ramayana*, another Veda epic which dates from the fourth or fifth century, B.C. In one passage, a vimana is described as a "chariot that resembles the sun... that aerial and excellent chariot going everywhere at will .... that chariot resembling a bright cloud in the sky .... and the king got in, and the excellent chariot ... rose up into the higher atmosphere."[17]

Another vimana is described in the *Mahabharata*, another ancient text. Here, one vimana measures twelve cubits in circumference, with four strong wheels. This seems quite small, roughly 20 to 25 feet in circumference, or about seven feet in diameter. Still, there have certainly been reports of flying saucers of that size.[18]

Unfortunately, most of what we hear regarding vimanas is connected to something that is not ancient, but entirely modern. That is the *Vaimanika Shastra*. Some sources have claimed it is an ancient Hindu manuscript, but this claim is spurious. Every single scholarly opinion agrees that it is an early 20th century Sanskrit text on aeronautics. In fact, It was claimed to be obtained by channeling. There is, in fact, no evidence of its existence prior to 1952, when the text itself was first revealed, and we are told it was dictated between 1918 and 1923. It is from this text that so many readers hear of the many allegedly technical features of the ancient vimanas. For instance, the claim that there were "31 essential parts" of the vehicles and "16 materials" from which they were constructed, and so on. The text gives a great amount of detail, it is true, but it is a 20th century creation.

Indeed, a number of studies of the technical illustrations make it clear that the vimanas as described in the *Vaimanika Shastra* are not even airworthy. One aviation engineer studied the technical illustrations, concluding the vimanas were "absurdly unaerodynamic." He added that "they look like brutalist wedding cakes, with minarets, huge ornithopter wings and dinky propellers. In other words, they look like typical early 20th century fantasy flying machines with an Indian

---

17 Dutt, Manatha Nath (translator). *Ramayana*, Elysium Press, Calcutta, 1892 and New York, 1910. Cited in "Vimana" From *Wikipedia, the free encyclopedia*.
18 *Mahabharata* VIII.31.80

twist."[19]

The fantasies from the *Vaimanika Shastra* aside, the vimanas of the ancient texts do transport the gods through the heavens. However, before we have anything definitive to say about them, serious and careful work needs to be done on this topic. We deserve better than wild claims which are uncertain at best and fictitious at worst.

Speaking of wild, fictitious claims, this is a good place to lay to rest the claim that the *Mahabharata* has a passage that describes nuclear devastation. The ancient text most certainly does not, although more recent ancient astronaut theorists have taken liberties in claiming otherwise.

It is unfortunate that this claim has continued for nearly fifty years, when it is clear that no one making it has been a Vedic scholar, nor even bothered to provide a sound citation of the original text. The Mahabharata, after all, is ten times longer than the *Iliad* and *Odyssey* combined. It has roughly 100,000 verses, many long prose passages, and about 1.8 million words. Who among students of UFOs has read any significant portion of that, or even can read the Sanskrit? Nevertheless, within that massive text, we are told there is a description of ancient aerial warfare involving nuclear weapons. Here is the key passage:

> Gurkha, flying a swift and powerful vimana,
> hurled a single projectile
> charged with all the power of the Universe.
> An incandescent column of smoke and flame,
> as bright as ten thousand suns,
> rose in all its splendor.
>
> It was an unknown weapon,
> and iron thunderbolt,
> a gigantic messenger of death,
> which reduced to ashes the entire race of the Vrishnis and Andhakas.
>
> The corpses were so burned
> as to be unrecognizable.

---

19 "Ancient Flying Machines, Vimanas - Vaimanika Shastra" [www.thelivingmoon.com] and Hindu Vivek Kendra, "Flights of Fancy?" *The Week*, June 24, 2001 [www.hvk.org/2001/0601/100.html]

Their hair and nails fell out.
Pottery broke without any apparent cause,
and the birds turned white.

...After a few hours, all foodstuffs were infected...
...to escape from this fire,
the soldiers threw themselves in streams
to wash themselves and all their equipment.

The passage appears in several books and many websites. But, as researcher Jason Colovito clearly shows, this translation bears hardly any relationship to the original sanskrit. This translation derives from earlier (misleading) translations, primarily one by Louis Pauwels and Jacques Bergier in their book, *Morning of the Magicians,* from 1960. The original sanskrit says nothing at all about nuclear bombs. Colovito sums up the situation well:

> Pauwels and Bergier seem to have intentionally mistranslated Sanskrit sentences into French to create a false impression, but were honest enough to allow that the sentences weren't related to each other and to leave in some baffling details . . . . [others] and their followers are content to mangle a bad English translation of a French mistranslation of a Sanskrit original without ever checking the original source material. Texts are conflated, separate incidents combined into one, and no context is considered or analyzed. Details that do not support [their] ideas are eliminated with no indication that they were dropped. Mistranslations are purposely created and copied uncritically. Then they are changed at will to support the author's views and repeated endlessly as revealed truth.[20]

The quotation has been repeated endlessly from website to website, copied and pasted at will, with no thought to checking for original citations. We can do better.

Ancient Writings: Egypt

Beyond the realm of mythologies and other sacred texts, the ancient world has left us with several interesting UFO accounts. Calling them reports is going too far, but they are certainly interesting stories.

The earliest of these, if legitimate, is from the annals of Thutmose

---

20 Colavito, Jason. "The Case of the False Quotations: How Ancient Astronaut Theorists Faked a Hindu Nuclear Explosion," 2011. www.jasoncolavito.com/the-case-of-the-false-quotes.html

III of Egypt's 18th Dynasty, who reigned 3,500 years ago. This document is known as the Tulli Papyrus, after Alberto Tulli, a director of the Egyptian section of the Vatican museum, who found it in a Cairo antique shop in 1933.[21] However, the price was too high, so a copy was made of the text, which was then recopied, this time replacing the original hieratic script with more common hieroglyphic. Years later, an Italian Prince named Boris de Rachewiltz claimed to have found the original papyrus, "untranslated and unpublished," among the papers which had been left by the deceased Tulli. He described his find to the Fortean *Doubt* magazine in 1953, and stated that the noted Egyptologist, Étienne Drioton of the Egyptian Museum in Cairo, had retranscribed it from the original hieratic script into hieroglyphics. De Rachewiltz claimed that the papyrus formed part of the library of Thutmosis III. Although nothing in the document refers to a pharaoh by name, this is not uncommon.[22]

Further complicating matters is that the document's location is currently unknown, so that no scholarly analysis can be performed on it; and, while the credentials of the associated individuals are not under dispute, there is always the possibility that the accuracy of the translations can be disputed. It is possible that the original papyrus was accidentally destroyed; if so, we may never be able to prove the authenticity of this compelling story.

More serious is the allegation in 2006, by Egyptologist Franco Brussino, that the *Tulli Papyrus* is a forgery, prepared from fragments of nine different papyruses described in a 1927 book by Egyptologist Sir Alan Gardiner.[23] However, another Egyptologist, R. Cedric Leonard, argues strongly against this conclusion. The forgery would have been made years before the world knew of "flying saucers," and indeed no motivation can be seen for it. More to the point, the documents Brussino claimed were used in this alleged forgery show "obvious textual differences" with several long phrases in the Tully

---

21 See "Tulli Papyrus," Wikipedia, the free Internet encyclopedia for a good overview of this.
22 de Rachewiltz, Boris, *Doubt* Magazine, No. 41, official magazine of the Fortean Society, pp. 214-15, Arlington, 1953;
23 Brussino, Franco (2006). "Il papiro di Tulli"
[www.egittologia.net/portals/0/articoli/IlPapiroTulli.PDF]

Chapter 2: Theories of Ancient Visitation

papyrus. "In regard to the short phrases," Leonard continued, "I have no doubt that I could locate identical short phrases by looking in Budge's hieroglyphic text of the *Book of the Dead*. Would that prove that Tulli cribbed the text in question from Budge's book?"[24]

Here is the translation of R. Cedric Leonard.

> In the year 22, of the third month of winter, sixth hour of the day [...] among the scribes of the House of Life it was found that a strange Fiery Disk was coming in the sky. It had no head. The breath of its mouth emitted a foul odor. Its body was one rod in length and one rod in width. It had no voice. It came toward His Majesty's house. Their heart became confused through it, and they fell upon their bellies. They [went] to the king, to report it. His Majesty [ordered that] the scrolls [located] in the House of Life be consulted. His Majesty meditated on all these events which were now going on.
>
> After several days had passed, they became more numerous in the sky than ever. They shined in the sky more than the brightness of the sun, and extended to the limits of the four supports of heaven [...] Powerful was the position of the Fiery Disks.
>
> The army of the King looked on, with His Majesty in their midst. It was after the evening meal when the Disks ascended even higher in the sky to the south. Fish and other volatiles rained down from the sky: a marvel never before known since the foundation of the country. And His Majesty caused incense to be brought to appease the heart of Amun-Re, the god of the Two Lands. And it was [ordered] that the event [be recorded for] His Majesty in the Annals of the House of Life [to be remembered] for ever.

An interesting aspect to this story, incidentally, is that Thutmose III, along with his stepmother and aunt, Hatshepsut, initiated one of the most glorious periods of ancient Egypt. Thutmose III extended Egypt's empire to the greatest extent in its history. In fact, that dynasty—the 18th—is the most famous of all. In addition to Thutmose III and Hatshepsut (who became one of the few female Pharaohs in Egyptian history), it included Akhenaten, (known as the "heretic pharaoh" who instituted the first known instance of monotheism in history) his queen Nefertiti, and his son Tutankhamun (King Tut).

---

24 Leonard, R. Cedric, Fire Circles, A Revised Translation of the Tulli Transcription, [www.atlantisquest.com/Firecircle.html]

Ancient Writings: The Bible

In the 1950s, a writer named Morris Jessup wrote an interesting book called *UFOs in the Bible*. This was the first true attempt to interpret the Bible with a connection to UFOs and extraterrestrials. Jessup wrote about unusual elements within the Book of Exodus, during which Moses led his people out of Egypt. Over and over during that time, powers from the sky interacted with them, sometimes dropping plagues from some kind of aerial conveyances, sometimes keeping them alive with "manna from heaven." Some of these passages are quite interesting.

Exodus 3:2 reads, "and the angel of the Lord appeared unto him in a flame of fire out of the midst of a Bush: and he looked and behold the Bush burned with fire, and the Bush was not consumed."

In Exodus 4:3, "he cast it (his rod) upon the ground, and it became a serpent; and Moses fled before it."

Or Exodus 13:21: "And the Lord went before them by day in a pillar of cloud... and by night in a pillar of fire." In Jessup's opinion, this seems like "an intelligently guided UFO."

There are enough passages in Exodus that suggest an extraterrestrial connection, that Exodus certainly warrants a fresh re-read from interested students.

A decade after Jessup, Erich von Daniken followed up on this line of thought. In *Chariots of the Gods?*, von Daniken offered an interesting interpretation of Ezekiel's vision, which he interpreted as a detailed description of a landing spacecraft with angels in the likeness of humans. Here is the most relevant passage from Ezekiel:

> As I looked at the living creatures, I saw a wheel upon the earth beside the living creatures, one for each of the four of them... like the gleaming of a chrysolite, and the four had the same likeness being as it were a wheel within a wheel ... [containing] rims and ... spokes, and the rims were full of eyes round about.... The living creatures were in each wheel.[25]

A fascinating sidelight to this is that a former NASA scientist named Josef Blumrich, who had thought von Daniken's interpretation to be

---

25 Ezek.1, *Bible, Revised Standard Version*. [quod.lib.umich.edu/cgi/r/rsv-idx?type=DIV2&byte=3114646]

ridiculous, set out to design a craft based on the passage in Ezekiel. Blumrich analyzed six different translations of the Bible in conjunction with his experience in engineering.

In a book he wrote in 1970s, *The Spaceships of Ezekiel*, Blumrich presented technical specifications of the spacecraft that, he argued, fit Ezekiel's description perfectly. Of course, we should remember that Ezekiel presumably was describing something well beyond his experience for his time of 2,500 years ago. If he did see a descending spacecraft, he would have lacked the language or technological understanding to describe it in any way other than he did. Ezekiel's description seems rather vague to be taken as an actual craft. Then again, why would it be impossible for ancient people to have seen genuine UFOs? And if so, why would we expect them to describe such phenomena the same as we would today?

Ancient Astronauts

It was von Daniken who put ancient astronauts into the public spotlight. Before him, the idea had barely registered anywhere, but by the early 1970s, it was everywhere. The thesis was that the technologies and religions of many ancient civilizations were bequeathed by ancient astronauts, who were welcomed as gods. Von Daniken's interpretation of the Bible was only a small part of his effort.

We may admire the audacity of such a grand interpretation—it was the 1960s, after all. *Enough said.* However, nothing in the book is scientific, precious little of it plausible. Von Daniken argued that a number of the structures and artifacts of the ancient world were highly advanced technology, explainable only by extraterrestrials. Very prominent in his book were structures like Stonehenge, the Egyptian pyramids, the huge heads on Easter Island, and the Nazca lines in Peru, the last of which he explained as landing strips for an ancient airfield. All of these, he argued, were connected to the presence of extraterrestrials. While the Great Pyramid clearly constitutes a genuine mystery in many important respects, most of these other monuments and artifacts do not require unconventional explanations.

Von Daniken also discussed the Piri Reis map, described earlier, and presented the image, now famous, of the tomb of the Mayan ruler Pakal, which he interpreted as depicting an astronaut in his spaceship. Again, this is interesting, perhaps suggestive. Most scholars, however, have no problem interpreting this in conventional Mayan terms, and it is certainly not proof of ancient astronauts.

Mayan artifacts. Statuette from ruins at Tikal (l) and an illustration of the lid of the tomb of the ruler Pakal (r).

Von Daniken has been ridiculed and attacked by mainstream scholars, and they certainly have picked apart his claims that the Easter Island statues, Stonehenge, the Nazca lines, or other monuments were built as a result of human contact with extraterrestrials.

However, despite his uncritical enthusiasm for any and all apparent ancient mysteries, a few of von Daniken's claims may have landed somewhat closer to their mark. For instance, although his account of the Great Pyramid is far from the best, he did bring attention to some of the oddities and mysteries of that structure. And try though we might to deny it, some of the ancient petroglyphs that appeared in his book do indeed look like people wearing spacesuits.

The Annunaki

Let us review another figure whose impact on the discussion over our origins equals that of von Daniken: Zechariah Sitchin.

Sitchin spent much of his life studying ancient Sumerian clay tablets, which is the earliest form of human writing. This includes cuneiform and ancient cylinder seals, and not surprisingly is understood by only a handful of scholars around the world. In addition to including information about ordinary things such as commercial transactions and the like, some of the tablets tell stories about "the gods" of Sumer. In general, scholars have interpreted these as they have interpreted all stories of gods from other ancient cultures: as myths told by people as a way of making sense of their world.

Sitchin, who did not undertake formal university study of these ancient tablets and was entirely self-taught, argued otherwise. Starting in 1976, he began publishing a series of books arguing that the stories told by the Sumerians were quite specific and detailed, and that they appeared to be describing, more or less accurately, what really happened. And what did these tablets say? According to Sitchin, they said that the ancient Sumerian gods, called the *Annunaki*, were an extraterrestrial race who came to Earth about 450,000 years ago. Their planet was known as Marduk or Nibiru. This planet, according to the tablets, followed a highly elongated, elliptical, orbit in Earth's solar system, making one transit around the Sun every 3,600 years.

The Annunaki originally came to Earth looking for minerals, argued Sitchin, especially gold, which they found in a mine in Africa. These so-called gods, he said, were essentially rank and file workers of a colonial expedition from Nibiru to Earth, undertaken during one of the periods when Nibiru's orbit took it close enough to Earth. Sitchin wrote that one of them, named Enki, suggested the creation of a better class of worker by genetically engineering man to mine for the gold. In other words *Homo Erectus* was crossed with genetic material from the Anunnaki to create modern *Homo Sapiens*.

The Anunnaki also taught humans the means of civilization, although presumably this was hundreds of thousands of years later. Sitchin argued that the Sumerians even knew that the Sun was the center of our solar system, (a fact unknown by our own civilization until Copernicus) and that all the planets were known to them, including Nibiru. There is a Sumerian cylinder seal, known as VA 243, that seems to depict the Sun surrounded by twelve smaller circles, (one of which is difficult to discern) presumably planets. In the same cylinder, a seated figure, seemingly a king of some kind, is significantly larger in size than the two men facing him. In Sitchin's opinion, this King was of the Annunaki, who were "much bigger, at least by a third ... than the average human being. They were giants."[26]

Sitchin expanded on this thesis over the course of many books, incorporating the Bible, for instance, when stating that the Anunnaki were the Nephilim as depicted in Genesis. When the Anunnaki returned after thousands of years, they found Earth females attractive. As it is written in Genesis:

> The sons of God saw that the daughters of men were beautiful, and they married any of them they chose. . . . The Nephilim were on the earth in those days—and also afterward—when the sons of God went to the daughters of men and had children by them. They were the heroes of old, men of renown.[27]

That is, the descendants of the Anunnaki continued to live on, until the Great Flood apparently wiped everyone out except for Noah and his descendants.

Sitchin's scenario is fascinating, and he has many followers, but professional Sumerian and Hebrew scholars are not among them. His detractors have argued that his translation skills were spotty and his documentation poor. A key criticism is that other scholars have no way to know what the original tablets actually show, because Sitchin provided few references or citations to enable them to look up the tablet. Certainly, the scientific difficulties of a planet like a Nibiru supporting life ought to be evident. A planet that far out from the sun, vastly more distant than Neptune or Pluto, yet supporting life? Of course, one might defend Sitchin on the basis that this is only what the tablets themselves say, but simply because the Sumerians may have recorded such a thing does not make it automatically true.

Sitchin's interpretation of the image on VA 243 has also been

---

26 Zecharia Sitchin, interview. Youtube video, "Were the Anunnaki the Nephilim in the Bible?" [www.youtube.com/watch?v=Hp0DAwy0-xM]
27 Genesis 6:2, 6:4. *Bible, New International Version.*

Chapter 2: Theories of Ancient Visitation

roundly criticized. Scholars point out that hundreds of Sumerian astronomical seals and calendars have been decoded and recorded, and the total count of planets on each seal has always been five. That is, the Sumerians knew of five planets only, not twelve as Sitchin asserted (the nine planets, plus the Sun, the Moon, and Nibiru—the Twelfth Planet). It is true that seal VA 243 has a sun-like image, plus twelve circles around it. Of course, it is easy to think it looks like the Sun, but apparently that symbol has no resemblance to the many other documented Sumerian sun symbols. According to researcher Michael Heiser, the Sun image on that seal is not the Sumerian symbol for the sun. It is only a star, as are the surrounding circles. In fact, scholars have translated this seal as a message from a nobleman to a servant reading simply, "you are his servant."[28]

Sumerian cylinder seal VA 243. Note the sun-like image at the upper left.

Similar objections are evident regarding Sitchin's interpretation of how the human race was engineered. As mentioned earlier, the rapidity of human evolution is a true marvel. One might easily wonder if we were engineered in some way, but it is difficult to get a good understanding of Sitchin's timeline. He wrote that the Annunaki arrived 450,000 years ago. As far as the most current science tells us, this is more than 200,000 years before the appearance of the earliest

---

28 Heiser, Michael. "The Myth of a 12th Planet in Sumero-Mesopotamian Astronomy: A Study of Cylinder Seal VA 243" [www.michaelsheiser.com/va_243%20page.htm]

anatomically modern human beings, whose remains have been found in Ethiopia, not Southern Africa (where Sitchin said humanity was created). Does this mean that it took them several hundred thousand years before creating anatomically modern humans? Why the long delay? Does this mean that such humans mined for gold in southern Africa for 100,000 years or even more? None of this really makes sense. Sitchin's scenario, which he formulated during the 1970s, simply does not fit with the increasingly complex understanding scientists have developed concerning human origins.

An argument supporting Sitchin's thesis has come from Michael Tellinger and Johan Heine, have explored ancient stone circle formations in their country that has led them to argue that an advanced civilization existed at the southern tip of Africa more than 200,000 years ago, and that they were mining gold. These formations, Tellinger argues, housed advanced technology that was designed to create tunnels to reach the gold deposits below the Earth.

The formations are certainly interesting. The stones are usually a few meters high, sometimes in complex arrangements, almost weblike. Traditional academic arguments that they are cattle enclosures seems absurd, given their structure, and the fact that many have no openings.[29]

Skeptics abound, and one of many problems has been to find a way to date the ruins in such a way that convinces outsiders. Another is to make a persuasive case about their use, while another still is to find evidence of sophisticated human settlements in South Africa dating back through those years. The presentation is intriguing, but the claims are generally recent. The task is to take the argument beyond speculation and incorporate corroborative evidence. Given the problems with Sitchin's work, it does not help that it is used as the inspiration and source.

It is not *a priori* impossible that humanity could have been engineered as the property of some extraterrestrial race, and Sitchin did create a fascinating interpretation of human origins. Still, the evidence

---

29 Tellinger, Michael. *Temples Of The African Gods. Slave Species of God, Adam's Calendar.* Inner Traditions, 2012.

he marshalled from the Sumerian and Biblical texts has been problematic. For this thesis to work, better arguments need to come from elsewhere.

Having said that, we would be rash to dismiss all possibilities that the ancient gods were nothing more than mythical figures. For instance, there has been a great deal of research (most of which is outside the academic mainstream) on ancient traditions and scriptures from the different continents that describe God figures in such a way that certainly give one pause.

Consider the many stories of serpent beings with superhuman powers. In India, for instance, they were known as the Naga. According to one Vedic tradition, the serpent Naga instructed humanity in knowledge of good and evil. It is interesting how the serpent is seen as a symbol of wisdom or knowledge across many cultural traditions. Cultures such as the Scandinavian, Slavic, Hebrew, Tibetan, Hopi, and West African all depict serpent gods possessing esoteric wisdom.

There are also occasional ancient depictions of deities that look decidedly reptilian. In particular are some well-known early Sumerian lizard-headed figurines from the fifth millennium B.C., from what is known as the Ubaid period, found in the Mesopotamian city of Ur. Are these actually the Anunnaki, as some ancient astronaut theorists argue? Such a conclusion seems unwarranted. After all, why would the Anunnaki be reptilian, when, according to Sitchin, they created mankind in their image? In fact, the female figure shown here, commonly described on the web as an Anunnaki god, is actually nursing a child. In all likelihood we are seeing a stylized form of art, the full interpretation of which we may never fully grasp.

There has also been discussion over the beings known as the *Elohim*. The word is Hebrew, and one valid way to translate it is Shining Ones. A number of researchers, including Richard L. Thompson, author of *Alien Identities*, believe that "these beings created modern humans from earlier human forms by genetic manipulation. Along these lines, some of these beings, called Watchers, mated with humans. This, however, was considered a crime by the Shining Ones." If you read the word *Elohim* in this manner, then Yahweh was one of the Shining Ones, but not the only one. Not all scholars accept the plural nature of Elohim. Indeed, Michael Heiser analyzed all instances in the Bible in which the God of Israel is the *elohim*, and the verbs are singular.[30] There is, however, the suggestive passage in Genesis which states "the sons of Gods (bene ha-elohim) saw the daughters of men that they were fair.[31]"

In summary, we must conclude that the stories and myths left from the ancient past generally do not stand up to scrutiny when we consider them as evidence for the idea of ancient extraterrestrial contact. But, that does not necessarily mean there are no reasons to speculate about an "ancient alien" connection to humanity. There remain some intriguing possibilities. Unfortunately, we may never get to a point where we can acquire enough evidence to settle the matter.

More Ancient Stories

During the last two millennia, interesting UFO-related events have continued to occur. Having already discussed the famous sighting of the prophet Ezekiel, let us move on to another famous apparition, that of the Emperor Constantine during the period of ancient Rome. According to legend, while Constantine marched with his army amid a Roman Civil War, he looked up to the sky. High above him he saw the early Christian symbol, two Greek letters: *chi* (X) and *rho* (P). These are the first two letters in the name of Christ. Accompanying these two symbols, we are told, were Greek words in the sky meaning "by this, be victorious." We are told that Constantine did not understand the apparition, but the following night he dreamed that Christ explained to him that he should use the sign against his enemies. That became the military standard used by Constantine, and he soon won control of the Roman Empire.

To put it mildly, such an account cannot be taken seriously by scholars. Who really can imagine not merely two Greek letters in the sky, but a complete phrase? And who can envision Christ coming to

---

30 Heiser, Michael. michaelsheiser.com/PaleoBabble/tag/gods/
31 *Genesis* 6:2a

Constantine in a dream, persuading him to use a Christian symbol for victory in war? Of course, it was Constantine's dream, not ours, and the man was a General. Perhaps there is a speck of truth somewhere in that story, some sort of strange apparition in the sky on that day.

The ancient world has other stories like this. A ninth century Latin manuscript, called *Liber contra insulam vulgi opinionem*, contains a passage which, a thousand years later, inspired the title of one of ufology's most original books: *Passport to Magonia*, by Jacques Vallée. In this document, the Archbishop of Lyons complained about a persistent belief among the French peasantry regarding a "certain region called Magonia from whence come ships in the clouds." According to the belief, the occupants of these vessels would "carry back to that region those fruits of the earth which are destroyed by hail and tempests; the sailors paying rewards to the storm wizards and themselves receiving corn and other produce." The Archbishop even said three men and a woman who had claimed to have "fallen from these same ships" had been stoned to death, an event he personally had witnessed.

An even more interesting story comes down to us from 13th century England. In the year 1211, Gervase of Tilbury, a chronicler of historical events and curiosities, recorded this bizarre story:

> There happened in the borough of Cloera, one Sunday, while the people were at Mass, a marvel. In this town is a church dedicated to St. Kinarus. It befell that an anchor was dropped from the sky, with a rope attached to it, and one of the flukes caught in the arch above the church door. The people rushed out of the church and saw in the sky a ship with men on board, floating before the anchor cable, and they saw a man leap overboard and jump down to the anchor, as if to release it. He looked as if he were swimming in water. The folk rushed up and tried to seize him; but the Bishop forbade the people to hold the man, for it might kill him, he said. The man was freed, and hurried up to the ship, where the crew cut the rope and the ship sailed out of sight. But the anchor is in the church, and has been there ever since, as a testimony.

This tale is like no other British legend or supernatural tradition. In the words of folklorist Katharine Briggs, it is "one of those strange, unmotivated and therefore rather convincing tales that are scattered through the early chronicles." Even so, Gervase wrote about a number of bizarre "marvels." Apparently, these included ghosts, lamia, fairy creatures, "the phoenix arising from the flames," "women with boars' tusks and men with eight feet and eyes." In short, this is not necessarily a source that inspires confidence.[32]

Another fascinating event, one that has received much attention on UFO-related websites, took place at dawn on April 14, 1561, over the town of Nuremberg, Germany. On that morning, people noted that the sky seemed filled with "cylindrical objects." Emerging from these objects were disks and globes colored red, black, orange, and blue. Crosses and tubes resembling cannon barrels also appeared. Then, the objects "began to fight one another." After about an hour of battle, they seemed to catch fire and fell to Earth, where they turned to steam. The witnesses took this display as a divine warning and were deeply affected. A few years later, an artist named Hans Glaser created a woodcut of it.

Commentators have occasionally attributed that spectacle to the effects of a sundog over the city. One supposes that anyone can say anything, since everyone who saw the apparition has been dead for five centuries. It seems, however, that this description is quite specific, and many of the effects do not resemble a sundog. Unfortunately, we encounter this problem with all ancient UFO stories. They are fascinating, but none of them were subjected to anything more than a cursory description. Nothing like proper investigations and reports were done, in which multiple witnesses were interviewed, measurements taken, and so on.

Such is also the case with a fascinating and baffling story from a century later. In some ways, this deserves to be called the first true, modern UFO report, except that, once again, it received no investigation. Even so, it was written up as a report to a higher authority, from whom it was hoped some sort of answer would come. Of course, given the circumstances of the event, no action could possibly have been

---

32 Joynes, Andrew. *Medieval Ghost Stories*, (Boydell Press, 2006), p. 74. See also Siebert, Eve, "The History Channel Discovers the REAL Cause of the Black Death," May 16, 2011, [skepticalhumanities.com].

Chapter 2: Theories of Ancient Visitation

Woodcut depiction of an aerial display over Nuremburg, 1561.

taken, and there is no evidence that any answer ever came.

The event took place in Russia, in the town of Roboziero, on August 15, 1663. Russia at that time was the very definition of a backwater area. Utterly remote, effectively cut off from the rest of the world, with no industrialization whatsoever. The case came to light around the year 1800, when a researcher in the St. Cyril Monastery discovered a letter to a Bishop from a concerned priest. The priest was relating a story that had been told to him by a villager.

According to the priest, people who were in church at the time heard a great sound in the heavens. They came outside and looked above. They saw "a large ball of fire [come] down over Roboziero, arriving from the clearest part of the cloudless heavens… it moved toward the lake passing over the church."

This is surely interesting. The size of the object appears to have been fairly substantial, perhaps between 100 feet and 150 feet in length. Two rays of light extended from it, then it left. But then, less than an hour later, it returned, coming to within 1,500 feet when it disappeared.

And then, "to the great terror of all those who watched it," it came back for a third time, remaining over the village for an hour and a half. According to the priest, fishermen in their boat on a nearby lake were burned by the heat. The waters of the lake were fully illuminated down to its bottom depth of thirty feet, and the fish swam away to the shore. The water also seemed to be covered with rust under the reddish light of the object.

If such a story were to be told today, we would certainly find it interesting, but without corroboration, not much more could be done with it. Of course, we might suppose this seventeenth century villager was pulling the leg of his local priest. We know nothing about the priest himself, or whether or not it might have been considered fun to tell a tall tale to the village priest. However, most historians of medieval Russia would consider this very unlikely. Priests held positions of great power in traditional villages. To put it mildly, Russian villagers would never have considered such a thing. What we have instead is a fascinating early UFO report, one which, incidentally, is reminiscent of the account from the era of Thutmose III in ancient Egypt. The object, as described by the priest, moved with too much deliberation for this to have been a natural phenomenon. We would seem to be dealing with either a hoax or a genuine UFO type of event, centuries before the world ever heard of flying saucers.

During the 18th century, the trickle of strange stories continued. Some of these undoubtedly are meteoric events, or even ball lightning (which, incidentally, is an unexplained phenomenon to this day). Others presumably could be One was said to have happened over the Isle of Man on February 15, 1716. As reported that year in *The Boston News Letter* "... there was a Strange Appearance of Ships in the Air, which engaged each other for about half an hour; when a Cloud of Divers Colours covered and prevented any further sight of them."[33]

One of the more interesting ones is from Westminster, England, from December 16, 1742. The phenomenon was witnessed by a highly educated man who wrote of his sighting in a journal called *Philosophical Transactions*.

---

33 "Daniel Guenther's Just the Cases UFO database." [www.jtc-ufo.com/database/sightings/5]

I saw a light arise from behind the Trees and Houses ... which I took at first for a large Sky-Rocket; but when it had risen to the Height of about 20 Degrees, it took a Motion nearly parallel to the Horizon, but waved in this manner [in his drawing of the object, he drew a wavy line]. Its Motion was so very slow, that I had it above half a Minute in View, and therefore Time enough to contemplate its Appearance fully ...

His drawing of the object made it appear somewhat acorn-shaped, with a long straight flame coming out of it as it moved across the sky. Needless to say, there was nothing in 1742 that could have explained this sighting.[34]

Charles Fort

By the 19th century, the trickle of UFO events became a small but steady flow. It is not necessarily that there was more activity, but simply that we became better at recording them. In this regard, the contribution of Charles Fort is of key importance. Fort was the first person in modern history to look at the anomalies of our past with a fresh eye, understanding these anomalies as, at least in part, the result of an intelligence beyond our civilization.

Fort lived through the turn of the 20th century, spending years at the New York Public Library, doggedly sifting through old newspaper reports, collecting many bizarre stories that, on the face of it, simply made no sense. For instance, all sorts of things falling out of the sky: frogs and fish, both living and dead, stones, and even blocks of ice.

He also collected an array of astronomical oddities. Some of these are certainly intriguing. One report was from 1799, describing a "luminous spot seen moving across the disk of Mercury."[35] Another, from November, 1821, was from the *Proceedings of the London Royal Society*, concerning unusual bright spots on the Moon. Yet another report, from the journal, *Philosophical Transactions*, in 1847, concerned a very odd moving light. According to the writer, "it looked like a star passing over the Moon which, on the next moment's consideration I knew to be impossible." He added, "it was a fixed, steady light upon

---

34 *Philosophical Transactions*, Vol. 42, p. 524.
35 Jenkins, B.G. "The luminous spot on Mercury in transit." *Monthly Notices of the Royal Astronomical Society,* 38 (April 1878): p. 338. Fort, Charles, *Book of the Damned*, p. 198

the dark part of the Moon.[36]" Another astronomical oddity found by Fort was recorded in the 1894 issue of the *Astrophysical Journal* about "a light reflecting body, or a bright spot near Mars seen November 25, 1894, by Prof. Pickering and others at the Lowell Observatory, above an unilluminated part of Mars...."[37]

One might try to argue that the astronomers of the 18th and 19th centuries were not as precise or capable as astronomers today. But, in fact, their equipment was up to the job, and they were certainly capable observers.

Fort collected more than astronomical oddities. Indeed, he collected many of what we can only call UFO sightings. Since they are predominantly from the 19th and early 20th century, we are clearly not talking about "ancient aliens." Even so, they are still early enough that they do not make sense in terms of secret or classified technology explanations. Moreover, they reinforce the idea of UFOs as something that goes back before our modern era.

For instance, Fort recorded a number of interesting ocean-based UFO sightings. One of them, from 1845, Is especially intriguing. It took place in the Mediterranean Sea, not far from Sicily and Malta. The latitude and longitude were given with precision by the Captain, who described three luminous bodies rising up from the sea about half a mile from the ship. The objects were visible for 10 minutes. A Malta newspaper reported the event:

On June 18th, at 9h 30m p.m., the brig *Victoria*, from Newcastle to Malta, in lat. 36° 40' 56", long. 13° 44' 36", was becalmed, with no appearance of bad weather, when her topgallant and royal masts suddenly went over the side as if carried away by a squall. Two hours it blew very hard from the east, and whilst all hands were aloft reefing topsails, it suddenly fell calm again, and they felt an overpowering heat and stench of sulphur. At this moment three luminous bodies issued from the sea, about half a mile from the vessel, and remained visible for ten minutes (it is not said what became of them). Soon after it began to blow hard again, and the vessel got into a current of cold

---

36 Fort, Charles, *Book of the Damned*, Cosimo Classics, 2004, p; 199.
37 Fort, Charles, *Book of the Damned*, Cosimo Classics, 2004, p; 195.

fresh air.

The sulphur connection is intriguing, since many UFO accounts have been connected to the smell of sulphur, as are accounts of so-called ball lightning. The latter is sometimes used as an explanation for UFO sightings. This is ironic, since there is no adequate understanding or explanation for ball lightning itself. Unfortunately, we have nothing more on this event from 1845.[38]

Another interesting ocean-based UFO report came from March 22, 1870, from F.W. Banner, captain of a ship named *The Lady of the Lake*. As he wrote in his ship's log, this occurred just north of the equator in the Atlantic Ocean, almost dead center between South America and Africa. For one thousand miles in any direction, there is nothing but water. On that day, the sailors of the ship saw a remarkable object, somewhat resembling a cloud, but not exactly. This object was circular and divided into four parts. According to the Captain, it had a "central dividing shaft beginning at the center of the circle and extending far outward, and then curving backward." In other words, it was a circular object with something that looked like a hook. The object started from a point south-southeast, about 20 degrees above the horizon, to a point northeast of the ship, about 80 degrees above the horizon. It was light gray in color, and much lower than the clouds. According to the sailors, it traveled against the wind. They watched it for thirty minutes, when it finally was lost in the evening darkness.[39]

Save a small, devoted, following, Fort received little attention for most of his life. Such is the price to pay for being so far ahead of your own time. It was not until fifteen years after his death that the modern UFO age was born in 1947, with the sighting of "flying saucers" by the pilot Kenneth Arnold. It was only then, in the following years, that many others began to look at the earlier period of human history in a different light.

Summary

When we think about early UFOs, we ought to shed many of the

---

38 *Malta Mail Times*, August 18th, 1845.
39 Fort, Charles, *Book of the Damned*, p. 267.

arguments that are currently used to justify them. Too many collapse under scrutiny, too many have relied upon sloppy translations of ancient texts, or even spurious texts. Too many others have made unwarranted interpretations of ancient artwork. And all too many commentators have done little more than trustfully copy and paste information from one website to another, without the slightest bother to investigate claims. As a result, many arguments have been made with poor evidence, speculation has taken on the status of "proven fact" in the mind of the public, and hyperbole has infested the entire subject.

Responsible investigators are obligated to do more. As we work to understand this difficult topic, we must take care to draw conclusions that are warranted by the evidence, and to know where to draw the line. There is nothing wrong with experiencing uncertainty.

Having said that, there is some reason for the hype regarding ancient UFOs. When looking at the big picture with an open mind, we can see there are reasons to think that *they* have been here for a very long time. The evidence we have may never be enough to make it a certainty, but even now there is enough to persuade a reasonable mind that highly advanced beings may well have been interacting with Planet Earth and its inhabitants, including humanity, for millennia.

In other words, we seem to have a hole in our history.

Chapter 3
Into Modernity: Airships, Foo Fighters, and Flying Saucers, 1896 to 1969

Even before the term "flying saucer" became a global catchphrase in 1947, unknown and unexplained aerial objects had become surprisingly common. As early as the turn of the twentieth century, the phenomenon had become a genuine mystery, even if no one quite realized it at the time.

Of course, the twentieth century was the century of human aviation. It is natural that, once people took to the air, some contraptions would genuinely mystify onlookers back then, just as they do today. Even so, by the year 1900 there were reports of things seen in the sky, sometimes on the ground, and sometimes in the waters of this great Earth, which baffled people then and a few of which baffle us today.

A good UFO story can be a bit like a good ghost story. Both are inexplicable and incredible; both challenge our beliefs and can make us uncomfortable. Yet, simply because we are generally taught that neither phenomena really exists, there will always be people who follow their own mind, who have an innate curiosity about their world. For such people, stories like the ones that follow can be fascinating, even exhilarating.

The Airships

Many people think of 1947 as the starting point of the UFO story. This is understandable, since that was when the phenomenon truly entered popular awareness. But as the previous chapter has shown, unknown aerial phenomena were being seen long before then.

Yet, sightings were sporadic and hardly of much public notice. That is, until the end of the nineteenth century.

In 1896, save for birds, occasional balloons, and a few early gliders, the skies of Planet Earth were clear. On rare occasions, one could see an experimental airship, essentially early blimps. But these were few indeed, and nearly all of them were in Europe. They were also primitive. The range of these airships did not exceed five or ten miles. They had terrible steering and were prone to crashes and deaths. Not until 1900, when the first Zeppelin was launched, did the golden age of airships begin, and that was across the Atlantic Ocean in Europe.

All of which makes the American airship sightings from 1896 to 1897 the first true wave of UFO sightings in the modern world. To this day, they remain a genuine mystery. Over 1,500 newspaper articles discussed them. They flew with intensely bright searchlights, sometimes very high up, sometimes low, occasionally lighting an area as though it were daylight. Amid the fuss, people sometimes claimed to meet (the entirely human) occupants of these ships, who unfortunately never seemed to give away much valuable information. For six months, people claimed to see them. Then, just as suddenly, the airships were gone.[40]

Traditionally, the story began in Sacramento, California on November 17, 1896, although later research has shown that sporadic sightings of vague aerial phenomena had been reported up and down the U.S. west coast in the previous months.[41] Newspapers reported that hundreds of people saw a light pass over the city, like "an electric arc lamp propelled by some mysterious force.[42]" It traveled so low to the ground that it took evasive action as it approached buildings and hills, and people claimed to hear voices coming from it. Then it flew away. We are told that it returned to Sacramento three days later, and then on the following day (November 21), it was seen over nearby Oakland. In this case, we have an artist's illustration showing a large airship, perhaps 200 feet long, with powerful headlights shining down. It is worth remembering that the source of power needed for an intensely bright searchlight at that time would have been extremely

---

40 A fine website devoted to airships, complete with original newspaper articles, is ufologie.patrickgross.org/htm/airship.htm
41 See ufologie.patrickgross.org/airship/index.htm
42 *California Bee*, Sacramento, California, November 18, 1896.

Chapter 3: Into Modernity

Sketch of a mystery airship seen over San Fransicso, November 19, 1896.

heavy, and definitely was not a practical item carried by airships back then.

The airship, or *something*, returned to Sacramento on November 25. People reported seeing a bright light circling the city at "high speed," whatever that would have been. We are told that many observers, including high-ranking state officials, saw it, and they were convinced it was not an astronomical body. What was it? We do not know.

Some of these airship sightings were obvious hoaxes, and American journalism at the time did enjoy the occasional tongue-in-cheek story. One man, for instance, claimed that while driving his buggy through the countryside, he happened across a landed metallic spacecraft roughly 150 feet long. Three slender seven-foot tall beings approached him while "making a strange warbling noise." They tried to force him into their ship, but were not strong enough, so they simply flew off in their ship. This is the first modern claim of an attempted alien abduction. It is also an amusing yarn.[43]

Another witness said the group he met claimed to be from the lost tribe of Israel. Yet another group of airship pilots allegedly claimed to be going off to fight Spain (this was shortly before the Spanish-

---

43 *Stockton Daily Mail*, November 19, 1896.

American War). One witness said an airship landed on his pasture in Rockland, Texas. One of the pilots, an ordinary man, asked for lubricating oil, chisels, and bluestone. Then he paid for them, presumably with valid currency. When the witness tried to inspect the airship, another occupant stopped him, although he promised to return to take him for a ride. The airship then took off "like a shot out of a gun."[44] Incidentally, bluestone has a high silica content that can generate electricity under pressure; one cuts it by soaking it in water and striking it with a chisel.

Two of the most dramatic airship cases occurred in Chicago, Illinois, and Aurora, Texas. Chicago's event took place on April 9, 1897. The local newspaper reported that thousands of people saw bright, intense, lights circling the city that night. No one was sure if this was a true airship, but it seemed to be some sort of floating object "miles above the earth." A few people claimed to see two cigar-shaped objects joined together and with great wings. From time to time it was illuminated by the rays of two giant searchlights.[45]

However, the town of Aurora, Texas takes the prize for the most dramatic airship story. Early in the morning of April 17, according to a story in the *Dallas Morning News*, one of these airships crashed into a local windmill. The occupant, who was declared to be "not an inhabitant of this world," was dead and mangled. The wreckage was said to be a mixture of silver and aluminum, and was said to have weighed several tons. Whatever happened to it was never mentioned, other than that locals descended upon it and presumably scavenged all the pieces. Some of it was allegedly dumped into a nearby well.[46]

The deceased occupant had been carrying "papers" which were indecipherable and, *a la* Roswell, written in some unknown hiero-

---

44 *Houston Post*, April 22, 1897. See ufologie.patrickgross.org/press2/houstonpost22apr1897.htm
45 "That airship now at Chicago." New York *Herald*, April 11, 1897.
46 An interesting addendum to this was the story of Brawley Oates, who bought the property around 1945. Some years later, apparently during the late 1950s, Oates cleaned out the debris in the well and soon after developed a severe case of arthritis. He claimed this was because of contaminated water from the wreckage dumped into the well. As a result, he sealed the well with a concrete slab and placed an outbuilding atop it.
[en.wikipedia.org/wiki/Aurora,_Texas_UFO_incident]

glyphic. The dead alien had even been buried in the town cemetery, according to the article. An interesting addendum to this story is that, years later in 1973, investigators with the Mutual UFO Network (MUFON) discovered the alleged stone marker used in this burial. Their metal detectors indicated that something unusual might have been buried there, but they were not allowed to dig. A few years later, when they returned to try again, the headstone was gone, as was whatever metallic material lay beneath it.

There has been a great deal written about the Aurora case, both pro and con, as with the airship mystery itself. Unfortunately, throughout the period of airship sightings, no investigator is known to have performed a true investigation or analysis. More recently, the television show *UFO Hunters* aired an episode in which investigators were allowed to unseal the well where it was believed the remains of the wreckage had been deposited. Water taken from the well tested normal, except for large amounts of aluminum. Although the well contained no apparent wreckage, it was stated that large pieces of metal had been removed from the well by a past owner of the property. The investigation also refuted earlier statements from an elderly resident in 1979, that the property in question never had a windmill. On the contrary, the *UFO Hunters* investigation found the remains of a windmill base near the well site. Does this mean that what happened at Aurora was a genuine UFO event? We are still far from any confirmation.[47]

Many people at the time suspected the airships were a new American invention. So many inquiries reached the inventor Thomas Edison that he made a public statement denying any connection to the airships. Recently, there have been claims that there were American inventors who were developing state-of-the-art airships at the time. It has been suggested that an unknown inventor with financial backing was responsible. One supposes that this could be possible, and it does seem that there were a few prototype airships being flown around the

---

47 See the UFO Hunters episode of November 19, 2008 entitled "First Contact," at *Aurora Texas UFO Crash - Paranormal Alien Documentary* on YouTube [https://www.youtube.com/watch?v=eEfRQ3h8WQM]

Midwest in the mid-and late 1890s.[48]

Yet, the airships of 1896 and 1897 were at least ten years ahead of the rest of the world. That may not sound like much, but it is of great importance. The entire matter comes down to whether or not one credits the newspaper accounts, since the performance capabilities of these airships were vastly superior than even the Zeppelins of a few years later. That takes some doing if we are considering a clandestine human agency. How could these prototypes have remained secret to this day?

It is also helpful to recall that many of the sightings were merely presumed to be airships. A number of them were of unusual lights in the night sky, very much like UFO reports of today. A number of them truly could have been anything, but that surely does not make them alien craft.

In considering the airships, is it possible that we are dealing with some extraordinary agency? Could it be that some group, whether from "here" or not, allowed themselves to appear in a more-or-less conventional manner so as not to terrify witnesses? Perhaps, too, to inspire them toward new developments in aviation? Could the airships have been a demonstration by an extraterrestrial agency for the purpose of sparking human innovation? Or simply a confusion caused by a variety of factors, including misidentification, hoaxes, and hysteria? Questions and more questions. Few answers.

After the Airships

It was once assumed that UFOs were not seen between the airship sightings of 1897 and the 1940s. In reality, unexplained sightings, while much less reported than today, continued through the early decades of the twentieth century. Some were extraordinary.

One such case occurred at sea on February 28, 1904 when crew members aboard the USS *Supply*, a Navy ship 400 miles southwest of

---

48 For instance, Busby, Michael, *Solving the 1897 Airship Mystery* (Pelican, 2004) and Danelek, J. Allan, The Great Airship of 1897, both propose variations of the argument that a mysterious American inventor (or group of inventors) were behind the sightings. While both are conjectural, they attempt to make a reasonable case for human-made airships.

San Francisco saw three large, red, glowing objects in a close triangle formation. For two minutes, the objects were seen passing beneath the clouds at about a mile in altitude. They approached the ship, levelled off, then climbed back through the clouds and out of sight. The ship's Commander, Lieutenant Frank Schofield, who later became an Admiral and Commander-in-Chief of the U.S. Pacific Battle Fleet, appears to have been one of the witnesses. The event was reported in the *New York Times*, which described the largest of the objects [described as "meteors" in the article] as having an apparent area of six suns and being egg-shaped, with the sharper end forward. The other two objects were round.[49]

In 1908 and 1909, there were some odd aerial events in New England, several in December 1909. Mostly these were very bright lights, either circling in the sky or moving across. Airplanes were still not common at all, so it remains strange. Still, we have to be careful. During the following month, for instance, similar sightings occurred in the American South. For several days in January, 1910, there were airship sightings in Chattanooga, Tennessee. Thousands of people rushed out of their homes in broad daylight to see a huge, white, cigar-shaped object, plainly in view, flying around above the city. This went on for several days in a row, until the so-called airship was captured. It was a 15 foot-long home-made balloon set aloft as a prank.[50]

One of most interesting sightings of the early twentieth century occurred in northeastern Tibet on August 5, 1927. The person who recorded it was an artist and philosopher named Nicholas Roerich, who was leading a trek in the Himalayas. In his diary, he described how members of his party were observing a large black eagle in the sky, when someone noticed something more interesting far above the bird. Roerich wrote:

> We all saw, in the direction north to south, something big and shiny reflecting sun, like a huge oval moving at great speed. Crossing our camp

---

[49] "Navy Officer Sees Meteors.; They Were Red Ones, the Largest About Six Suns Big." *The New York Times*. 9 March 1904. See also
brumac.8k.com/RemarkableMeteors/Remarkable.html
[50] "Chattanooga Airship of 1910," *Examiner*, Jan. 15, 2013
[www.examiner.com/article/chattanooga-airship-of-1910?cid=rss]

this thing changed in its direction from south to southwest, and we saw how it disappeared in the intense blue sky. We even had time to take our field glasses and saw quite distinctly the oval form with the shiny surface, one side of which was brilliant from the sun.

This would appear to be a very solid UFO incident. After all, what silvery, oval, huge object could fly through northeastern Tibet in 1927? Still, no case is immune from attempts at conventional explanation. In this instance, some researchers believe they found the answer. Amazingly, it turns out that Roerich's group were not the only explorers traveling through China and Tibet at that time. A Swedish expedition was also in the general region and, believe it or not, they launched several weather balloons at around this time. We do not have precise dates, unfortunately, but some appear to have been launched in August, 1927, the month of the sighting.[51]

Could one of these balloons have been what Roerich's group saw? It would seem logical to conclude yes, especially when recalling that weather balloons were quite rare and could well have fooled an observer. On the other hand, there is reason to doubt the balloon explanation.

The main problem is that the Swedish group was never closer than 400 miles to Roerich's party, and the balloons were not larger than four feet in diameter; many were smaller. Realistically, for any of those balloons to have been visible to Roerich's group, they would had to have been launched much closer. One researcher pointed out that, even if launched a mere one mile away, it would have been nearly impossible to see such a balloon with the naked eye. Consider how insignificant a three- or four-foot balloon would have appeared at a distance of even two or three miles. Yet, Roerich described the object as huge, brilliant, and oval-shaped.

The clincher, however, is that 400 miles appears to be beyond the range of *any* weather balloon. Most never travel more than 100 miles from their point of origin before bursting, although the jet stream

---

51 Sparks, Brad. "1927 Roerich Sighting Analyzsis," [www.nicap.org/270805himalayasdir.htm]

Chapter 3: Into Modernity

might enable some to travel around 150 miles in a few cases.[52]

All of which leaves us with a genuine mystery. Still, there are those who find extraordinary explanations distasteful. One supposes that such people could, if pressed to the wall, argue that a small balloon miraculously traveled more than 400 miles to be seen by a completely separate expedition. A stretch, obviously, but what else is there? Unless, of course, it was a genuine alien craft.

No doubt there were many other startling sightings from the 1920s and 1930s which are now lost to us forever. People essentially had no way to report such things. However, some years ago while visiting the Canadian National Archives in Ottawa, I came across several extraordinary reports. These were sightings that ordinary people reported to their government, hoping that somehow it would be of interest. In fact, the Canadian government did nothing with these reports, but they are archived for anyone to read. A few of them describe events that took place as far back as far as the 1930s.

One was submitted in the early 1980s by an elderly man who described his experience in the Northwest Territories in 1936. This is a remote area, nearly as large as Alaska, inhabited by very few people. His exact location, Aylmer Lake, was especially remote. This is within a large region known as the Barren Grounds, a tundra zone in the Canadian Arctic where trees do not grow and where, to this day, nobody lives. The writer was 25 years old at the time, employed by the government in aerial mapping operations. He wrote:

> At the time of the sighting, I was standing on the float of my aircraft performing a before-flight inspection when I happened to glance skyward and detected the vehicle in question, completely stationary. How long it had been there and for whatever reason I have no idea. At the time the sky was azure blue, completely clear of all cumulus and cirrus clouds (C.A.V.U.), making it virtually impossible to determine the height of the object in question.
>
> In trying to describe this vehicle, I can only say that it was the most magnificent configuration of an airship one could imagine. I would say it was very large, but this would depend on the height, which as stated could

---

52 See wiki.answers.com/Q/Where_do_weather_balloons_go; and www.ehow.com/way_5745254_homemade-weather-balloon.html.

not be determined.

He then described some salient features of the object, including a light aluminum color but no shine, an elliptical shape, and no portholes.

The object was stationary for a moment, then it rotated. He continued:

> From a north/south stationary position it turned east in a moment. The turning was hardly detectable to the eye. After the turn, it took off at a fantastic speed going east. From the time of takeoff until it vanished was a matter of moments.

He added that it made no contrail when it departed. The writer attached his service record in order to confirm his identity.[53]

Truly an amazing story. Incredible technology in one of the most remote regions on Earth.

World War Two

It was during the Second World War that UFO reports became more common. Of course, this makes perfect sense. It was only during the 1940s that large numbers of people began to fly in the skies. Above the clouds with perfect visibility, there were now many more chances to see what was up there. Radar was another new development, enabling electronic detection of aerial objects. Thus, our ability to sense the world around us increased dramatically. Sure enough, people began to notice many more strange things in the skies. These strange objects were eventually given a name: *foo fighters*. Even today, researchers disagree on what they were. But there is no question they remain the greatest mystery of the war.

The first important UFO sighting of the war was so significant that it has its own name: the Battle of Los Angeles. This happened early in the morning of February 25, 1942, a mere three months after Pearl Harbor. The U.S. was in a heightened state of alert regarding the Japanese threat. In fact, Japanese submarines were off the U.S. coast

---

53 To (Canadian) National Research Council; Re: UFO Sighting, NWT 1936 Alymer Lake, NWT. Canadian National Archives, Ottawa. Record Group 77 ACC 1992-1993/308 N92/15.

Chapter 3: Into Modernity

Photograph of an object over Los Angeles, early morning hours of February 25, 1942. The small white dots are artillary bursts.

at the time, and there had been a minor military engagement just a few days before. Then, at around 2 a.m. on February 25, several radars detected an unidentified target over the ocean, about 120 miles west of Los Angeles. Within minutes, anti-aircraft batteries were on alert, ready for action. A small number of fighter planes were on the ground but also ready. The target was tracked on radar to within a few miles of the coast. At 2:21 a.m., a city blackout was ordered.

This is when things became a bit confusing. In the first place, the radar target vanished. Next, personnel started reporting enemy planes. One colonel thought he saw about twenty-five planes over Los Angeles. Shortly after 3:00 a.m., anti-aircraft batteries opened fire. Some 1,430 rounds were fired into the sky—not over the ocean, but right over the city. Three citizens actually died from the shelling, and three more from heart attacks attributed to the shelling. A great deal of property damage was also inflicted. This is not surprising, considering that roughly nine tons of ordnance had been fired into the air. Oddly, no debris of the object (or objects) was ever known to have been recovered.

So what was in the sky that night?

Army Chief of Staff George Marshall wrote to President Roosevelt that, "unidentified airplanes, other than American Army or Navy planes, were probably over Los Angeles." But, in fact, these could not have been Japanese planes. The only possible source for any such planes would have been an aircraft carrier, and none were nearby. In all the records of the war, nothing even hints of Japanese planes flying over Los Angeles at any time.

If not enemy military aircraft, could they have been commercial aircraft? The question is a fair one, but, once again, there is no evidence suggesting anything of the sort. Commercial aircraft were certainly not coming in over the Pacific at 3:00 a.m. Moreover, no commercial aircraft would have withstood the artillery barrage; they would have been shot out of the sky.

Navy Secretary Frank Knox suggested it was all a big mistake caused by "war nerves." Nothing flew over the city, he said. That statement earned him a heap of scorn from the Los Angeles media, and even some of the area military.

Could our old friends, balloons, have been behind this?

In fact, meteorological balloons *were* in the thick of the action that night. They may even have triggered the shelling itself. Because wind conditions affected the trajectory of a shell, regiments often released balloons to determine how the wind was blowing.

At 3:00 a.m., when all of Los Angeles was in a state of red-alert, when searchlights were on and anti-aircraft gunners were ready to fire, two of these balloons were set aloft, each one with a candle inside to improve its visibility. Since the barrage also started at 3:00 a.m., it is reasonable to conclude that the balloons triggered it. In fact, this is what some historians conclude: the excitement of that night stemmed from a faulty radar reading, balloons, and inexperienced, nervous gunners.

On the face of it, this seems reasonable. It may even be true. The only problem is that most of the eyewitness accounts do not support it. In the first place, several witnesses stated that they saw anywhere from fifteen to twenty-five objects in the sky. There were two balloons in the sky, possibly a few others that remain unaccounted for, but

Chapter 3: Into Modernity

certainly not fifteen. Additionally, people were reporting objects in the sky fifteen minutes before the first balloon was launched.

Many witnesses also maintained that the objects were unaffected by the shelling. One witness, an experienced Navy observer, counted nine silver-colored planes through high-quality binoculars. He said they passed from one battery of searchlights to another, all while under heavy fire from the guns below.

There is also a photograph from that night, a truly remarkable image. The small lights scattered around the searchlights are exploding shells, visually interesting but not unusual. It is the object in the center of the searchlights that some believe is a genuine extraterrestrial craft.

Dr. Bruce Maccabee, an expert in photographic analysis, believed the object to be roughly 100 feet or more in diameter. If correct, this would be a problem for the balloon theory, since the balloons launched were a mere four feet in diameter.

Ultimately, while we cannot entirely rule out a conventional explanation such as balloons, there is reason to consider that the objects over Los Angeles were genuine UFOs. Indeed, why not? The balloon explanation presents enough problems to make a reasonable mind wonder.

If these were UFOs from some agency not of our own society or civilization, we might naturally ask what were the operators of those craft trying to do? Were they conducting a test of some sort? Did they make a mistake? Were they joyriding?

Unfortunately, when reflecting on these possible answers, the UFO explanation feels equally dissatisfying. This is a key problem of the entire phenomenon. Not only is the apparent UFO technology well beyond contemporary human capabilities, but whatever motivates their operators remains a mystery. They simply refuse to make sense to us.[54]

So much for the Battle of Los Angeles.

---

54 Helpful resources on the Battle of Los Angeles include: Littleton, C. Scott, *2500 Strand: Growing Up in Hermosa Beach, California, during World War II*. (Red Pill Press, 2007), p. 59.; Young, Donald J., "Phantom Japanese Raid on Los Angeles During World War II," *Word War II* (September 2003), reprinted at www.historynet.com/phantom-japanese-raid-on-los-angeles-during-world-war-ii.htm/1; Marshall, George C., "Memorandum for the President," 26 February 1942; and the website of Bruce Maccabee at brumac.8k.com/BATTLEOFLA/BOLA1.html.

Its interesting that the next day, on February 26, 1942, a fascinating UFO sighting is said to have taken place in the Timor Sea, north of Australia, by the crew of the Cruiser *Tromp* of the Royal Netherlands Navy. Years later, a man named William Methorst, claiming to have been on the ship, wrote that a large metallic-looking disk flew toward the ship at "tremendous speed." It circled high above for three to four hours, and finally flew off at an estimated speed of more than 3,000 mph.

Did it really happen? Australian researcher Keith Basterfield tried to confirm the account. He discovered that the *Tromp* had indeed been in the Timor Sea, although a few days prior to the date of the alleged encounter. By February 26, it was moving down the western side of Australia, probably near the coast. Of course, this is hardly a problem, since people can easily misremember certain details, especially dates. Unfortunately, no one has yet confirmed that a man named Methorst was on the *Tromp* at that time. If that can ever be confirmed, we would have a stronger case, although, once again, a skeptic can fall back to the argument that, ultimately, the story is just one person's allegation. Still, it could well be that the story is true.[55]

There are a number of UFO stories from the war, either confirmed in military records or obtained through witness interviews. U.S. marine sergeant Stephen J. Brickner said in August 1942 while on the island of Tulagi, just west of Guadalcanal, that he saw a huge formation of over 150 objects, faster than Japanese planes, with no wings or tails, wobbling slightly, and dropping no bombs. He called it "the most awe-inspiring and yet frightening spectacle I've ever seen in my life."[56]

In 1944 and 1945 reports of UFOs came in from Allied pilots over Europe, soon dubbed "foo fighters" in the press. A typical account came from B-17 pilot Charles Odom on a daylight raid over Germany. He said that objects "the size of basketballs" approached his aircraft to within three hundred feet, then almost seemed magnetized to the

---

55 Basterfield, Keith. "26 February 1942 Timor Sea, north of Australia 1200hrs Methorst," *Project 1947; a Catalogue of the More Interesting Australian Ufo Reports, as of 6 December 2012*. [www.project1947.com/kbcat/kbmoreintoz.html].
56 Pfeifer, Ken. "Marine Sergeant Spots Silvery Ufo's West of Guadalcanal August 12, 1942 Island of Tulagi" [worldufophotosandnews.org/?p=5746]

Chapter 3: Into Modernity

formation and flew alongside. After a while, they peeled off and left. In other reports, such objects shot straight up into the air.[57]

The *New York Times* suggested the foo fighters were new German weapons. Even today, one hears the claims that these were a type of German technology. The Germans were indeed working on novel and advanced concepts in science and aviation at this time, including objects such as the Horton brothers' flying wing, that were shaped somewhat like flying saucers. Other, more extreme types of craft, have been alleged but their existence rests upon assertions that have not led to hard evidence. It comes down to whether or not what the Germans had was operational, and whether their creations had capabilities comparable to those described in these reports. It is also worth asking about the Pacific sightings. Did the Germans send their experimental revolutionary aircraft to the opposite side of the Earth to help the Japanese, especially when they were desperately trying to stay alive themselves?[58]

While we are asking such questions, we might wonder why the foo fighters didn't attack the Allied planes? Explaining the foo fighters as German technology does make sense on a certain level, but in other ways it does not (more on this in the next chapter). Incidentally, we know that U.S. and British intelligence both investigated the foo fighters. What we do not know are their formal conclusions. As of this writing, that has remained classified for seven decades.

One of the last good UFO reports of World War II is the *Delarof* case. Years later, a radioman named Robert Crawford reported a sighting he had with fourteen other crewmen aboard the U.S. attack transport ship, *Delarof*, during the summer of 1945. The ship was on its way back to Seattle, at the edge of the Alaskan Aleutian Islands near the town of Adak. This is in the very northern Pacific, almost exactly halfway between North America and Asia. At around sunset in the open sea, an object appeared out of the water about one mile from the

---

57 Cook, Nick. *The Hunt for Zero Point: Inside the Classified World of Antigravity Technology* (Broadway Books, 2001). p. 42.
58 The Germans and Japanese did not coordinate their respective war efforts and cooperation between them was minimal.

ship. It was dark against the sunset, circular in shape, perhaps two hundred feet in diameter. It flew almost straight up, then made a turn and circled the ship two or three times. Then it flew away and disappeared, leaving flashes of light in its wake. Yet another story of a craft emerging from the water. Crawford told this to several researchers, including atmospheric physicist Dr. James E. McDonald of the University of Arizona. The case looks good. If this event actually happened, we would be hard-pressed to explain this as technology from our civilization.[59]

Ghost Rockets

With the end of something as violent and all-encompassing as the Second World War, one might suppose that UFO sightings would cease. In fact, they escalated.

During the spring and summer of 1946, unknown objects were seen traversing Scandinavia, primarily Sweden. These were soon dubbed "ghost rockets." Unlike the sporadic sightings that had occurred during the World War II, or even the flurry of sightings from the airship era of 1896-97, sightings now reached into the hundreds. Not only that, but the reported maneuverability of these "things" was extraordinary. Several were observed descending very low or even landing. By the summer, things had became serious enough to warrant an unofficial visit to Sweden by two American generals. By the late summer, the ghost rockets were being reported elsewhere in Europe, most prominently France and Greece.

The Cold War was beginning and tensions between the U.S. and Soviet Union were already high. Some analysts wondered if the Soviets, perhaps with their own group of captured German scientists, were sending rockets over Europe in some act of intimidation. Of course, to do so, they would have had to have tripled the range of the German V2 rockets within less than a year, something for which there has never been any evidence. Today, it is clear that the Soviet Union

---

[59] Hall, Richard H. *The UFO Evidence, National Investigations Committee of Aerial Phenomena*, 1964, p. 30. See also "The Case of the USAT Delarof," at ufologie.patrickgross.org/htm/delarof45.htm#doc.

Chapter 3: Into Modernity

was not behind the ghost rocket mystery.

Years later, the Greek physicist Paul Santorini made a fascinating statement on the matter of the ghost rockets. Santorini had been involved in the Manhattan Project, and returned to Greece after the war. When the ghost rockets were seen over his country, he was charged with leading a group of scientists to determine what they were. Speaking in 1967 to a private researcher, Santorini said that his team concluded the ghost rockets were neither Soviet nor rockets. At that point, the Greek government, after conferring with an unnamed foreign government (presumably the U.S.), ended the investigation.

To this day there is no official answer to the mystery of the ghost rockets. However, after fifty years, the conclusion of the Swedish Air Intelligence Service finally became known. It reads:

> ... some reliable and fully technically qualified people have reached the conclusion that 'these phenomena are obviously the result of a high technical skill which cannot be credited to any presently known culture on earth.' They are therefore assuming that these objects originate from some previously unknown or unidentified technology, possibly outside the earth.

It would have been nice to have made that conclusion public in 1946. Or would it?[60]

1947

Then came 1947. This was when matters really became interesting. As we have seen, there was no shortage of unexplained aerial activity in the years before, but it was the sighting by private pilot Kenneth Arnold, on June 24, 1947, that made international headlines and created a new global awareness. Arnold was flying near the Cascade Mountains in the state of Washington, when he saw a formation of nine bright, very fast objects moving along in a column. He was startled because he saw no tail on them, and initially thought they were experimental jets. What struck him, though, was their speed. He decided to estimate their speed between two mountain peaks that he

---

60 Good, Timothy, *Above Top Secret: The Worldwide UFO Cover-Up* (William Morrow & Co. 1988), p. 23; Keyhoe, Donald, *Aliens From Space*, (Doubleday & Co, 1973) p. 142; USAFE Item 14, TT 1524, (Top Secret), 4 November 1948, declassified in 1997, National Archives, Washington D.C..

knew were fifty miles apart. They covered this distance in less than two minutes, which he calculated to be an astonishing 1,700 mph. That seemed too fast, so he reworked his numbers, allowing for all possible errors, arriving at the still amazing speed of 1,200 mph. In 1947, no flying craft could reach much more than half that speed.

When he landed, there were reporters nearby. Arnold told them all about his sighting, describing the movement of the objects "like speed boats on rough water" or "like a saucer would if you skipped it across water." The phrase "flying saucer" was born.

Not only that, but so was a mania. For the next several weeks, people around the United States reported seeing flying saucers. Many of these were mistaken sightings of aircraft, balloons, and God knows what else. Not surprisingly, there were hoaxes from people wanting to poke fun at it all. A number of reports, however, appear to be legitimate. Several were military reports with multiple witnesses. A good example is the series of sightings from Muroc Army Airfield in the California desert, on July 8, 1947 (later renamed Edwards Air Force Base). That day, there were four separate sightings of a highly unusual object that maneuvered in ways that defied explanation.

The big event of 1947 was the crash of *something* in the New Mexico desert, not far from the Roswell Army Air Field. The Roswell story has been studied and debated endlessly. On July 8, the local newspaper reported that Roswell Army Air Field had announced the "capture of a flying saucer." The story made the newswires, and the town was besieged with inquiries from around the world. Then, within hours, the Army made a second announcement, this time saying that what had crashed had simply been a weather balloon. For more than thirty years, people simply forgot about Roswell.

Then in 1978, by sheer luck, UFO researcher Stanton Friedman met the retired Lieutenant Colonel Jesse Marcel, who had been at the crash site. Marcel told Friedman that what had crashed there was no weather balloon but, in his opinion, was technology not from our world. Through the 1980s and 1990s, and into the 21st century, investigators have reopened the Roswell case, finding other witnesses

Chapter 3: Into Modernity

and family members of deceased witnesses. A good argument has been made that the Roswell crash was indeed something exotic. Could this something be extraterrestrial? In my own view, I would say the answer is yes. Many witnesses have come forward with explicit statements that support the story in one way or another. We shall return to this in greater detail in Chapter 5.

From this point onward, unknown craft were more or less being reported with regularity within the U.S. military. Just a month after Roswell something extraordinary was seen over Harmon Field, an American base on the island of Guam in the Pacific. This case is not as well-known as it ought to be. A report about it was sent to Army intelligence and 6th Army headquarters. It stated that three U.S. soldiers saw two "unidentified flying objects" on the morning of August 14, 1947. The objects were "small, crescent shaped and traveling at a speed twice that of a fighter plane." This was roughly the speed Kenneth Arnold calculated for his flying saucers two months earlier. The report stated that the objects passed over the field in a zig-zag motion at roughly 1,200 feet altitude, which is fairly low. They then went west and disappeared into clouds. Shortly afterward, one of objects emerged from the clouds and proceeded west. Nothing else is known of the case. Suffice to say that zigzagging was not then, and is not today, part of the capabilities of any known human created aircraft.[61]

Some of the best UFO reports of this period are connected with the U.S. military. From the end of 1948 and well into 1949, a phenomenon known as the Green Fireballs was seen and tracked over Los Alamos Laboratories in New Mexico, the main center of nuclear technology in the world. These "fireballs" traveled low, horizontally, and silently. Within classified meetings, leading scientists and military officers discussed the phenomenon. To this day, more than sixty years later, we still do not have a good explanation. It must be added that the man who studied them the most carefully, Dr. Lincoln LaPaz, a meteor expert from the University of New Mexico, came away

---

61 Headquarters Fourth Air Force, Office of the Assistant Chief of Staff, A-2 Intelligence, Hamilton Field, California, 27 August 1947. Subject: Flying Disc.

```
                    DEPARTMENT OF THE ARMY
                    STAFF MESSAGE CENTER
                  INCOMING CLASSIFIED MESSAGE

CONFIDENTIAL                              PARAPHRASE NOT REQUIRED
PRIORITY

From:    CO Kirtland AFB New Mexico

To:      Chief of Staff USAF attn Dir of Special Investigations
         Officer of the Inspector General

Nr:      OSI-1-90                              31 January 1949

         Reference previous reports, subject; unknown, aerial
phenomena, file number 24-8. Sighting of identical object
reported at 2355Z 30 Jan 49 by aprx 30 people. Estimate at
least 100 total sightings. AEC, AFSWP, 4th Army, local
commanders perturbed by implications of phenomena. Sighting
reported from El Paso, Alburquerque, Alamogordo, Roswell,
Socorro, and other locations. All appear to be same object at
different points in trajectory. Unless instructed to contrary
this office will make all out investigation with view to
location of impact point if any. Request reply.
```

Classified memo pertaining to UFOs seen at Kirtland AFB, 1949.

convinced they were artificial—not meteors—and perhaps one of the keys to the whole UFO phenomenon.[62]

The Army recorded UFOs over and over again. A January 1949 memo from Kirtland AFB, in Albuquerque spoke of a UFO being reported by around 30 people and estimated, "at least 100 total sightings" at the base.

During the summer of 1950, a memo from Hanford Atomic Energy Commission in the State of Washington—another nuclear connection—also mentioned multiple sightings of unknown "round" objects over the plant. Intriguingly, it mentioned failed interception attempts by Air Force jets.

Up to this point, there had been a handful of photographs taken of alleged UFOs. But two pictures taken on May 11, 1950 surpassed anything up to that point, as well as most photos since. These were taken in McMinnville, Oregon, by Mr. and Mrs. Paul Trent, a farming couple who saw a classic flying saucer over their land in the

---

62 Ruppelt, Edward J. *Report on Unidentified Flying Objects* (Double Day, 1956), p. 47-48; Maccabee, Bruce, *The UFO-FBI Connection*, Llewellyn Publications, 2000.

Chapter 3: Into Modernity

The second of the two Trent photographs, with the object enlarged in inset.

early evening. They took two clear photographs of it.

Over the years, skeptics made several attempts to prove the photos were a hoax. This is the only viable method to debunk them, as there is no other way to interpret them as anything other than images of a "flying saucer." Several computer enhancement tests, however, proved conclusively that the object was not a model suspended on a string—the only evident hoax possibility. Everyone who knew the Trents judged them as good, honest people. To the end of their lives in the 1990s, they stood by their story, and the photographs remain a major piece of UFO evidence.[63]

Belgian Congo Mines

The number of serious military and government UFO records we have is quite impressive. One is a CIA report from 1952, released years later via the U.S. Freedom of Information Act (FOIA). It is a reprint of a news account of two craft over a uranium mine in the Belgian Congo. The report described "two fiery disks" over the uranium mines in the southern part of the country. They were said to glide in "elegant curves and changed their positions many times." After hovering in one

---

63 For a detailed analysis of the Trent photographs, see Maccabee, Bruce, "The Trent Farm Photos" [http://brumac.8k.com/trent1.html].

spot, they took off in a zigzag motion to the northeast. People heard a hissing and buzzing sound. The sighting lasted 10 to 12 minutes.

The report continued:

> Commander Pierre of the small Elizabethville airfield immediately set out in pursuit with a fighter plane. On his first approach he came within 120 meters of the disks...The disks traveled in a precise flight maneuver... the disks often shot down to within 20 meters of the tree tops...Pierre had to give up pursuit after 15 minutes since both disks, with a loud whistling sound which he heard despite the noise of his own plane, disappeared in a straight line toward Lake Tanganyika. He estimated their speed at 1500 kilometers per hour...Pierre is regarded as a dependable and zealous flyer.

There is no other information on this case, but for sure, in addition to incredible performance characteristics, we are seeing much interest by the UFO operators in nuclear technology.

1952 and Washington, DC

1952 was a critically important year for UFOs. Within the U.S. and throughout the world, there were many perplexing sightings. This included several weekends in a row of baffling objects over the Capitol in Washington, D.C. To this day, these events remain unexplained in any conventional sense.

There are a number of statements from air traffic controllers and pilots regarding visual and radar contact during the nights of July 19-20, and July 26-27. According to Harry Barnes, the senior air traffic controller during the first weekend, the movements of the UFOs "were completely radical compared to those of ordinary aircraft.... For six hours, there were at least ten unidentifiable objects moving above Washington. They were not ordinary aircraft." [64]

I was fortunate to interview the last surviving air traffic controller who worked during those weekends. Howard Cocklin was 90 years old when I spoke with him in 2008. His testimony clearly supported what others had also said, namely that there were visual and radar unidentifieds tracked by traffic controllers and pilots that night. He believed they were not of our civilization. Two months after our

---

64 Ruppelt, Edward J. *Report on Unidentified Flying Objects.*

Chapter 3: Into Modernity

interview, he passed away.[65]

Air Force interceptors were sent, but never with success. On the second weekend, one interceptor made radar and visual contact—the pilot saw several glowing objects, but no one could catch them. The Air Force told the nation that all the confusion was caused by false radar returns and unusual weather. Suffice to say, many disbelieved that assessment, particularly in the classified world, but more on that in the next chapter.

Aerial Encounters and Air Space Violations

Fascinating UFO cases continued throughout the 1950s, many of which were military encounters. One memo discusses a black colored UFO over Oak Ridge, Tennessee, another key atomic facility, in August, 1953. According to the document:

> No sound was heard. The object flew east at a tremendous speed for what appeared to be three miles where it stopped. The object was then joined by two more of these same objects. A formation similar to a spread 'V' was formed, and the objects, at a tremendous speed, flew in an eastward direction.

This is yet another report that describes exceptional performance that was not supposed to be possible.

Quite a few reports describe intrusions of sensitive airspace, such as one from August, 1954 (with the heading "Emergency") which originated from the flight service center at Maxwell Air Force Base in Alabama. This was sent to the Commander of Air Defense Command (ADC) in Colorado. The report describes a "strange, stationary object, variable in brilliance" which moved rapidly, and then returned to its original position. The base sent a helicopter to investigate. The pilot's assessment: "definitely not a star." Personnel in military and civilian towers watched this object, as the object dimmed, glowed red a little bit, then disappeared.

Could it have been a star? The personnel involved at the time

---

65 Some of my interview with Howard Cocklin can be seen at "1952 UFO Witness Howard Cocklin Interview" [http://www.disclose.tv/action/viewvideo/45206/1952_UFO_Witness_Howard_Cocklin_Interview/]

certainly wondered the same thing. They concluded, however, that it was not. According to the report: "...pilot of helicopter wished to stress fact that the object was of a saucer-like nature, was stationary at 2000 ft., and would be glad to be called upon to verify any statement and act as witness." This report was sent to the CIA, the NSA, the Joint Chiefs of Staff, and each of the military services. Apparently a number of people thought it was important.

Several of the military encounters not only involved visual confirmation, but simultaneous radar tracking. One is described in a CIA document dated July 12, 1955, an extraordinary case that lasted a full 49 minutes over Newfoundland, Canada. Another such case occurred on July 17, 1957. This involved the six-man crew of an Air Force RB-47 electronic warfare aircraft. For 800 miles, while this aircraft flew over the southeastern U.S., it was accompanied by a craft that showed incredible maneuverability and speed. At one point the object simply stopped suddenly in midair as the plane flew past it; at another point, it easily pulled away, even though the plane had accelerated to its top speed. At yet another time, it blinked out simultaneously, both visually and on radar, and then reappeared. All instruments were functioning perfectly. Needless to say, the experienced crew was very uneasy about their escort. After 800 miles of this, the UFO disappeared over Oklahoma City.

Encounters with Beings

The U.S. military did not have a monopoly on interesting UFO encounters during the 1950s. People from around the world were experiencing and reporting such impossibilities.

During the fall of 1954, from September through December, something strange was being reported throughout much of the world. It started in France and Italy, then spread to Britain, Germany, and other European countries. Reports then sprang out of the Middle East, and the focus eventually shifted to South America, primarily Venezuela and Brazil.

Quite simply, people were claiming to have encounters with small humanoid beings who had landed in strange craft. This was not the first time people had made such claims, but it was the first time so many were reported within such a short period of time. The number of cases was unmatched for almost twenty years.

One of the first such reports came from Quarouble, France, near the Belgian border, on the evening of September 10, 1954. At around 10:30 p.m., Marius Dewilde heard his dogs barking outside and decided to see what was going on. On the nearby railroad track only twenty feet away, he saw a dark mass. When he heard footsteps, he turned his flashlight on the path, where he saw two very short beings (between three and four feet tall) wearing what he called "diver's suits." He approached to within a mere six feet, when a brilliant light came from the object on the tracks. This blinded and paralyzed him. The two creatures then moved toward the object. When the beam light went out, Dewilde continued to approach the track, but the object was now rising, giving off a "thick dark steam" and a low whistling sound. It glowed red, then it flew away. On the wooden railroad ties were found five imprints; later calculations were that a thirty-ton weight would have been necessary to produce them. Oddities continued to occur in the immediate aftermath of the incident. One of Dewilde's dogs died just three days after the event, and he began suffering from respiratory problems. Meanwhile, it was claimed that three cows in nearby farms were found dead, with subsequent examination revealing that their blood had been completely removed.[66]

Another case from the region, this time in Flanders, Belgium, occurred on the night of September 26. A man was returning to the village on his bicycle when he saw a saucer-shaped object in a field. He approached and hid in some bushes. He saw two small men wearing helmets and carrying instruments of some sort. They took something from the ground, and then one of the instruments emitted a flash of light. At this point, he saw a screen in which a face appeared to speak to him, although he could not hear anything. The instruments then were dismantled by the little men and reloaded into the object. They

---

66 Young, Edward, "Marius DeWilde - France, 1954" [www.vigilia.com.br/sessao.php?categ=3&id=891].See also Vallee, Jacques, *Passport to Magonia*, Henry Regnery Co, 1969, p. 218-239 and en.wikipedia.org/wiki/Marius_Dewilde.

Marius Dewilde describing his encounter.

then had an animated conversation between them, sometimes pointing towards the witness. Afraid, the witness shut his eyes and was unable to move. When he reopened his eyes, he saw one of the little beings entering the craft. As soon as it rose, he ran out, but was struck by a beam of light and did not see the craft leave. A fantastic story, to be sure.

Not all these reports consisted of small beings. Some were of very tall beings, and others of perfectly human-looking beings. One, from south-central France on October 4, typifies this. A man, regarded as trustworthy by the locals, saw a round flying object, about the size of a small truck, land in his field. A door slid open and two "normal" men in brown coveralls came out. They looked like Europeans and shook hands with the witness. Then they asked, "Paris? North?" The shocked witness could not even answer. The two strangers petted his dog and flew away. The story is reminiscent of some of the airship encounters from years before. It also seem odd, from a 21st century perspective, that such travelers would lack basic navigational tools (GPS, anyone?) to such a degree that they would ask someone for directions to Paris. Here, again, we see one of the core features of the

Chapter 3: Into Modernity

UFO phenomenon: reliable people reporting events that smack of the absurd.

There were many of these reports. The easiest thing to do is ignore them. But there are hundreds of them from 1954, from witnesses who were deemed to be sincere at the time they were interviewed, often by police.

Incidentally, even the U.S. Air Force had at least one official report of a UFO "occupant" during this period. The incident occurred in the Azores Islands on September 21, 1954. A guard at the Santa Maria Airport reported a ten-foot wide, metallic blue object with a clear glass or plastic nose. It made a humming sound, hovered, and landed vertically about fifty feet from the witness. A normal-sized blond man emerged from the object, spoke in an unknown language, and patted the witness on the shoulder. The strange blond man returned to the craft, attached a harness, pressed a button, and ascended vertically. The total encounter lasted three minutes. This incident was listed in the files of Project Blue Book, the Air Force's official UFO office, not as a hoax, but as an *unknown*![67]

Throughout the remainder of the 1950s, there were many alleged encounters with extraterrestrials. Many of these took the form of direct contact and communication from seemingly benevolent extraterrestrial visitors, sometimes referred to as "the space brothers." These claims are a distinct phenomenon altogether, and the "contactees" will be discussed in a later chapter.

There is at least one more encounter from the 1950s that deserves mention. This was not part of the 1954 sightings, but took place over a series of encounters on June 26 and 27, 1959, in the remote region of Papua, New Guinea. It involved multiple sightings of a hovering craft, with much mutual waving and apparent good will exchanged.

The main witness was Reverend William Booth Gill, a respected man on the island, known as scrupulously honest and decent. At around 6:45 p.m., Gill and thirty-eight other witnesses saw a shining object hovering in the air, quite low, a mere three or four hundred feet

---

67 Project Bluebook Case 3224. [www.cufos.org/BB_Unknowns.pdf]

away. The object was circular and had legs under it. Shining directly above it was a bright blue beam of light. Everyone saw four figures on what appeared to be a deck. It was about forty-five minutes after sunset, and the sky was becoming dark, although visibility remained good.

The visitors returned the next day, this time at around 6 p.m., which was just at sunset and therefore perfectly light. Once again, Father Gill and many others saw four figures on top of the ship. This time, two nearby smaller craft were also visible. According to Father Gill's detailed account of the incident (an 11-page single spaced report signed by over 25 witnesses):

> ... two of the figures seemed to be doing something near the center of the deck. They were occasionally bending over and raising their arms as though adjusting or setting up something not visible. One figure seemed to be standing, looking down at us.

At this point, Father Gill waved to the figures. To everyone's surprise, the beings waved back. A teacher among the witnesses then raised both of her arms and waved, and two of the figures did the same. The mutual waving went on for some time. When it became dark, Father Gill used a flashlight to make a series of movements toward the craft, and the craft eventually made several wavering motions back and forth.

A drawing (l) of the encounter by Father Gill and the local population in Papua, New Guinea. Father William Booth Gill (r).

The Reverend Norman E. G. Cruttwell (not present) who investigated the event wrote:

... the facts of this sighting and the waving by the men and the responses to the [flashlight] signals are fully corroborated by ... many of the other witnesses in personal interview with myself.

Cruttwell also reported that between June 26 and 28, there were several UFO sightings at nearby Giwa, Baniara, and Sideia. UFO researcher J. Allen Hynek also interviewed Gill some 15 years later, finding him to be wholly credible.

Skeptics Donald Menzel and Philip Klass wrote debunking pieces on the sighting. Menzel did not impugn Gill's integrity, but theorized that the whole encounter was an optical illusion of the planet Venus caused by Gill's bad eyesight. The malleable natives merely wanted to impress "their Great White Leader" who had a "god-like" status with them. Klass, for his part, did impugn Gill's character, claiming that the Reverend invented or imagined the encounter in order to please Cruttwell. Considering the incredible nature of the sighting, it is interesting that these were the most damaging arguments skeptics were able to offer.[68]

Abductions

Even during the 1950s, there was more than just sightings of beings; there were also claims of alien abduction. This will be explored in greater detail in Chapter 8, but it is helpful to mention here some of the better known cases of the era.

The first well-known UFO abduction case involved a young Brazilian farmer named Antonio Villas-Boas, who lived near Sao Paulo. Boas had an apparent abduction experience on the night of October 15, 1957. He gave a detailed description of the inside of the craft and its occupants: they wore tight, white clothing with a light on their belt, white shoes with no heels, large gloves, and opaque helmets with a slit at the level of the eyes. He claimed to have been stripped naked and given a medical exam in which one of the beings spread a liquid over his skin. He was then led to another room, where they took some

---

68 "Father Gill / Papua New Guinea Sighting" [ufoevidence.org/cases/case67.htm]; Booth, Billy, "1959-The Papua, New Guinea UFOs" [ufos.about.com/od/bestufocasefiles/p/papua.htm]; See also "Father William Gill about his encounter with UFO" YouTube video [www.youtube.com/watch?v=ua8MmT4bIHU].

blood from his chin, then left him alone. An unpleasant odor caused him to vomit.

Eventually, an alien female entered the room, entirely naked. She was attractive but seems very much like later descriptions of a human-alien hybrid: she had hair that was nearly white, large slanted blue eyes, an ordinary nose, small but ordinary ears, high cheekbones, and a pointed chin. They had sex, but this was no fantasy out of *Star Trek*. Boas later said he was "uncontrollably" excited, despite being physically repelled by the experience. He wondered whether the liquid that had been spread over him had contributed to this. When the sexual experience was over, the woman lost interest and left the room. Just before she left, she turned to him, pointed to her belly, then pointed to the southern sky.

Boas's case is tricky. He only discussed his experience on rare occasions and later became a practicing attorney. Everyone who interviewed him found him to be believable, and he maintained his story until his death in 1992. A year later, a skeptical writer argued the case was a probable fabrication, and that it seemed to be based on a Brazilian periodical that had a comparable story published in November 1957. In support of Boas's case, he was examined shortly after the event by Dr. Olavo Fontes of the National School of Medicine of Brazil. His symptoms included pain throughout the body, nausea, headaches, loss of appetite, burning sensations in the eyes, and lesions on the skin with slight bruising, all of which continued for months. Fontes concluded that Boas had been exposed to a large dose of radiation from some source and was suffering from mild radiation sickness. Of course, even though it would certainly be unusual for a Brazilian farmer to become exposed to such high levels of radiation, it is not proof he got it from an alien spacecraft. But it would seem that something unusual happened to him.[69]

Certainly one of the most famous abduction stories is that of Betty

---

69 Lorenzen, Jim and Coral. *Encounters with UFO Occupants*, p. 62-87; *Flying Saucer Review*, August 1966. Rogerson, Peter, "Notes towards a revisionist history of abductions – Part One" *Magonia* [magonia.haaan.com/1993/notes-towards-a-revisionist-history-of-abductions-part-one/]; Melanson, Terry, "Antonio Villas Boas: Abduction Episode Ground Zero," [www.conspiracyarchive.com/UFOs/boas-abduction.htm].

Chapter 3: Into Modernity

and Barney Hill. After a vacation, the couple was driving toward their home in New Hampshire on the night of September 19, 1961, when they had a UFO sighting. After arriving home, they were puzzled to realize they had lost two hours of time.

Two years later, they were hypnotically regressed by one of the nation's leading psychiatrists, Dr. Benjamin Simon. Throughout the extended process they underwent separate sessions, and for nearly all of that time Simon ensured that they did not consciously remember their experiences. These sessions were intense. Both remembered being taken aboard a craft by humanoid entities that physically examined them. This involved scraping off some skin, cutting off bits of hair, and examining their ears and throats. In Barney's case, it also included extracting his semen and the insertion of a rectal probe. In Betty's, it included the insertion of a long needle into her navel. There is little question that the Hills experienced something real and dramatic. More will be said on this case in Chapter 8.[70]

Operation Dominic: UFO Crash in the Pacific

The following account came to me personally and was prepared following a detailed interview with the witness in 2013, whose career with the U.S. Navy spanned from 1960 to 1980. It involves the attention of extraordinary, unknown craft in the vicinity of high-altitude U.S. nuclear tests in the Pacific Ocean during the early 1960s, and what appears to be the crash of a UFO—and a failed attempt to retrieve it.

During the 1960s, the witness (named David) completed tours of duty with a number of U.S. Naval vessels, one of which included the *USS Finch*, a destroyer escort. In 1962, recently promoted to Seaman, he was aboard the *Finch* when the vessel participated in Operation Dominic, a series of high-altitude nuclear detonations over the Pacific.

A little appreciated fact of modern history is that, from 1945 until

---

70 Fuller, John. *The Interrupted Journey: Two Hours Lost Aboard a Flying Saucer.* (The Dial Press, 1966); Marden, Kathleen & Friedman, Stanton T., *Captured! The Betty and Barney Hill UFO Experience: The True Story of the World's First Documented Alien Abduction* (New Page Books, 2007).

the late 1990s, the world experienced over 2,000 nuclear explosions. The bulk of these occurred in a few general regions: the U.S. Nevada Test Site, Soviet Central Asia, and the Pacific Ocean. The amount of damage caused by these detonations has seldom been acknowledged or studied in detail, particularly in the context of the environmental and atmospheric problems currently plaguing the planet.[71]

Following an intense barrage of nuclear tests in the late 1950s, the U.S. and Soviet Union agreed to a tacit moratorium on testing in 1958, which lasted until the Soviets broke it in September 1961. By early 1962, the Americans were again detonating nukes at the Nevada Test Site, and in April of that year resumed tests over the Pacific Ocean as part of Operation Dominic. From April until the end of October, 36 nuclear weapons were detonated at high altitudes over the ocean. Most of these bombs were dropped from B-52 bombers, but a number were launched by ground- and submarine-based missiles. During October, the final five detonations of the program were based out of Johnston Island Atoll, about five hundred miles southwest of the Hawaiian Islands. These detonations took place at altitudes as high as 160,000 feet—more than double the ceiling of the ultra-high flying U-2 spy plane.[72]

The second-to-last exercise of Operation Dominic took place on October 26, 1962 at 9:59 a.m.[73] This detonation appears to have caused the crash of a UFO.

Aboard the *Finch*, Seaman David was unaware that a missile had even been launched. Shortly after, however, the loudspeaker carried the voice of the Captain, ordering everyone other than a few essential personnel below deck. There, the men waited, preparing for damage control. After fifteen minutes, an officer selected about a dozen sailors,

---

71 A sobering video on this subject is "A Time-Lapse Map of Every Nuclear Explosion Since 1945" by Isao Hashimoto at http://www.youtube.com/watch?v=LLCF7vPanrY
72 For a complete list of Operation Dominic detonations, see the Wikipedia page at http://en.wikipedia.org/wiki/Operation_Dominic
73 The Wikipedia entry for Operation Dominic gives information that differs from David's account, listing this test as taking place on October 27, not October 26, and not from a missile launch, but rather an air drop from a B-52. However, the Wikipedia page for "High Altitude Nuclear Explosion" lists the information exactly as he gave it: October 26, 1962, with a warhead that reached an altitude of 50 kilometers (about 160,000 feet).

Chapter 3: Into Modernity

including David, to man the starboard side of the ship. Wearing jackets, gloves, and protective clothing against the virtual wall of sea spray, they were ordered to look forward toward the horizon. No conversation was allowed.

After some time, the officer in charge ordered the men to look ten degrees off the starboard bow. "Lo and behold," said David,

> ... what appeared in the sky—what I saw—was a huge cigar shaped object coming toward us at ten degrees and about 15-20 degrees off the horizon. It looked like it was two football fields in length. It appeared to have some kind of blue glow at the stern as it was moving past us at a moderate rate. My judgment is that it had to be traveling at least 400 mph. When it reached directly in front of us, it picked up speed. It just went from *there* to *gone*.

An interesting aspect of this sighting is that the object moved horizontally fairly close to the water. David also noticed what he thought might have been a wisp of smoke in the object's wake.

That constituted his entire observation. But David learned a bit more later that day while cross-training with the ship's radar technicians. Everyone, it seems, was talking about the UFO they had tracked. It had been a huge object with a significant heat signature. Moreover, they said, it had descended into the ocean. Pilots of several aircraft saw it enter the water, and several ships were currently en route to its position. Nobody knew for sure, but it was guessed that the high altitude detonation had caused the problem. Clearly, since this was a scheduled detonation, it was not an intentional attack on a bogey. The object just happened to be there.[74]

David was soon debriefed about the incident by a security officer who had boarded the *Finch* at Pearl Harbor. He was ordered to sign an agreement forbidding him to discuss the incident with anyone for twenty years.

This crash of this unknown object occurred in the context of a number of UFO and USO encounters that had accompanied Operation Dominic. Indeed, such stories are common among U.S. Navy

---

[74] Apparently, Navy brass had initially been concerned that one of their observing aircraft had gotten too close to the explosion. However, not only were all aircraft accounted for, but such an impact would have sent any aircraft straight into the ocean.

personnel, if only an investigator takes the time to learn of them. More than once during 1962, members of the *Finch* observed strange objects above and below the ship.

The objects below the ship sometimes inspired real fear. These might be recorded by sonar, or they might be seen visually. In the case of the latter, the sighting usually involved a luminous, fluorescent effect in the water. This is commonly given off by dolphins, whales, and other kinds of ocean life, but there were times when the fluorescence was simply enormous—far too large even for whales. Sometimes it came perilously close to the ship. On one occasion, the *Finch* nearly capsized from an intense swell which David believed was caused was a USO (the event caused the Captain to break his leg and be transferred off the ship). "I would say 75-80 percent of all these bogeys were logged," he stated. "If you could get access to these logs you would have a gold mine."

But it is in relation to the UFOs tracked high above that the crash of October 26 becomes even more significant. For one of the common things that radar personnel noticed during the course of Operation Dominic, especially shortly before scheduled tests, were large numbers of "bogeys" in the upper atmosphere. Nobody knew what these ultra-high altitude objects were, but they inevitably disappeared from the radar scope moments before detonation. The object that crashed on October 26, 1962 appears to have been unlucky.

For years after, David remained bewildered by his experience. Then, in 1976, he met a senior Navy diver while while stationed at Guantanamo Bay, Cuba. Over many drinks, the two traded stories. Amazingly, the diver told David of an experience he had in late October 1962, in the Pacific Ocean. He had been part of of a Top Secret salvage mission to pull a UFO out of the ocean floor! In fact, he was the first man in, volunteering to go alone for an initial reconnaissance of the situation. Wearing the traditional diving bell helmets and gear, the intrepid diver went down below the surface of the water. At first, he saw nothing unusual—until he realized he was standing on an enormous object. Loosing his footing, he slid down the object to the

Chapter 3: Into Modernity

ocean floor. At this point, he told his astonished listener, he was able to see part of it, even inside it. It was like a gigantic sponge, he said, with organic-looking compartments. He touched it, and his hand went through. Now in terror, the Navy diver admitted of losing bladder control. He was soon brought back to his ship, barely able to recount what he had seen. That was the end of his mission. Later, however, he diver learned from another member of the diving team that when they attempted a salvage the following day, the object was no longer there. Somehow, it had left.

David told the diver that he too had witnessed part of that UFO event, and the two met privately a few days later at the diver's home. They compared notes, discovering that each suffered from similar nightmares of beings (or hands) coming into their bedroom. Shortly after this meeting, however, the diver was dead—a freak accident from a faulty electrical conduit while in the shower.

I have been unable to confirm every element of this story, which includes even more detail than I have recounted here. However, all of the technical elements related by David concerning Operation Dominic, including several arcane details, turned out to be precisely correct upon investigation. Moreover, his complete lack of hesitation and fluidity of explanation, along with his willingness to answer my myriad questions, give me reason to believe his account is genuine. Like all UFO crash retrieval stories, this one will benefit from additional research, something I hope to undertake in the future. Perhaps other researchers will consider doing the same.

If true, the UFO encounter in the Pacific points to a strong interest by the operators of these objects in human nuclear technology. Obviously, there are many reasons why this should be so. If *they* have any kind of interest in this world, the detonation of some 2,000 powerful nuclear bombs over a fifty-year period would be certainly command their attention. Moreover, the fact that these high-altitude blasts discharged powerful electromagnetic radiation would be a matter of concern. Such blasts caused retinal damage and blackouts on the ground, and electromagnetic storms in the upper atmosphere. This alone could well explain the presence of so many bogeys during the stratospheric tests of Operation Dominic.

The Crescendo of the 1960s

The 1960s brought other intriguing sightings of so-called humanoid beings (or, as researchers were still calling them, UFO occupants). One of these, concerning New Mexico police sergeant Lonnie Zamora, is nearly as well known as the Hill case. During the late afternoon of April 24, 1964, Zamora was in the process of pulling over a speeding vehicle in the town of Socorro. Then he heard a roar from outside his police car, and saw what looked like a "flame in the sky." He thought that a nearby dynamite shack must have exploded so Zamora gave up the chase and drove part of the way up a hill, in the direction of the flame. Closer to the top, he got out of his car and walked the final part. At the top, he saw a shiny object in the distance. His initial thought was that a car had overturned. He walked toward it, and saw what looked like two children wearing white coveralls.

But then Lonnie Zamora got a closer look. He noticed the object was resting on four legs, and the "children" were examining or repairing the craft. They did not immediately notice him. When they did, however, they hurried back into the object.

Zamora became frightened. He started running back. Within moments, the object began to roar, a flame appeared on its underside, and it ascended slowly into the sky. Now, Zamora could see that it was oval in shape, and very smooth. Although he saw no windows or doors, he did notice an insignia in red lettering. He ran after the object as it continued to rise in the air and accelerate toward the southwest. Zamora was so shocked that he asked to see a priest before releasing his report to the authorities. Quite simply, he believed he had seen an alien craft.

Within hours, Army Intelligence and the FBI were at the site. More investigators arrived in the following days. They noticed deep landing marks left by the legs of the craft, as well as a charred area where it had taken off. For the next week, Zamora was interviewed constantly. Everyone was impressed by his honesty, his puzzlement, and his

Chapter 3: Into Modernity

detailed report.

Project Blue Book was the Air Force's office to investigate UFO reports. Publicly, Blue Book debunked and even ridiculed Zamora's story. However, in a 1966 classified article, the head of Blue Book, Major Hector Quintanilla, wrote something different:

> There is no doubt that Lonnie Zamora saw an object which left quite an impression on him. There is no question about his reliability . . . He is puzzled by what he saw and frankly, so are we.[75]

This statement sounds like an endorsement. Despite various attempts to explain the case in conventional terms, whether as the testing of a classified craft or a prank, the case has stood the test of time. Lonnie Zamora saw something extraordinary. What was it?[76]

Through the mid-1960s, there was a gradual crescendo of UFO reports. On July 1, 1965, in the south of France, a rather strange encounter occurred, somewhat like Zamora's, which was also reminiscent of the 1954 sightings. Farmer Maurice Masse, of the village of Valensole, heard a strange noise outside his home early one morning. He saw an egg-shaped object in his lavender field, only one hundred feet away. It sat on a central pivot with six legs, was about twenty feet long, and had a door showing two seats back to back. Nearby were two small beings, the size of children. They had large bald heads and tiny mouths, but normal human eyes and hands. They seemed to be examining one of his plants. When they saw him, they aimed a small device at him which paralyzed him. Meanwhile, they spoke between themselves in gargling-type sounds, and Masse actually wondered if they were making fun of him. Soon, they entered their craft through a sliding door, and it quickly took off at a forty-five degree angle,

---

75 Quintanilla, Hector. "The Investigation of UFOs," *Studies in Intelligence*, Vol. 10. No 4. Fall 1966.
76 An extended discussion recently ensued following the assertion that the Socorro UFO was the result of a prank. See Bragalia, Anthony, "The Ultimate Secret of Socorro Finally Told: New Details on World-famous 1964 UFO Hoax." [http://bragalia.blogspot.com/2012/08/the-ultimate-secret-of-socorro-finally.html]. See also Stanford, Ray. *Socorro "Saucer" in a Pentagon Pantry* (Blueapple Books, 1976); Edwards, Frank, *Flying Saucers: Serious Business*, p. 186-190; Hynek, J. Allen, *The Hynek UFO Report*, p. 223-229; Lorenzen, Jim and Coral, *Encounters with UFO Occupants*, p. 8-11; 182-186.

making a whistling sound as it left. For another twenty minutes afterward, Masse was paralyzed. Holes were left in the ground by the object, and quite a few people examined them. Masse himself was a former Resistance fighter during the Second World War, and the police who investigated this case regarded him as reliable.

Another interesting water-based UFO sighting occurred on July 6, 1965. Crew members of the Norwegian tanker ship, *Jawesta*, saw a UFO. The ship was in the North Atlantic, on route from Venezuela to the Canary Islands, about a thousand miles west of the African coastline. In all directions, for thousands upon thousands of square miles, the ship was surrounded by ocean. A look-out insisted that something appeared to come up from under the sea and then change course to approach the ship. The First Officer watched it with binoculars. According to his entry in the ship's log:

> It was bright like a star, and the moonlight was shining through between the low clouds, and I could clearly see the outlines of the upper part of it. Its shape was that of a cigar, and I could clearly see a row of square windows and the faint golden-orange coloured light from inside it. There was no sign of wings or rudder. The object had a bluish tongue of fire behind it, which was most concentrated near the tail, fanning out a little further back.
>
> A little farther back still, behind the body, I could see a tremendous number of globes, and from every globe there was streaming out a blue beam, away from the body. The length of the fiery tongue would, I should think, have been about 100 metres. The object seemed to be far bigger than any aircraft known up to this present day.
>
> Its speed was tremendous and it was visible for about 30 to 40 seconds. It was moving at the time in N-S direction . . . I can say with complete certainty that it was no question of an aircraft of conventional type, or rocket, or meteor, or ball lightning.

Several of the ship's crew saw this unusual object, and apparently someone sketched it. Report and sketch were both apparently sent to the Geophysical Institute at Bergen. It is not known what the Institute had to say about this matter. In all likelihood, its scientists did *not* say, "flying saucer over the North Atlantic? You betcha!" But it seems that a large, low-flying, silent object moved with remarkable agility and great speed above an immense ocean. It appears to have taken note of

Chapter 3: Into Modernity

a lone ship, and then departed.⁷⁷

There are several more interesting cases from 1965, including two UFOs that were photographed in the U.S. in early August.

The first photo was taken in Tulsa, Oklahoma, on August 2 at 1:45 a.m. by a 14 year-old boy named Alan Smith. This was during an evening in which thousands of people from South Dakota to the Mexican border were reporting unusual objects in the night sky, often in formations. Alan, along with his father and three other people, were watching an unusual, multi-colored object which moved slowly toward them, then paused and hovered. At that moment, Alan snapped a photograph with an inexpensive camera, and the object soon left. His picture was extensively analyzed, pronounced authentic, and later published in *Life* Magazine. There are detractors to this day, arguing that the object in the photo was simply a camera defect, but Alan and the other witnesses maintained that it was an accurate photo of the object they had seen.⁷⁸

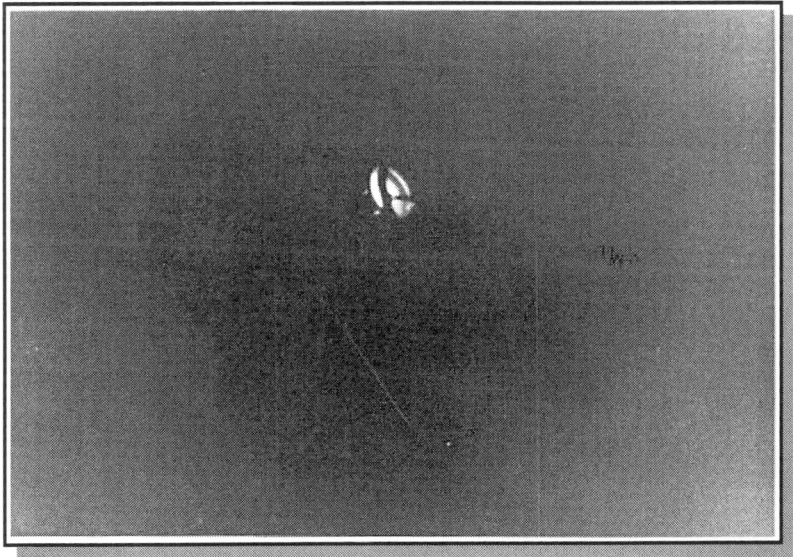

Photograph of an object taken by Alan Smith, Tulsa OK, August 2, 1965.

---

77 *Flying Saucer Review*, Vol. 12, No. 5, September/October 1966, p. 32; *Gaceta Ilustrada* (Spain), July 31, 1965, and *Moss Dagbled* (Norway), December 27, 1965. See also www.waterufo.net/item.php?id=313.
78 "First Night Color Shot of Flying Saucer Bared," *The Oklahoma Journal*, October 5, 1965 [ufologie.patrickgross.org/press/oklahomajournal5oct1965.htm]. Smith, Michael, "Tulsa's UFO Still Unidentified" *Tulsa World*, March 11, 2011, [www.tulsaworld.com/

Amazingly, on the very next day, another striking UFO photograph was taken, this time in California, on August 3, 1965. Actually, this was three photographs of a UFO, plus a fourth of a smoke ring that was left behind. These were taken by a Highway Accident Investigator named Rex Heflin. While sitting inside his vehicle on a lonely stretch of road near Santa Ana, Heflin saw a hat-shaped UFO hovering close by. It was silent, and a beam of white light seemed to rotate underneath it. Heflin tried to radio his supervisor, but he said the radio went dead. He then took his four Polaroid photographs. Back at his office, he put the pictures in his desk drawer. A few days later, one of Heflin's co-workers sent the pictures to United Press International (UPI), and from there they were published in many newspapers.

After this, the story became even more interesting. Heflin stated that, shortly after UPI returned his photos to him, he was approached by a man claiming to be from NORAD Intelligence, who demanded the prints. Heflin gave them to the man, and the photos were gone. Of course, this story has never been confirmed, and no one has ever heard of a "NORAD Intelligence." But during the 1970s, when computer analysis of photographs was in its infancy, several analyses were performed on copies of the images, and at one point they were pronounced fake. Then, in 1995, twenty-eight years after the photos had disappeared, and long after Heflin had retired, the original photos mysteriously reappeared in his mailbox. A detailed analysis of the originals was performed by researchers Ann Druffel, Dr. Bob Wood, and Eric Kelson. This was published in the *Journal of Scientific Exploration* in 2000, and vindicated the photos.[79]

Some doubters remain. More recently, researcher Anthony Bragalia argued the photos were hoaxes by Heflin, based on the testimony of someone who claimed to have seen them before they were published, who said Heflin claimed he had hoaxed them.[80] Most researchers do

---

scene/article.aspx?subjectid=268&articleid=20110311_282_D1_CUTLIN174559&allcom=1.
79 Druffel, Ann; Wood, Robert M.; Kelson, Eric: "Reanalysis of the 1965 Heflin UFO Photos," *Journal of Scientific Exploration*, Vol. 14, No. 4, pp. 583–622, 2000 [www.scientificexploration.org/journal/jse_14_4_druffel.pdf].
80 Bragalia, Anthony, "The UFOs That Never Were: Classic Photos Now Exposed As Fakes!," 2010 [ufocon.blogspot.com/2010/10/ufos-that-never-were-classic-photos-now.html].

Chapter 3: Into Modernity

not appear to be convinced by this, however. Hearsay testimony cannot be considered superior to a detailed photographic analyses. So far, it looks like Rex Heflin took three amazing UFO photos.

The first of Rex Heflin's photographs, Santa Ana, CA, August 3, 1965. Note the apparent ground disturbance below the object.

Minot AFB

As active and interesting as 1965 had been, subsequent years of the decade appear to have matched it. Several UFO cases directly affected the U.S. military.

One report came from Minot Air Force Base, in North Dakota from August 25, 1966. Minot was a major Strategic Air Command base at the time, housing ICBMs and manned bombers. That night, a team was ordered to investigate a very high multi-colored light, well above the position of the base. The team confirmed that, indeed, there was such a light there, as well as a second object. At the same time, base radar was tracking the object, which was as high as 100,000 feet (almost twenty miles). Several times, it rose and descended; each time it came down, the missile chief found his radio disrupted by static, even though he was sixty feet below ground. The object eventually descended to ground level ten to fifteen miles south of the area. Consider the capabilities of any object that could perform such a controlled descent from twenty miles above, particularly at night, in the mid-1960s.

A team was sent to investigate. Apparently, they saw the object, either on the ground or hovering very low. According to the report: "When the team was about ten miles from the landing site, static disrupted radio contact with them. Five to eight minutes later, the glow diminished, and the UFO took off." The report mentioned that a second UFO was seen visually and confirmed by radar. One object passed beneath the other, also confirmed on radar. Then they both departed.[81]

The entire incident lasted almost four hours. It was confirmed by three different missile sites. Who was playing games over this American air force base?

Malmstrom AFB

But such games continued. The following year, on the morning of March 16, 1967, at Malmstrom AFB in Montana, one of the most extraordinary events in the history of military-UFO encounters occurred. This base controls a huge, sprawling network of ICBMs. Under a clear and dark Montana sky, an airman with the Oscar Flight Launch Control Center (LCC) saw a star-like object zigzagging high above him. Soon, a larger and closer light also appeared and acted in a similar way. The airman called his non-commissioned officer, and the two men watched the lights streak through the sky, maneuvering in impossible ways. The NCO phoned his commander, Lieutenant Robert Salas, who was below ground in the launch control center. Initially, Salas was not impressed. He ordered the NCO to keep watching the display and report back if the objects got any closer. Minutes later, that is precisely what happened. Shouting into the phone, the NCO told Salas that a red, glowing UFO was hovering outside the front gate.

Salas woke his commander, Lieutenant Fred Meiwald. As he briefed

---

81 Report, Department of the Air Force, Headquarters 862nd Combat Support Group (SAC), Minot AFB, North Dakota. Subject: UFO Report. to: AFSC (FTD) Wright-Patterson AFB, Ohio. Date: 30 Aug 1966. Letter, Department of the Air Force, Headquarters 862nd Combat Support Group (SAC), Minot AFB, to Dr. J. Allen Hynek, 4 January 1967.

Chapter 3: Into Modernity

Meiwald, an alarm went off in the small capsule, and both men saw a "No-Go" light turn on for one of the missiles. Within seconds, about ten of the missiles went down in succession.

Twenty miles away, at the Echo Launch Control Center, the same scenario took place. First Lieutenant Walter Figel was at his station when one of the Minuteman missiles went into "No-Go" status. He called the missile site and learned that a UFO had been hovering above. Like Salas, Figel doubted the UFO story. But just then, ten more ICBMs in rapid succession reported a "No-Go" condition. The entire flight was down.

Strike teams were sent to the two launch facilities, where maintenance crews were at work and had been watching UFOs hover over each of their sites. The missiles were down for most of the day. Neither the Air Force investigation, nor Boeing's tests found any cause for the shutdown. According to the Boeing engineering chief, "there was no technical explanation that could explain the event."

Over the years, a number of additional Air Force personnel have come forward to confirm that something truly strange did happen at Malmstrom AFB that day. In 2010, Salas and researcher Robert Hastings organized a news event at the National Press Club in Washington, D.C., which included a number of these additional witnesses of this and similar types of events. At the same time, a controversy arose which called the veracity of these claims into question but which, after my own close examination, fell short of making their case—again, at least in my view. Moreover, having met Bob Salas on a number of occasions, I have no question as to his truthfulness, reliability, and integrity. Something highly irregular did take place, and it involved the sighting of a UFO at the same time that ICBMs, which were all separately controlled and should not have gone offline, did go offline for reasons that remain unexplained.[82]

---

82 Salas, Robert and Klotz, James. *Faded Giant: The 1967 Missile/UFO Incidents*, Privately Published, Revised Edition 2004. Hastings, Robert. *UFOs and Nukes: Extraordinary Encounters at Nuclear Weapons Sites*, AuthorHouse, 2008. To see the news event at the National Press Club, see "Disclosure Conference, National Press Club 27 Sept 2010" on YouTube [www.youtube.com/watch?v=BtmpaM0PqyI]. For a description of the controversy regarding the Malmstrom incident, see Dolan, Richard M., "The Malmstrom UFO Event: Did It Really Happen?" [richarddolanpress.com/33-the-malmstrom-ufo-event-did-it-really-happen/]

Shag Harbor

Throughout 1967, UFOs were being reported across the world. South America was a hotbed of activity that year, including several reports of humanoid beings, as well as water-based craft, several of which involved disk-like UFOs coming out of the water. Not all were perfectly recorded or transmitted to U.S. researchers, but something was going on.

Still, the best-known water-based UFO story of the decade took place not in South America, but near the town of Shag Harbor, Nova Scotia Canada. On the night of October 4, 1967, witnesses saw several lights joining together in a straight line, forming a 45-degree angle, flashing on and off in sequence as they moved over the water. The lights then seemed to glide into the sea about a half-mile offshore.

For a while, a single white light bobbed on the water, and people heard a hissing noise. The light disappeared before anyone could reach it, but witnesses also noticed a yellowish, bubbling froth about eighty feet wide when they went out there. No one had ever seen this before. The Royal Canadian Navy reported no missing aircraft or ships in the area, and no planes had been operating in the area at the time.

For two days, Canadian Navy divers searched the waters and ocean bottom. They found nothing. Then, a week after the incident, several people saw more lights in that area, less than a mile offshore, very low over the water. They disappeared, then reappeared, and finally seemed to descend into the water.

Years later, Canadian researchers Chris Styles and Don Ledger interviewed several of the divers and military personnel involved in the search. According to what they learned, all unofficial of course, the searchers determined that there was indeed an underwater object, and that it had moved northeast. This was near a top-secret submarine detection station run jointly by Canada and the U.S. As a flotilla of ships positioned themselves over the submerged craft, a second underwater object joined the first, and apparently engaged in a repair operation. The members of the ships observed, but did not interfere. A Soviet submarine later appeared but was escorted away. Eventually, the two unknown objects moved off toward the Gulf of Maine.

Chapter 3: Into Modernity

Emerging from the water, they ascended rapidly and flew away.

Such is the fascinating story.[83]

Mutilations and More

Incidentally, 1967 also happens to be the year of the first widely publicized animal mutilation. Disagreement exists to this day as to whether or not such mutilation cases are connected to the UFO mystery, but it does appear that an unknown agency is behind at least some of them. In this case, a horse named Lady was found on September 9, 1967, in southern Colorado's San Luis Valley. When her owners found her, she had been stripped of flesh from the neck up. The exposed skeleton was so white and clean that it looked as though it had been bleached in the sun for days. There was also a medicinal odor about her. Yet, Lady had been known to be alive and well only two nights before. Oddly, her tracks stopped one hundred feet from her body. Several holes in the ground were nearby, as if (some thought) from a landed craft.

According to Dr. John Altshuler, a veterinary doctor who examined her, Lady's internal organs had been removed "surgically with heat ...There was no blood and the cuts were surgically precise."

Was this UFO related? Either way, it certainly was a mystery. But it is not unreasonable to wonder about a UFO connection, and there were indeed UFO sightings in the area around the time Lady died. Over the years, the San Luis Valley has remained a hotbed for UFO sightings, bizarre encounters, and animal mutilations.[84]

As the 1960s came to a close, UFO reports dwindled a bit in America. Elsewhere, sightings continued at a steady pace, especially in Europe and South America. A number of reports concerned sightings

---

83 Ledger, Don, "The UFO Crash at Shag Harbor," *International UFO Reporter*, Jan. 1998, www3.ns.sympatico.ca/dledger/Shag_Harbour_article.html; see also Clark, Jerome, *The UFO Book*, Visible Ink, 1998, p. 134-136.
84 "Dead Horse Riddle Sparks UFO Buffs," *The Pueblo Chieftain*, October 7, 1967. Howe, Linda Moulton, *An Alien Harvest: Further Evidence Linking Animal Mutilations and Human Abductions to Alien Life Forms*, Special Limited Edition, 1989, p. 1-8. O'Brien, Christopher, *Enter the Valley: UFOs, Religious Miracles, Cattle Mutilations, and Other Unexplained Phenomena in the San Luis Valley*, St. Martin's Paperbacks, 1999. See also O'Brien, Christopher, *Stalking the Herd: Unraveling the Cattle Mutilation Mystery* (Adventures Unlimited Press, 2014). One website discussing the case of Lady is www.snippy.com/.

of alien beings. The *New York Times* joked about this in an article in July 1968, ("UFOs Add Spice to Life of Latins") but did quote an Argentine government official who said: "I have no doubt that flying saucers have arrived here. I worry about what they are up to. I just can't understand why they have picked on Argentina." In fact, they had not picked solely on Argentina. It is evident that "they" were everywhere.[85]

A review of the cases in this chapter suggests that the group or groups behind the UFO phenomenon were not necessarily hostile to humanity. Of course, they may not have been on the most friendly terms, either, and there are a few cases in which human fatalities are linked to encounters with UFOs.[86] For those who wonder why they have not provided more open assistance for a species that clearly could use it, we might recall that "assistance" is often the wrong way to promote healthy development. We often need to struggle through our problems if we are to become better than we were. Then again, there remains the possibility that they see humanity as their property, as livestock to be managed. We do not have certain answers.

Still, there are some instances in which these "Others" appear to have acted in a beneficial manner to individuals on a limited basis. Such was an encounter that took place in France on the night of November 1, 1968. A prominent French Doctor (referred to as Dr. X to maintain his anonymity) was home during a thunderstorm with his fourteen-month old son. Outside the boy's window, the doctor saw two luminous objects come close together, then merge. As the object tilted, it emitted a beam of light at him for about a second. Then, it vanished with a flash, leaving only a slowly-dissolving cloud.

Shortly after this, the man's leg, which had been wounded in the Algerian War years before, healed. Several days later, he experienced pain in his abdomen, and a red pigmentation appeared around his navel, forming a triangle. Dermatologists who examined him had no answers. The case was reported to the French Academy of Sciences,

---

85 Browne, Malcolm W., "UFOs Add Spice to the Life of Latins," *New York Times*, July 13, 1968.
86 See the Valentich case, described in Chapter 7.

Chapter 3: Into Modernity

although without the UFO connection. The baby also developed a red triangle. This case was unusually well-tracked and investigated. In the words of researcher Jerome Clark, "this is one of the most fantastic UFO stories ever, but is accompanied by "physical evidence of an eerily compelling sort."[87]

* * *

One thing should be clear at this point: there is no shortage of astonishing UFO stories, and they appear to have existed throughout our recorded history. Even a cursory review such as this makes it evident that the full range of UFO cases are far more difficult to explain than simply resorting to natural phenomenon, or even secret human technology. Something important, something strange, is very much a part of our history.

As the following chapters will show, this phenomenon has also had serious political, economic, and social implications.

---

87 Clark, Jerome, *The UFO Book*, Visible Ink, 1998, p. 172-175; Michel, Aime, "The Strange Case of Dr. X," in Charles Bowen, ed. *UFO Percipients: Flying Saucer Review Special Issue No. 3*, Sept. 1969, 3-16. *Flying Saucer Review*, 1969.

Chapter 4
UFO Secrecy and Those Who Fought It

Delving into the world of UFO secrecy is not the easiest of tasks. It must be explored layer by layer, and this chapter explores the top layer. It comprises the public history of the UFO controversy, garnered from easily confirmed and open sources. Before plunging into the deep waters, we must learn how to swim. Before we speculate about the coverup, we must first understand what is easily confirmed. That is, we need to get our facts straight.

The topic of UFOs is not simply an intellectually interesting exercise (like asking, *I wonder if there is life out there in the universe?*). It is not a hypothetical matter, but has several pragmatic implications for our society.

One of the more obvious implications is that UFOs constitute a national security problem. As the last chapter demonstrated, there have been many UFO encounters by the various militaries of this world, especially that of the U.S. With so many violations of sensitive airspace taking place, caused by unknown objects with extraordinary capabilities, it would have been impossible for responsible national security officials to have ignored the situation.

This leads to the second important practical implication of UFOs, even more important from a public policy point-of-view: government by secrecy. Clearly, certain implications of UFOs prompted a decision that the matter had to be kept away from detailed public inquiry. Over the years, there have been many contributing factors to our current culture of expansive government secrecy, and UFOs have been one of them, typically overlooked by the more conventional students of history and political science. It is, of course, entirely understandable that military and political leaders would wish to conceal such a serious problem from the public. Yet secrecy is a cancer that, if unchecked, kills the body politic it is ostensibly trying to protect.

Another implication of the UFO phenomenon concerns exotic technology and science in general. Consider a craft that can zigzag silently across the sky: one simple maneuver encapsulating a science that is utterly revolutionary. If we ever grasp the various sciences behind UFOs, our society will be dramatically transformed, in ways that are probably beyond our wildest imagination. Indeed, we appear to be on the cusp of making several such breakthroughs.

Finally, a study of UFOs brings us inevitably to an existential crisis. Who are these other beings? What is their agenda? Are they friend or foe? Are people really being taken by them, and if so why? These questions are of the greatest importance, with deep implications for human society.

The American power elite appears to have agreed. Those who were *in the know* decided that, for the time being at least, this was a reality too awesome, too terrifying, too destabilizing to share with the world. What they needed, above all else, was time: time to gather information, time to plan, time to stall.

Although a lifetime has gone by since those initial decisions were made, the basic plan has continued. Denial and deception remain the rule.

So UFOs are important to us. And yet, they are almost entirely ignored by the open and official organs of power in our society, despite being seen worldwide. It is time to redress the imbalance.

The Early Cover-Up

As the 1942 "Battle of Los Angeles" shows, the U.S. military was learning to lie about UFOs at least five years before Roswell. The public, incidentally, knew it was being lied to. One of the local newspapers, the *Long Beach Independent*, wrote of "a mysterious reticence," and that "some form of censorship [appears to be] trying to halt discussion of the matter." Indeed it was, and so it continued throughout the war. Of course, warfare breeds secrecy, but all the other secrets of World War Two have long since been revealed.

Everything, it appears, except UFOs. Or, as they were called at the time, *foo fighters*.

Throughout the war, some strange events were reported, and there was always a discrepancy between what the classified community discussed and what the public was told. Hardly anything about foo fighters was considered openly. When the Associated Press and *New York Times* covered the topic in early 1945, it was speculated that this might be a new form of German weaponry.[88] In fact, no one had a clue. Even today, despite continued speculation about the German connection to the foo fighters, there is still no proof, nor even much in the way of evidence. Yet, we do know there was great interest in these strange . . . *things*. We have rumor after rumor that the U.S. Eighth Air Force under General James Doolittle, the Office of Strategic Services (the forerunner of the CIA), and British intelligence all conducted investigations of the foo fighters. The conclusion, it is said, was that they were neither American nor German technology.[89] While we are left to speculate and piece together what history we can, studies were done in secret years and years before us. Even now, we do not know for certain what they concluded. Why?

Nevertheless, some researchers are making strides. Joseph P. Farrell, in a series of books, has built a case for a range of highly advanced German technology that intersects with the UFO phenomenon, and this includes at least some of the foo fighters. Although the case has often been made by some UFO researchers that the foo fighters were not overtly hostile, Farrell found cases in which they seemed to be experimental technologies designed to interfere with Allied missions.

One event cited by Farrell was from a 1943 bombing run over Schweinfurt, a German city in Bavaria, and home to a ball-bearing factory that was targeted by the Allies for destruction. A report on the event was dated October 24, 1943, and described interviews with American B-17 pilots of the 384th Bomb Group who reported that the

---

88 "Balls of Fire Stalk U.S. Fighters in Night Assaults Over Germany", Associated Press, January 2, 1945.
89 See Grant Cameron's Presidential UFO website, [www.presidentialufo.com/old_site/harrys.htm].

Germans had inexplicably not sent up any fighter planes to attack them, when instead they encountered a cluster of silver discs that closed on them. These objects were very small, estimated as one inch thick and three inches wide (the exact size of a hockey puck). The pilots were astonished when the clusters directly struck at least one of the B-17s (apparently) on the right wing and definitely on the tail. Although the cluster had no effect on the performance of the aircraft, the strange absence of German Luftwaffe led Allied intelligence officers to suspect (in Farrell's words) "that the incident reflected the combat use and experimentation with some sort of unusual weapon." Indeed, an incident had occurred during a mission over Stuttgart on September 6, 1943 in which another cluster of "small round objects, silvery in color," fell in the path of Allied bombers. According to one report, "some was observed to fall on the wing of a B-17 belonging to our group. The wing immediately started to burn." In Farrell's judgement, "clearly, the Luftwaffe was deploying and combat-testing some sort of strange technology, and that technology was anything but harmless."[90]

Farrell also studied the more common foo fighter reports over Germany which were connected to sightings of "red balls of fire." He noted that "the overwhelming body of foo fighter reports could never pin them down to anything explicitly German . . . *except* in one instance." This was when the IX Tactical Air Command Allied aircraft reported that a German Messerschmitt-109 fighter joined a formation of Allied aircraft and "was seen to emit what appeared to be a red ball of fire which followed the aircraft for some 2-3 seconds."[91]

This is certainly fascinating. While the above is not quite enough to serve as firm confirmation that some foo fighters were of German manufacture, it's a reasonable position to take. Farrell is furthermore on point in his suggestion that Nazi technology bears a relationship to post-World War Two UFOs. The U.S. brought the lion's share of the

---

90 Farrell, Joseph P., *Roswell and the Reich: The Nazi Connection* (Adventures Unlimited Press, 2010), p. 336-339. See also Farrell's *Reich of the Black Sun: Nazi Secret Weapons and the Cold War Allied Legend*, (Adventures Unlimited Press, 2004); and *Saucers, Swastikas and Psyops: A History of A Breakaway Civilization: Hidden Aerospace Technologies and Psychological Operations* (Adventures Unlimited Press, 2012) and *The SS Brotherhood of the Bell: Nasa's Nazis, JFK, And Majic-12* (Adventures Unlimited Press, 2006).
91 Farrell, Joseph P., *Roswell and the Reich*, p. 345.

German intelligence and scientific community into its sphere after the war ended, and would presumably have kept the best developments classified for as long as possible. More on this in Chapter 5.

Still, when considering that equally baffling foo fighter accounts came from the Pacific Theater of war, including the summer of 1945 after the Germans had surrendered, we need to question the viability of explaining all of these as German-derived technology. Did the Germans, even while fighting literally for their lives, share their most dprecious technological secrets with the Japanese (with whom, by the way, communications became increasingly difficult as the war drew to a close, and trade-transport nearly impossible)? When we look for historical evidence to support such a line of speculation, we come up empty, or at least woefully insufficient.

There is a truth somewhere behind these foo fighters. After all these years they continue to leave us with nagging questions unanswered by our official organs of truth, that is, academia and the media.

The same can be said of the ghost rockets of 1946. Once again, the classified world showed great interest in an unknown phenomenon, none of which was transmitted to the public. Two American generals visited Sweden, one of whom was General James Doolittle (leading us to consider that the Eighth Air Force may have reached some interesting conclusions about the foo fighters). After this visit, the Swedish government stopped talking to the newspapers. And while public speculation centered on the Russians as the likely culprits, the classified world concluded differently. By late 1946, the Swedish Air Intelligence Service arrived at a truly remarkable assessment. Unfortunately, it was not declassified until the late 1990s. It read, in part:

> . . . some reliable and fully technically qualified people have reached the conclusion that 'these phenomena are obviously the result of a high technical skill which cannot be credited to any presently known culture on Earth.' They are therefore assuming that these objects originate from some previously unknown or unidentified technology, possibly outside the Earth.[92]

---

92 USAFE Item 14, TT 1524, (Top Secret), 4 November 1948, declassified in 1997, National Archives, Washington D.C.

Chapter 4: UFO Secrecy and Those Who Fought It

Given the close contact between the Swedes and the Americans, the Americans obviously knew everything the Swedes knew. So here is an early example of the Extraterrestrial Hypothesis (ETH) making its way through the U.S. military command structure. Whether America's top generals and admirals supported these arguments is another matter. But their Swedish counterparts seem to have.

When recalling the statements of the Greek scientist Paul Santorini, mentioned in the previous chapter, the argument for cover-up becomes more powerful still. Years after the fact, Santorini said that the so-called ghost rockets were neither Soviet nor rockets.[93] He also described American interference in the Greek investigation. Just as with the Swedes, the Americans were obviously familiar with his team's conclusions. One can only wonder if Doolittle was involved here, too.[94]

1947: The Dam Breaks

Now we come to 1947. Despite the continual and steady upsurge of sightings, none of the prior events had proved durable in the public psyche. The Battle of Los Angeles and foo fighters were already a distant memory. The ghost rockets had vaguely been ascribed to the Soviets. As far as the public could tell, there were no connections among these obscure events, and hence no phenomenon.

Not so, however, among the national security elite. Every indication is that they knew full well that they were dealing with something extraordinary. Maybe they knew even more than that.

Then, in late June and early July of 1947, the dam broke. Finally, the public was talking about this new phenomenon called flying saucers, and Roswell was the culmination. Something went down near Roswell in July 1947. An FBI memo from that week tells us that, whatever it was, it was sent to Wright Field in Dayton, Ohio for analysis—that is, the U.S. Air Technical Intelligence Center (ATIC).

---

93 We might also ask if these Ghost Rockets could have been derived from a secret post-war Nazi base somewhere else in Europe, and are left with no historical evidence to support such a conclusion.
94 Good, Timothy, *Above Top Secret: The Worldwide UFO Cover-up*, p. 23.

Since the Air Force has continued publicly to assert that the Roswell debris was a balloon known as Mogul, we are obligated to ask: why would *any* type of balloon be sent to ATIC? There is also a great deal of anecdotal testimony supporting the idea that an exotic and advanced craft went down near Roswell. For instance, General Arthur Exon, who was a junior officer at Wright Field at the time, told researchers that, in 1947, he had heard about the materials arriving from New Mexico as being incredibly exotic and mystifying to the best scientists who studied them. During the 1960s, Exon was Base Commander at Wright-Patterson Air Force Base. As he said in 1990:

> They knew they had something new in their hands. The metal and material was unknown to anyone I talked to. Whatever they found, I never heard what the results were. A couple of guys thought it might be Russian, but the overall consensus was that the pieces were from space. Everyone from the White House on down knew that what we had found was not of this world within 24 hours of our finding it. . . . Roswell was the recovery of a craft from space.[95]

For a brief moment one day, the world was treated to a headline confirming the capture of a flying saucer. Three hours after the initial press release, however, the story was ordered pulled, retracted, and then debunked. In the aftermath of Roswell, press coverage of flying saucers practically ceased. The *New York Times, Life* Magazine, and other major print media published dismissive articles. From this point onward, UFO witnesses increasingly began to be portrayed as crackpots.

The press was simply following the lead of the military. In volume one of *UFOs and the National Security State,* I wrote, "the Army baked it, the press served it, and the public ate it." There were no independent civilian investigations of UFOs in 1947, hence no one to challenge the national security apparatus, which was the only group investigating this matter seriously.

And what was occurring within that apparatus? According to Captain Edward Ruppelt, who later headed the Air Force's Project

---

95 Randle, Kevin, *Roswell UFO Crash Update,* Inner Light-Global Communications, 1995. See also "Brig. Gen. Arthur Exon" [roswellproof.homestead.com/exon.html]

Blue Book, and who had the opportunity to review the records of 1947, the situation in Air Force Headquarters was "confusion almost to the point of panic," and that the security lid was down tight. This is perfectly logical.[96]

Consider the situation. The U.S. military had just fought the most terrifying and consuming war in history. The world was broken, exhausted, and just beginning the long road to recovery. In the two years since the war's end, the Soviet Union and communism had given the U.S. something new to fear. Then there was the new and terrifying technology of atomic weapons. There was a fear, almost in the air, that such weapons portended the destruction of mankind, or even of all life on Earth. More than anything else, people everywhere wanted to return to some sense of normal.

And yet what was happening? A mysterious phenomenon had appeared. Its source and intentions were as yet unknown, likewise its full capabilities. Nevertheless, whoever and whatever was behind the flying saucers, they appeared to be "ahead" of the most advanced human technology.

Under such conditions, could anyone expect national security policymakers to announce the presence of such things to the world? Wouldn't it make more sense to keep this as secret as possible, while trying to understand what they were dealing with? Surely it would, and this appears to be exactly what happened.

It is also helpful to remember that no organization as large as the U.S. military can ever operate in a completely organized manner, without some level of confusion. Throughout the summer of 1947, it was obvious that many senior officers and decision-makers were not in the loop on the matter of flying saucers. Not everyone had a "need-to-know." As a result, there were attempts by various offices to find out just what this business was all about. One such attempt was by Brigadier General George Schulgen at the Pentagon when he wrote to Lieutenant General Nathan Twining of Air Material Command. Schulgen believed these so-called flying discs were probably classified

---

96 Ruppelt, Edward. *Report on Unidentified Flying Objects*, Doubleday & Company, Inc., 1956. For an online text version, see www.gutenberg.org/cache/epub/17346/pg17346.html.

American technology, but he wanted confirmation. After all, was this something he needed to be concerned with?

In reply, Twining wrote one of the most remarkable memos on the flying discs that has ever been made public. Dated September 23, 1947, he told Schulgen that the saucers were "real, not visionary or fictitious." Although he conceded the possibility that they may be natural phenomena such as meteors, he added:

> ... the reported operating characteristics such as extreme rates of climb, maneuverability (particularly in roll), and action which must be considered evasive when sighted ... lend belief to the possibility that some of the objects are controlled either manually, automatically, or remotely.

Twining listed several common descriptions of UFOs. They generally were silent, had a metallic or light reflecting surface, no trail, were circular or elliptical in shape, and often flat on the bottom. Many descriptions indicated a dome on top. Several reports indicated they flew in formation. Quite specific information, indeed.

UFO skeptics have pointed to Twining's statement that no wreckage of a flying disc had been recovered. It is true that he was probably in a good position to know. But what we do not know is whether Twining would have been able to tell Schulgen about a UFO crash, if such a thing had happened. Simply put, if Schulgen lacked a "need to know," Twining could not have told him. On the other hand, Twining did state that UFOs were not secret American craft. This came as a surprise to Schulgen, who expected to learn that there was nothing to the affair, that everything was under control.

Was Twining hiding the fact that UFOs were classified technology? It is a fair question, and he appears to have left the door open. He wrote:

> Due consideration must be given to the following: The possibility that these objects are of domestic origin—the product of some high security project not known to AC/AS-2 or this command.... The possibility that some foreign nation has a form of propulsion, possibly nuclear, which is outside of our domestic knowledge.

Clearly, there was much more going on than what we read in Twining's memo. To start, we might ask, *how much was Schulgen*

Chapter 4: UFO Secrecy and Those Who Fought It

cleared to know? For instance, what does it mean that Twining wrote there were no crashed UFOs—such as at Roswell? Logically, it would seem to mean one of three things: either there was no crash of a UFO at Roswell, or Twining did not know about it, or Schulgen was not cleared to know about it.

If nothing else, we can see by this three page, typewritten, memo that the UFO issue was being taken very seriously by the highest levels of the American national security community.

Twining later earned his fourth star and became Chief of Staff of the U.S. Air Force. As a result of his letter to Schulgen, the Air Force established Project Sign, based out of Wright-Patterson Air Force Base. Sign began work in the beginning of 1948, charged with studying the flying saucers and coming to some sort of conclusion about them.

Before leaving the Twining memo, we are obliged to ask a few more obvious questions. First, is there any credible evidence that either the U.S. or anyone else had any craft in 1947, experimental or otherwise, that could duplicate the reported maneuvers of flying saucers? What aerial object in 1947 had those performance capabilities, and which was flat on the bottom and domed on top?[97]

As mentioned earlier, much of this hinges on whether or not the Germans developed technology during the Second World War that could have accounted for a portion (whether small, large, or entire) of the UFO phenomenon at this time. It is well understood that German science and technology were quite advanced, and that the Allies were aware of this fact during the last phase of the war as they scrambled to acquire as many German science and intelligence specialists as they could. There may well be a connection with what the Germans had been working on, although it remains problematic to ascribe all of the UFO sightings to this. There were simply too many of them, and there were too many that predated any possible German-Nazi technology. Moreover, there has never been a reasonable account of the manufacturing infrastructure needed to develop and build these objects, especially in a decimated post-1945 world, nor of their mission, nor of

---

97 See Dolan, Richard M. "Twelve Government Documents that Take UFOs Seriously," [richarddolanpress.com/30-twelve-government-documents-that-take-ufos-seriously/].

how, in how in subsequent years, they were able (presumably) to create the illusion among so many witnesses that they were not normal human beings but extraterrestrial aliens.

Another interesting question arises. If Roswell was the crash of something highly exotic, even extraterrestrial, does that mean Project Sign was something other than what we have been told for years and years? Was Project Sign, instead, a kind of busy-work for certain groups in the military that did not need to know the full truth of the matter? Might it have been an exercise to see just how vulnerable the UFO reality was to being accurately assessed and perceived by reasonable analysis, and which would therefore provide guidance on how further to hide it from prying eyes? After all, if material and bodies from Roswell or elsewhere had already been recovered, surely the conclusions of Sign would not have been needed for those people who were truly in the know. But it would be necessary to keep enough people busy "searching" for answers. So, was Project Sign something like busy-work? The short answer appears to be *yes*.

In any case, by the beginning of 1948, the scientists at Project Sign agreed that the phenomenon of "flying saucers" was real, and not merely illusory, nor all hoaxes. They shared a broad consensus that somebody's technology was responsible, probably either a secret project of the Soviets or Americans, or else of "interplanetary" origin. They also agreed that this was serious business, and that secrecy was needed to study it. Everything was to be conducted away from prying eyes.[98]

1948: Estimating the Situation

The new year began with an ill-fated attempt to intercept a UFO. On January 7, 1948, while chasing an unknown object near Goddard Air Force Base in Kentucky, Air Force Captain Thomas Mantell crashed to his death. He had climbed too high without oxygen, and certainly passed out. What he chased remains unclear to this day. The team at Sign initially thought he had misidentified Venus, which was in the general direction he was going, until it was realized there was too

---

98 A good overview of Project Sign can be found in Ruppelt, Edward J., *The Report on Unidentified Flying Objects* (Doubleday & Co., 1956).

much daylight for Venus to have been visible. They then changed their solution to "unknown." Some years later, astronomer J. Allen Hynek suggested Mantell might have chased one of the Navy's classified Skyhook balloons. This answer is possible, although there still remains doubt. We may never know.[99]

For the next few months of 1948, there were few good UFO reports within the U.S. There was a crescendo that began in May, however, and included several military aerial encounters. Matters came to a head on July 24, when an Eastern Airlines flight over Montgomery, Alabama had a near collision with a large UFO. Both pilots and one of the passengers saw a brilliant, rocket-like object rushing straight at them. Then it veered to the side, gave a long gust of red exhaust, and shot up into the clouds. Both pilots stated they were able to see the object clearly. They agreed that it had double decked rows of square windows along the side, and was about one hundred feet long. It was moving at an estimated speed of between five hundred and seven hundred miles per hour: roughly the top speed attained by any aircraft in the world at that time. They were convinced this was no natural phenomenon. A meteorite, for instance, would have been much faster and would not have maneuvered as this object did.[100]

Upon reflection, this is a very perplexing sighting. First, if this was an extraterrestrial craft, we have ask: what were its operators thinking? Did they have a mechanical failure? Were they trying to terrify the locals in some celestial game of chicken? Moreover, the craft's level of technology did not seem more than perhaps a few decades ahead of the rest of the world, if that. After all, it was clearly burning some sort of fuel. Indeed, there were a few experimental designs (existing on paper only), which bore a superficial resemblance to the description of the strange object. These were the Air Force/RAND "World-Circling Spaceship," the Navy/Martin "High Altitude Test Vehicle" (HATV), and the Navy/North American HATV. All were early designs to launch an artificial satellite into Earth orbit, and all—if they had been

---

99 "1948, The Death of Thomas Mantell" [www.ufocasebook.com/Mantell.html].
100"Watershed: The Chiles-Whitted 'rocketship' sighting," [www.project1947.com/gr/chileswhitted.htm].

UFOs for the 21st Century Mind

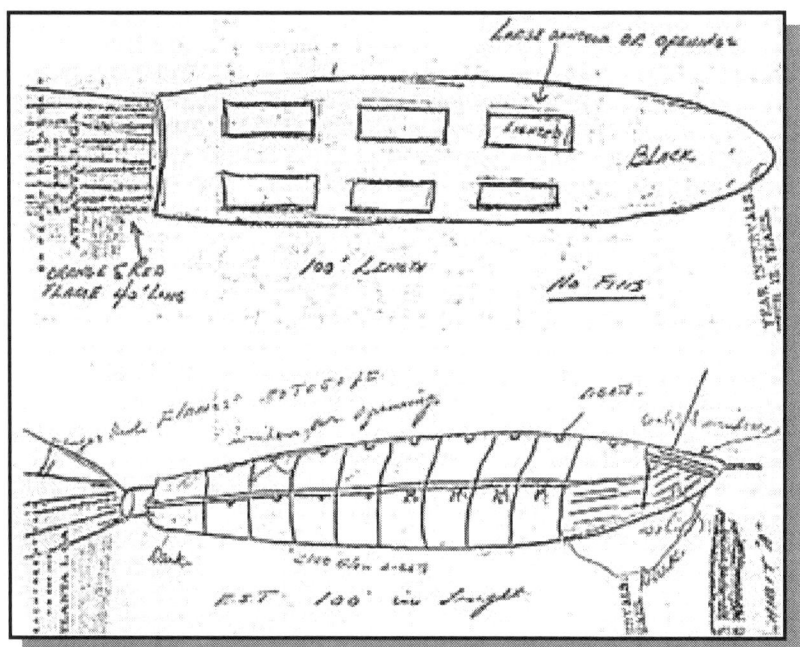

Drawings by the witnesses of the object they saw on July 24, 1948.

built—would have been roughly the size of the object described by the pilots.[101] For all we know, this object was less advanced than the F-117A Stealth Fighter, although admittedly it had much better maneuverability and acceleration. This sighting also prompts us to recall the airships of the 1890s, which also seemed to have been a decade or so ahead of the rest of the world.

So what is the ultimate meaning of this July, 1948 encounter? Extraterrestrials? Extraterrestrials that live here permanently, but somehow in secret? Or, were they possibly an entirely human group, but secret? If the last of these, it remains frustrating that, even after all these years, no one ever leaked information to that effect. We are as stumped today as people were back then.

Publicly, the military did everything possible to downplay interest in this case, even initially calling the unknown object a weather balloon, a statement it was forced to retract. Behind the scenes, however, there was great interest. Indeed, it led the team at Sign to

---

101 "The RAND World-Circling Spaceship and the 1948 Chiles-Whitted 'rocketship' sighting," [www.project1947.com/gr/worldcircling.htm].

Chapter 4: UFO Secrecy and Those Who Fought It

create a document entitled, *The Estimate of the Situation*. It was handed to Air Force Chief of Staff, General Hoyt Vandenberg, most likely in August of that year. This document, which has taken on a legendary status, has never been made public. Yet, a number of people have attested to its reality, including Edward Ruppelt. As he put it: "the situation was the UFOs; the estimate was they were interplanetary!" The most likely scenario, according to the report, was that extraterrestrials were making a full-scale observation of Earth, although attack did not seem imminent. A rather shocking assessment, to be sure.[102]

Vandenberg, we are told, rejected the report's conclusion, either because it could not be proven, or (more likely) because he simply did not desire it. The Estimate then died a quick death. According to Ruppelt, all but a few copies were burned, and the personnel involved in creating it were reassigned. Later during the 1950s, Ruppelt spoke privately with retired Marine Corps Major Donald E. Keyhoe, probably the most important UFO researcher of the 1950s. Ruppelt told Keyhoe, "the general said [The Estimate] would cause a stampede.... how could we convince the public the aliens weren't hostile when we didn't know it ourselves?"

Researcher Kevin Randle had another interesting story about the Estimate. Randle had met an Air Force colonel who also confirmed the existence of the Estimate. This colonel had worked with Air Technical Intelligence Command (ATIC) during the late 1940s, and told Randle that after it had been hand-delivered to Vandenberg, he returned it with instructions that two paragraphs be removed. These paragraphs were said to have referred to physical existence of alien craft recovered in New Mexico. Randle was told this before the Roswell case was rediscovered in the late 1970s.[103]

One way or another, the Estimate of the Situation led to a policy change on UFOs. Essentially, it portended the end of Project Sign and

---

102 Good discussions of the Estimate of the Situation can be found at Aldrich, Jan. "1948 UFO Documents: Background" [www.project1947.com/fig/1948back.htm] and Swords, Michael, "Project SIGN and the Estimate of the Situation," [www.bibliotecapleyades.net/sociopolitica/sign/sign.htm].
103 Clark, Jerome, *The UFO Encyclopedia: The Phenomenon from the Beginning*, Vol. 2, (Omnigraphics, 1998) p. 138-139.

the demise, albeit temporarily, of the extraterrestrial hypothesis.

But let us reflect on what had just happened. A strong and compelling UFO sighting takes place, something so profound that it shakes up the Air Force and prompts the staff at Sign to write a report favoring the ETH. Then, the report is batted down, and an anti-ETH mood sets in. The people at Sign were not ill-trained, gullible, or naive. On the contrary, they were level-headed and skeptical in the best sense of the word, and serious about the problem of UFOs. In this context, what seems most likely is that this was an attempt to keep the low-level investigation at Project Sign from straying into highly classified territory. The staff had stumbled onto the correct answer, but that correct answer was beyond their pay grade.

Certainly, the attitude of President Harry Truman would have been of great importance to this matter. Yet in Truman's two-volume autobiography, there are no references to anything connected to UFOs or flying saucers. One would think that UFOs were simply not part of his Presidency.

In fact, however, Truman was regularly briefed about UFOs. A statement from Major General Robert B. Landry makes this clear. In 1974, after he had retired and Truman had died, Landry gave an interview about his career, which included a time when he served as President Truman's Air Force Liaison. In the course of his interview, Landry said that from the summer of 1948 until the end of Truman's presidency in January 1953, he was responsible for coordinating with the CIA to provide quarterly briefings for President Truman on the subject of UFOs. Immediately after mentioning this, Landry downplayed its importance. All reports were made orally, he said, and "nothing of substance considered credible or threatening to the country was ever received from intelligence."[104]

Considering that these briefings lasted for four and a half years, it would seem that President Truman received seventeen or eighteen

---

[104] "Oral History Interview with General Robert B. Landry." Scottsdale, Arizona. February 28, 1974. by James R. Fuchs, Harry S. Truman Library. [sunsite.unc.edu/lia/president/TrumanLibrary/oral_histories/Landry_Robert.html].

briefings on UFOs. It certainly would have been nice to hear those conversations, unimportant though Landry professed them to be. But were they really unimportant? In the first place, they started at the time of the Eastern Airlines incident and The Estimate of the Situation. This alone would indicate that there was some urgency to the matter. Moreover, for a man as busy as President Harry Truman to be briefed every three months on flying saucers indicates that *someone* thought it was important. Ditto the fact that Landry worked with the CIA on this. As for Landry's insistence that nothing important was discussed, and that nothing was written down, perhaps a telling statement from former CIA director Richard Helms would be helpful: "the first rule in keeping secrets is nothing on paper."

It would appear that President Truman and his national security team considered the matter of UFOs to be very important.

The Case of James Forrestal

Another person of interest during this early period was America's first Secretary of Defense, James Forrestal. He held that position from the time of the great national security reorganization of mid-1947 until the spring of 1949. Forrestal ran America's military through the early tensions of the Cold War, as well as during the first upsurge in reports about the "flying saucers." He was fired by Harry Truman at the beginning of Truman's second term (for meeting with Truman's Republican opponent, Thomas E. Dewey, during the Presidential campaign season). At the end of March 1949, he formally left his position. He then immediately had a nervous breakdown and was hospitalized. On the early morning of May 22, 1949, Forrestal died after falling from the 16th floor window of the Bethesda Naval Hospital, in Washington, D.C. His death was immediately ruled a suicide, and that, apparently, was that. All standard biographies of Forrestal agree with this assessment.

Not everyone, however, has agreed. A number of people, including his brother Henry, suspected that he had been murdered. There are many suspicious elements of Forrestal's death:

(1) His near complete isolation during his hospitalization, even

several times from his brother, as well as his chaplain. (2) He was seen to be improving during the final weeks before his death. (3) He had befriended one of his security guards and had discussed having the young man serve as his assistant after his release. (4) On the night of his death, that security guard had been replaced by a new guard. (5) At 1:30 a.m., just minutes before Forrestal's death, the new security guard allegedly saw him reading and taking notes in bed, and said Forrestal declined a sedative to help him sleep. (6) The notes were said to be a transcription from a morbid speech from Sophocles' play *Ajax*. This was played up in the media as a kind of suicide note. Yet the note was barely considered a matter of interest during the U.S. Navy's Review Board, which investigated his murder. Most importantly, it was decidedly not in his handwriting. (7) Forrestal died by falling from the kitchen window in the hallway of his hospital. Yet he did not merely jump. His body was found with his bathrobe cord tied very tightly around his neck. Supposedly, he had tried to hang himself by tying the other end to a radiator just below the window, certainly an odd—probably unique—way to attempt suicide. He did not hang himself in his own room, which would have been far easier. (8) Scuff marks were found on the outer window sill where he fell. If Forrestal had decided suddenly to kill himself, he apparently changed his mind right away. (9) His brother, Henry, had just informed the hospital that he was going to report his brother's isolated detention to the press, and was going to have him taken out on Monday, May 23. James Forrestal died at 1:45 a.m. on the morning of May 23.[105]

Several analysts, including the author, have reviewed Forrestal's death in detail. Murder, not suicide, is the obvious probability. If so, we might ask why?

Here is where the UFO connection becomes interesting. Anyone as powerful as a Secretary of Defense has enemies coming from many directions. The UFO connection is not the only one that could have resulted in people wanting to kill him. But, without a doubt, if one

---

105 Dolan, Richard M. "The Death of James Forrestal," [richarddolanpress.com/the-death-of-james-forrestal/]. See also Martin, David, "Who Killed James Forrestal? Part 3" [www.dcdave.com/article4/041120a.html].

considers the UFO problem to have been real to the national security elite, then Forrestal would have been considered a security risk. Over 1948, his mental state had become delicate, and who knows what he might have said once he was released from the hospital?

Unknown Objects Over Sensitive Airspace

Throughout the late 1940s and early 1950s, a number of classified memos were written about UFOs. What we take away from them is that something was happening that gravely concerned people in the know. None of these documents was written with the expectation that they would ever be made public. It was during the brief window in American history when the Freedom of Information Act was somewhat user-friendly (that is, during the Jimmy Carter administration of the late 1970s) when most of these UFO-related documents were released. It is incredible but true that, of the thousands of pages of UFO-related documents that have been declassified by the U.S. government, more than half are from that now-distant period of time. Moreover, most of those are of lower levels of classification, seldom as high as Top Secret.

One of these, however, an FBI memo from January 31, 1949, stated bluntly that the matter of flying saucers was "considered top secret by intelligence officers of both the Army and the Air Forces." It went on to describe disturbing, unexplained events over Los Alamos and a variety of other military installations. This, at a time when government spokespersons had been assuring the public that flying saucers were simply a combination of hoaxes, hallucinations, conventional aircraft, and misidentification of natural phenomena. In reality, the memo described this phenomenon as positively dangerous. Once again, there is indication that the Eastern Airlines encounter of 1948 was considered very important. This memo explained that:

> . . . recent observations have indicated that the unidentified phenomena travel at the rate of speed estimated at a minimum of three miles per second and a maximum of twelve miles per second, or a mean calculated speed of seven and one-half miles per second, or 27,000 miles per hour.

The memo noted furthermore that several times "a definite vertical change in path was indicated." Whatever these things were, they were not only incredibly fast, but had maneuverability that was off the charts.

This classified memo also described incursions of unknown objects over Los Alamos, New Mexico throughout December 1948 (on the 5th, 6th, 7th, 8th, 11th, 13th, 14th, 20th, and 28th). The witnesses of these "unexplained phenomena" included Special Agents of the Office of Special Investigation, airline pilots, military pilots, Los Alamos base security personnel, and private citizens. A few sightings were of multiple craft, and analysts rejected the notion of meteorites as an explanation. Some wondered whether or not the objects were Soviet in origin, but this seemed to be a stretch.[106]

Several other memos of the period stand out. Indeed, on the same day that the FBI memo was prepared, another one was dispatched from Kirtland Air Force Base in Albuquerque. As mentioned in the previous chapter, this one declared that at least one hundred UFO sightings had been recorded in that area, and described concern from many quarters. Agencies such as the Atomic Energy Commission, the Armed Forces Special Weapons Project, the Fourth Army, and local commanders were "perturbed by implications of phenomena." Clearly, the implications of over one hundred UFO sightings in the area would perturb anyone.

Another document, this one from the summer of 1950, stated that round UFOs had been seen over the Hanford Atomic Energy Commission plant. Air Force jets had attempted to intercept the objects, but failed. Many units had been alerted, including anti-aircraft battalions and more. In other words, the matter was serious. Within such an environment of confusion and uncertainty, how could the military possibly desire to inform the public about it?

But, despite all efforts to keep UFOs secret, to erase them from the public mind, they would not go away. People continued to see them, and the U.S. military was in the uncomfortable position of attempting to explain them away. As long as the sightings were relatively few,

---

106 For an analysis of this and other interesting declassified U.S. government documents on UFOs, see Dolan, Richard M., "Twelve Government Documents that take UFOs Seriously," [richarddolanpress.com/30-twelve-government-documents-that-take-ufos-seriously/].

Chapter 4: UFO Secrecy and Those Who Fought It

```
MEMORANDUM FOR RECORD:

SUBJECT: Flying Discs

The following information was furnished Major Carlan by
Lt Colonel Mildren/on 4 August 1950:

    Since 30 July 1950 objects, round in form, have been
sighted over the Hanford AEC Plant. These objects re-
portedly were above 15,000 feet in altitude. Air Force
jets attempted interception with negative results. All
units including the anti-aircraft battalion, radar units,
Air Force fighter squadrons, and the Federal Bureau of
Investigation have been alerted for further observation.
The Atomic Energy Commission states that the investiga-
tion is continuing and complete details will be forwarded
later.

                                    U. G. C.
                                    U. G. CARLAN
                                    Major, GSC
                                    Survey Section
```

Classified memo describing UFOs over the Hanford Atomic Facility in the summer of 1950.

perhaps this could be done.

Then came 1952.

The Air Force had begun to revitalize the remnants of Project Sign, which had been recreated under the name Project Grudge. Through most of 1951, Grudge looked moribund. Then, after a dramatic military UFO sighting over New Jersey during the fall, Grudge was handed to Captain Edward Ruppelt. In the spring of 1952, Grudge received a new name: Blue Book. Ruppelt had a small staff to work with, just in time to deal with a huge increase in UFO sightings.

The Crisis of 1952

High up within the Pentagon, someone had decided to promote UFOs to the public. In April 1952, *Life* magazine published an article that had been sponsored by the Air Force, entitled, "Have We Visitors From Space?" *Life*'s answer was, *maybe*. The article ruled out the main excuses commonly attributed at the time: psychological phenomena, products of U.S. research, Russian developments, atmospheric effects from atomic activity, or Skyhook balloons. This was not the type of debunking piece that was typical of the era. Admittedly, the *New York Times* quickly rebutted it, but it was nevertheless true that the Air

Force had been the main source for the article. Project Blue Book had even declassified certain UFO reports for it. On several occasions, Ruppelt was asked whether the Air Force was really behind the piece. The official answer was *no*, that *Life*'s conclusions were its own. However, he stated that certain high-ranking Pentagon officers ("so high that their personal opinion was almost policy") had unofficially inspired the article. One of these men had even given his opinions to the journalist of the article.[107]

But what does it mean? Had the power elite decide to soften UFO secrecy? Or, perhaps, was the sudden openness a smokescreen for something else? Perhaps an inside faction wanted to hedge its bet, just in case events were to spiral out of control and a full disclosure became needed? Indeed, sightings had been quite frequent throughout 1950, 1951, and early 1952. Some had been unsettling. If the secret-keepers were concerned that the agencies behind UFOs might soon make an open appearance, they might seek to prepare the public, if only just a bit.

Yet another question arises in connection with the article: did the policymakers know that UFO sightings were about to spike so high? For, oddly enough, UFOs were reported at a record pace all through the spring and summer of 1952.

In April, two powerful members of America's defense establishment had a dramatic UFO encounter. U.S. Secretary of the Navy, Dan Kimball, was flying from California to Hawaii, when he saw two disc-shaped objects moving at an incredibly fast speed, later estimated to be about 1,500 mph. They circled Kimball's plane twice and then departed. Fifty miles to the east, another aircraft, carrying U.S. Navy Admiral Arthur Radford, encountered what appeared to be the same objects. They circled his aircraft, then zoomed upward and out of sight. Kimball reported the encounter to the Air Force, and was unhappy with what he believed was its stonewalling on UFOs. The

---

107 Darrach, H. B. Jr. and Ginna, Robert. "Have We Visitors from Space?" *LIFE* Magazine, April 7, 1952 [www.project1947.com/shg/csi/life52.html]. Ruppelt, Edward, *The Report on Unidentified Flying Objects*, p. 131-132. Also see: books.google.com/books?id=ElYEAAAAMBAJ&pg=PA80&source=gbs_toc_r&cad=2#v.

Chapter 4: UFO Secrecy and Those Who Fought It

story leaked to retired Marine Corps Major, Donald Keyhoe, which is how the rest of the world eventually learned about it. But Kimball's and Radford's sightings were only two of several hundred intriguing UFO encounters that took place during the spring and summer of 1952.[108]

April and May were busy months for Project Blue Book, with 99 and 79 reports, respectively. In June, the total increased to 149. Ruppelt described that month as "one big swirl of UFO reports." That month, he gave a briefing on UFOs to the head of Air Force Intelligence, General John Alexander Samford. The small room was crowded. Samford's staff was there, as were two Captains from Naval intelligence. There were also a few individuals that Ruppelt said he would not name. The meeting was tense, until one of Samford's staff members, a Colonel, argued that Blue Book's investigation was biased against the interplanetary thesis. At that point, wrote Ruppelt, "you could almost hear the Colonel add, 'okay, so now I've said it.'"

Opinions were split fairly evenly and, in Ruppelt's view, this reflected a split in opinions at the very top. On one side were those who wanted to continue keeping an "open mind" about UFOs, without forming a provisional conclusion as to what they were. The other group had apparently formed a conclusion and was "dead serious about the situation." They wanted a policy starting from the assumption that UFOs were interplanetary, and they wanted to stop any further release of information. He argued that this group had taken a firm hold in the Pentagon, and many other agencies throughout government.[109]

But the crescendo of sightings had not ended. Although June 1952 had been a busy month for Blue Book, July was the busiest of all. An incredible 536 reports came to the group, and unknowns were running at about forty percent. Ruppelt later wrote of rumors that the Air Force was braced for an invasion by flying saucers. And yet, the

---

108 Keyhoe, Donald, *Flying Saucers: Top Secret*, (Putnam, 1960), p. 85-86; Keyhoe, Donald, *Aliens from Space: The Real Story of Unidentified Flying Objects* (Doubleday, 1973), p. 79-80.
109 Ruppelt, Edward, *The Report on Unidentified Flying Objects*, p. 147-149, 152-153.

situation on the inside was even worse than that. "Had these rumor mongers been at ATIC in mid-July," he wrote, "they would have thought the invasion was already in full-swing."[110]

Matters culminated for two consecutive weekends over the nation's capital, when multiple UFOs were tracked on radar and seen visually by quite a few people. On both occasions, Air Force interceptors were sent. Pilots got close enough to track the unknowns but were unable to catch up. The events were so significant that they made the front page of the *New York Times*, even bumping the Democratic national presidential convention from the top spot. There is a famous photograph of the objects over the Capitol building, often argued to be reflections of lights from below, and this is very likely the case. Nevertheless, the radar and visual testimony is compelling. I was fortunate to speak to one of the key radar operators and air traffic controllers at the time, Howard Cocklin. Howard described how he saw the unknown objects visually at the same time they were being tracked on radar. He was ninety at the time of our interview, and passed away two months later.[111]

When unexplained objects are seen and tracked over the nation's capital, flying at will and easily evading the top interceptors available, this is a problem. Above all else, what had to be done was to defuse the situation. Thus did General John Samford speak to the press on July 29, 1952. He explained the recent UFO activity as the result of faulty radar returns caused by "temperature inversion," a particular type of weather phenomenon in which a layer of warm air becomes trapped between two layers of cooler air, and which can affect radar returns. While this is a real phenomenon, nearly all the radar operators involved disputed this explanation. None, however, were permitted to speak at the press conference. It is interesting, incidentally, that accompanying Samford was General Roger Ramey. Five years earlier,

---

110 Ruppelt, Edward, *The Report on Unidentified Flying Objects*, p. 155.
111 The author's interview with Howard Cocklin is on YouTube "First Contact Special Edition: 1952 UFO Eyewitness Howard Cocklin" at [https://www.youtube.com/watch?v=UQwwl1ln30Y&list=UUfuGn-5TVgftiL6kBDFr0CQ&index=4]

Chapter 4: UFO Secrecy and Those Who Fought It

Ramey had been the man to squash the Roswell story.[112]

The press conference effectively managed public opinion. Within the classified world, however, no one seems to have believed the explanation. Within days, a classified memo from the Air Intelligence Estimates Division stated that the Air Force had failed to arrive at any satisfactory conclusion to the UFO mystery. It also concluded that the Soviets were probably not behind the phenomenon, and acknowledged the possibility that UFOs were interplanetary. In other words, the classified conversations continued to be much more interesting than the public explanations.

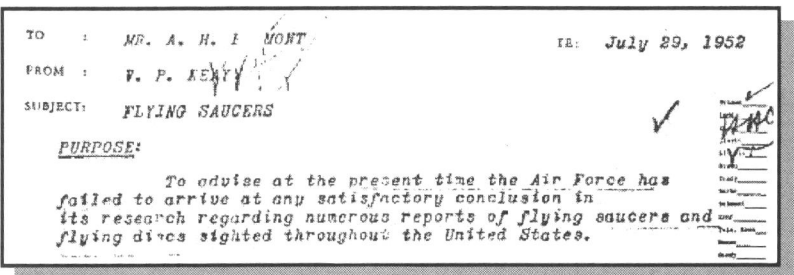

U.S. Air Force memo from July 29, 1952, stating that "the Air Force has failed to arrive at any satisfactory conclusion" regarding flying saucers.

This certainly applied to the CIA, where an analysis from August 1952 gave credence to the reality of UFOs. One statement in particular stands out:

> . . . sightings of UFOs reported at Los Alamos and Oak Ridge, at a time when the background radiation count had risen inexplicably. Here we run out of even blue yonder explanations that might be tenable, and are left with numbers of incredible reports from credible observers.[113]

Throughout this period, classified documents continued to acknowledge the possibility that UFOs might represent some bizarre natural phenomenon, as yet unknown. But no one had any idea what that could be. Most discussions centered over whether UFOs were either a secret American project or something extraterrestrial. In fact,

---

112 Clips of Samford's press conference can be seen at "General Samford's UFO press conference Pentagon, July 29, 1952," [www.youtube.com/watch?v=tcRtkA1Rmvw]
113 Mr. Eng, "Flying Saucers," CIA Special Study Group, August 19, 1952. Reproduced at the CUFON 1952 CIA UFO-Related Document Sampler [www.cufon.org/cufon/cia-52-1.htm].

very few analysts by this point considered them to be a secret American project. When considering this possibility, it is worth asking: what secret American technology would be employed over and over again to trigger U.S. Air Force interceptors? It made no sense then, nor does it today. Certainly, an occasional errant Skyhook balloon may have caused some confusion, but to think such types of events could regularly cause such concern at high levels within the military and intelligence community goes beyond the most generously applied boundaries of belief. Moreover, if such sightings of the early 1950s were secret American technology, what became of it? Why would there have been no sign of it in later decades? Ruppelt, who briefed many branches of the military throughout 1952, had a good idea of the mood among military decision-makers, and it is clear that the extraterrestrial explanation was always the elephant in the living room—that is, the obvious explanation, but one which unfortunately was not allowed to be discussed openly.

During the fall of 1952, the Truman presidency was nearing its end. Within the CIA, the matter of UFOs took on greater urgency. In particular, the CIA's Office of Scientific Intelligence was moving ahead toward creating a panel that would study UFOs scientifically. From this would come a formal policy recommendation. On December 2, the Director of that Office, H. Marshall Chadwell, made an important statement attesting to the reality of UFOs. Chadwell wrote to his boss, the Director of the CIA, Walter Bedell Smith. Chadwell's statement was breathtaking:

> ... at this time, the reports of incidents convince us that there is something going on which must have immediate attention. . . . Sightings of unexplained objects at great altitudes and traveling at high speeds in the vicinity of major US defense installations are of such nature that they are not attributable to natural phenomena or known types of aerial vehicles.[114]

This statement bears close scrutiny. A high-level U.S. official stating

---

114 Memorandum for Director of Central Intelligence from the Deputy Director for Intelligence. Subject: Unidentified Flying Objects. Date: 2 December 1952. Reproduced at the CUFON 1952 CIA Ufo-related Document Sampler, [www.cufon.org/cufon/cia-52-1.htm].

Chapter 4: UFO Secrecy and Those Who Fought It

to the Head of the CIA that UFOs were real, probably artificial, probably intelligently operated, and apparently not American; nor was there serious consideration that these were Soviet.

If not American, if not Soviet, if not natural phenomena, and if they appeared to be technological and under intelligent control, one begins to run out of conventional options. Chadwell's memo makes it obvious that he understood this, although he was loathe to state the obvious.

This led to what became known as the Robertson Panel, a CIA-sponsored group of scientists which met secretly from January 14 to January 17, 1953. Their job was to review UFO reports and to make a recommendation. All of the scientists involved were Nobel-caliber. The Chairman was H. P. Robertson, one of America's leading mathematicians and physicists. During the Second World War, Robertson had become very familiar with foo fighter reports (as had another Panel member, Dr. Luis Alvarez).

The Panel concluded that UFOs were not a direct threat to national security. Yet, they could pose an indirect threat if reports from the general public or within the military were to overwhelm communication channels. Members of the Panel therefore emphasized a need to manage public opinion regarding UFOs, particularly by debunking the topic. They discussed the value of working with Walt Disney and other media figures to convey the message that UFOs were mundane and nothing to get excited about.

Rather insidiously, the Panel recommended that civilian groups studying UFOs be monitored, citing "their potentially great influence on mass thinking . . . the apparent irresponsibility and possible use of such groups for subversive purposes." Two groups in particular were singled out: the Aerial Phenomena Research Organization (APRO) and Civilian Saucer Investigations (CSI). Several times over the years, the leaders of APRO expressed their belief that they were being monitored. Unquestionably, during its final years in the 1970s and 1980s, the organization was infiltrated by intelligence operatives. Most likely it had been so all along.

There is also good evidence that the disbanding of CSI was caused directly by the U.S. government. Researcher Michael Swords located FBI documents indicating that the noted engineer Walther Riedel was pressured to resign from CSI. The group disbanded not long afterwards. In response, Robertson wrote to H. Marshall Chadwell: "[t]hat ought to fix the Forteans," a reference to Charles Fort and hence UFO researchers. There is also a strong case that the UFO organization NICAP, which was founded in 1956, was infiltrated by CIA operatives.

Indeed, Swords and other researchers later determined that the Robertson Panel's conclusions were written before its members even met. In retrospect, this ought not to be so surprising. Realistically, how much work could one expect them to accomplish in a mere twelve hours? One of the Panel members, Dr. Lloyd Berkner, did not even show up until the final day of the gathering.

One fact of great significance regarding this Panel, something always overlooked by historians, is that it was the final act of any importance of the Harry Truman Presidency. The Panel constituted the administration's final act of housecleaning. Its effect throughout the military and intelligence community was profound. In particular, Blue Book was gutted, and it became all but impossible to inquire within the military into the matter.

What appears to have happened is that the split in opinion Ruppelt had described had been definitively resolved. The extraterrestrial hypothesis was accepted and secrecy became the rule. Clearly, the matter had already been strictly secret at the highest levels. Now, however, the clampdown extended much farther down the ladder. After all, for those few already in possession of the secret, why seek any more input from the lower levels? What was to be gained from continually stirring the pot?

For the remainder of the 1950s, the U.S. Air Force and the American government assigned flying saucers to the realm of oblivion. One official statement after another claimed that UFOs were either misidentifications of known aircraft or natural phenomena; or hoaxes. There was no national security threat, so they stated, and, with enough data, every so-called unknown case could be identified. Flying saucers existed solely in the imagination. During that period of time, project Blue Book was ordered to bring its percentage of unknowns to the lowest number possible. Solutions that previously had been considered as "possible" now became the definitive answer, case closed. Whereas during the 1940s and early 1950s, official unknown totals had generally been between fifteen and twenty percent, by the mid-1950s the numbers were regularly two percent or lower. In 1956, for example, Blue Book unknowns were listed at 0.4%. None of this was due to better investigative techniques. How could there be better investigations, when the staff now consisted of only one or two people? In reality, Blue Book became better at one thing only: discarding scientific principles for the purposes of propaganda. Blue Book cooked its books. At the same time, UFOs all but disappeared from American news coverage, at least compared with earlier years.

Challenging the Air Force

From the moment that flying saucers had become a public issue in 1947 until the mid-1950s, the extent of public participation had been nothing more than a handful of small research groups. People relied on their newspapers and radio to enlighten them on the matter. In terms of local reportage, those institutions generally did well enough. The newspapers of that era published many accounts of saucer sightings that were dramatic and baffling. However, in terms of national media, that is, major wire services, established radio networks, very early television broadcasting, and newspapers such as the *New York Times*, the situation was different. These organs were the opinion makers and shapers of the nation, and they worked closely with the military and intelligence community. A great deal of research in subsequent years has highlighted that relationship. But during the 1950s, the myth of a Free Press was important in stifling public inquiry into UFOs. The 1953 movie, *The War of the Worlds*, contains a telling scene in which newspaper and radio journalists openly interview an Army general about the landed flying saucer that was plainly and openly in public view. Seen today, the scene is downright humorous in its absurdity.

Hardly a person alive in the 21st century can imagine such a thing taking place. And yet, that was indeed how America saw itself during that era. Most people fervently believed that, If something important like that were to happen, their journalists—the watchdogs of the public—would be there to report it, rather than isolated far from the scene by the military.

Except that those watchdogs never barked. More accurately, they were little more than lap dogs, and the laps in which they sat were those very agencies seeking to erase UFOs from the public mind.

However, something else began to happen: the beginnings of public dissent. First among these dissenters was Major Donald Keyhoe, who stumbled into the flying saucer mystery in 1950. Keyhoe was a retired Marine Corps Major who had once flown with Charles Lindbergh. He was well-connected. Among his friends were Admiral Roscoe Hillenkoetter, who had directed the CIA from 1947 to 1950. Keyhoe was also friendly with Admiral Delmar Fahrney, known within the Navy as the father of the guided missile. In 1950, Fahrney had privately told Keyhoe, "there have been too many convincing reports, and if the flying saucers do exist they must be interplanetary. Certainly neither we nor the Russians had anything remotely like that."

Through the 1950s, Keyhoe wrote a series of books that discussed the reality of flying saucers and their cover-up by the military. He was a conduit for many important leaks. During the important year of 1952, he obtained roughly fifty accounts of military encounters with UFOs which had been declassified specifically to be shared with him. He was the first person to write about the Robertson Panel, having immediately received leaks about it. He was prolific, and released a great amount of information to the rest of the world.

Another thorn in the side of secrecy was Air Force Captain Edward Ruppelt, the head of Project Blue Book until 1953, who in 1956 published an important book, *The Report on Unidentified Flying Objects*. Even today, it remains among the most important books ever written about UFOs. Ruppelt's treatment of the matter was sober and evenhanded. Considering his prior position as head of Blue Book, it

Chapter 4: UFO Secrecy and Those Who Fought It

U.S. Marine Corps Major Donald E. Keyhoe

was also unflinching in his willingness to acknowledge the difficulties that UFOs posed to the military. The publication of his book also posed a serious problem. Not surprisingly, it came under strong attack from establishment publications such as the *New York Times,* which labeled it "cultist," and "the longest and dullest of the current crop of saucer books." This was not merely unfair, but exactly the opposite of the truth.

In late 1956, a new organization was founded not only to study UFOs seriously, but also to fight the cover-up. It was called the National Investigation Committee on Aerial Phenomena (NICAP). By early 1957, Keyhoe was running NICAP and had committed the organization to promoting open congressional hearings on UFOs. Yet, while pressing for change, the people at NICAP were far from revolutionaries. Indeed, the organization was positively establishment-oriented, and most of its board members were retired senior officers of the U.S. military (including Hillenkoetter, Fahrney, and many others).

Even so, Keyhoe believed that the public had a right to know the truth about UFOs. Like all Americans of his generation, he believed that the American political system was the most open in the world, and that the best strategy for change was to work within it. Several times during the late 1950s and early 1960s, it looked as though this faith would be justified, and that NICAP might succeed in getting those congressional hearings. Every time, however, seemingly at the eleventh hour, the initiative would fizzle out. This saga continued for several years.

Matters came to a head in 1962. During the previous summer, Hillenkoetter had made a public statement that urged "immediate congressional action to reduce the dangers from secrecy about unidentified flying objects." Now, early in 1962, Keyhoe talked with him about making an even stronger statement to Congress. Hillenkoetter agreed, and they determined that spring was the best time to do it. Then, however, Hillenkoetter disappeared. Keyhoe wondered if his old Annapolis classmate was avoiding him. Finally, after weeks of silence, a letter arrived. The Admiral and former CIA chief did a complete about-face. Now, he defended the Air Force's policy on UFOs. "I believe we should not continue to criticize their investigations," he wrote to Keyhoe, "I am resigning as a member of the NICAP Board of governors." It was a hard blow for NICAP.

Such changes of heart seemed to be the order of the day. Just a few years earlier, the same thing had happened to Ruppelt. After the publication of his book in 1956, someone, somehow, appears to have gotten to him. In 1957, Ruppelt was still making pro-UFO statements to the press. In 1960, however, he published a revised version of his book, adding three chapters at the end which debunked his prior thesis, that UFOs constituted a genuine mystery. The three additional chapters, sophomoric and mocking in tone, were of a completely different character from his earlier book. Now, Ruppelt actively ridiculed the people, such as Keyhoe, with whom he had previously been collegial. In his new conclusion, he referred to UFOs as the space age myth. "I'm positive they don't exist," he wrote. "There's not even a glimmer of hope for the UFO."

Then, as if to underscore the mystery, Edward Ruppelt died from a heart attack the following year, at the age of 37. Who knows how it all happened. Perhaps, as some researchers believed, he really did change his mind, and then simply died of natural causes. Maybe not. It is not difficult to see that there would be real pressure placed on outspoken figures like Ruppelt and Hillenkoetter to alter their public positions on this question. Such pressure can be made in a friendly way, or not so friendly. Whether some agency caused Ruppelt's heart attack is something that we will surely never know, unless some fresh document spills out of the archives. Such capabilities did exist back in the 1950s; assassination techniques had already become sophisticated by that time, including the ability to surreptitiously induce a seeming heart attack.

More Sightings and A New Crisis

Thus, by the early 1960s, it appeared that the Air Force, the CIA, and their allies had succeeded in removing the UFO phenomenon from public discussion. But there is always one factor beyond anyone's control: those beings behind the phenomenon itself. Time and again, they never seem to get the memo that they are not supposed to exist.

Starting in 1964, a dramatic rise in well-documented and publicized UFO reports took place. Such reports peaked over the next few years, and once again UFOs were a *problem,* first of national security, secondly as a matter of public credibility. In the past, Blue Book's debunking policy had helped to submerge the problem. Now, however, it only seemed to make things worse. Newspapers started to demand better Air Force investigations of UFOs.

By 1965, Blue Book consultant, astronomer J. Allen Hynek, recommended that the Air Force improve its UFO investigation. Essentially, this meant more money for Blue Book and presumably a healthier philosophy toward investigating the truly difficult cases. The Air Force, which wanted as little public attention on UFOs as possible, had always been loathe to do this. Indeed, the Air Force for years had been trying to unload the program, but had not found a politically viable way to do so. Still, Hynek's suggestion gained ground. By late

1965, the Air Force Scientific Advisory Board met to discuss the UFO question and the idea of an independent study of the problem. Within a year, this would lead to the announcement of the Air Force decision to commission a study of UFOs by the University of Colorado, otherwise known as the Condon Committee. More on that in a moment.

Before that happened, however, an explosion of UFO reports occurred in the United States. In terms of media coverage, this culminated in March 1966. In the town of Dexter, Michigan, night after night, students at Hillsdale College and people elsewhere reported UFOs. On March 14, two deputy sheriffs in Dexter saw what looked like disc-shaped objects maneuvering above the town. Three other police agencies reported similar sightings. Selfridge Air Force Base confirmed that it had tracked objects on radar moving at extreme speeds and maneuverability. On March 17, in Milan, Michigan, another police officer saw a UFO approach his patrol car to within seventy-five feet, then follow him for half a mile, then fly off. Something strange was going on. On the evening of March 20, near Dexter, several people saw a lighted object hovering over a swamp. It was very well defined, in their opinion. Then, it rapidly flew away while making a whistling sound. That night, several lights were reported moving around the swamp.

These sightings received national attention, and Blue Book dispatched Hynek to make a statement. What happened next, however, was a public relations disaster. Immediately upon arriving in Michigan, Hynek gave a press conference. Although he called for a thorough investigation, he focused on the lights over the swamp, suggesting they could have been marsh gas caused by decaying vegetable matter in the swampy area. In other words, swamp gas. The statement was obviously premature, even absurd. The press ridiculed Hynek and the Air Force, which had never looked so incompetent, even duplicitous, about UFOs as it did in that moment. The press conference severely damaged the image of Project Blue Book.

The national media tried its best to calm things down. One such

Chapter 4: UFO Secrecy and Those Who Fought It

Allen Hynek at the March 1966 "swamp gas" press conference.

effort was a CBS television special, narrated by Walter Cronkite, which took a straightforward, debunking approach to UFOs. Researchers later proved that this special was explicitly connected to the recommendations of the Robertson Panel, the guidelines of which were still being followed more than a decade later. Even so, too many voices were speaking openly against the Air Force position. One of these was a Michigan Congressman and the House Minority leader, Gerald R. Ford. Many of the recent sightings had occurred in his district. Ford stated:

> I think there may be substance in some of these reports and because I believe the American people are entitled to a more thorough explanation than has been given them by the Air Force to date.... I think we owe it to the people to establish the credibility regarding UFOs and to produce the greatest possible enlightenment on the subject.[115]

This statement is normally interpreted in a straightforward manner, to the effect that Congressman Ford was genuinely working on behalf of his constituents to get some honest answers about UFOs. Yet,

---

115 News Release, House Republican Leader, March 28, 1966 [www.checktheevidence.com/disclosure/web%20pages/] and [www.presidentialufo.com/ufotalk.htm].

Gerald Ford had also been an active member of the Warren Commission, which obfuscated the assassination of President Kennedy under the guise of an independent review. In addition, he was a five-time attendee of the infamous (though still secret) Bilderberg meetings during the 1960s. It therefore seems probable that there was an ulterior motive to his statement on UFOs. Indeed, the Condon Committee may very well have been the intended result.

The immediate result of Ford's news release, however, was the first-ever open hearing on UFOs within the U.S. Congress, which took place on April 5, 1966. It met for one day only, and was an exclusive gathering. Indeed, only three people were invited to testify in person: Hynek, Blue Book Chief Hector Quintanilla, and Air Force Secretary Harold Brown. It was rather a snub to NICAP, which had been pressing for ten years for this moment and was not invited.[116] The results were predictable. Hynek, still licking his wounds, said UFOs deserved more scientific attention. Brown and Quintanilla were more dismissive, but Brown did direct the Air Force to arrange for a scientific team to investigate and review the Blue Book sightings that remained unidentified, which by then had totaled more than 600.

That spring, a Gallup poll revealed that forty-six percent of Americans believed UFOs to be real. Five percent thought they had seen one personally, which projects to roughly nine million people. This was yet more evidence that UFOs posed a potential public relations problem for the Air Force and Blue Book.

Matters worsened still, at least from the perspective of the Air Force. During the spring of 1966, another personality entered the UFO debate. This was Dr. James McDonald, an atmospheric physicist from the University of Arizona. McDonald had a longstanding private interest in UFOs, but now became publicly involved. The Office of Naval Research awarded him a small stipend to examine the Blue Book material at Wright-Patterson Air Force Base, ostensibly to learn whether certain kinds of clouds accounted for the occasional radar

---

116 Although NICAP, of course, was not a government agency. Moreover, it was permitted to submit material for the record.

Chapter 4: UFO Secrecy and Those Who Fought It

trackings of UFOs. In June, while at Wright-Patterson, McDonald discovered an unedited copy of the Robertson Panel report. It had been classified for more than a decade, and no one outside the military had ever read it. Seeing what surely appeared to be evidence that the CIA was directing a cover-up, McDonald was distressed. Two days later, he was at Hynek's office, pounding his fist on the table and demanding to know why Hynek had not spoken publicly about the cover-up he had obviously known about for years. It was soon evident that McDonald was the cover-up's worst nightmare: a fearless, world-qualified scientist who was willing and able to dismantle the many pseudoscientific explanations of UFOs proffered by the authorities.[117]

Dr. James McDonald.

McDonald's visit seemed to light a fire under Hynek, who now began to distance himself publicly from Blue Book and the Air Force. He wrote several articles that year that highlighted the difficulty of the UFO issue, and stated that the Air Force *did* have unexplained radar reports and photographs of UFOs. He called for an end to witness ridicule and said a truly scientific program had never been undertaken

---

117 Clark, Jerome, *The UFO Encyclopedia: Encyclopedia of the Extraterrestrial* (Visible Ink Press, 1998) Vol. 3, p. 293-294.

regarding UFOs. This was a direct slap at Blue Book.

The Condon Committee

Although it appeared that the Air Force had reached a dead end in its public handling of the UFO problem, the chess pieces were well positioned. Now, the endgame was at hand. By late summer, the Air Force had settled on a solution: the University of Colorado would be selected to undertake an independent, formal study of UFOs. Leading the study was a physicist of world renown, Dr. Edward U. Condon. Many hoped this study would settle the matter once and for all. For a brief, shining moment, it looked as though perhaps there would be an appropriate resolution to this long-standing controversy.

Except that it did not work out that way. In the first place, it became evident from the beginning that Condon's public statements about flying saucers were limited to ridicule. There was a fixation on the most fantastic, absurd stories. If he knew anything of substance about the topic, he surely was not revealing it in public. Worse still, he seemed uninterested in learning anything new. A number of private researchers were brought in to brief the Colorado group, and frequently found Condon napping during the sessions.[118]

Other academicians and scientists on the team did approach the subject with the idea that they were involved in a serious, scientific endeavor. Not surprisingly, after some time reviewing the cases that were brought to them, a number of them began to consider that there was a genuine UFO mystery. Suspicions surfaced regarding Condon's apparent lack of commitment to the truth. To some, it seemed that he had decided from the beginning upon a negative outcome regarding UFOs. This was the claim of Dr. David Saunders, one of the team members who eventually confronted Condon on the matter. Saunders asked him, *What if you determine that these UFOs are in fact real? What then?* According to Saunders, Condon replied that, if such were the case, he would take the report in a locked briefcase to the President of United States. Evidently, there would be, no matter their conclusions,

---

118 Keyhoe, Donald, *Aliens from Space*, p. 130-134.

Chapter 4: UFO Secrecy and Those Who Fought It

no public validation of UFOs coming from the Condon Committee.[119]

Morale worsened still when a particular memorandum was discovered a year into the project. It had been written by the Project Director, Robert Low. Low was second only to Condon in the hierarchy, and had written the memo during the summer of 1966, shortly before the University of Colorado had won the Air Force contract. The statement and tone made it look very much as though the game had been rigged from the outset. Low wrote:

> . . . the trick would be to describe the project so that, to the public, it would appear a totally objective study, but to the scientific community would present the image of a group of nonbelievers trying their best to be objective but having an almost zero expectation of finding a saucer.[120]

The memo had been buried in the project files and was found by one of the project scientists, Dr. Roger Craig. It was circulated and eventually ended up in the hands of James McDonald. From there, matters became ugly.

Early in 1968, McDonald wrote a long, masterful letter to Low. By this time, morale and research problems abounded within the project, something McDonald was well aware of, despite not being a member. It was clear, McDonald wrote, that Condon was a problem: his repeated negative comments in the press, his disturbing preoccupation with the crackpot aspects of UFOs, the obvious conclusion that Condon himself was not personally examining the kinds of witnesses and cases that had made many UFOs so compelling, the obvious lack of communication between Low and Condon on the one hand, and the bulk of the investigators on the other, and the failure of the project to investigate cases of "obfuscation," that is, of cover-up.[121]

Then, finally, McDonald mentioned Low's memorandum itself. "I am rather puzzled by the viewpoints expressed there, but I gather that they seem entirely straightforward to you. . . "

It was a bold statement and a thinly veiled accusation of scientific

---

119 Saunders, David and Harkins, Roger. *UFOs? Yes! Where the Condon Committee Went Wrong.* (New York, World Pub. Co., 1968), p. 140.
120 See Robert Low "Trick" Memo at www.nicap.org/docs/660809lowmemo.htm.
121 Keyhoe, Donald, *Aliens from Space*, p. 175.

dishonesty. McDonald sent a copy of his letter to the project's open files, which meant that it was available for everyone to read.

Condon was furious. Immediately, he summoned each project member to meet with him, one-on-one. He then fired anyone who had been present when McDonald had been given a copy of Low's memorandum. As a result, he was forced to hire several new investigators, just as the project was supposed to be winding down. These replacements comprised a major part of the team that wrote what became known as the Condon Committee Report.[122]

Meanwhile, on July 29, 1968, while the Condon drama was unfolding, the U.S. Congress held a symposium on UFOs sponsored by the House Science and Astronautics Committee. This was a very different affair from the 1966 hearing. Many of the major UFO researchers testified, including McDonald, Hynek, astronomer Carl Sagan of Cornell University, and several others. McDonald made the greatest impression, providing thirty pages of verified UFO reports. He stated:

> I have become convinced that the scientific community, not only in this country but throughout the world, has been casually ignoring as nonsense a matter of extraordinary scientific importance. . . . My own present opinion, based on two years of careful study, is that UFOs are probably extraterrestrial devices engaged in something that might very tentatively be termed surveillance. . . . I have interviewed several hundred witnesses in selected cases, and I am astonished at what I have found. I had no idea that the actual UFO situation is anything like what it appears to be. . . . I now regard the [extraterrestrial] hypothesis as the one most likely to prove correct.[123]

Despite the impression made by McDonald and other presenters, the symposium had no political impact. However, it is now part of our public history, part of Congressional history, which is no small achievement.

Meanwhile, the Colorado team worked on completing its report, and on October 31, 1968, it delivered its *Scientific Study of Unidenti-*

---

122 Saunders, David and Harkins, Roger, *UFOs? Yes!*, p. 186-200, 244-252.
123 McDonald's complete text can be read at www.anomalies.net/archive/Text-Archive/txt1/508.ufo

fied Flying Objects to the Air Force. Condon's conclusion was definitive. "Nothing has come from the study of UFOs in the past twenty-one years," he wrote in the report's Introduction, "that has added to scientific knowledge." Further study of UFOs, he wrote, "probably cannot be justified in the expectation that science will be advanced thereby." In other words, he was recommending that the Air Force shut down Project Blue Book.[124]

The report certainly was massive. It also contained quite a few cases that were investigated with reasonable sophistication by the scientists involved. Yet, there was a striking discrepancy in the report between its contents and conclusions. Condon had concluded that science could gain nothing from studying UFOs. Yet roughly thirty percent of the cases within the report had failed to be explained. This was a vastly higher percentage of unknowns than the U.S. Air Force had offered in years. It was as though Condon had not bothered to read his own report, which in fact has been a common claim and may well have been true. Condon never did show the slightest genuine interest in the topic, and there is little evidence that he gave much energy to its scientific aspects.

In addition to the high percentage of unknowns there were a small number of cases that bordered on virtual acknowledgment of an alien reality. One such case was from 1956, at RAF Lakenheath, a British air base. The report's statement was clear enough: "the apparently rational, intelligent behavior of the UFO suggests a mechanical device of unknown origin as the most probable explanation of this sighting."

Just as powerful was the conclusion regarding two famous photographs from 1950, taken in McMinnville, Oregon:

> this is one of the few UFO reports in which all factors investigated, geometric, psychological, and physical appear to be consistent with the assertion that an extraordinary flying object, silvery, metallic, disc shaped, tens of meters in diameter, and evidently artificial, flew within sight of two witnesses.

---

124 *Final Report of the Scientific Study of Unidentified Flying Objects*, Edward U. Condon, Scientific Director, Daniel S. Gillmor, Editor, Bantam Books, 1968. The report can be read online at www.bibliotecapleyades.net/sociopolitica/condonreport/full_report/contents.htm.

UFOs for the 21st Century Mind

Edward Condon presenting his committee's report, capped by a friendly flying saucers.

Yes indeed, there was gold within the Condon Report. Yet, from a public relations point of view, none of this mattered. As messy as it was, the Condon Report did its job. Although many scientists individually criticized it, it received an endorsement from the National Academy of Sciences. One has to wonder whether those scientists actually read the report. The national media, too, focused on Condon's conclusions rather than the details inside the report. How could they do otherwise? Under pressure to write about a report that was more than nine hundred pages, and considering the time constraints journalists were under, they went to Condon's brief statement, despite its being only marginally related to the actual report.

The End of an Era
The Condon Committee Report accomplished two main things. First, it provided an official scientific dismissal of UFOs. Second, it

resulted in the closing of Project Blue Book. The Air Force had long sought this outcome, and now with the recommendations of an independent scientific body, it was able to do so without major public outcry. In October 1969, Brigadier General Carroll H. Bolender, the Air Force's Deputy Director of Development, wrote a classified memo recommending the termination of Project Blue Book. He wrote: "we agree, that the continuation of Project Blue Book cannot be justified, either on the ground of national security or in the interest of science." Blue Book data, he said, simply did not serve any useful intelligence function. But the important point was that "reports of unidentified flying objects which could affect national security... are not part of the Blue Book system."[125]

Bolender pointed out that such reports were made in accordance with JANAP-146 or Air Force Manual 55-11. These were explicit U.S. Air Force reporting procedures that had long dealt with UFOs, and had done so in a serious matter.[126] In other words, Bolender was saying, if it was an important UFO sighting, it was not supposed to go to Blue Book, anyway. In effect, this was an admission of Blue Book's longstanding role as a public relations exercise. Naturally, it could be let go with no fuss, no muss.

The closing of Project Blue Book might seem to have been no great loss. After all, it had been clear for many years that Blue Book's job was not to explain UFOs, so much as to explain them *away*. In fact, that was true. It had become a national joke, and could scarcely conduct a minimally valid investigation of any UFO encounter, much less a scientific one.

Yet, if Blue Book was a farce, at least it was the people's farce. That is, the public paid for it through tax dollars, and at least in theory Blue Book was responsible to the American people. During the 1950s and 1960s, American citizens who witnessed a UFO may or may not have believed what they saw to have been extraterrestrial, but they were able to report it to their local Air Force Base with the expectation that

---

125 The Bolender memo can be read at www.nicap.org/Bolender_Memo.htm.
126 JANAP-146 can be read at www.cufon.org/cufon/janp146c.htm. AF Manual 55-11 can be read at www.cufon.org/cufon/AFM55-11A.htm.

Project Blue Book would somehow look into it. This enabled a level of engagement with the UFO topic by the American public in a way that would not otherwise have happened.

This also meant that Blue Book served as a wedge with which to pry open the UFO problem. Its very existence begged an obvious question: if the Air Force claimed UFOs were not real, why did it have an office devoted to investigating them? As long as that office existed, maintaining a serious cover-up was problematic. As a number of declassified military records have demonstrated, UFOs *were* a serious matter to the U.S. national security establishment. Blue Book's role, especially after the Robertson Panel of 1953, was to pacify the public. This policy worked for a few years, but by the late 1960s, the office had become a lightning rod. Blue Book therefore needed to go.

Ultimately, the closing of Project Blue Book undermined democratic rule. It removed UFOs from the realm of public-government interaction. After 1969, any citizen who saw a UFO had no government agency to which to report it.

In other words, people now had to cope with this most awesome and sometimes terrifying phenomenon without cooperation from the government that was supposed to be responsible to them. In a society that theoretically gave sovereignty to the people, this was, and is, a discrepancy and a problem. By the end of 1969, it appeared that secrecy had won.

And indeed, the bottom had fallen out for supporters of a UFO reality. NICAP was in financial ruins and effectively leaderless following the removal of Keyhoe from its leadership. This was accomplished by a group of NICAP board members with strong CIA connections.[127] In 1971, James McDonald died of a self-inflicted gunshot wound to the head, a terrible conclusion to a brilliant career.[128] It appeared that all the efforts of those people working to end UFO secrecy had resulted in abject failure.

---

[127] Zechel, Todd, "NI-CIA-AP OR NICAP?" *MUFON UFO Journal*, January-February, 1979.
[128] Druffel, Ann. *Firestorm: Dr. James E. McDonald's Fight for UFO Science* (Voyagers, 2003).

Chapter 4: UFO Secrecy and Those Who Fought It

Yet, if there is one thing that can always be counted on, it is that today is not yesterday, and tomorrow will not be like today. UFO research would regroup in the 1970s, 1980s, and beyond. New attempts would be made to understand the problem and to crack open the secrecy.

Chapter 5
Digging Deeper—The Breakaway Civilization

Imagine the year is 1947, and you are President Harry Truman. Key advisers have just informed you that the U.S. military has recovered technology from a crashed flying disc. You learn that this technology does not appear to have come from any known source, nor even human civilization itself.

Surely, that would be a lot to handle. What might President Truman do in such a situation? It is possible that his initial instinct would be to tell the world about this momentous discovery. After all, it would make him forever famous as the man who announced that an extraterrestrial race was visiting Earth. It would probably ensure his re-election, too, no small consideration for a career politician.

But then again, Truman would have had second thoughts. He would have been reminded, as if he needed to be reminded, of just how upsetting, traumatic, and even revolutionary such a revelation would be. Because this would pose a serious threat to the human structure of power, perhaps even the stability of human society itself.

That is because in 1947, the people of Earth were lying flat on their backs, exhausted from the titanic struggle that had been the Second World War. Europe and Asia were devastated, filled with rubble, refugees, and an overwhelming task of rebuilding. Even in America, which emerged from the war powerful and vibrant, the American people were also desperately seeking a return to normalcy—that is, to put all the stresses, uncertainties, and terror of the war behind them, and to resume their lives. An announcement of extraterrestrials could create genuine public panic. The question was, how severe would it be?

Such factors by themselves would be enough to give anyone pause before announcing the reality of extraterrestrial visitors. In addition,

Chapter 5: Digging Deeper—The Breakaway Civilization

however, there was the nascent Cold War. In 1947, Soviet military power rivaled that of the United States. Soviet troops appeared to threaten all of Western Europe at that very moment. Communism was the great enemy to the Western world—that is certainly how America's leadership saw the matter. It seemed no sure thing that Europe would remain a free enterprise zone. Under such conditions, giving the secret to the Soviets would mean that they, too, would possess ET technology.

There is no way the American national security establishment could assent to such a thing. That very establishment was unwilling to share its newly exploited atomic technology, an important political issue at the time. The United Nations had already suggested that atomic technology was too important for any one nation to possess, and that the U.N. itself ought to control it. The U.S. position was, *absolutely not*. Such a development would be the quickest way to give the nuclear secret to the Soviets.

If not atomic technology, clearly not something as exotic as alien technology. Cold War requirements demanded secrecy about UFOs.

Then there was the matter of oil. Even a child can understand, after some basic observation, that that these objects do not require oil to travel from Point A to Point B. Any object that can hover indefinitely, accelerate instantly, zigzag, and do all this silently, is surely using an exotic means of propulsion and surely a highly advanced energy system. If the President were to announce the reality of these flying saucers, it would not be long before scientists around the world began to study the nature of their propulsion and power systems. This could quickly lead to a replacement of petroleum as the world's leading source of power.

Today, in the 21st century, most people are fine with that idea, at least in theory. Petroleum may underlie our world, but it is also at the center of many of today's important problems. But in the 1940s and 1950s, the petroleum industry was the largest business in the world, and the very foundation of the global infrastructure. It had been growing for generations. It provided millions of jobs. It supported

America's constantly growing automotive industry, an industry that defined so much of American and world culture.

Recognition of UFOs would pose a grave threat to all of this, even to the global financial structure itself. After all, what if this new source of energy, whatever it was, could not be as easily monetized as petroleum? Could the global financial structure afford free energy? A perverse question, to be sure, but one that had to be important to those people at the top of the human power structure.

All of this would have been daunting enough to President Truman. And yet, there was more to consider. He had to wonder how this disclosure would affect society. Aside from the likelihood of some level of panic, he had to think about the changes that might take place once the public had access to the radical technologies being studied in secret. Was it really a good thing to let everyone have their own flying saucer, zipping around the world at whim? Most people, undoubtedly, would say *yes*. From the perspective of those individuals making national and global policy, however, and whose first goal is usually stability and control, the answer would be, *certainly not*.

More serious still would be the potential of weaponizing this new technology. The world had just been shown the awful power of the atomic bomb. With access to alien technology, might some scientist or nation create a weapon even more powerful, more terrifying? How could such technology be controlled? The only certain way would be to keep it completely secret.

Finally, there was the matter of assessing these unknown beings themselves. Truman and his people could not possibly have known the full scope of what they were dealing with. Did they have anything to worry about? Were these other beings a threat? As the previous chapter showed, the U.S. military had continual encounters with UFOs from the 1940s onward. These objects had the ability to penetrate U.S. airspace with total ease, evading interception time and again. What were they trying to do? This matter caused concern at the highest levels of the U.S. national security establishment. U.S. Air Force Captain Edward Ruppelt, who had managed Project Blue Book during the early 1950s, put the matter well: "how could we convince the public the aliens weren't hostile when we didn't know it ourselves?"[129]

All of these factors—public panic and destabilization, Cold War realities, petroleum and infrastructure issues, weaponization fears, and concerns over these *Others*—had to make their weight felt in the decision to keep UFOs as secret as possible. It was not simply a matter that strange technologies and beings were operating on the Earth. More to the point, their materials and even bodies had probably been acquired. It is this factor that made all the difference, and which, more than anything else, required the secrecy.

In other words, it would have been one thing for the military to hide the existence of the UFO reality, as long as the UFOs and ETs remained safely "out there." In that case, it would simply be a matter of preventing public panic and perhaps to avoid looking helpless. But, if it were acknowledged that this same military had recovered alien hardware, everything would change. It would mean that there would need to be a program to study, replicate, and exploit that technology. Such a program would have to have been funded secretly, away from Congressional oversight. After all, admitting such a secret to Congress would be the same thing as admitting it to the world.

UFO Crash: Roswell

Of course, before discussing the possession of alien technology, we should first make a case for it.

Upon review of the history, it appears that, not only at Roswell but in several other instances, military authorities came into possession of UFOs. In his book, *Majic Eyes Only*, Ryan Wood listed more than seventy cases of possible UFO crash retrievals. With enough information, many undoubtedly would turn out to be something else. But some of these cases are compelling.

Roswell, for instance, remains a strong case, even after all these years, despite being mired in confusion, argument, and obfuscation. On Saturday, July 5, 1947, a sheepherder named Mac Brazel, foreman

---

129 Keyhoe, Donald. *Aliens from Space*, p. 27.

of the Foster Ranch, a very remote place outside Roswell, New Mexico, found debris scattered over a large pasture. It seemed to him to consist mostly of metal, plastic I-beams, lightweight material, foil, and string-like material. All of it seemed to be unusually lightweight and strong. After showing some of it to his nearest neighbors, he contacted the Roswell Sheriff, George Wilcox. Wilcox contacted the Roswell Army Air Force Base, home of the 509th Bomb Group, under the command of Colonel William Blanchard.

On Monday, July 7, Blanchard sent three men to the Roswell debris field. These were intelligence officer Captain Jesse Marcel, and two counterintelligence officers: Sheridan Cavitt and William Rickett.

Many years later, Jesse Marcel told his story to researcher Stanton Friedman. He said that Brazel took him and Cavitt to the debris field, which was three quarters of a mile long and two hundred to three hundred feet wide. There was a gouge in the ground about five hundred feet long. Marcel noticed debris as thin as newsprint, but which was incredibly strong. Later, another soldier told Marcel that this debris could not be dented, not even by a sledgehammer. There was also foil which, when crumpled, would return to its shape without wrinkles. Marcel noticed I-beams with odd symbols on them; the beams would flex slightly, but not break. Marcel told Friedman, "it certainly wasn't anything built by us."

After spending the afternoon and evening gathering as much debris as possible, Marcel drove back to the base. Along the way, he stopped at his home. It was 2 a.m. when he awakened his family to show them what he had found. His son, eleven-year-old Jesse Marcel, Jr., remembered the incident for the rest of his life. Later that morning, Marcel and Cavitt arrived at Roswell Army Air Field, each with a carload of debris. Blanchard then notified the Eighth Air Force in Fort Worth, Texas, and ordered Marcel to take the debris there.

The *Roswell Daily Record* of Tuesday, July 8, 1947, then issued one of the most famous newspaper headlines in history: "RAAF Captures Flying Saucer On Ranch In Roswell Region." Lieutenant Walter Haut, the public information officer at the base, on orders from Blanchard,

Chapter 5: Digging Deeper—The Breakaway Civilization

wrote "the intelligence office of the 509 Bombardment Group at Roswell Army Air Field announced at noon today that the field has come into possession of a flying saucer."

Headline of the *Roswell Daily Record*, July 8, 1947.

Immediately, the town of Roswell was overwhelmed with media requests from around the world. Just as immediately, a decision was made from up high to kill the story. Thus, three hours after the announcement, Jesse Marcel was in Fort Worth, Texas, with the head of the Eighth Air Force, General Roger Ramey. There, Marcel was made to pose with scraps of a dilapidated weather balloon. Ramey announced it had all been a misunderstanding. No flying saucer, just a weather balloon. Sorry for the confusion, everyone.

At the same time, a memo from the FBI offered some description of the object and added some interesting details. The relevant passage reads:

THE DISC IS HEXAGONAL IN SHAPE AND WAS SUSPENDED FROM A BALLON [sic] BY CABLE, WHICH BALLON [sic] WAS APPROXIMATELY TWENTY FEET IN DIAMETER. FURTHER ADVISED THAT THE OBJECT FOUND RESEMBLES A HIGH ALTITUDE WEATHER BALLOON WITH A RADAR REFLECTOR, BUT THAT TELEPHONIC CONVERSATION BETWEEN THEIR OFFICE AND WRIGHT FIELD HAD NOT BORNE OUT THIS BELIEF. DISC AND BALLOON BEING TRANSPORTED TO WRIGHT FIELD BY SPECIAL PLANE FOR EXAMINATION.

It is not often realized that the description of the Roswell object follows the one given by Ramey himself, as well as a Major Curtin, to the Reuters wire service. It also appears that the technicians at Wright Field were skeptical of the claim that a balloon was what had crashed. The debris that was photographed in Ramey's office certainly appeared to be the badly torn up part of a balloon. How Ramey could describe it as hexagonal defies any logic or observational common sense. Of course, just how Marcel, Blanchard, and the rest of the people at the 509th could make such an egregious error and identify it as a flying disc is an even greater leap of logic, especially since no disc was ever photographed in Ramey's office. An important aspect to this memo is that it stated the debris was "being transported to Wright Field by special plane for examination." Somehow, it was considered important enough for serious analysis by the technicians there. Why would a downed balloon warrant such treatment? Ultimately, what seems glaringly obvious is that Ramey released a cover story about what had crashed, and some of this information got into the FBI memo.[130]

The Roswell news made a brief splash, and then submerged so deep as to be forgotten for more than thirty years. In 1978, purely by chance, Stanton Friedman met Marcel, beginning the resurrection of Roswell into the iconic case it has now become. Through the 1980s, 1990s, and indeed into the 21st century, researchers such as Friedman, William Moore, Donald Schmitt, Kevin Randle, Tom Carey, and others had interviewed hundreds of individuals with connections to the case.

Still, efforts to get to the bottom of the Roswell mystery have been thwarted again and again. Part of the problem appears to be the national security apparatus, which naturally has controlled access to key data. For instance, during the 1990s, New Mexico Congressman Steven Schiff began to look into the case, after hearing requests from his constituents. After stonewalling and rebuffs from the Pentagon, Schiff contacted the General Accounting Office (GAO), the official investigative arm of Congress. Unfortunately, the GAO similarly got

---

[130] A good analysis of this appears in roswellproof.homestead.com/Rameys_hexagon_story.html

nowhere. In fact, one Pentagon liaison reportedly told the GAO representative to "go shit in your hat." Ultimately, the GAO report concluded that the outgoing messages from Roswell Army Air Field for the period of time in question "were destroyed without proper authority." This is very unfortunate, since these messages would have shown how military officials in Roswell explained to their superiors what had happened. As Schiff put it, "these outgoing messages were permanent record, which should never have been destroyed. The GAO could not identify who destroyed the messages, or why."[131]

The investigation of Roswell is a perfect example of how the formal government apparatus, in this case Congress, was inadequate when dealing with the true center of power, the clandestine secret keepers of the National Security State. Meanwhile, the U.S. Air Force had taken the initiative to generate two reports on Roswell, stating first that all the confusion was caused by a downed, Top Secret, Mogul high-altitude balloon, and later by air drops of six-foot tall test dummies, which presumably were mistaken for tiny extraterrestrial bodies.[132] Nitpicking these Air Force explanations is easy and has become something of a hobby among some researchers. Nevertheless, the Air Force's official explanation of Roswell, despite the fact that so few people believe it, has been able to maintain its standing within official media and political circles.

There is much more to the Roswell story and subsequent debates. Much discussion has occurred over how many debris fields there actually were. More recently, the claim has been made that some researchers have found quality Kodachrome images of a dead alien, presumably from Roswell. As of this writing, no images have been released, but such discussion at least proves that Roswell continues to

---

131 *MUFON UFO Journal*, August 1995, p. 23.
[www.scribd.com/doc/131772404/MUFON-UFO-Journal-1995-8-August]
132 *Roswell Report: Fact verses Fiction in the New Mexico Desert*, Col. Richard Weaver and 1st Lt. James McAndrew, Headquarters United States Air Force, 1995. [www.airforcehistory.hq.af.mil/Publications/fulltext/roswell.pdf]. *The GAO Report on The Roswell Incident Records* [www.roswellfiles.com/Articles/TheGAOReport.htm]. *The Roswell Report: Case Closed*, James McAndrew, Headquarters United States Air Force, 1997 [www.dod.gov/pubs/foi/homeland.../RoswellReportCaseClosed.pdf].

be a fertile ground for investigation, and heated debate.[133]

UFO Crash: Aztec

It is not possible here, nor is there need, to include all of the UFO crash retrieval stories that exist. But, it is useful to describe a few of them, if only to point out that claims of such retrievals include much more than the Roswell story.

One such case, much-debated, took place in Aztec New Mexico, in March 1948. Aztec is located at the four corners area where New Mexico, Colorado, Utah, and Arizona meet. Like the Roswell crash site, it is quite remote, nearly surrounded by Indian reservations. Few people today realize that for years it was the Aztec case, not Roswell, which was the best known alleged UFO crash. It was first discussed in a 1950 book, *Behind the Flying Saucers*, by journalist Frank Scully. Scully had two primary sources for this story, a friend named Silas Newton, and an acquaintance and sometime business partner of Newton, a scientist Scully called "Dr. Gee."

According to the story, an alien saucer came down essentially intact, whereupon the U.S. military gained access to it via a punctured porthole. Inside were anywhere from 2 to 16 alien bodies: small, humanlike, dead, and charred. The UFO was dismantled and taken to Wright Field in Dayton, Ohio for study.

Within three years of the book's publication, a journalist named J.P. Cahn wrote a series of devastating exposés regarding the accuracy and truthfulness of Silas Newton and Dr. Gee, whom he identified as Leo GeBauer. The two were simply a pair of con men in the oil industry, wrote Cahn, who had hoaxed Scully. Newton had lied about his education and had defrauded business associates. Indeed, soon afterwards, both were convicted of discrediting a Colorado businessman.

However, Scully maintained that, while Dr. Gee was modeled primarily on GeBauer, he was actually a composite of multiple inside

---

133 Bragalia, Anthony. "Authentic Alien Images from Roswell Finally Found?" Friday, September 27, 2013 [ufocon.blogspot.com/2013/09/authentic-alien-images-from-roswell.html].

Chapter 5: Digging Deeper—The Breakaway Civilization

sources. And while GeBauer did not study at the University of Berlin (as Dr. Gee supposedly had), and did not manage 1,700 scientists doing experimental work in secret magnetic research related to the flying saucers, he was Chief of Laboratories of Air Research Company in Phoenix and Los Angeles, although in charge of maintenance equipment, not research.

What is interesting is that GeBauer was the subject of an FBI file totalling at least 398 pages. Even more interesting is that less than 200 of these pages have been declassified under the Freedom of Information Act. The rest remain classified, exempt, according to the FBI, "in the interest of national defense." One cannot help but wonder why this is so, after all these years.

But what makes Aztec intriguing is that several researchers have found elements of the story that continue to give pause. In 2002, investigative journalist Linda Moulton Howe interviewed members of the Pace family in Farmington, New Mexico, who recalled hearing news of a crashed UFO during the late 1940s. They said this took place either in March 1948, or March 1949. The family recalled reading a newspaper article which stated a UFO had crashed near Aztec, in an area known as Hart Canyon. However, that article has never been found.

Scott Ramsey did even more research and investigation into the Aztec crash.[134] Supported in this endeavor by this wife, Suzanne, the Ramseys made contact with relatives of two former New Mexico police officers from the area, who told their families that they saw a crashed disc in Hart Canyon. The year they gave was 1948, probably March.

An intriguing part of Ramsey's research related to a witness who claimed to have worked at Roswell Army Air Field, and said there was a concrete slab at the crash site used to support the crane that removed the craft. Ramsey searched for the slab, which initially was not visible. Then, however, with help from an assistant, he found it at the suspected site by probing the soil. The rebar in the concrete was dated to the 1940s, although further tests are needed to obtain a more precise

---

134 Ramsey, Scott and Suzanne. *The Aztec Incident*, Aztec.48 Productions, 2011.

date.[135]

Just as compelling as this, however, was the research by the Ramseys into Scully, Newton, GeBauer, and Cahn. Regarding the latter, they discovered an agenda against Scully that was nothing short of a vendetta. Cahn, it turned out, had been captivated by the Aztec story, fully accepting its authenticity. He had approached Scully with a view to collaborating on a book about it. Denied this, he never forgave Scully and set out to destroy him and his main sources. The Ramseys' research on Newton and GeBauer do not show them to be dishonest in the least, but rather smeared by Cahn's unethical journalism. After all these years, it appears that something exotic did go down near Aztec.

There are quite a few alleged retrievals of exotic, or even extraterrestrial, UFOs—far more than the average person suspects.[136] What follows are only a few of the better known cases, and which have received a reasonable investigation by private researchers. Naturally, no government has ever confirmed any of these cases. Still, they remain intriguing possibilities, and some of them, at least in my own opinion, appear to genuine.

UFO Crash: Kingman

One of these may have occurred near Kingman, Arizona, on May 21, 1953. During the early 1970s, a man spoke to two private researchers, identifying himself as an engineer with graduate degrees in physics and engineering, stated that twenty years earlier he had been part of a group of specialists who were taken in a bus (with blacked-out windows) to the crash site to study the craft. It was thirty feet in diameter and embedded in sand. Inside a nearby tent, under armed guard, was a humanoid figure, roughly four feet tall, and apparently dead.

Researcher Raymond Fowler began looking into the case and met

---

135 kevinrandle.blogspot.com/2012/05/aztec-incident-by-scott-and-suzanne.html
136 In addition to many sources on the web, two books that discuss this subject are Kevin Randall's *History of UFO Crashes* (Avon Books, 1995); and Ryan Wood's *Majic Eyes Only: Earth's Encounters with Extraterrestrial Technology* (Wood Enterprises, 2005).

with the witness. He concluded that something significant did appear to have happened, and wrote a long report, giving the witness the pseudonym "Fritz Werner." There were some discrepancies in Werner's account of the craft, compared with what he had told the two previous researchers, although these could conceivably be explained by memory lapses, or the fact that Werner claimed to Fowler that he had had a number of martinis before talking with the other researchers. Yet much seemed legitimate. Although Fowler was unable to find other witnesses to the event, he wrote that "the peripheral names, positions, tests, dates, and places mentioned within Mr. Werner's personal account all check out exceptionally well." Werner's diary entry for May 21, while not confirming a crash retrieval, does appear to show that he was on some sort of special mission at the time: ". . . Got picked up at Indian Springs AFB for a job I can't write or talk about."

Other researchers came across tidbits pointing to a UFO crash at Kingman in 1953. One of these was Charles Wilhelm, whose father had an acquaintance, a "Major Daly," who had been flown to a UFO crash in April 1953. Leonard Stringfield, one of the key researchers on the matter of UFO crash retrievals, described this in one of his reports and lectures on the subject. Daly was blindfolded and driven to a hot desert location where there was an undamaged metallic ship that was twenty-five to thirty feet in diameter. He spent two days there, determining that the craft was not made on Earth. There are other intriguing details to this account. Other than the exact date (which may have been misremembered), this account is consistent with that of Werner's.

Don Schmitt, author of several books on Roswell, once spoke with a woman named Judy Woolcott, whose husband had told her of "something strange" he had seen in 1953. Although she could not recall the month exactly, she was certain that the location was Kingman, Arizona. Her husband had been an officer, on duty at an air base control tower, when something strange was picked up on radar. The target lost altitude and went off the screen. He and several others went in jeeps to the location where the object was believed to have crashed. They found a domed disc, embedded in the sand, which seemed undamaged. Before they could get close, however, they were escorted from the area and told never to discuss it. Although Woolcott's husband saw no bodies, he told his wife that some of the military police said there were casualties and they were "not human."

Another interesting element to the Kingman story was provided by Bill Uhouse, a man who served ten years in the U.S. Marines as a fighter pilot, then four more years as a civilian with the Air Force at Wright-Patterson AFB, performing flight testing of experimental aircraft. For many years after that, he said, he worked for defense contractors as an engineer of antigravity propulsion systems. This included flight simulators for exotic aircraft as well as actual flying discs. Uhouse claimed that several times he met with an extraterrestrial being, who assisted the physicists and engineers with the engineering of the craft. This being, known as J-Rod, was said to have arrived on Earth in 1953 from the Kingman crash. According to the account, four entities survived altogether, although two were disabled and taken to an unspecified medical facility. The recovery crew that entered the craft at Kingman to inspect it came down with a mysterious illness. J-Rod was reportedly over 200 years old, a typical gray extraterrestrial biological entity (EBE), suffering from cell deterioration, and said still to be located at Papoose S-4, just south of Area 51. Researcher Bill Hamilton said that he had read a document purporting to be a technical paper on tissue samples taken from an EBE known as AQ-J-ROD. The AQ is believed to stand for Project Aquarius.[137]

UFO Crash: Brazil

Another interesting crash, of sorts, took place in Brazil on September 10, 1957, although the date is approximate. According to an anonymous letter sent to a Brazilian journalist, a crash of a UFO occurred near Sao Paulo, in a town known as Ubatuba, where several

---

137 Stringfield, Leonard, *Situation Red: The UFO Siege*, Doubleday, 1977, p. 179-186; Stringfield, Leonard, *Retrievals of the Third Kind*, MUFON, 1978; Hamilton, William, *Cosmic Top Secret: America's Secret UFO Program*, Inner Light, 2002, p. 106-111; Wood, Ryan, *Majic Eyes Only*, p. 111-114.

Chapter 5: Digging Deeper—The Breakaway Civilization

people saw a disc dive down and explode, showering the area with flaming fragments. The writer mailed some small samples, which soon made their way to a Brazilian UFO researcher named Dr. Olavo Fontes. Fontes had the samples brought to a laboratory, which showed the fragments to be apparently of nearly pure magnesium. Although this could have been produced by earthly technology, creating it would not have been an easy thing to do, and only a very few companies in the world were capable of manufacturing it. There is no easy explanation as to why such nearly pure magnesium was found there.[138]

Even if this was the crash of non-human technology, there was never an indication that bodies were recovered, and indeed the story is so threadbare that nothing remains of it, especially following the loss of the samples from the files of the American organization that housed them, the Aerial Phenomena Research Organization (APRO). That organization dissolved in the 1980s after the deaths of its two founders, and its files were sequestered by a private group that has never allowed public viewing of them ever since.[139]

UFO Crash: Las Vegas

Yet another fascinating UFO crash case took place on April 18, 1962, not far from Las Vegas, Nevada. One might think that the arrival of aliens in Las Vegas would help to explain some of the city's current character, but of course it was already a wild town by then. Perhaps it was already an ET tourist attraction.

In fact, an unidentified, and very fast, object was tracked by the military moving across the United States, from Oneida, New York all the way west to the outskirts of Las Vegas. The entire sighting lasted 32 minutes, giving the object an average speed of 4,500 mph. If nothing else, this was no meteor, which would have travelled at a much faster speed, and would not inspire the scrambling of jets.

---

138 Lorenzen, Coral E., *The Great Flying Saucer Hoax*, William Frederick Press, 1962; Gillmor, Daniel, *Scientific Study of Unidentified Flying Objects*, Bantam Books, 1968, p. 138-143; Wood, Ryan, *Majic Eyes Only*, p. 121-122.
139 A description the tragedy of the APRO files can be read in Dolan, Richard M., *UFOs and the National Security State: The Cover-up Exposed, 1973-1991*, Keyhole Publishing Co., 2009, p. 440-441.

Yes, whatever this object was, it triggered the scrambling of interceptor jets from Luke Air Force Base in Phoenix and Nellis Air Force Base in Las Vegas. In fact, it appears to have landed briefly at the town of Eureka Utah, where several witnesses saw it as a glowing orange oval that gave off a low whirring sound. As it landed, it disrupted the electrical service from a nearby power station. Then it rose, maneuvered, and headed toward Nevada. People in Reno saw it, where it turned south and was seen just east of Las Vegas. At that point, it vanished from the radar screens. Many people described it as looking like a tremendous flaming sword. Thousands of witnesses saw this object. It then exploded near Mesquite, Nevada, at which time it was being pursued by armed jet interceptors from Nellis Air Force Base.

Project Blue Book investigated the event, doing a thoroughly unsatisfactory and probably dishonest job. It separated the sighting into two distinct events, making them appear unrelated to each other. Years later, investigator Kevin Randle interviewed several witnesses and reviewed the Blue Book files, where he discovered the major discrepancies. He also communicated with an anonymous man who claimed to have been an officer at Nellis Air Force Base at the time of the crash. This person claimed that he and thirty others were driven into the desert early the next morning to retrieve the crash debris. They were loaded into a bus with blacked-out windows, but one window was not entirely covered, and the man claimed to have seen a damaged saucer-shaped craft.[140]

UFO Crash: Kecksburg

Next to Roswell, this incident may be the best-known possible crash and retrieval of a UFO. It took place in 1965, near Kecksburg, Pennsylvania. Also like Roswell, it has been the subject of much debate among researchers. The Blue Book files officially listed it as a meteorite, but whatever it was, it was certainly not a meteorite.

On the evening of December 9, 1965, a brightly glowing object

---

140 Randle, Kevin. *A History of UFO Crashes*, p. 79-94.

streaked eastward across Canada, Michigan, and Ohio before striking ground at 4:47 p.m., near the small town of Kecksburg. Thousands of people saw the object streaking across the sky, which left a vapor trail that was visible for more than twenty minutes. Many people thought it was an aircraft on fire. At around 6:30 p.m., a woman called the local radio station, stating that an object or fireball had crashed into the woods near her home. She and her two sons saw smoke rising from the trees, and a bright object off to one side. State police and firefighters soon arrived.

One person who arrived on the scene was John Murphy, the news director of a local radio station, WHJB. Murphy asked questions of everyone he saw. Then he drove to the state police barracks in Greensburg, Pennsylvania. There, he saw not only members of the state police, but also U.S. Army personnel, and two men in U.S. Air Force uniforms, one of them a lieutenant. Murphy asked the police officers what had happened, and was told that there was nothing whatsoever going on in the woods. Skeptical of that explanation, to put it mildly, Murphy returned to the crash site. He found an investigator for the State of Pennsylvania and the two decided to enter the woods. At that point, he learned he was not allowed in, and the entire area was cordoned off. Still, Murphy had taken pictures and recorded audio while on the scene, and decided he would prepare a radio documentary about the event.

Other citizens had more success in entering the woods than did Murphy, several of whom were firefighters. One of them, Jim Romansky, was interviewed years later by researcher Stan Gordon. Romansky had reached a streambed where the object apparently had first touched down. A deep furrow had been cut into the bed, and the object itself was nearby. It was acorn-shaped, between nine and twelve feet in diameter. It had no wings, no visible motors, no fuselage. Around the bottom was a gold band with writing on it. To Romansky, it looked like "ancient Egyptian hieroglyphics." More precisely, with characters of broken and straight lines, dots, rectangles, and circles. The body was dented, but without visible rivets, seams, or welds.

Gordon found another witness, Bill Bulebush, who had gotten nearly as close as Romansky. He described the object in a near-identical manner. Bulebush could see bright blue sparks emanating from it, but heard no sound. Another man, Bill Weaver, was farther away from the object, but claimed to see it glowing. He saw four men dressed in what he called "moon suits," carrying a large white box on a stretcher into the woods. Soon after, Weaver was ordered out of the area by men in dark suits, something Romansky had also claimed.

The media covered the Kecksburg story almost exclusively as a fireball. A number of astronomers were brought in to make statements to this effect, essentially ending public interest in the story. But even the most conservative calculations of the object's speed make it much much slower than any meteorite ever recorded. The Blue Book files also state that a three-man team had been dispatched to investigate and pick up an object that started a fire in the woods. This was certainly part of Project Moon Dust, a classified program designed to retrieve unidentified flying objects for military custody.

One researcher, James Oberg, a NASA employee and former Air Force intelligence officer, suggested in an article for *Omni* magazine that the crashed object was a Soviet Kosmos 96 satellite, which he believed would have caused the activation of Project Moon Dust. But this is incorrect. The Kosmos 96 satellite was later confirmed to have crashed thirteen hours earlier in Canada.

All that is known within reason is that, within two hours of the crash, the military sealed off the site, but not before witnesses got a good look at the object, and not before others claimed to see a flatbed truck, with a tarp covering a large object, leave the area at high speed.

John Murphy's story in this adventure is of special interest. According to his wife, Murphy was convinced the object was not a meteorite. Following the crash, he became deeply interested in the case and wrote a news story about it, called *Object in the Woods*. Just before the show was supposed to air, however, he was visited at the station by two men in black suits, identifying themselves as government officials. They met with him alone for thirty minutes, an event recalled by another WHJB employee, Linda Foschia, who added that the men confiscated some of Murphy's audio tapes, and probably his photographs also, since these were never seen again. Soon after, Murphy aired a censored version of his documentary, which essentially told nothing of interest. He then seems to have gone into a depression, pulling away from the case and refusing to discuss it. In February 1969, Murphy was struck and killed by an unidentified car in an apparent hit-and-run while on vacation in Ventura, California.

There were still more witnesses to the Kecksburg crash who came forward years later. One of these claimed to have worked at Wright-Patterson Air Force Base at the time, and said that a strange object was shipped there on December 16, 1965. Before he was escorted away, he saw the object, describing it in nearly identical terms as had the other witnesses.

It certainly appears that something highly unusual came down at Kecksburg, which could well have been a genuine crashed UFO.[141]

UFO Crash: Bolivia

Another UFO crash retrieval took place in the mountains of Bolivia on May 6, 1978. According to a declassified U.S. State Department memorandum, many people saw an object streak across the sky and slam into a mountain near El Taire on the Bermejo River, very close to the Argentine border. On May 14, the Bolivian Air Force discovered the crash site, apparently working with the local police, with the police chief reporting "our men have discovered the object and inspected it." It was "a dull metallic cylinder twelve feet long with a few dents. No one knows what is inside it."

In one of the declassified memos, the U.S. Ambassador to Bolivia wrote:

> ... the Bolivian Air Force plans to investigate to determine what the object might be and from where it came.... The general region has had more than its share of reports of UFOs this past week. Request a reply ASAP.

---

141 Randle, Kevin, *A History of UFO Crashes*, p. 95-120. Wood, Ryan, *Majic Eyes Only*, p. 152-160.

One might wonder why a U.S. Ambassador would know about the intensity of a UFO wave in Bolivia. It is known that Project Moon Dust was activated for this event. Furthermore, two U.S. intelligence officers arrived on the scene and seem to have taken over the investigation. To this day, the identity of what came down in Bolivia has not been made public.[142]

```
@ 151939Z MAY 79
FM SECSTATE WASHDC
TO AMEMBASSY LA PAZ IMMEDIATE
S E C R E T STATE 126725
E.O. 11552: GDS
TAGS: TSPA, BL
SUBJECT: REPORT OF FALLEN SPACE OBJECT
REF: LA PAZ 3824
. PRELIMINARY INFORMATION PROVIDED IN REFERENCED CABLE
AND FBIS CABLES PANAMA 142357Z AND PARAGUAY 161931Z HAS
BEEN CHECKED WITH APPROPRIATE GOVERNMENT AGENCIES. NO
DIRECT CORRELATION WITH KNOWN SPACE OBJECTS THAT MAY HAVE
REENTERED THE EARTH'S ATMOSPHERE NEAR MAY 6 9AM FE MADE.
HOWEVER WE ARE CONTINUING TO EXAMINE ANY POSSIBILITIES.
YOUR ATTENTION IS INVITED TO STATE AIRGRAM A-6343.
SECRET
SECRET
AGY 22         STATE  126725
JULY 26, 1973 WHICH PROVIDES BACKGROUND INFORMATION AND
GUIDANCE FOR DEALING WITH SPACE OBJECTS THAT HAVE BEEN
FOUND. IN PARTICULAR ANY INFORMATION PERTAINING TO THE
PRE-IMPACT OBSERVATIONS, DIRECTION OF TRAJECTORY, NUMBER
OF OBJECTS OBSERVED, TIME OF IMPACT AND A DETAILED
DESCRIPTION INCLUDING ANY MARKINGS WOULD BE HELPFUL.  VANCE
SECRET
```

A declassified Secret memo to U.S. Secretary of State Cyrus Vance about the crash of an unknown object in Bolivia.

Other Crashes

There are a few possible UFO crashes from more recent years. All are spotty, unconfirmed, and mostly uncorroborated. One, rather sketchy indeed, is said to have occurred on April 15, 1992, near Buffalo New York. An investigator known to the author looked into this case, in which a large disc-shaped craft was seen coming out of Lake Ontario. It then flew erratically south towards the city of Lockport, then crashed. Not much more is known about it. A better-known case took place in the Brazilian town of Varginha. In addition to involving a crash retrieval, it included the alleged sighting of a live alien being by three young girls, involvement by Brazilian medical personnel, and of course U.S. military involvement. The case fascinates

---

142 Wood, Ryan, *Majic Eyes Only*, p. 193-197. Stringfield, Leonard, *The UFO Crash/Retrieval Syndrome, Status Report II: New Sources, New Data*, MUFON.

because it has generated a number of compelling witnesses that attest to its reality. On the other hand, very little has been verified, and naturally the Brazilian government denies that anything of the sort occurred.

Finally, a lesser known case, but one which seems suggestive, is said to have taken place in March, 1997, in Peru. The sole witness is U.S. Marine Corps Lance Corporal John Weygandt, who gave a detailed description of a crashed object and recovery operations, all run by the U.S. military, for the Disclosure Project, headed by Dr. Steven Greer. Weygandt's opinion was that this UFO had been shot down by a Hawk missile.

It is worth mentioning that not only did the U.S. military recover apparent crashed UFOs, but so did the Soviet military. One case occurred near the far eastern city of Dalnegorsk, in January 1986. Another possible case took place in August 1987, near the town of Vyborg, close to Leningrad, and yet another possible UFO crash occurred in Tyumen, east of the Ural Mountains, in 1989. In this last instance, alien bodies were said to have been recovered. It is very difficult to confirm these cases, but the Dalnegorsk case at least was investigated extensively, and has been argued with some force to have been a legitimate UFO crash retrieval. It is sometimes referred to as the Soviet Roswell.

If even one of these, or any other instances, were genuine retrievals of UFOs, we are talking about something of great importance. Clearly, such retrievals would require programs to study the technology and (presumably) biology. It is obvious that the acquisition of alien technology would demand a program to study it. Indeed, there have been many leaks from the classified world exactly to that effect.

Stringfield's Leaks

Such leaks go back to the 1950s and 1960s, but not until the late 1970s did large numbers of them begin to appear. The researcher Leonard Stringfield published a book in 1977, titled *Situation Red: The UFO Siege*. It was the first serious book in years to discuss crash retrievals as a legitimate phenomenon. Stringfield's mention of such stories was brief, but it was enough to capture the attention of quite a few people who had stories of their own. These included stories not only of UFO crash retrievals, but sometimes of individuals who had seen dead alien bodies.

The stories Stringfield collected were astounding. He was able to investigate a number of these, unable to investigate others, and at all times used his best judgment and common sense in evaluating them. Overall, they tell a consistent story.

Several intriguing stories had reached Stringfield prior to publishing *Situation Red*. One came through Sherman Larsen, a UFO researcher with a background in the U.S. Army's Counter Intelligence Corps (CIC). Larsen had known a Presbyterian minister who, as a boy, had been with his father (also a minister) on a visit to the Museum of Science and Industry in Chicago. After straying into a "labyrinth of corridors" and becoming lost, they entered a room in which they encountered a large, glass-covered case. "Peering inside, they were shocked to see a number of small, preserved humanoid bodies. They were immediately grabbed by security and taken to another room. The boy's father was forced to sign papers before they were allowed to leave the museum. By chance, Larsen also learned that the Security Intelligence Corps office in Chicago was in that very building. Stringfield wrote, "Perhaps forever unanswered is the question: Was there a secret link between the SIC and the preserved little creatures?"

Other stories came to him through Charles Wilhelm. As an adolescent in 1959, Wilhelm listened to a deathbed "confession" from a neighbor whose lawn he used to cut. The woman was dying of cancer, and told him that she once held a Top Security Clearance at Wright-Patterson Air Force Base and had seen two saucer-shaped craft in a secret hanger. One craft was intact, the other damaged. She also knew of two small "creatures" preserved inside another secret building, and had personally handled the paperwork on their autopsy report. "Uncle Sam can't do anything to me after I'm in the grave," she told him. Wilhelm related another story to Stringfield of something he was told in 1966 by a friend whose father had worked with Project Blue

Book at Wright-Patterson. It was nearly identical to what his dying neighbor had told him. On the father's deathbed, he told his son that he had seen two disc-shaped craft, one intact and one damaged, along with four preserved small alien bodies "packed in chemicals.[143]"

Leonard Stringfield, one of the most important American UFO researchers of the 1970s and 1980s.

But such stories were a mere smattering compared with what Stringfield collected after publishing *Situation Red*. They came in, dozens and scores of them. One source said that the U.S. military was designing a radar system to detect UFOs, and that Navy nuclear submarines were equipped with instruments to detect submerged UFOs. Another related a retrieval of a UFO somewhere in the American southwest in 1957, in which four humanoid bodies were recovered with great difficulty. In another, a witness claimed to see nine alien bodies at Wright-Patterson Air Force Base in 1966. They were four feet tall. He added that the craft was also at the base, and at certain military bases, mobile units were ready at all times to recover downed UFOs. Yet another of Stringfield's witnesses—a doctor whom he interviewed several times—claimed to have autopsied an alien body himself. This doctor gave Stringfield a great deal of information while they were in communication.

---

143 Stringfield, Leonard. *Situation Red*, p. 177-178.

There were more witnesses. One, a contractor at Wright-Patterson during the 1960s, claimed to have seen seven alien bodies under conditions of extreme security. Yet another, a former Air Force intelligence officer, said that in 1948 he saw a top-secret manuscript about a UFO crash in New Mexico in which craft and bodies were recovered. Yet another witness, a radar specialist at Fort Monmouth, New Jersey, told Stringfield that in 1953 he had been shown a film of a crashed UFO in the desert, which included the interior of the craft, and dead alien beings inside a tent. This individual had been given no explanation or debriefing regarding what he had been shown.

Stringfield held onto the stories quietly for a while, but eventually published them for the UFO research community.[144]

Going Deeper Still: The Sarbacher-Walker Saga

During the 1970s and 1980s, Stringfield was not the only researcher uncovering a fascinating saga supporting the existence of a UFO retrieval program. The Canadian UFO researcher, Arthur Bray, gained access to the papers of the deceased Canadian government scientist, Wilbert Smith. Smith had had a longstanding interest in UFOs dating back to the 1950s. It had already been known from a released Canadian government document that in 1950, during a trip to Washington D.C., Smith had discussed the matter of flying saucers with a senior American defense scientist. It was known that this scientist confirmed the reality of UFOs to Smith, and stated that the matter of UFOs was "the most highly classified subject in the United States government, rating higher even than the H-bomb."

What was not known, however, was the identity of this scientist. Bray discovered this because he located Smith's original handwritten notes describing the interview. The scientist was Dr. Robert Sarbacher, a brilliant physicist who was a prominent consultant to the U.S. defense community. This was a stroke of very good fortune, because Sarbacher was still alive in the early 1980s, when Smith discovered his identity. Two researchers, Stanton Friedman and William Steinman,

---

144 Stringfield, Leonard, *The UFO Crash/Retrieval Syndrome, Status Report II: New Sources, New Data*, MUFON.

Chapter 5: Digging Deeper—The Breakaway Civilization

both interviewed Sarbacher, and Steinman hit paydirt, receiving a two-page, single-spaced, typewritten letter from Sarbacher. Not only did the letter confirm all the essentials of what Smith had written about long before, but it went much further. Sarbacher told Steinman that, yes, there have been crash retrievals of UFOs, and that there was a program in place to do this. He even named famous names, such as Dr. Robert Oppenheimer, Dr. Vannevar Bush, and Dr. John von Neumann. He wrote:

> ... about the only thing I remember at this time is that certain materials reported to have come from flying saucer crashes were extremely light and very tough. I am sure our laboratories analyzed them very carefully. There were reports that instruments or people operating these machines were also very light weight.... I remember in talking with some of the people at the office that I got the impression these aliens were constructed like certain insects.

Sarbacher's letter was written in 1983, and he died shortly thereafter. Before he died, he gave one more clue to help unravel the mystery. During a telephone conversation with Steinman, Sarbacher said that although he had not attended the UFO meetings at Wright-Patterson Air Force Base, he knew of another scientist who had. This was Dr. Eric A. Walker. Sarbacher was certain about it.

Steinman and several other researchers, including Grant Cameron and T. Scott Crain, interviewed Walker a number of times through the 1980s. Walker had been President of Penn State University, but more important was his work as a member of the elite think tank, the Institute for Defense Analyses (IDA), which he chaired for many years. Cameron and Crain wrote extensively on Walker and the IDA, describing the organization as "the think tank to the highest echelons of the Pentagon " and "the principal advisory organization serving the office of the Secretary of Defense as a whole."

In a conversation with Steinman, Walker said, "yes, I attended meetings concerning that subject matter." When asked about the group known as MJ-12, argued to be the secret group in charge of managing everything related to UFOs, Walker said that he did know about it and then told Steinman that he was "delving into an area that you can do absolutely nothing about." Leave it alone, he told Steinman. In subsequent communications, however, Walker became less and less forthcoming. He apparently decided that perhaps he should not have been talking about this topic, after all.[145]

Bodies, Technology, and Area 51

There is no shortage of stories from impressive people attesting to the reality of UFO technology or extraterrestrial bodies held in secret at Wright-Patterson Air Force Base, or near Area 51, or elsewhere. One such person was Senator Barry Goldwater, who not only was a General in the U.S. Air Force Reserve, but ran for President on the Republican Party ticket in 1964. Goldwater was as military-friendly a politician as one could find in Washington, and that is no small matter. He was even one of the first civilians to take a ride in the legendary aircraft, the SR-71 Blackbird. One of his closest friends was General Curtis LeMay, Chief of Staff of the United States Air Force. Several times, Goldwater discussed how LeMay had rebuffed his attempt to gain access to the area in Wright-Patterson where alien bodies and technology were believed to be held, sometimes referred to as the Blue Room. According to Goldwater, this was the only time in their friendship that LeMay had gotten angry with him. He told the Senator never to mention the topic again. In a letter to a constituent, Goldwater wrote "this thing has gotten so highly classified... it is just impossible to get anything on it."[146]

LeMay may have gotten testy with his friend Barry Goldwater, but he did let his guard down at least one time. I met a gentleman who told me of his encounter in 1987 with the retired Air Force legend. After meeting with this witness and learning his key personal details, I will only add that there is no doubt in my mind that his account is truthful.

The witness ("Jim") was an active Ham radio operator living in

---

145 An excellent resource on this topic is Cameron, Grant and Crain, T. Scott, *UFOs, Area 51, and Government Informants*, Richard Dolan Press, 2013.
146 Barry Goldwater letters to constituents and researchers, dated March 28, 1975, October 19, 1981, and June 20, 1983.

Orange County, California. During early October 1987, he struck up an engaging radio conversation with an elderly gentleman about various aircraft, when he overheard the operator refer to his companion as "General." Jim did not know the identity of his new friend until he called the FCC office in Long Beach to look up the address of "W6EZV." The result: Curtis E. LeMay, in Newport Beach.

A week later, Jim found LeMay on the air talking with "K0dwc" (who turned out to be three-star General Francis H. "Butch" Griswold). After that conversation ended, Jim contacted LeMay again for another pleasant conversation about aircraft and the band leader Tex Beneke, whom Jim had previously encountered on the Ham airwaves, and of whom LeMay was a fan.

Jim decided to try meeting with LeMay. He drove to Newport Beach and found his home. At 11:00 a.m., he rang the security door button as a camera swivelled to face him. Helen LeMay, wife of the General, answered. When she learned this was "Curt's" friend, her voice brightened and she let him through. Inside the LeMay house was a four-foot high bust of the general—and then the man himself.

For a short while, the two talked cordially about aircraft, and then Tex Beneke. Then, Jim asked a different sort of question. "General," he said, "was the 1947 crash at Roswell related to an alien craft?" LeMay looked at him silently. Without saying a word, he nodded his head up and down. He was obviously saying "yes" and just as obviously did not want to say it out loud. Perhaps he was being monitored, Jim wondered.

Meanwhile, in the next room, Helen had answered the telephone. Jim heard her speaking with someone, and then saying, "Butch, you would not believe what Curt is talking about right now!" A moment later she entered the room. Butch Griswold was on the phone, she said to her husband, and he wants to talk with you.

Jim took the opportunity to say goodbye to the four-star general and drove home, his head swimming. Later that afternoon while on his Ham radio, he saw the address "K0dwc" make a statement: "Well, we figured out who the mystery guest was." General Butch Griswold was clearly none-too-pleased about his friend's indiscretion.

That was the end of Jim's communication with Curtis LeMay. The general died three years later. Perhaps some people might not believe that Jim's encounter with Curtis LeMay really happened. To those people I will only say that having met with Jim and reviewed his Ham radio information—including Curtis LeMay's Ham radio information, which was legally available—and going over the encounter repeatedly in detail, I am entirely convinced this event took place as told. LeMay, nearing the end of his life, for reasons we will never know, decided to make an important admission to a new acquaintance. Stranger things have happened.

Through the 1980s and 1990s, other leaks continued to emerge. One important source during this period was aerospace journalist, James Goodall, who wrote for such publications as *Jane's Defense Weekly*, *Aviation Week and Space Technology*, and *Interavia*. Goodall interviewed quite a few members of the clandestine world, especially from within Groom Lake, Nevada, including Area 51. As a result of his interviews, Goodall concluded that there were at least eight "black" programs flying out of Groom Lake, not counting the ones that were already known, such as the B-2 stealth bomber. One of those programs, he determined, was a silent flying triangle. Many of these used radical and highly unconventional technologies.

Goodall also had several contacts telling him that the technology at Groom Lake was essentially out of this world. When asking one Groom Lake insider if he believed in UFOs, his contact replied, "absolutely, positively they exist." When Goodall asked if he would expand on that statement, the man said he would not, although he later said, "we have things in the Nevada desert that would make George Lucas envious," a clear reference to *Star Wars* technology and beyond. Another source told Goodall, "we have things out there that are literally out of this world. . . . better than *Star Trek* or anything you can see in the movies." He, too, would not expand on this statement.[147]

---

147 James Goodall interview, "Jim Goodall of classified programs at Groom Lake" YouTube video [www.youtube.com/watch?v=vM0PvvIHAnM].

Some of these accounts make the story of Bob Lazar seem almost pedestrian by comparison. And yet, it was Lazar's story, which came out at the end of 1989, that once and for all blew open the secrecy and anonymity of Area 51. More accurately, Lazar discussed an area just south of it, which he said is known as S-4. He claimed to have seen discs at S-4 several times in 1988 and 1989. All in all, he said there were nine extraterrestrial vehicles there. A great deal has been said about Lazar, both pro and con, but it is worth consideration that George Knapp, a journalist with KLAS-TV in Las Vegas, investigated Lazar extensively, and was able to confirm key elements to the story. He also interviewed more than two dozen Area 51 and Groom Lake insiders who corroborated many of the kinds of things Lazar was discussing. None, however, were willing to go public.[148]

If Lazar's basic account is true, the U.S. black budget world has been in possession of extraterrestrial technology and attempting to duplicate it since well before the 1980s. This rather confuses the matter of what a witness sees, when they look up and see what looks like a UFO. Is it one of *ours*, or *theirs*?

Despite the frequency of leaks coming from people like Bob Lazar and so many others from within the classified world, they still lack the power of a confirmed government statement. But how does one deal with leak after leak, claim after claim, coming out of that world, saying essentially the same thing? What does one make of the statements given by Ben Rich, for instance, the man who for many years headed Lockheed's legendary Skunk Works division. Ben Rich has been called the Father of Stealth, having overseen the development of the stealth fighter, the F-117A *Nighthawk*. Before Rich died in January 1995, he made several startlingly open statements about the reality of UFOs and extraterrestrials.

One was in a 1986 letter to friend and colleague John Andrews, one of Lockheed's great engineers. Andrews had written to Rich, stating his own belief in "lots" of UFOs, both man-made ("Category A") and extraterrestrial ("Category B"). Andrews asked Rich if his own belief

---

148 George Knapp, personal discussion with the author, July 2007.

covered extraterrestrial as well as man-made UFOs.

Rich's reply was succinct, yet a tad enigmatic. "Yes," he wrote back to Andrews, "I'm a believer in both categories. I feel everything is possible. Many of our man-made UFOs are <u>U</u>n-<u>F</u>unded <u>O</u>pportunities" (and here he underlined the U, F, and O of that phrase).

It is important to recognize Rich's stated belief that extraterrestrials were here on Earth. True, he stated this as *belief* rather than *knowledge* to Andrews, but one must remember that Ben Rich was the CEO of a large organization. Such people are not prone to making blatant statements about anything, certainly not something as sensitive as UFOs. Rich was in an excellent position to form his opinion. During the course of his career, he had access to individuals of the highest intellectual caliber, who in turn were exposed to some of the most sensitive secrets in the nation. He himself was one such person, having managed the stealth fighter program. Ben Rich was in as good a position as anyone to have genuine information on the matter of UFOs.

The most provocative part of his reply to Andrews was his remark about <u>U</u>n-<u>F</u>unded <u>O</u>pportunities. What might that mean? There seem to be two possibilities. One is that the program to build UFOs was so secret, so "black," that funding would be so deeply hidden as to be "nonexistent"—hence the project would be unfunded, so to speak. The other possibility is that man-made UFOs were derived from the active study of extraterrestrial UFOs, presumably in the form of crash retrievals or other *freebies*. Hence, unfunded.

Ben Rich had more than this to say on the matter of UFOs. On March 23, 1993, he spoke at the UCLA School of Engineering, presenting a generally standard history of Skunk Works. Then, however, he ended his presentation with a remarkable statement: "we now have the technology to take ET home."

This happens to have been a tagline that Rich used for many of his lectures over the years, and seems to have been more coy and humorous than provocative in intent. Since 1983, in various lectures, he had referred to Skunk Works getting a contract to "take ET home" (a

Chapter 5: Digging Deeper—The Breakaway Civilization

Ben Rich, a man with an interest in UFOs, and evidently some knowledge.

reference to Steven Spielberg's movie, *ET: The Extraterrestrial*, which came out in 1983).

Nevertheless, the statement startled a few in attendance, and after most attendees filed out, some stayed behind, in the hopes that Ben Rich would clarify or expand on what he meant. Two of these people were Jan Harzan, a senior executive with IBM, and also Director of the Orange County Mutual UFO Network (MUFON), and Tom Keller, an aerospace engineer who has worked as a computer systems analyst for NASA's Jet Propulsion Laboratory.

According to both of them, Rich was surrounded by a small group of people and made a few other statements.

"We now know how to travel to the stars."

"There is an error in the equations, and we have figured it out, and now know how to travel to the stars and it won't take a lifetime to do it."

"It is time to end all the secrecy on this, as it no longer poses a national security threat, and make the technology available for use in the private sector."

And, finally, said Harzan, a statement which he considered to be a very close paraphrase: "there are many in the intelligence community who would like to see this stay in the black and not see the light of day."[149]

Rich did not explicitly state that extraterrestrials were among us. Nor did he even state explicitly that UFOs were real. On the other hand, he did make a very clear statement that the technology within the classified world was vastly beyond anything imaginable in the public realm. After all, he essentially said that the classified world had the capability for interstellar travel.

James Goodall knew Ben Rich very well, and also had something to add about the aerospace legend. In a video interview, Goodall said that he spoke to Rich about ten days before he died, which would have been shortly after Christmas of 1994. According to Goodall:

> About ten days before he died, I was speaking to Ben on the telephone at the USC Medical Center in Los Angeles. And he said, Jim, we have things out in the desert that are fifty years beyond what you can comprehend. They have about forty five hundred people at the Lockheed Skunk Works. What have they been doing for the last eighteen or twenty years? They're building something.[150]

As if these stories were not enough, there is a final, very intriguing story about Ben Rich. This came from Bill McDonald, a forensic illustrator for the aerospace industry, and a good friend of John Andrews. After Andrews died in 1999, McDonald wrote in a private email, since republished many times, that Andrews had told him of claims made by Ben Rich during private communications.

First, Rich told Andrews that there were two types of UFOs: "the ones we build, and the ones they build." According to this account, Rich said that the U.S. government actively managed the UFO program until a 1969 purge by President Richard Nixon. After this, administration over the program was handled by an international Board of Directors in the private sector. Rich also reportedly described

---

149 Keller, Tom, "Extraterrestrial UFO Are Real : Ben Rich Lockheed Skunk Works Director Admitted In His Deathbed Confession," *MUFON UFO Journal*, May 2010. See also www.abovetopsecret.com/forum/thread965970/pg1 and www.garuda.co/2013/01/31/extraterrestrial-ufo-are-real-ben-rich-lockheed-skunk-works-director-admitted-in-his-deathbed-confession/.
150 Interview from documentary: *Stranger Than Fiction: The Real Flying Saucers*, Produced by David Monaghan. (Top Notch & Off the Fence, 2004), www.dmptv.co.uk/pro/saucers/index.htm.

to Andrews the attitude taken by his predecessor at the head of Skunk Works, Kelly Johnson. According to Rich, Johnson's attitude toward the extraterrestrials was negative. In private conversation with Rich, Johnson implied that factions from "out there" were more of a threat than they were a blessing, and that the cost of having them around was "unimaginable" and "unbelievable."[151]

McDonald's letter on the subject continued.

> It was Ben Rich's opinion that the public should not be told. He believed they could not handle the truth—ever. Only in the last months of his decline did he begin to feel that the 'international corporate Board of Directors' dealing with the 'Subject' could represent a bigger problem to citizens' personal freedoms under the United States Constitution than the presence of off world visitors themselves.[152]

Ben Rich appeared to be conflicted about what he knew. He may not have believed most people could handle the truth about UFOs and extraterrestrials, but he also appears to have felt the need to confide to a few people on a limited basis toward the end of his life.

There are other stories, fascinating but so far unprovable. One is the the alleged Alien Reproduction Vehicle, or ARV, allegedly seen at a secret display at Lockheed's Helendale facility in November 1988. The source for this account was a technical design engineer named Brad Sorensen, who told his friend and respected aviation/aerospace illustrator, Mark McCandlish. The design was of a classic flying saucer, except that this was made in the USA, and designed from acquired alien technologies. According to a lecture from a four-star general that Sorensen heard while there, some form of antigravity was in effect, and the ARVs in operation had already traversed much of the solar system by then. The story is fascinating, and a number of prominent individuals have interviewed Sorensen about his account. Those who listened to him stated that he seems entirely truthful, but the story of

---

151 On this matter, one well-placed individual told me "For what it's worth, Kelly Johnson's viewpoint ... is significantly more widespread among the cognoscenti than most would imagine."
152 "Extraterrestrial UFO Are Real: Ben Rich Lockheed Skunk Works Director Admitted In His Deathbed Confession," [www.garuda.co/2013/01/31/extraterrestrial-ufo-are-real-ben-rich-lockheed-skunk-works-director-admitted-in-his-deathbed-confession/].

course remains officially unconfirmed.[153]

One more final high-profile individual ought to be mentioned in this context: former Apollo 14 astronaut, Dr. Edgar Mitchell, who was the sixth man to walk on the moon. As such, Mitchell has had access to elite figures throughout the U.S. national security structure. Certainly, he has been in a good position to know matters of importance relating to space and national security. Therefore, it is of no small significance that for many years on various occasions, Mitchell has spoken publicly about the reality of a deeply secret program to study extraterrestrial technology and bodies. In several private conversations with myself, he added that he learned this from two "very elite" connections who told him about the existence of this program at "great risk personally, professionally, and to their families." The fact that mainstream news media has ignored, marginalized, or belittled his various statements will remain a black mark as long as such a policy continues.

When considering the likelihood of actual retrievals of crashed UFOs, combined with the many leaked accounts emanating from the world of national security, there is a compelling argument that exotic technology in the form of UFOs came into the possession of the American military, and almost certainly others such as the Soviet military. This technology appears to have been studied for many years. Indeed, the observations of many citizens from California's Antelope Valley, where many of the leading aerospace and aviation designs are created and tested, confirm that extremely advanced technologies are being seen and flown there. The same can be said for the Area 51/Groom Lake region. What does one make of the 1994 video of a very bizarre UFO being flown over the Nevada Test Site? This video was leaked in early 1995. It shows an object moving in ways that defy conventional aviation physics. Multiple analyses indicate that it was roughly fifteen feet wide and ten feet high. Within minutes its speed ranged from as low as 20 mph to as high as 500 mph. It made very sharp-angled turns, including a right angle turn at approximately 140

---

153 For a detailed account of this event, see Greer, Steven M., M.D., "Testimony of Mr. Mark McCandlish, U.S. Air Force December 2000," in *Disclosure*, p. 497-510.

Chapter 5: Digging Deeper—The Breakaway Civilization

mph. What can do this? Since it was recorded inside one of America's most secret testing facilities, it is reasonable to assume that we ourselves made it. Can this be related to the program to study crashed UFOs? The answer may well be *yes*.[154]

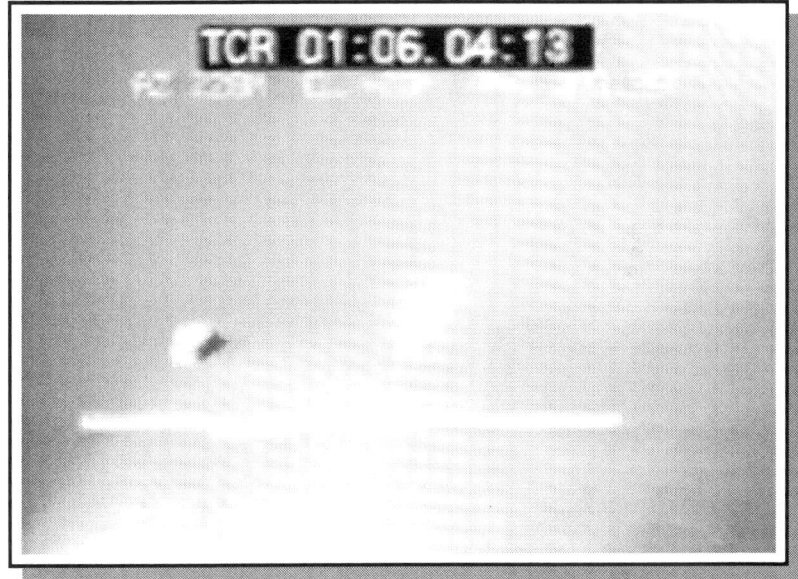

From the 1994 video of an unknown object recorded at the Nellis Test Site.

German Technology

Starting in the 1960s, another idea was introduced into the UFO research field, one which has received significant attention throughout the 21st century. It is the idea that a certain portion of what we call UFOs has derived from clandestine German technology from the Second World War, technology which continued to develop during the 1950s and beyond.[155] There are a number of permutations on this

---

154 See "UFO over Nellis AFB, Nevada 1992" [sic] on YouTube at www.youtube.com/watch?v=1oCl2kROv1Y.
155 The most historically important studies in this area are probably Vesco, Renato, *Intercettatelli Senza Sparare* (U. Mursia & Co., 1968; Vesco's book was republished in 1974 as *Intercept -- But Don't Shoot*); Cook, Nick, *The Hunt for Zero Point: Inside the Classified World of Antigravity Technology* (Broadway Books, 2002); and several books by Joseph P. Farrell, most notably *Reich of the Black Sun: Nazi Secret Weapons and the Cold War Allied Legend* (Adventures Unlimited Press, 2005), *SS Brotherhood of the Bell: The Nazi's Incredible Secret Technology* (Adventures Unlimited Press, 2006), and *Roswell and the Reich: The Nazi Connection* (Adventures Unlimited Press, 2010).

195

idea, including a covert research and development program based in the U.S. with the help of Nazi scientists, various programs in South America (most notably Argentina and Bolivia) run by escaped Nazis, and even a secret Nazi base in Antarctica.

It is worth remembering that from the very beginning of the modern flying saucer era, many researchers speculated that the mysterious objects were classified technology, presumably from either the Americans or Russians. During these early years, very little was known of the importation of Nazi scientists (Project Paperclip), but the idea was there that these objects were of entirely terrestrial manufacture, and it has never gone away. Starting in the late 1960s, Italian researcher Renato Vesco argued that the Germans had developed several types of alternative energy devices, even some form of antigravity. Disc-shaped and tubular craft were built and tested near the end of the Second World War, which, he argued, was the proper explanation of the foo fighters. These concepts, he maintained, were developed by the Americans and Soviets and led directly to flying saucers.

In 2002, aviation writer Nick Cook investigated this possibility further. His conclusion was that the Nazis had experimented "with a form of science the rest of the world had never remotely considered," and which has continued to be suppressed to this day. The most famous of the Nazi achievements was said to be a flying disc, the so-called V7, which flew out of Prague on February 14, 1945. It was said to have climbed to an altitude of 40,000 feet within minutes and reached a speed of 1,200 mph, far and away beyond what any fighter aircraft could achieve at the time. According to the source, it was either destroyed at the war's end, or captured by the Soviets. Cook also discussed the work of Viktor Schauberger, who investigated alternative energy and "levitational flight," including flying saucer-shaped craft. During the war, his work was taken over by the S.S. under the direction of the notorious General Hans Kammler. According to one of Cook's sources, a Schauberger prototype, using "wholly unconventional" science, successfully rose twice to the ceiling and then was

Chapter 5: Digging Deeper—The Breakaway Civilization

wrecked.[156] Shortly after this, Schauberger himself was captured by the Americans and detained until March 1946.

Cook also investigated the so-called "Bell Experiment," something that received significant follow-up in the work of Joseph P. Farrell. In the region of Lower Silesia, under Kammler's management, work was underway that seemed to be related to antigravity. It involved using large amounts of electricity feeding into a below-ground chamber with two contra-rotating cylinders filled with mercury (said to produce terrible side effects on humans). Sixty-two scientists working on the program were allegedly shot by the S.S. just before the German surrender. It has even been suggested that the Bell experiments were possible efforts into time travel.

Farrell's research goes further still. In his judgement, the Bell was:

> ... a *gateway* technology, a hyper-dimensional torsion-based technology that the Nazis had developed to investigate its potential applications in three areas:
> 1) As a means to tap into the zero-point energy, or, to phrase it differently, the energy of the physical medium of space-time itself;
> 2) As a means to manipulate gravity itself, i.e. as an advanced prototypical field propulsion technology; and,
> 3) As a means to the ultimate, potentially planet-busting, weapons.

The conceptual key to the Bell, as both he and Cook noted, was the manipulation of rotating magnetic fields via the two contra-rotating mercury-filled cylinders.[157]

It is unclear how much of "The Legend" (as the story of Nazi UFOs has sometimes been called) is true, and how much fantasy. The existence of the Bell, for instance, relies on a small handful of witnesses who claimed knowledge of it after the war. None of the stories have benefitted from solid documentation, and some of them, such as the Prague flying saucer, seem outlandish. One wonders how a pilot would have managed a feat of flying in a completely new type of airframe at

---

156 Some years ago, the author was shown what was claimed to be the only remaining Schauberger disc, held at the time in an American research facility. It was saucer-shaped, brass colored, and roughly three feet in diameter. The scientist who discussed it said he believed it was of sound design and could fly, although he did not believe the material science was advanced enough, and that the craft could probably not withstand the rigors of flight.
157 Farrell, Joseph P. *The SS Brotherhood of the Bell*, p. 77.

three times the speed of the world's best fighter aircraft at the time. But even these speeds pale in comparison with the speeds said to have been attained by the fabled Haunebu craft, a literally unbelievable 17,000 kph (over 10,000 mph). The technology enabling this fantastic performance was described as:

> ... a revolutionary electro-magnetic-gravitic engine which improved Hans Coler's free energy machine into an energy Konverter coupled to a Van De Graaf band generator and Marconi vortex dynamo (a spherical tank of mercury) to create powerful rotating electromagnetic fields that affected gravity and reduced mass.[158]

Some descriptions of Nazi manufacture of these discs are quite specific. Their only problem is they lack evidence. Sources are not cited; photographs are either indistinct or look Photoshopped. Moreover, claims of such speeds lack any semblance of credibility. Two problems that immediately come to mind are heat shielding and human survivability (let alone control over such a craft). In the context of the 1940s, these would be insurmountable. What we appear to be left with are claims of individuals, some of which may have had validity, some not, but which nearly all lack supporting documentation.

Still, Farrell's work bears close scrutiny, as he makes a strong case that, at the very least, the fundamentals of the Nazi's fringe research continued on after the war, especially in Argentina but perhaps elsewhere, with substantial cooperation from within the U.S. First, the massive Nazi intelligence group led by Reinhard Gehlen was brought into the Anglo-American fold organizationally intact and run essentially by the same people after the war as during it—and with a great amount of independence. Secondly, not only did the importation of so many Nazis into the CIA via Project Paperclip fundamentally undermine the nature and purpose of that organization, but many Paperclip Nazis who went elsewhere (such as into the U.S. rocket program in the Southwest) also exhibited a striking level of independ-

---

158 Arndt, Rob, "Haunebu (H-GERÄT, Hauneburg Device,1939-1945)," at discaircraft.greyfalcon.us/HAUNEBU.htm. This thesis is also offered in Vesco, Renato and Childress, David Hatcher, *Man-Made UFOs, 1944-1994: 50 Years of Suppression* (Adventures Unlimited Press, 1994).

Chapter 5: Digging Deeper—The Breakaway Civilization

ence from U.S. military authority. These Nazis, Farrell suggested, were a "classic Trojan Horse operation." Thirdly, these U.S.-based Nazis were in all likelihood collaborating with Nazis elsewhere in the world, most importantly Argentina but probably other places, too. "'Our Nazis,' he wrote, "may not really have been 'ours' after all."[159] Argentina under Juan Peron provided them with a secure home and infrastructure, in return for Nazi gold and whatever other ample financial resources they brought with them.[160]

To his great credit, Farrell went further still and analyzed declassified U.S. military documents, especially the "Schulgen Intelligence Collection" memo of October 1947, which clearly showed a belief that the flying saucer phenomenon not only may have been derived from Nazi technology, but that a rogue Nazi group may well have existed at the time and had to be dealt with. Not only this, but he demonstrated that a forged version of this document, which almost certainly was crafted by UFO researcher Bill Moore in the 1980s, was designed to take attention away from the Nazi connection in favor of an ET connection that never existed in the original memo.[161]

If I have a quibble with this analysis, it is that Schulgen's conclusions should not in any way be taken as definitive for the U.S. national security community as a whole. In the first place, during the 1940s and 1950s, opinions varied widely within that community regarding the flying saucers. Some included speculations along the lines of Schulgen, others were explicitly along extraterrestrial lines. Secondly (and as Farrell also showed), Schulgen was essentially guided into his position by a previous memo from Air Force General Nathan Twining, who may well have had good reason for steering the lower-ranked Schulgen into the direction he did.

Few of the critical details can be known for sure. Clearly, if the saucers were being manufactured by a rogue post-war Nazi group that was beyond the reach of the American military machine, this would have been explosive news for the American and world public. Espe-

---

159 Farrell, Joseph P. *Roswell and the Reich*, p. 352.
160 Farrell, Joseph P. *Roswell and the Reich*, p. 355.
161 See Farrell's engaging discussion of this memo in *Roswell and the Reich*, pp. 374-403.

cially if it were learned that thousands of hard core and unrepentant Nazis were working illegally in highly sensitive scientific and intelligence positions throughout the U.S. On the other hand, a truly alien (e.g. extraterrestrial or similar) answer to the flying saucer phenomenon would have required just as much secrecy and disinformation.

Still, there is cause for believing that some Nazi technology during the war was of a genuine proto-UFO nature. There is even good reason to consider that, somewhere, someone was trying to build genuine flying saucers in the immediate aftermath of the war. But it must be emphasized that the evidence for this is slender, and based on a surprisingly small number of claims. Nor has it ever been answered satisfactorily where they were based, who built them, what their missions were, or what relation (if any) they had with pre-war sightings of apparent UFOs. And again, most important is the lack of any historical documentation leading us to a firm conclusion.

One scenario that has often been raised is that the Nazis set up a base in Antarctica (Neu-Schwabenland) which became a major problem after the war's end, as it contained all their advanced science and weaponry. This in turn underlies the claim that the American expedition known as Operation Highjump, which took place in late 1946 and early 1947, was in reality a failed military expedition against the secret Nazi base. Highjump was indeed a large expedition, including 13 ships and nearly 5,000 men, and as recent scholarship has shown, "it was designed to train the U.S. Navy for a possible war with the Soviet Union in the Arctic, and not to attack an alleged German base in Antarctica."[162]

The Operation did end earlier than scheduled, and there were also deaths, but all of the problems appear explainable by bad weather, which became quite serious by February 1947. The Commander of Highjump, Admiral Richard Byrd, gave a statement to the March 5, 1947 edition of the Chilean newspaper, *El Mercurio*. This is sometimes used to indicate that Byrd was hinting at the reality of dangerous,

---

162 Summerhayes, Colin and Beeching, Peter. "Hitler's Antarctic Base: The Myth and the Reality." *Polar Record*, V. 43, Issue 01, pp. 1-21, January 2007. Abstract available at journals.cambridge.org/action/displayAbstract?fromPage=online&aid=64811

Chapter 5: Digging Deeper—The Breakaway Civilization

revolutionary, technology in Antarctica. In fact, his statement does not appear to do this. The article, in part, reads as follows:

> Admiral Richard E. Byrd warned today that the United States should adopt measures of protection against the possibility of an invasion of the country by hostile planes coming from the polar regions. The admiral explained that he was not trying to scare anyone, but the cruel reality is that in case of a new war, the United States could be attacked by planes flying over one or both poles. This statement was made as part of a recapitulation of his own polar experience, in an exclusive interview with International News Service. Talking about the recently completed expedition, Byrd said that the most important result of his observations and discoveries is the potential effect that they have in relation to the security of the United States. The fantastic speed with which the world is shrinking—recalled the admiral—is one of the most important lessons learned during his recent Antarctic exploration. I have to warn my compatriots that the time has ended when we were able to take refuge in our isolation and rely on the certainty that the distances, the oceans, and the poles were a guarantee of safety.[163]

Unless one decides to speculate that Byrd was speaking in code, there is no justification for interpreting his statement any other way than how it was reported, barring new facts or developments. Moreover, if Highjump ended in disaster, why then were subsequent, smaller expeditions sent to the same region later in 1947 and 1948? Such was Operation Windmill, described as an exploration and training mission in 1947-1948. In addition, the private explorer Finn Rone organized an expedition to the same area at this time. In other words, the idea of a Nazi base in Antarctica has no foundation, only speculation.

So the Nazi-UFO connection, just like the ET-UFO connection, offers its own frustrations and dead-ends. And yet, we can at least acknowledge the genuine possibility that there was a connection, and that the Americans, British, Russians, and others were very interested in such Nazi technology. As Cook, Farrell and others have pointed out, it has always been suspected that Hans Kammler, who disappeared at the end of the war, went to work for the Americans.

---

163 "A bordo del Monte Olimpo en Alta Mar," *El Mercurio* (Santiago). March 5, 1947. English translation

Moreover, there can be no question that a clandestine "flying saucer" program would have been desirable within the U.S. and possibly elsewhere in the immediate post-war era. This would presumably include science related not only to acquired technology—whether from Nazis or extraterrestrials—but also to the pioneering research of people like Nikola Tesla and Townsend Brown (both discussed in Chapter Eleven).

The question is not was there a terrestrial effort to build flying saucers. Rather, whether or not this scientific work comprised the sum total of what we call the UFO phenomenon. That is, are UFOs a *completely* man-made phenomenon, and is the alien connection merely disinformation and a distraction? For those researchers who believe this, the reasoning is (a) that aliens from another planet, arriving in "flying saucers" that look like human designs from the 1940s, is implausible; (b) human science and technology is more than sufficient to explain the operation of UFOs, as long as we include hidden, suppressed technologies; and (c) the "alien" connection is pure disinformation designed to confuse the public from the reality of a fully terrestrial breakaway civilization that has no intention of sharing its technology with the masses.[164]

As I have been suggesting, and will continue to argue in this book, there is a certain logic to the position, but only if a substantial body of other evidence is ignored. Moreover, there is more evidence that the core UFO phenomenon derives from *others* not from our civilization.

The Requirements of Secrecy

Let us return to 1947, to President Harry Truman, facing the shattering news that other beings of some sort were here. Moreover, that the U.S. military had recovered some of their technology, and even bodies. We may assume that this would require the creation of black budgets. After all, it would be necessary to fund these programs,

---

164 Although I coined the phrase "breakaway civilization" with a specific meaning in mind in *UFOs and the National Security State: The Cover-Up Exposed, 1973-1991*, the phrase has been adopted and used by other researchers to describe a wide range of covert possibilities. One thing is evident: the concept resonates with many, and is certainly worthy of more research and investigation.

and it would not exactly be the wisest idea to inform Congress about it, considering that so little would be known about these beings, considering the desire to keep such technology away from enemies real or perceived, and for so many other reasons already discussed. Thus, layer upon layer of secrecy would need to be established to hide these UFO-extraterrestrial technology programs. As we know has become the norm within the black budget world, such a program would be nested within other classified programs, providing deep layers of protection from outside observation.

Such a program of secret study would also require ongoing influence and even control over mainstream radio, newspapers, and television. This does not mean that the CIA would control every piece of information coming through the media. It might mean, however, that there would be key, strategically placed, individuals who would influence stories as they came out. In other words, spin control: promoting certain types of stories and killing others. Over the years, there have been a number of exposés detailing the relationship between the CIA and the news media. One was from 1977 by journalist Carl Bernstein, of Watergate fame. Bernstein concluded that since the end of the Second World War, the CIA had recruited more than four hundred U.S. journalists and placed them secretly on its payroll.[165] Any private citizen might well ask what he or she could accomplish with four hundred journalists, many in highly influential positions, as secret employees? Certainly there would be a great ability to influence the news, and therefore influence public opinion.

The same situation applies to the academic and scientific communities, as well as to Hollywood and the entertainment industry. Influencing them is easier than most people realize. With a few leading professors at the right institutions—Harvard, Princeton, UCLA, Berkeley, University of Chicago—the guard dogs would be in place.

---

165 Bernstein, Carl. "The CIA and the Media: How America's Most Powerful News Media Worked Hand in Glove with the Central Intelligence Agency and Why the Church Committee Covered It Up." *Rolling Stone*, October 20, 1977 [www.carlbernstein.com/magazine_cia_and_media.php].

A young professor who develops an interest in UFOs would then be smacked down by the leading lights. In fact, this is known to have happened. Harvard astronomer Donald Menzel fulfilled precisely this role during the 1950s and 1960s. Not only was he the leading debunker of UFOs in the world during that period of time, but he had a secret relationship with the National Security Agency. Not even his wife knew about that.

In today's world, such relationships are sometimes barely even concealed, as if no one cares. There is a virtual revolving door between the government/intelligence community and the most prestigious elements of the academic world. The situation is even worse in the world of scientific research, where everything is controlled by funding, and the largest share of funding for the scientific community comes from the U.S. government. Scientists who stray into areas not approved by their paymasters quickly find that they lose their funding, after which a loss of standing and prestige are a constant threat. These are very big incentives to toe the line.

Thus, control moves beyond the classified world to become cultural.

The Breakaway Civilization

What happens when teams of brilliant scientists, under conditions of total secrecy, and utilizing limitless black budget money, are able to study recovered extraterrestrial technology for many years, and even decades?

Consider the Roswell crash. More likely than not, technologies recovered there would have been well beyond the understanding of the scientists studying them. But, given enough time and effort, we might assume that even if they could not replicate what they found, they might have learned new things. Such claims have been made, and it is reasonable to suppose that new breakthroughs in understanding would have been made from such technology. Breakthroughs such as solid-state electronics, fiber optics, high-tensile fibers, lasers, and an array of other money-making opportunities for the defense and other industries. None of this has been proven, of course, but it is also true that the private research undertaken in deeply classified environments is not easy for outside researchers to observe. In fact, it would be be very easy to hide the Roswell connection in the historical treatment of these and other technologies.

Another relevant consideration of such breakthroughs is that they would reduce to zero any incentive to reveal the secret to the public. Why give up the goose that lays golden eggs?

But now matters become even more interesting. For what if some of the breakthroughs were even more significant than defense industry money-makers? What if they included secrets to antigravity, for example? What if they included an understanding of a new source of energy, something that could make petroleum obsolete? It would seem that these would be breakthroughs of vastly greater importance than anything imaginable. In the first place, they would threaten the world's largest industry, one that is entrenched within most aspects of our lives.

If, hypothetically, such breakthroughs were made during the 1950s or 1960s, it is conceivable, even likely, that those managing the program would make sure that the secrets never see the light of day. Certainly, those scientists engaged in the investigation would need to continue their research to learn everything they could about electrogravitics, antigravity, new sources of energy, and any related studies.

Science does not progress in a haphazard fashion. It is more like a series of connections in which knowledge must progress in a certain way for breakthroughs to be achieved. One does not simply go from the discovery of fire straight to rockets leaving Earth's atmosphere. There are necessary steps along the way. But what happens when a necessary link in the chain remains unavailable to the rest of the world, known only to a few clandestine scientists? It would mean that those scientists have the ability to add more links to the chain, moving farther and farther away in their knowledge from the rest of the world.

Without question, the classified world is far ahead of the rest of us. Some years ago, I had a conversation with a scientist who had worked for the National Security Agency during the mid-1960s. I know this man fairly well. He stated that in around 1965, the NSA had computers running at a clock speed of 650 MHz. Today, that is decidedly slow, but in 1965 it was extraordinary. In the first place, computers were virtually absent outside the classified world. Moreover, that clock speed was not reached by the personal computing market until the year 2000; that is, thirty-five years later. It is worth adding that in 1965, the NSA was still virtually unknown to the world. It had only been outed for the first time in a book the prior year.[166] In other words, during the early 1960s, an agency that nobody knew existed had the most advanced computing capabilities in the world.

Returning to our hypothetical UFO technology group, we might ask, how many years ahead of us might they be? What new understandings of our world and universe might they have that we lack? Would they have the ability to develop a fleet of clandestine flying saucers, with the ability to leave Earth's orbit and enter space? Would such capabilities allow them to have interactions or encounters with non-human intelligences? Would they have a significant infrastructure, perhaps some of it underground?

What are the features that constitute a distinct civilization? Admittedly, this is not always easy to quantify, yet we can identify certain key factors. The level of technology would be one. Scientific and cosmological understanding—that is, how one sees oneself in the grand scheme of things—would be another. By both of these features, the deeply clandestine black budget group might be so far ahead of the rest of us, that we might justly consider them to be a separate civilization, one that has broken away from our own, or a breakaway civilization. Undoubtedly, its members would continue to interact with our own society, since in all likelihood Earth is where the action is. But their level of knowledge, and the technologies at their disposal, would give them a unique and very advanced position in the grand scheme of things.

It seems unlikely that such a group would answer to the President of the United States. Simply based on the known structure of power

---

166 Wise, David and Ross, Thomas B., *The Invisible Government*, Random House, 1964.

in the world today, it seems much more likely that private international finance would exercise dominant control over the group, or somehow be merged with it. The office of the U.S. President, while still important, is no longer the central pivot that it was just after World War Two. Studies of the black budget world, for instance, have emphasized that at the deepest levels of secrecy, it is not official Defense Department personnel, but private contractors who usually dominate most of the Special Access Programs—that is, black budget programs.[167] Why should it be any different regarding the UFO secret?

Paying For It All

Funding such a program would be a nightmarish prospect, at least if done through formal legal channels. What we call the black budget is usually understood to be classified appropriations and, within the U.S., part of the normal budgetary process which must be approved each year by Congress. In other words, while it may be secret, it would at least have the veneer of legality. Officially speaking, the U.S. black budget is estimated to be around $50 billion.[168] This is an enormous sum, but keeping in mind that it is allocated for the entire U.S. defense community, only a certain portion would be available for an undoubtedly expensive UFO research and development program. Not nearly enough. One conversation I had with an insider with some knowledge of such matters is that, if nothing else, this program is *expensive*.[169]

In this context, it is worth pondering the research of several analysts, notably Catherine Austin Fitts, John Perkins, and Joseph Stiglitz. Fitts was Under Secretary of the U.S. Department of Housing and Urban

---

167 Sweetman, Bill. "In Search of the Pentagon's Billion Dollar Hidden Budgets: How the U.S. Keeps its R&D Spending Under Wraps." *Jane's International Defence Review*. January 5, 2000 [www.combatsim.com/cgi-bin/ubbcgi/ultimatebb.cgi?ubb=get_topic&f=53&t=001149]. Also, Priest, Dana and Arkin, William. "Top Secret America: A Washington Post Investigation," *Washington Post*, July 19-21, 2010 [projects.washingtonpost.com/top-secret-america/].
168 In 2013, the *Washington Post* reported the U.S. black budget to be $52.6 billion, based in large part on relevations leaked by Edward Snowden. See Gellman, Barton and Miller, Greg. "U.S. spy network's successes, failures and objectives detailed in 'black budget' summary" *Washington Post*, Aug. 29, 2013. [http://www.washingtonpost.com/world/national-security/black-budget-summary-details-us-spy-networks-successes-failures-and-objectives/2013/08/29/7e57bb78-10ab-11e3-8cdd-bcdc09410972_story.html]
169 Almost as an aside, he indicated that the security measures for the clandestine UFO research program vastly outstripped formal scientific R&D.

Development (HUD) from 1989-1993; Perkins worked during the 1970s for the international engineering consultancy Chas T. Main as an "economic hitman," and Stiglitz was Chief Economist for the World Bank from 1997-2000. The first conclusion of importance reached by these and similar analyists is that international financial power is irredeemably corrupt and controls entire nations. The next conclusion, for our purposes at least, is that there is a great deal of money floating around the world that is free for the taking and requires no open accounting, at least for those groups in a position to take advantage.

Perkins described how he was charged with enticing developing countries to borrow money for poor infrastructure investments which were ultimately designed to cheat them out of trillions of dollars, increase their debt to the West, and make them dependent in every way. This was pure economic colonization on behalf of powerful corporations and banks that use the United States government as their tool. Significantly, Perkins added that behind his formal employment, the U.S. National Security Agency was essentially calling the shots, and was even behind hiring him for his job.[170]

Stiglitz described precisely the same process via the operations of the World Bank via its "four-step plan" for debter nations. Step One involves pressure for those nations to privatize state industries. Step Two involves capital market liberalization, meaning that speculative investment money comes—and then goes, draining national reserves and prompting IMF demands for large interest hikes. This destroys property values, industry, and national treasuries. He describes Step Three as "Market-Based Pricing," meaning higher prices on food, water and cooking gas. That inevitably leads to "Step Three and a Half: The IMF Riot." Such riots have occurred in Indonesia, Bolivia, Ecuador, and elsewhere, and according to Stiglitz is entirely expected by the Bank. This is also when foreigners pick off remaining assets at firesale prices. Finally, we reach Step Four, which is "free trade," in which the last barriers to sales are destroyed and domestic markets are

---

170 Perkins, John. *Confessions of an Economic Hitman*. Ingram Pub Services, 2004.

barricaded against their own local produce.[171]

Other international organizations, such as the World Trade Organization, enforce this financial misrule. The WTO is not part of any government and is wholly an instrument of corporate power. It enforces privatization of natural resources like water and deems the environmental, health, and food safety laws of nations to be barriers to trade. Effectively, it gives corporations a veto over national environmental and labor laws.

Fitts's analysis perfectly rounds out this scenario with special attention on the black budget. Recognizing that the rule of law does not apply to the global financial elite, she has described how the "real" black budget involves more than classified appropriations but also includes monies obtained by intelligence groups by way of narcotics trafficking, predatory lending and numerous other forms of financial fraud. She concluded that at least 85 percent of the U.S. federal budget is unauditable. Furthermore, that HUD (and probably other federal agencies) served effectively as a cut-out operation for drug trafficking and securities fraud. She wrote about the lack of accountability of billions of dollars in several classic analyses, "What's Up With the Black Budget?," "The Myth of the Rule of Law," and "Dillon, Read & Co. Inc. & the Aristocracy of Stock Profits." Fitts also argues that the housing bubble collapse and financial crisis make sense when viewed through the lense of mortgage and securities fraud used to finance the black budget.[172]

Getting to the financial roots of the UFO cover-up may well require the skills of a large team of financial wizards, wending their way through layer upon layer of classified (and largely privatized) programs, nested within each other like an elaborate Matryoshka doll. Just as

---

171 Palast, Greg. "IMF's Four Steps to Damnation." *The Observer*. April 28, 2001. [http://www.theguardian.com/business/2001/apr/29/business.mbas]. Stiglitz, Joseph. "Thanks for Nothing," *Atlantic Monthly*, October 2001 [http://www.globalpolicy.org/component/content/article/209/42948.html]
172 Fitts, Catherine Austin. "What's Up With the Black Budget?" Sept. 23, 2003. [https://solari.com/blog/whats-up-with-the-black-budget/]. See also Fitts, Catherine Austin, "The Myth of the Rule of Law. Or How the Money Works: The Destruction of Hamilton Securities Group." *Sanders Research Associates, Third Quarter Commentary*, 2001. [http://solari.com/assets/PDFs/myth_of_the_rule_of_law.pdf]. Fitts, Catherine Austin. "Dillon, Read & Co. Inc. & the Aristocracy of Stock Profits." [Dunwalke.com]

ordinary national and international policy of most nations has long been hijacked for private financial interests, so too almost certainly for the UFO cover-up. For this is a subject that most assuredly involves a tremendous amount of power, and therefore money.

What this means is that we have an upside down reality. The things that are real are the things that are denied to us. The things that we see in our entertainment-dominated mass media are the most illusory. This is no accident. Given the long-term relationship between the intelligence community and mainstream media, it is most reasonable to assume that the public is being subjected to a pacification program, one in which people are explicitly being distracted and brainwashed for the purpose of getting them to sit down and shut up.

But not everyone can do this. Not everyone can sit quietly, passively, unwilling to ask the difficult questions. It is up to those people who care enough to become truth warriors. To fight for the truth, however, it is necessary first to realize that the deception exists. Next, in order to discern the truth amid a tissue of lies, perseverance is necessary. This is not always easy to cultivate, for Truth does not simply appear in all her shining glory. Like a rare archaeological find, Truth must be excavated. She must be dug out. And, even then, interpreting Truth can be maddeningly difficult. Finally, one must learn to speak out on behalf of Truth. In so doing, we find ourselves at odds with a formidable structure of power. Becoming a truth warrior requires intelligence, perseverance, and courage. It means remembering that the nail that sticks out is the one that gets hammered.

Still, upon reflection, in the context of something as brief and ephemeral as a human life, what can be more rewarding, what more worthy, than an unswerving dedication to the fight for Truth?

Chapter 6
High Strangeness—UFOs from 1970 to 1990

As 1970 began, the Condon Committee of the University of Colorado had just debunked UFOs to the scientific community, and the U.S. Air Force had closed down Project Blue Book, its long-standing office which accepted and investigated UFO reports from the public. UFOs had become passé. The world had *been there, done that*.

The operators of these unidentified craft never seem to get the message. For not only have UFOs failed to go away, but since 1970 they have become more numerous than ever. In the 21st century, thousands upon thousands of reports are filed every year at various online repositories. But even during the 1970s and 1980s, before the Age of the Web, UFO reports rose steadily in the United States. More importantly, they spiked elsewhere in the world. UFOs had always been noticed worldwide, of course, but now reporting and communication systems were improving enough that they could be recorded more readily.

The Delphos UFO of 1971

One of the most memorable UFO events of the early 1970s occurred in the small town of Delphos, Kansas.

On the evening of November 2, 1971, sixteen-year-old Ronald Johnson was tending sheep on the family farm when he and his dog saw an object hovering two feet off the ground about twenty five yards away, among some trees. According to Ronald, it was shaped like a mushroom, covered with multi-colored lights, roughly nine feet in diameter and ten feet tall, and made a sound like a vibrating washing machine. Suddenly, it became bright at the base. Then it took off at an angle, temporarily blinding him. Although his dog was extremely quiet during the sighting, the sheep had been bleating nervously.

After his eyes adjusted, Ronald went into the house and told his parents. Once outside, they also saw the object, easily visible in the sky before it vanished toward the south.

The three approached the site where the object had been seen. They found a glowing ring on the ground, about eight feet in diameter, and some sort of glowing material on nearby trees. One tree had been crushed; presumably the object had landed on it. They also noticed the broken limb of a live tree; this seemed to have been caused by the object as it descended. The limb snapped easily, as if it had been dead for some time, yet it was green under the bark, and the upper area still had green leaves on it. When Mrs. Johnson touched the glowing area on the ground, her fingers went numb. When she wiped the substance onto her leg, she became numb there as well. For two weeks, her fingers remained slightly numb, although she never saw a doctor about it. Meanwhile, Ronald's eyes became red and irritated for some time after the event, and he also suffered from nightmares.

Police investigated and found a corroborating witness to the event. A few miles away, someone else had reported "a bright light descending in the sky in the Delphos area" just at the time of the Johnson sighting.

The ring was visible for a month afterwards, and was examined by UFO investigator Ted Phillips. He found the soil beneath the ring to be dry to a depth of at least twelve inches, whereas the soil outside the ring was wet and dark. Samples were brought to a laboratory, which determined that the soil within the ring was resistant to water. It also contained more calcium and more soluble salts, and was also more acidic, than soil from outside the ring. In addition, the soil from inside the ring contained an unidentified hydrocarbon and an organic material composed of white, crystal-like fibers.

Researcher Jacques Vallée discussed the findings of a French biologist, who asked to remain anonymous, but who identified the white fibers as a fungus-like organism of the order *Actinomycetales*.

This organism apparently can cause a circular pattern to form on the ground. In addition, the biologist stated that the fungus is often found growing with another fungus of the order *Basidiomycetes*, which may fluoresce under some conditions.

The Delphos ring after 10 minutes, 16 hours, and 3 1/2 years (top to bottom).

Accordingly, some analysts have labeled the case as *solved*. However, this does not explain the witness accounts of the UFO. One may also ask, even if the ring was not related to the UFO sighting, how did the fluorescent material get onto the surrounding trees? How did the branches break? What crushed the dead tree? Police told Phillips that the Johnsons were well-respected, and that they did not believe it possible that the family had perpetrated a hoax. There the case remains, still a puzzle after so many years.[173]

The Wave of 1973: Two Interesting Cases

Despite several interesting reports, there was no identifiable "wave" of UFO sightings until the latter part of 1973. During October, particularly in the southeastern United States, there were a number of startling and disturbing encounters, by ordinary people, with the extraordinary.

Probably the best known of these is the so-called Pascagoula Incident, which took place on October 11, 1973. This involved two men, Charles Hickson, in his forties, and Calvin Parker, age nineteen, who were fishing in Mississippi's Pascagoula River when they heard a buzzing noise behind them. They turned and were terrified to see a glowing egg-shaped object with blue lights in front, hovering just above the ground. It was not especially large, roughly ten feet wide and eight feet high—in other words, of a very similar size to the object seen two years earlier at Delphos, Kansas. The men watched in terror as a door appeared in the object and three strange beings came out of it, floating over the river towards them.

They were extremely odd-looking. They were the size of a short human adult, perhaps five feet tall, and they had arms and legs, but there the similarities ended. These beings had no necks, but instead had bullet-shaped heads coming straight from the shoulders. There seemed to be no eyes, and mere slits served as mouths. Instead of normal looking noses and ears, they had thin, conical projections, described "like carrots from a snowman's head." Their skin was grey and wrinkled. Instead of human-looking hands, they had claws of some sort. Frankly, a body plan that makes no sense to us.

---

173 "Delphos, Kansas Landing Ring," [ufoevidence.org/cases/case192.htm]. "1971, "The Delphos Kansas UFO Landing Ring," [www.ufocasebook.com/Kansas.html].

Two of the beings seized Hickson; the third one grabbed Parker, who then fainted. According to Hickson, his body went numb and he was floated into a brightly-lit room inside the craft. He received a medical examination with a floating eyelike device. The beings then left Hickson, still floating and paralyzed, apparently to examine Parker. Fifteen or twenty minutes later, he was floated back outside and released. Parker was weeping and praying on the ground. The object then rose straight up and shot out of sight.

How does one tell people a story like that? Not surprisingly, the two men initially decided to keep quiet. But they soon changed their minds and spoke to the local sheriff, who interviewed them carefully, then left them alone in a room wired for sound. The sheriff assumed that if the men were hoaxing, this would be when he found out. It became obvious, however, that the men were very serious. The case soon received a great deal of attention and was investigated by a number of researchers. Both men passed polygraph tests, and Hickson underwent hypnotic regression which had to be terminated when he became too upset.

The two men consistently impressed people with their account and demeanor. Scientist J. Allen Hynek, giving an opinion shared by many, said: "There was definitely something here that was not terrestrial."[174]

Another interesting case from that period occurred the following week near the town of Mansfield, Ohio, involving a U.S. Army Reserve helicopter crew commanded by Captain Lawrence Coyne. On October 18, 1973, just after 11 p.m., the helicopter was at an altitude of 2,500 feet with good visibility, when the crew noticed a red light abruptly change course and move directly toward them. Captain Coyne put the helicopter into an emergency descent at the rapid speed of 2,000 feet per minute. At the same time, he noticed that all radio frequencies went dead. When the helicopter was an altitude of 1,700 feet, the object streaked in front of the crew and remained directly in

---

174 "The 1973 Pascagoula, Mississippi Abduction (Hickson/Parker)" [www.ufocasebook.com/Pascagoula.html]. "The Air Force and Pascagoula: A Transcript of the Hickson-Parker Interrogation," *MUFON UFO Journal*, May-June 1984 [www.theblackvault.com/encyclopedia/documents/MUFON/Journals/1984/May_June_1984.pdf].

front of them for ten seconds. All four crew members said it looked like a gray cigar with a small dome on top. The red light was still there, but now there was a white light on the side and a green one on the bottom. The bottom light swung around like a searchlight and bathed the entire cabin in green light. The object then accelerated to the west, made a sharp turn, and was lost above Lake Erie.

Just as astonishing, when Coyne next checked his altimeter, he saw that his chopper was rapidly *climbing*, and was already past the altitude of 3,500 feet. There was no reason his helicopter should have been that high. Somehow the object had pulled them up. It took Coyne several minutes to regain control of the helicopter. Later inspections showed no mechanical problems. This is considered by many researchers to be a very good case, and Coyne later described it to a United Nations subcommittee in 1978.[175]

High Strangeness in Spain

Spain was another area of interesting UFO activity during the early 1970s. Something very unusual was going on there during the spring of 1974. Several dozen reports made it to local police and newspapers, a number of which included descriptions of apparently alien figures. For some reason, they were collected by the U.S. Defense Attaché and were later released to the public through the Freedom of Information Act. Very interesting, very odd. Unfortunately, only the summaries are available, but they are suggestive enough.[176]

One, from March 23, concerned a sighting near the Gulf of Cádiz. A local politician and his chauffeur were driving along an empty stretch of road at 3 a.m., when they were shocked to see what was described as a "luminous, metal like" object. The two men felt a strange sensation as the car came to a near stop. The object soon took off.

---

175 "Coyne Helicopter Incident" [www.ufoevidence.org/cases/case104.htm]. "Coyne Helicopter/UFO Incident" [www.ufocasebook.com/coyne.html]. "The Coyne UFO incident - Mansfield, Ohio 1973" at YouTube [www.youtube.com/watch?v=4uxF9tRPIhM].
176 The following cases, and many more, are described in "Department of Defense Intelligence Information Report" in six pages, United States Defense Attache Office, Madrid, Spain, 1974.

A few nights later, about 100 miles west of Madrid, a truck driver claimed to see "three silver ships on the highway" with intensely bright lights. He said that figures approached him, and he ran. When they followed, he threw himself onto the road. They came to within six feet of him. They were allegedly very tall, roughly six-and-a-half feet, but the man could not see their faces. They returned to their ships and left. A police investigation the next day found a hole in the ground which the driver said he had not made.

Another report described a "round intense torchlike light" which in the words of the report, "rose out of the water near a huge rock, traveled at low altitude, then fell into the water again. This happened twice."

And so it went for the next few months. It is not clear what the U.S. Defense Attaché thought about these reports. They were merely passed on to Washington, as he put it, "strictly for the information of those parties interested." No doubt, there were some parties that were quite interested in these reports.

The Strange Year of 1975

Within North America, UFO sightings increased dramatically in 1975, making it one of the most important years in the history of UFO reports, ranking along with 1947, 1952, or any other year. Several important developments became prominent at this time. One was cattle mutilations. Going back to the 1960s, there had been reported cases of bizarre mutilations of cattle. But starting in late 1974, the number of these skyrocketed, especially in the American West. Another new development was reports of unmarked, black helicopters. These were frequently noticed in the same areas where mutilations occurred, and also often where UFOs were being reported. Perhaps these helicopters were part of a covert military group that monitored the mutilations or UFOs, or had something else to do with all this. Some analysts have argued they have been behind the mutilations themselves.

Another important development of 1975 was the rise in the number of credible accounts of alien abduction. There will be more to say about this in later chapters, but it is noteworthy that several of these cases occurred in the midst of all the other activity that was going on, that is the American West during late summer and fall of 1975. Among these was the famous Travis Walton case, sometimes known by the title of the book and movie based on it: *Fire in the Sky*.

When examining the long history of U.S. military encounters with UFOs, the more you search, the more you find. The U.S. military has engaged UFOs throughout the post-World War Two period, with good cases from nearly every single year. Nevertheless, several years stand out, one of which is 1975. Perhaps it is simply a matter of good fortune to have received confirmation of many cases from that year via the U.S. Freedom of Information Act. During the late 1970s, when FOIA was at its peak effectiveness, many of the most dramatic confirmed military cases were revealed. That includes the events of October and November of 1975.

What happened, as far as can be determined, was a systematic incursion of military bases along both sides of the vast US-Canadian border. Several compelling but unconfirmed reports describe such cases throughout the summer, but confirmed cases via official documentation start from late October.[177]

Intruder Alert

On the evening of October 27, 1975, a low-hovering object invaded the airspace of Loring Air Force Base in northern Maine. This object penetrated the perimeter at an altitude of just 300 feet. Personnel inside the base said it had a white strobe light, and what appeared to be a red navigation light. It circled inside the base and came to within 300 yards of the nuclear weapons area. By that time, it was only 150 feet above the ground. For about an hour, while the object was being observed, the base was on high alert status. All attempts to identify the

---

177 The declassified documents on these events are available at many websites, including www.cufon.org/cufon/foia_002.htm, but a very good book on the subject remains Fawcett, Lawrence and Greenwood, Barry, *The UFO Cover-Up: What the Government Won't Say* (Formerly titled *Clear Intent*), Foreword by J. Allen Hynek. (Prentiss Hall Press, 1984).

object failed. It then left and went north toward Canada.

Twenty-four hours later, the scene was repeated. Security personnel saw an object approaching from the north at an altitude of 3,000 feet. It had flashing white lights and a solid amber light. Even though it was under constant radar and visual observation, it somehow disappeared several times. On the previous night, the base commander had been denied air support; this time he received permission for a National Guard helicopter to be dispatched. Before the helicopter arrived, however, this object did something rather impressive. It had been keeping a distance of at least three miles from the base all the while; now, somehow, it penetrated the base perimeter and appeared over the end of the runway, not more than 150 feet off the ground. Personnel nearby described it as red and orange, and resembling a stretched out football. The object hovered in mid-air, then turned out its lights and seemingly disappeared. Its lights went on and off several times. When, on one occasion, the lights turned back on, the object had gotten very close to the weapons storage area. By now, it was 1 a.m., which means the encounter had been going on for more than five hours. There is a record stating that the National Guard helicopter unsuccessfully attempted to contact and identify the object at this time. Then, for another two hours, the object remained inside or very close to the base, as it was seen over the weapons storage area once again at 3 a.m., completely unlit but visible to ground personnel. Consider how ominous and provocative this action was. When the helicopter again arrived to investigate, its crew members could not see the object, even though the frustrated ground personnel plainly saw both objects. Shortly after, the unknown craft flew off. It had been inside the base for seven hours.

Those who insist upon conventional explanations to this event might consider the possibility of the intruder being a helicopter. Indeed, one of the declassified documents refers to the unknown object as a helicopter. The problem is that no one heard any sounds from the object, despite its low altitude. Moreover, several times, personnel could see its shape, yet none described it as a helicopter. As with the other incursions of this period, the identity of this intruder has never been confirmed. In fact, in all the decades since the event, the military has never even offered a reasonable guess.

There were equally baffling incursions over other U.S. bases at this time. On October 30, an unidentified object entered restricted space at Wurtsmith Air Force Base in Michigan. This was a Strategic Air Command (SAC) base off the coast of Lake Huron. Again, we have an object that acted like a helicopter, but then again not exactly, and demonstrated interest in the weapons storage facilities. In this case, a tanker aircraft which was on approach was vectored in to observe and follow the object, which had just departed, going south down the lake. An interesting cat and mouse chase ensued, until the object rapidly accelerated and was gone.

Equally fascinating were the events of November 7 and 8, 1975, at Montana's Malmstrom Air Force Base. The base contained ICBMs over an area of many square miles. At 3 p.m., electronic sensors detected an intrusion at one of the missile sites. A Sabotage Alert Team was ordered to investigate, and when the members came to within a mile of the site, they reported by radio that they could see a bright, glowing, orange disk as large as a football field. It was simply hovering there, over the missile site. It was apparently an unsettling sight to behold, because when they were ordered to proceed to the site, the men refused to go any further. The object soon began to rise, whereupon it was registered on NORAD radar. F-106 interceptors were scrambled, but the object continued to rise to the incredible altitude of 200,000 feet. This is more than double the ceiling of the ultra-high flying U-2 spy plane, and the intercepting jets never saw the object. Upon inspection, a missile at the site showed indications that its computerized targeting system had been tampered with, and it had to be removed. It would appear that the UFO was responsible.

More UFOs were reported the following night at the base. Once again, two F-106s were scrambled, whereupon ground personnel observed a cat-and-mouse game during which the UFOs turned off their lights each time the jets approached. When the jets departed, the

Chapter 6: High Strangeness—UFOs from 1970 to 1990

objects would turn their lights back on. Clearly, these objects were able to outclass American intercepting jets with ease.

```
MEMORANDUM FOR RECORD

Subject: Unidentified Sightings

1. 0308 EST FONECON from NORAD Command Director: at 0253 EST
Malmstrom AFB Montana received seven radar cuts on the height-
finder radar at altitudes between 9,500' and 15,500'. Simultaneously,
ground witnesses observed lights in the sky and the sounds of jet
engines similar to jet fighters. Cross-tell with FAA revealed
no jet aircraft within 100NM of the sightings. Radar tracked the
objects over Lewistown, Montana at a speed of seven (7) knots.
Two F-106 intercepters from the 24th NORAD Region were scrambled
at 0254 EST and became airborne at 0257 EST. At the time of the
initial voice report personnel at Malmstrom AFB and SAC sites
K1, K3, L3 and L6 were reporting lights in the sky accompanied
by jet engine noise.

2. 0344 EST FONECON, same source:

   Objects could not be intercepted. Fighters had to maintain a
minimum of 12,000' because of mountainous terrain. Sightings
had turned west, increased speed to 150 knots. Two tracks were
apparent on height-finder radars 10-12 NM apart. SAC site K3
reported sightings between 300' and 1,000' while site L-4 reported
sightings 5NM NW of their position. Sightings disappeared from
radar at position 4650N/10920W at a tracked speed of three (3)
knots.

3. At 0440 EST, NMCC intiated contact with the NORAD Command
Director who reported the following:

   0405 EST: Malmstrom receiving intermittent tracks on both
search and height-finder radars. SAC site C-1, 10NM SE of
Stanford, Montana, reported visual sightings of unknown objects.

   0420 EST: Personnel at 4 SAC sites reported observing inter-
cepting F-106's arrive in area; sighted objects turned off their
lights upon arrival of interceptors, and back on upon their
departure.
```

A declassified memo on UFOs over Malmstrom AFB in November, 1975.

These were only the best known events. There were several others that followed them. For instance, there is an interesting report of two UFOs over Cannon Air Force Base in New Mexico, on January 21, 1976. A report by security police stated they were "25 yards in diameter, gold or silver in color with [a] blue light on top, hole in the middle and red light on bottom." This is a very specific observation.

Records also exist of UFO incursions at Eglin Air Force Base in Florida on January 31, 1976, and over Fort Ritchie in Maryland, on July 30 of that year. In the latter case, it was reported that the object hovered over the ammunition storage area at low altitude, just as had happened at Loring and Wurtsmith Air Force Bases the previous year.

In lieu of obtaining a public confirmation from the U.S. government, something we have not gotten, all we have are these declassified reports. They tell us nothing of substance regarding the motivations of whomever or whatever was responsible for these UFOs. Common sense would indicate that they were observing various North American weapons facilities, possibly even tampering with them. In other words, there appears to have been some kind of confrontational relationship between these objects and the U.S. military.[178]

A Sphere over the Canaries

UFOs were never restricted to the United States. In every decade, they have been reported worldwide. Some of the events reported from around the world during the 1970s were truly amazing.

One spectacular case occurred in the Canary Islands on the night of June 22, 1976. Witnesses from several locations saw what can only be described as a transparent, spherical craft containing two very tall human-like figures. One witness, a medical doctor, described the object to be the size of a three-story building, and perfectly round. It was transparent enough that he could see stars through it, and two human-like figures inside.

Witnesses elsewhere on the island gave comparable, or even identical, descriptions. Astronomers at a nearby observatory saw it with their unaided eyes, as it was below the line of sight of their telescopes. One astronomer stated that, whatever this was, it was definitely not a planet. Nor did he have any scientific explanation for it. The object was also seen by the crew of the Spanish naval vessel, *Atrevida*, which was several miles offshore.

James Oberg, writing for *Omni,* was skeptical this event was anything from beyond. He suggested that witnesses had probably seen the launch of Poseidon ballistic missiles by the U.S. Navy. The U.S. Navy did indeed launch those missiles somewhere in the Atlantic Ocean at that time. However, the exact location of the launch is not known, and considering the vastness of the ocean, this explanation is a stretch. Even on the chance the launch had been visible to the Canaries, it is hard to imagine how witnesses could have described it

---

178 For a more detailed description and analysis of the 1975 incursions, see Dolan, Richard M., *UFOs and the National Security State: The Cover-Up Exposed, 1973-1991*, p. 87-100.

as they did.[179]

Incident over Tehran

More fascinating still was a case that occurred a few months later, one of the most astonishing in the history of UFOs. This was the incident over Tehran, on the night of September 18, 1976, and has been described many times over the years. We are fortunate to have a four-page U.S. Defense Intelligence Agency report describing it in detail. In addition, both of the pilots involved discussed the event years later.

That evening, residents of the city noticed an unusually brilliant object in the sky. After enough phone calls to the local airport, the traffic controller decided to look. He saw exactly what had been reported to him: an intensely bright object that was not supposed to be there. He contacted the Iranian Air Force, which dispatched two F-4 fighter jets, one after the other. Iran, at this time, was still under the rule of the Shah, and was a close ally of the United States. An unknown intrusion like this was of interest not only to the Iranian government, but also to the U.S. government. Indeed, a report of what happened was sent to the top national security officials in the U.S.: President Gerald R. Ford, CIA Director George Bush, and National Security Advisor Henry Kissinger, among others. A rather impressive distribution list.

Each of the F-4 interceptor pilots saw the object visually and tracked it with their airborne radar. In both cases, critical electronics and instrumentation went offline at a distance of twenty-five nautical miles from the object. In one case, the pilot was about to fire a missile when his controls ceased to work. In the case of the second pilot, an excerpt from the report is worth noting:

> ... as the F-4 approached a range of 25 nautical miles it lost all instrumentation and communications. ... When the F-4 turned away from the object and apparently was no longer a threat to it, the aircraft regained all

---

179 Benitez, J. J., *OVNIS: Documentos Oficiales del Gobierno Español/UFOs: Official Documents of the Spanish Government* (Plaza & Janes, 1977). See also "1976: The Canary Island Alien Sphere" [www.ufocasebook.com/CanaryIsland.html].

> instrumentation and communications... Another brightly lighted object ... came out of the original object. The second object headed straight toward the F4.

A rather alarming development. The report then went on to describe how this second object turned inside the arc of the F-4 itself and then rejoined the original object for a perfect rendezvous.

It is worth asking what could do that today, much less almost four decades ago? Officially speaking, nothing. Yet, something clearly did. The Iranian UFO case is strong because it is a spectacular event on its own merits, but also because it has supporting documentation, proving that UFOs have important national security considerations. An exotic object that can disable key instrumentation and electronics from top jet fighters is something that needs to be taken seriously. Indeed, it was. It is simply that national security groups continually try to hide that fact from the rest of us.[180]

Around the World During the Late 1970s

The late 1970s saw many bizarre and disturbing UFO cases. An intriguing event occurred over NATO's Aviano Air Base, near Venice, Italy, on July 1, 1977. During the evening, several U.S. Air Force personnel saw an unknown object hovering just outside the base perimeter. While the object was there, part of the facility lost electrical power. One prosaic explanation attributed the event to an electrical phenomenon related to geological stresses in the earth. Clearly, this does not square with witness accounts that claim to have seen a structured craft, if one chooses to accept witnesses testimony, of course.[181]

Meanwhile, South America, and especially Brazil, was experiencing dramatic sightings that appear to have caused the death of some

---

180 A very fine description of the event and good starting point for further research is the Wikipedia page at en.wikipedia.org/wiki/1976_Tehran_UFO_incident. A pdf copy of the original report can be read at foia.abovetopsecret.com/ultimate_UFO/UFO_GOVT/UFO_Cases/Sept1976iranufo.pdf.
181 Chiummiento, Antonio, "UFO Alert at a NATO Base in Italy," *Flying Saucer Review* (V. 30. No. 2 1984) (translated into English by Gordon Creighton). Available to read at www.ignaciodarnaude.com/avistamientos_ovnis/Chiumiento,AFO%20Alert%201977,NATO%20Base,Italy,FSR84V30N2.pdf. See also "Aviano AFB, Italy, July 1st, 1977" [ufologie.patrickgross.org/htm/aviano77.htm].

individuals. Obtaining certain proof of this has not happened, although Brazilian military officers off the record told this to investigators, and there is some corroboration that the Brazilian military investigated these events. This was throughout much of the late 1970s, frequently deep within the Brazilian rain forest.[182]

UFO sightings became much more dramatic during 1978. Like 1975, it was a very big year for UFO reports. Some people have attributed the high number of sightings to the release of Steven Spielberg's movie *Close Encounters of the Third Kind*. It is true that the movie made a major splash into popular consciousness. But, the UFO events of that year were of great specificity, occurring across every cultural and linguistic barrier. Looking into the details of the hundreds of cases from that year, one quickly realizes how ludicrous it is to suggest that all this was caused by Steven Spielberg, and yet some have tried to do this.

One key factor of that year is the number of sightings of alien or humanoid types of beings associated with UFOs. Nearly five hundred such reports have been collected from that year.[183]

One of these involves the shooting of an apparent alien being at McGuire Air Force Base in New Jersey, just over the fence from Fort Dix. This is said to have occurred on January 18, 1978. At around 3 a.m., a Fort Dix military policeman, who had been pursuing a low-flying UFO, saw a small being with a large head and a slender body appear directly in front of his car. He panicked and shot the being several times with a .45 caliber pistol. The being ran to a deserted runway at McGuire Air Force Base, where it died. Throughout the morning, the shooter was interrogated at McGuire Air Force Base. One of the men who spoke to him was Air Force Major George Filer, who has spoken about this event a number of times, including with the author. Other conservative, veteran researchers, such as Richard Hall and Leonard Stringfield, also interviewed this man, finding him

---

182 Pratt, Bob. *UFO Danger Zone: Terror and Death In Brazil. Where Next?* Foreword by Jacques Valee. (Horus House, 1996).
183 Rosales, Albert. "1978 Humanoid Sighting Reports" [www.ufoinfo.com/humanoid/humanoid-1978.pdf].

completely credible.

Filer, who arrived at the base at 4 a.m., about an hour after the shooting, noticed that something important was happening. When he arrived at the command post, he learned that UFOs had been flying over the base "all night." He was even more surprised when he learned that a military policeman had shot an alien. When he heard the word "alien," he replied, "you mean foreigner? That kind of alien?" "No," came the reply, "an alien from outer space." According to Filer, a C-141 transport plane from Wright-Patterson Air Force Base arrived to acquire the body. For a short while, Filer was told that he would brief the base commander on all this, but at the last moment he received a phone call informing him there would be no briefing.

Proving this case has been a frustrating experience. A document of unknown origin surfaced which described this event. However, a retired military police officer who studied it pronounced it as "probably a forgery." Seemingly on that basis alone, many researchers have shied away from the document and the case itself, which admittedly describes a rather extreme event. Nevertheless, the event may well have happened. This is yet another case demonstrating how difficult it is to obtain undeniable proof of what we are dealing with.[184]

Other UFO events of 1978 include the previously discussed crash of an unknown object in Bolivia on May 6, an event in which U.S. took over the operation, as a declassified document stated.

There was also the tragic case of Frederick Valentich, the young pilot who was flying across the Bass Strait from Australia to Tasmania, in October, 1978, but never reached his destination. The transcript of his radio conversation with ground control is chilling and unforgettable. In terror, Valentich described an object that continually buzzed over and around his aircraft. It obviously interfered with his radio, and ultimately interfered with the operation of his engine, causing him to

---

184 Stringfield, Leonard and Hall, Richard, "Dix-McGuire Update," *MUFON UFO Journal*, 6/87; Hall, Richard, *The UFO Evidence, Volume 2*, p. 22, 97-98. Filer's interview in Greer, Steven, *Disclosure*, p. 284-288. "Alien Being Shot Dead by MPs, January 18, 1978 (Ft. Dix & McGuire)" [www.ufocasebook.com/ftdix.html].

Chapter 6: High Strangeness—UFOs from 1970 to 1990

go down into the sea.[185]

Just days before, in the northwestern Chinese province of Gansu, several hundred military personnel were watching an outdoor movie, when they saw an enormous object pass over their heads. It had two searchlights and a glowing tail, and was close to the ground. They saw it for two or three minutes. Many of the witnesses were fighter pilots, but none had the slightest idea of what the object could be. According to a report in the CIA files, "it covered half the sky." The object has always been, and may forever be, unknown.[186]

Then, from November 9 through December 14, at least eight major UFO events occurred over the oilfields of Kuwait. At times, they appeared to have disrupted the operation of the equipment there. This received attention and generated reports from the Kuwaiti government, and not surprisingly, received attention from the U.S. Embassy and government.[187]

Perhaps most dramatic of all were two encounters on December 16 by the Chilean Air Force with a UFO utterly gargantuan in size. Early that afternoon, two pilots on a training mission, each flying an F-5 fighter aircraft, tracked the object on their airborne radar. It gave a return equal to ten or more aircraft carriers—except this object was in the air, not floating on the water. Each pilot assumed his radar equipment was faulty, until he learned that the other pilot was also getting the same return. Not only this, but ground radar from a nearby airport also picked up the object and confirmed its huge size. The pilots also saw the object with their own eyes. One pilot later said that at a distance of twenty miles, it looked "like a plantain banana swathed in smoke." The pilots were frightened, having no missiles or weapons.

---

185 A good summary of the case, an a copy of the transcript of Valentich's conversation with ground control, is in "Australian Pilot Frederick Valentich Disappears" www.ufocasebook.com/australianpilot.html].
186 Stevens, Wendelle and Dong, Paul, *UFOs Over Modern China*, UFO Photo Archives 1983, p. 119-120; Good, Timothy, *Above Top Secret: The Worldwide UFO Cover-Up*, 213-214.
187 U.S. Department of State Telegram, January 29, 1979, "'UFO' Sightings Cause Security Concern in Kuwait," From American Embassy Kuwait to Secretary of State, Washington, DC; *Kuwait Times*, Nov. 16, 18, 1978; *Arab Times*, Nov. 23, 25, 1978; "UFOs in Arab Nations," *MUFON UFO Journal*, Jan-Feb 1979; "UFOs Over Kuwait," *The APRO Bulletin*, Jan. 1979; Fawcett, Lawrence and Greenwood, Barry, *Clear Intent*, 90-91.

As they approached the massive object, which had been motionless all this while, it took off at an unimaginable speed. All at once, it vanished from the three radar screens.

Some hours later that evening, three more Chilean F-5s were sent to intercept a very large UFO. Whether this was the same object as earlier, or not, is not known. Two pilots saw it, describing it simply as very large and very bright. Several months later, the Chilean Air Force formally acknowledged the events of that day. Not surprisingly, no one could explain what had occurred. After all, what could be said?[188]

Thus, throughout 1978, it surely appears in retrospect that some sort of conflict, or at least confrontation, was occurring, very secretly, between the world's military forces and something far more advanced.

Enter the 1980s

During the 1980s, researchers sometimes commented on what seemed to be a slowdown in UFO sightings. Perhaps this was so for a few years during the middle of the decade, but UFO statistics are inherently spotty, if for no other reason than most people do not report them. This was especially true in the pre-Internet era. Still, there were excellent sightings throughout the decade, many of them quite dramatic.

1980 itself boasted several riveting military encounters with UFOs. We have the record of a tracking and attempted engagement of a UFO by the Austrian Air Force on May 7, 1980. The object was also seen by several commercial airliners. It was something extraordinary, whatever it was.[189]

Immediately after, on May 9 and May 10, the Peruvian Air Force had two successive encounters with an unknown object hovering just outside the airfield. Both times, the base commander ordered an SU-22 fighter bomber to intercept the object. This is an excellent aircraft, one of the best in the world at the time. During the first encounter,

---

188 Huneeus, J. Antonio, "A Chilean Overview," *MUFON UFO Journal*, 6/86; Huneeus, J. Antonio, "A Historical Survey of UFO Cases in Chile," *MUFON 1987 International Symposium Proceedings* (MUFON, 1987).
189 Hooper, Terry, "UFO Interceptions Attempted," *Flying Saucer Review*, v26, n4, 11/80; Gribble, Bob, "Looking Back," *MUFON UFO Journal*, 5/90.

Chapter 6: High Strangeness—UFOs from 1970 to 1990

the pilot fired a missile directly at the object. According to a declassified U.S. Defense report, the missile had no effect on the object. It apparently departed soon after that. On the second day, an SU-22 was again scrambled, but this time with orders not to fire on the object. Clearly, it made no sense to bother with obviously futile weapons, which were expensive and might serve only to annoy whatever this was.[190]

The Peruvian encounter is an incredible story, and yet it is supported by declassified U.S. military documentation. It deserves to be better known than it is. The next case, however, is very well known, deservedly so.

This concerns a series of events that took place in an area known as the Rendlesham Forest in late December, 1980. The action occurred between two military bases, one of which was RAF Woodbridge, the other RAF Bentwaters. For this reason it is often known as the Bentwaters case.[191]

It has been over three decades, and researchers are still learning new things about the Bentwaters case. That by itself is a rare thing. The incident received no publicity until 1983, when one of the airmen from the base, Larry Warren, alerted the media. Around the same time, researchers obtained a single page memo from the Deputy Base Commander, Colonel Charles Halt, succinctly (although somewhat inaccurately and incompletely) describing strange unidentified lights

---

190 Department of Defense Joint Chiefs of Staff Message Center, June 3, 1980. Title: UFO Sighted in Peru. Antonio Huneeus related the details of his interview with the Peruvian base commander to the author in April 2008.
191 The literature on this case is enormous. The major books are Butler, Brenda; Street, Dot; and Randles, Jenny, *Sky Crash: A Cosmic Conspiracy*, Grafton, 1986; Pope, Nick, *Open Skies, Closed Minds*, Pocket Books, 1997; Redfern, Nicholas, *A Covert Agenda: The British Government's UFO Top Secrets Exposed,* Simon & Schuster, 1997; Warren, Larry and Robbins, Peter, *Left At East Gate: A First-Hand Account of the Rendlesham Forest UFO Incident, Its Cover-up, and Investigation*, Marlowe & Company, 1997; Randles, Jenny, *UFO: Crash Landing? Friend or Foe? The True Story of the Rendlesham Forest Close Encounter,* Blandford Book, 1998; and Bruni, Georgina, *You Can't Tell the People: The Definitive Account of the Rendlesham Forest UFO Mystery*, Sidgwick & Jackson, Ltd, 2000. Among the many helpful websites, two are especially noteworthy: "The Rendlesham Forest Incident" at *ufoevidence.org*; "The Rendlesham Forest Incident" [rendlesham-incident.co.uk/rendlesham.php]. Primary documents associated with the case include Halt, Lt. Col. Charles I., USAF, Memorandum to Ministry of Defence, "SUBJECT: Unexplained Lights," January 13,1981; and British Ministry of Defence files on the Rendlesham Incident [www.mod.uk/DefenceInternet/FreedomOfInformation/PublicationScheme/SearchPublicationScheme/UnidentifiedFlyingObjectsufoRendleshamForestIncident1980.htm].

over and around the base.

On Christmas night, going into the early morning of December 26, airmen from the base investigated what initially appeared to be an aircraft that had gone down into the nearby woods. What they found instead was a landed or very low hovering craft. One of the men, Sergeant James Penniston, approached the craft and even touched it. He noticed strange markings or writing on it which he could not recognize. His companion, airman John Burroughs, was with him nearby. In the years that followed, both of these men struggled to regain all of their memories from that evening. An investigation of the site the next day found high levels of radiation, distinct impressions on the ground consistent with that of a landed craft, and other signs of evidence.

That was not the end of the Bentwaters case. On the night of December 27-28, security personnel saw lights floating in the sky above the forest. Ultimately, Colonel Halt, accompanied by a security team, went out to investigate personally. He had a cassette recording device with him, and he gave a running commentary throughout the evening. The recording and transcription are available online.[192] The men saw things they could not understand. Initially, they noticed an odd, intensely flashing, bright light in the forest. It is possible they had a close observation of a landed craft, although this has been disputed. They did see strange lights maneuvering in seemingly impossible ways. One of these lights shot down a beam of light which penetrated alternating layers of steel, earth, and concrete which housed a bunker containing nuclear weapons. (Which have yet officially to be acknowledged even to exist). In an off-the-record interview Halt gave some years later to Larry Warren and researcher Peter Robbins, he said that beam "adversely affected the ordinance."

According to Warren, there was also a third encounter. This has been disputed by Halt, Burroughs, and Penniston. It was, however, Warren's account that broke the story to begin with. Halt has always denied Warren was involved in the events, while Warren adamantly

---

192 Lt. Col. Charles Halt Rendlesham Audio Tape Dec 1980" at YouTube [www.youtube.com/watch?v=1eCmcmefTbM].

maintains that he was. Warren stated that he was part of a large group that went out with bright lights, Geiger counters, and other equipment, and came to within ten or fifteen feet of a landed UFO. He claimed that Base Commander, Colonel Gordon Williams, approached the craft and somehow communicated with the creatures or beings inside it. Warren said he could tell by their large heads and black eyes that they were not human beings. He claimed to have been subjected to a detailed debriefing during which mind control and memory erasure procedures were implemented. He later amended his statement to say the procedures had been done to his fellow airman, Adrian Bustinza, but that Bustinza was so traumatized by the event and unwilling to talk, that for years Warren told the world it had happened to him instead, simply to get the story out.

This case is fascinating for many reasons. It has a large number of witnesses and a declassified military document supporting it. Unfortunately, there has been confusion surrounding it from the beginning. Yet, the deeper one searches into the case, the more there is to find. This was a UFO encounter of great significance. Frustratingly, despite tremendous publicity and support from high-level officials, such as retired former British Admiral of the Fleet, Lord Hill Norton, the official statement from the British Ministry of Defence—without attempting to explain whatever had occurred—has been to brush off the matter as of "no defence significance." This is a position the MoD has taken to the present day: effectively a straightforward, straight-faced denial.

There are other fascinating events of that period which have received much less attention. One occurred near Huffman, Texas, just days after the Bentwaters events, and is known as the Cash-Landrum case, after the two women involved and the seven-year-old grandson of one of them. These three received radiation burns and poisoning from a bright, diamond-shaped object which happened to be accompanied by a large number of double-rotor Chinook-style helicopters. On that basis, one might think that the UFO would appear to have been one of "ours," but no agency has ever taken responsibility for the event. A lawsuit by Betty Cash, seeking damages for her burns and suffering, went nowhere.[193]

Another intriguing case took place less than two weeks after Bentwaters, in the French region known as Trans-en-Provence, on January 8, 1981. On this occasion, a small flying-saucer-type of object landed in a field belonging to a farmer. After it departed, ground impressions and other traces were observed and subject to detailed laboratory analysis.[194]

One of the more interesting photographs ever taken of a UFO dates from October 1981. Hannah McRoberts was vacationing with her family in British Columbia, when she decided to take a picture of a mountain. The image shows an absolutely perfect flying saucer nearby. Oddly—although, as it turns out, not unusually—no one saw it when she took the picture. The negative was subjected to detailed analysis by Dr. Richard Haines of NASA's Ames Research Center. Haines also interviewed the family. There was no evidence of hoaxing. The photo is real, and quite extraordinary.[195]

The Hudson Valley Sightings

During the early 1980s, a number of odd triangular craft were reported in Western Pennsylvania, mostly to researcher Stan Gordon. In fact, triangles had been reported sporadically in prior decades, particularly since the mid-1970s, but some fascinating cases going back much earlier.[196]

What happened in 1983, however, and for several years afterward, was a tremendous number of reports of triangular and boomerang-

---

[193] Schuessler, John, "Cash-Landrum Case, Investigation of Helicopter Activity," *MUFON UFO Journal*, 9/83; Baker, Dave, "MUFON's Schuessler Looks to the Future," *MUFON UFO Journal*, 1/00; Fawcett, Lawrence & Greenwood, Barry, *Clear Intent*, p. 106-108; Hall, Richard, *UFO Evidence, Volume 2*, p. 26, 226-229; Stancill, Nancy, "Women Seek Damages in UFO Sighting," *Houston Chronicle*, 1/21/84.
[194] Velasco, Jean-Jacques, "Report on the Analysis of Anomalous Physical Traces: the Trans-En-Provence 1981 UFO case," *Journal of Scientific Exploration*, Vol. 4, Number 1, 1990; Vallee, Jacques, "Return to Trans-en-Provence," by Jacques F. Vallee, *Journal of Scientific Exploration*, Vol. 4, Number 1, 1990; Berliner, Don, *UFO Briefing Document*, p. 112-120.
[195] Haines, Richard F., "Analysis of a UFO Photograph," *Journal of Scientific Exploration*, (Vol. 1, No.2) [www.scientificexploration.org/jse/abstracts/v1n2a3.html].
[196] Marler, David B. *Triangular UFOs: An Estimate of the Situation*, Richard Dolan Press, 2013.

Chapter 6: High Strangeness—UFOs from 1970 to 1990

Photo by Hannah McRoberts, October 1981. Object enlarged in inset.

shaped craft in the lower part of New York State, an area known as the Hudson Valley.[197] The sightings extended into Connecticut and northern New Jersey, as well. There are too many to recount here, but the month of March, 1983, deserves special attention. Whereas witnesses had reported large boomerang-shaped craft in January and February, what occurred on the night of March 17 went far beyond anything seen previously. On this evening, large numbers of people observed an extremely large boomerang-shaped object for thirty minutes. For much of that time, it hovered over Interstate Highway 84, but was also seen to make a right angle turn without banking. Motorists pulled over to see rows of multicolored lights along the sides of the object, as well as a bright light in the center. At one point, it bathed the area in very bright light. Local police stations received many calls; indeed, several police officers also reported the object.

Even at this early stage during the Hudson Valley flap, lies were spewing forth as a way of explaining (or more accurately *containing*) it. Police dispatchers, for instance, told frightened callers that they were seeing a type of experimental vehicle from nearby Stewart Air Force

---

[197] The best book on this subject remains Imbrogno, Philip J. Pratt, Bob, and Hynek, Dr. J. Allen. *Night Siege: The Hudson Valley UFO Sightings*. Second Edition Expanded & Revised. Llewellyn Publishing, 1998.

Base, a statement with no basis in fact. Moreover, to add to the confusion, the Sheriff's office later denied making such a statement.

Exactly one week later, on March 24, 1983, more people reported the same type of craft, behaving just as it had done before. Switchboards were jammed with reports of a large, boomerang-shaped UFO. It seems that there might have been two objects flying that night because witnesses fifteen miles apart simultaneously saw a low-flying object with red, blue, and green lights arranged in a boomerang pattern. The objects were silent. Astonished motorists pulled off the side of the Taconic Parkway, simply to gaze in awe. Several witnesses reported bright beams of white light coming from the underside of the craft shining down onto the cars.

So it was in the Hudson Valley for the rest of the spring, the rest of the year, and the next several years.

1984 was the peak year for sightings in that region. Once again, the month of March stands out. On the night of the 25th, off the Taconic Parkway near the town of Peekskill, drivers stopped their cars, stepped outside, and watched in amazement. Everyone saw the same thing: a slow moving, boomerang-shaped object with six intensely bright lights and a green light in the center. The lights moved like one object, even when making a sharp turn. The light was so bright that people had to shield their eyes. At least one witness, a professional photographer, discerned a dark structure connecting the lights, which he estimated to be at least three hundred feet long. Police were overwhelmed with calls that night.

It was like this all through the spring. On the night of June 14, a triangular or boomerang-shaped object entered the premises of the Indian Point Nuclear Facility. Several plant employees saw it, describing it as football-field-sized, with intensely bright lights along its sides. Despite high winds that night, it moved very smoothly and then departed.

That nuclear facility experienced another violation of its airspace on the night of July 24, 1984. At least a dozen plant workers and security personnel watched a boomerang pattern of lights approach. The

Chapter 6: High Strangeness—UFOs from 1970 to 1990

workers could plainly see that these were not disconnected lights, but a solid body of enormous size. In the words of one guard, it was about the size of three football fields. The enormous object moved toward the sole operational reactor at the plant, and then hovered directly over it. The guards stood, awestruck. Shortly before the order was given to activate National Guard helicopters, the object moved off and was gone. Guards were initially told to forget about the event, but received permission to speak to investigators shortly afterwards.

July 24, 1984, was an active night in the Hudson Valley. Nearby the Indian Point Nuclear Facility, another witness recorded video of a large object that has defied explanation ever since. It was studied by the Jet Propulsion Laboratory in Pasadena, whose analysts agreed the video was authentic, and that no one could explain the object.

Sightings like these continued in the Hudson Valley well into the 1980s. To this day, there has never been an adequate explanation of what these objects were. Occasionally, one hears attempts to explain them as illegal aviators flying ultralight aircraft in incredibly tight formation. While this is known to have happened on at least one occasion, this in no way explains the puzzling sightings of that period. In fact, it appears that those aviators flew with the express intention of causing confusion and providing a pretext to explain it all away. In the first place, they were never caught or arrested. Yet, they were expected to have been flying in such illegal and impossible formations for five years or more with impunity. Such an explanation has no merit.

Ultimately, however, what could the Federal Aviation Administration (FAA) or any other federal agency have said about these sightings? Any credence given to the reality of the situation could easily have caused panic. More seriously still, it could well have prompted a public investigation that would have led directly to the core of the UFO reality.

Around the World and in Space

The 1980s provided several good examples of UFOs recorded in space. Ronald Regehr, a former employee of the aerospace firm, Aerojet, accidentally, but legally, came into possession of an important database of the Defense Satellite Program, or DSP. This is a satellite made by Aerojet for military espionage purposes. The database was a list of objects known as *fastwalkers*, which were tracked by the DSP satellites. Fastwalkers, of course, is a term for space-based UFOs. The DSP database listed 283 fastwalkers recorded from the years 1973 to 1991, an average of more than one per month.[198]

One of the most amazing of these occurred on May 5, 1984. A UFO entered Earth's atmosphere from deep space, slowed down, turned, and returned to deep space. The observation lasted for nine minutes, and the object came to within a mere three kilometers of the satellite. A detailed investigation failed to explain what caused the sensor reading, other than a real object of some type. In fact, another deep space platform detected the same object optically, operated by a group that collaborated with Regehr's.

During the period of the Hudson Valley flap, there was another valley, elsewhere in the world, that also experienced recurring and baffling UFO sightings. But unlike the Hudson Valley, a densely populated suburb of New York City, this region—Norway's Hessdalen Valley—was remote and sparsely populated. The sightings began in 1982 and increased greatly in 1984. In fact, the Hessdalen sightings have continued sporadically to the present day. What makes them particularly interesting is that they had been subject to detailed tracking and recording by teams of dedicated scientists, braving the subzero temperatures for months at a time. The Hessdalen phenomenon has defied any simple explanation. It encompasses not simply mechanical craft, although some of the sightings appear consistent with that conclusion. Other sightings, however, appear to be the result of intelligent light phenomena. There have been trackings on radar and with other electronic means. The entire valley, roughly ten miles long, today has a population of 150 people; it was less during the 1980s. Loud noises can be heard for miles around. Something, however, has caused an unusual number of people to report these baffling phenom-

---

[198] Regehr, Ronald S., *How to Build a $125 Million UFO Detector*. Self Published by Ronald S. Regehr, 1998. p. 27-28, 84.

ena in the area.[199]

Throughout the 1980s, every region in the world at some point was the scene of an extraordinary encounter. One of these occurred in Brazil on May 19, 1986, in which an enormous portion of Brazilian airspace was the scene of UFO activity, including the scrambling of a large number of Brazilian jets to deal with the matter. This elicited a statement by the Brazilian military and government expressing its utter bafflement at what had just happened. In the words of the Brazilian Minister of Aeronautics, Brigadier General Otávio Moreira Lima:

> ... at least 20 objects were detected by Brazilian radars. They saturated the radars and interrupted traffic in the area. Each time that radar detected unidentified objects, fighters took off for intercept. Radar detects only solid metallic bodies and heavy (mass) clouds. There were no clouds nor conventional aircraft in the region. The sky was clear. Radar doesn't have optical illusions. We can only give technical explanations and we don't have them. It would be very difficult for us to talk about the hypothesis of an electronic war. It's very remote and it's not the case here in Brazil. It's fantastic. The signals on the radar were quite clear.[200]

Another took place over Alaska on November 18, 1986. This involved a commercial flight that was transporting expensive French wine from Japan to the U.S. For nearly thirty minutes, while flying over the Alaskan arctic, the crew tracked on radar, and saw with their own eyes, an enormous, gargantuan-sized object. Meanwhile, ground-based radar also recorded the event. At one point, in a manner similar to the Iranian case of 1976, the large object detached two smaller objects that remained directly in front of the airplane's cockpit. These objects maneuvered and danced about before returning to the mother craft.

---

199 Evans, Hilary, "Northern Lights," *MUFON UFO Journal*, 7/83; Stacy, Dennis, "Hessdalen: An Introduction," *MUFON UFO Journal*, 1/88; Havik, Leif, "Project Hessdalen," *MUFON UFO Journal*, 1/88. For up-to-date information on the Hessdalen phenomenon, see the Project Hessdalen website at www.hessdalen.org.
200 Department of Defense JCS Message Center, Subject: B6/BAF Has a Close Encounter of the First Kind. Date: 20 May 86. Subject: Numerous Unidentified Objects Were Cited in the Skies over Brazil. But BAF Fighters Were Unable to Intercept Them. Berliner, Don, *The UFO Briefing Document*, p. 121-127. Huneeus, J. Antonio, "UFO Alert in Brazil," *MUFON UFO Journal*, 11/86. Andrus, Walt, "UFOs Over Brazil," *MUFON UFO Journal*, 9/86. Smith, Dr. Willy, "The Brazilian Incident," *International UFO Reporter*, 7-8/86. Smith, Dr. Willy, "More on Brazilian OVNIs," *MUFON UFO Journal*, 9/86.

There was great pressure to keep this case out of the public eye, and then, once it became well-known, to disable it as something pedestrian. The pilot, Captain Kenju Terauchi, an ex-fighter pilot with more than 10,000 hours flight experience, reported the encounter and was promptly assigned to a desk job for several years. Philip J. Klass, on behalf of the Committee for the Scientific Investigation of Claims of the Paranormal (CSICOP), initially stated the UFOs were the planets Jupiter and Mars, despite the object being in a part of the sky opposite the position of these planets; despite, the two smaller objects having moved from positions one above the other to side by side. CSICOP later issued a second explanation that the UFO was light reflecting off of clouds of ice crystals, even though the sky was clear at the reported altitude of the UFO. These explanations, bogus though they were, received positive mainstream coverage. The FAA had no explanation for the visual sighting, but attributed the ground-based radar images to a "split radar return from the JAL Boeing 747." FAA official John Callahan later described how the CIA and other intelligence groups sought to confiscate all information pertaining to the case and to silence relevant personnel.[201]

U.S. defense records reported an interesting UFO sighting by the Ghana Air Force on July 27, 1987. This involved a large, silent object over southeastern Ghana and the Gulf of Guinea, shortly before midnight. Some people recorded the sound of explosions that seemed to be connected to the sighting, making us wonder if this was a military encounter. According to the U.S. Defense memo, a Ghana Air Force pilot was not flying, but standing on the ground near the city of Accra, when he saw the object. It was two or three times larger than a

---

201 Federal Aviation Administration (FAA), "Chronological Summary of the Alleged Aircraft Sightings by Japan Airlines Flight 1628," January 6, 1987. Andrus, Walter H., "Strange Alaskan Encounter," *MUFON UFO Journal*, February 1987. Maccabee, Bruce, "The Fantastic Flight of JAL 1628," *International UFO Reporter*, March-April 1987. "Extraterrestrial Object Involved in Japan Air Lines Pilot's UFO Sighting, According to Leading UFO Investigator," Committee for the Scientific Investigation of Claims of the Paranormal, January 22, 1987. "FAA Releases Documents on Reported UFO Sighting Last November," by Paul Steucke, Office of Public Affairs, Alaskan Region, Federal Aviation Administration (FAA), U.S. Department of Transport, March 5, 1987. Klass, Philip J., "FAA Data Sheds New Light on JAL Pilot's UFO Report," *The Skeptical Inquirer*, Summer, 1987. Greer, Steven, *Disclosure*, p. 79-93. *Filer's Files*, 6/19/02. For more resources, see "JAL Flight 1628 Over Alaska" [ufoevidence.org/topics/jalalaska.htm].

Boeing 747, he said, and shaped like a missile. The object dropped altitude, then gained altitude, then was replaced by small bluish lights arranged in a circular formation.[202]

Gulf Breeze

As the 1980s came to a close, sightings increased in many parts of the world. A few areas seemed to be hot spots, and the most prominent of these was near the town of Gulf Breeze, Florida, where sightings seemed to begin in November, 1987. A great deal has been written and said about Gulf Breeze, both pro and con. Most of the negative conclusions were directed at the town's most prominent witness, Ed Walters. Several times, Walters was accused of hoaxing his astonishingly vivid photographs, pictures which gained worldwide attention.

One of Ed Walters' photos from November 1987.

However, Walters was by no means the only witness of UFOs at Gulf Breeze. These numbered in the hundreds. Second, an apparent model of the UFO he had photographed was found in the attic of his former home. This was used to discredit him on the grounds that it supposedly proved that he was busy making UFO models as part of his hoaxing campaign. In fact, a study of the model proved the opposite.

---

202 U.S. Defense Department Information Report, August 20, 1987. From JCS; To AIG; Subject Unidentified Flying Object; Item Number 00427453.

The model was constructed with Walters' own discarded architectural plans. Crucially, these plans were dated *after* the time he moved out of that house. It is this date that proves the case. In other words, someone went trash-picking in front of Walters' new residence and acquired some of his discarded architectural papers. Then, they created a UFO model out of these papers, and then planted the model in the attic of his former home. There is certainly no reason in the world why Walters would do such a thing. At the time, he was regularly complaining of people fishing through his garbage. Clearly, someone or some group attempted to discredit him and gave the story immediate publicity.[203]

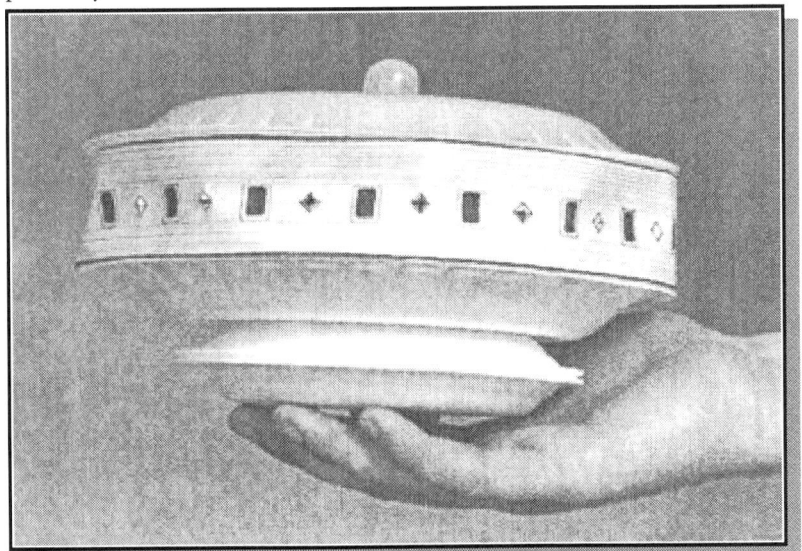

The so-called Gulf Breeze model. An analysis of the paper used to make it proves beyond a reasonable doubt that it was created solely to discredit Ed Walters.

That Ed Walters was a *repeater* seemed to cause a great deal of skepticism among many people. In other words, he had multiple encounters with these objects, and claimed to experience telepathic communication with the entities involved. For many researchers, this was simply too much to believe. Adding to the skepticism in some quarters was that Walters eventually published a book about his

---

[203] This scenario is analyzed in greater detail in Dolan, Richard M. *UFOs and the National Security State: The Cover-Up Exposed*, 1973-1991, pp. 513-516.

experiences, which sold rather well.

But when one analyzes the specific sightings, not merely those of Ed Walters but of the many other witnesses, the Gulf Breeze phenomenon becomes very compelling. The entire area is replete with military bases. It has often been speculated that that some of the UFOs people witnessed were military craft. Perhaps this is so, although that would need to account for the many cases of high strangeness. What remains evident, however, is that something very advanced and unusual was traversing the skies over Gulf Breeze, Florida.[204]

Area 51

While Gulf Breeze was heating up, so to speak, there was another region where unusual craft were being seen on a regular basis. This was Groom Dry Lake in Nevada, better known as Area 51, as well as the nearby Antelope Valley in the California desert. The entire region contained, and still contains, high-end military research and development projects. Based on the many sightings (to say nothing of the insider leaks discussed previously), it seems obvious that revolutionary technologies were being developed and tested there, possibly with an extraterrestrial boost. By the late 1980s, a number of people were aware of what was happening, and began to trek to these remote regions with cameras and video recorders.

This was when Bob Lazar's claims, discussed in the previous chapter, were being publicized. Instantly, Area 51 went from being one of the most secret places on Earth to one of the most notorious and sought-after. From 1989 until 1995, UFO hunters, aviation watchers, and curious tourists, most of them armed with cameras and binoculars, journeyed to "Freedom Ridge," where there happened to be a clear line of sight to the base. There were frequent sightings of highly unusual craft, often disc-shaped and moving in ways that were beyond ordinary aerodynamics. In April, 1995, the Air Force purchased the land around

---

204 Walters, Ed and Frances, *The Gulf Breeze Sightings, The Most Astounding Multiple Sightings of UFOs in U.S. History*, William Morrow, 1990. Booth, B.J., "The Gulf Breeze, Florida, UFOs" [www.ufocasebook.com/gulfbreeze.html] and [ufos.about.com/od/visualproofphotosvideo/p/gulfbreeze.htm]. Maccabee, Bruce, "The Scale Remains Unbalanced," *MUFON UFO Journal*, 4/89.

Freedom Ridge, effectively ending an era. After that, there remained the more distant Tikaboo Peak, offering a clear view of the base for those bringing a telescope.

One important UFO video from Groom Lake came not from the observers at Freedom Ridge, but from inside the base. In early 1995, a video was leaked to the television show *Hard Copy*. It was later determined to have been recorded by an Air Force surveillance camera in November, 1994, somewhere within the Nellis Test Range, which includes Area 51 at Groom Lake. The object bears more than a passing resemblance to the so-called Alien Reproduction Vehicle (ARV), discussed in the previous chapter. Moreover, its movements were truly radical. It accelerated rapidly from speeds as low as 30 mph to over 500 mph, and made right angle turns at roughly 140 mph. The video is authentic. We can assume it is one of *ours*. If so, then the clandestine military-industrial complex developed extremely advanced technology two decades ago, which has still not been officially recognized to this day. Unless, of course, it is one of *theirs*.[205]

Soviet UFOs

Not only were UFO reporting systems wildly uneven during this period, but there were entire regions that were essentially cut off from elsewhere. Most notably, this was so in the Communist nations of China and the Soviet Union. Certainly these and other relatively closed societies had their share of UFO sightings, but reports only seeped out sporadically. Then came the late 1980s: Gorbachev and *glasnost*. It is an interesting fact that as the Soviet Union spiraled into disunity and oblivion during the final years of the 1980s, until the end of 1991, UFO reports increased dramatically. Certainly, most or even all of this can be accounted for by the new period of openness in that nation. But it is worth wondering if the rise in reports had any relationship to the demise of the Soviet Union itself.

Many of these have probably been lost to us, but a good number did become available. One of the most interesting Soviet UFO events of

---

205 Powell, Martin. "The Nellis UFO Video" [www.aenigmatis.com/nellis-ufo-video/part-one/nellis-1.htm].

the 1980s is the Dalnegorsk case, sometimes referred to as the Soviet Roswell. Dalnegorsk was a mining town in the eastern Soviet Union. On January 29, 1986, only eighteen hours after the explosion of the U.S. space shuttle, *Challenger*, local people saw a reddish orange sphere flying at a low altitude. It moved on a level flight path and was absolutely silent. It was fairly low in the sky, probably not higher than 2,500 feet altitude, and was very slow moving, with estimates of roughly 30 mph (slower than the stall speeds of most aircraft). The object approached a low mountain near the town and apparently slowed down. Some witnesses claim to have seen it raise and lower itself several times. Each time it rose, the light became brighter; each time it descended, the light dimmed. Then, suddenly, it dropped like a stone.

A Soviet scientific team arrived days later. Researchers today are divided as to whether the object was a Russian military probe or something extraterrestrial. A few have argued that it was some sort of natural event, perhaps an electromagnetic phenomenon caused by anomalous stresses within the Earth's crust. This seems least likely. The analysis of the investigation team made a case for the object being of artificial origin. An answer to what crashed there may be very long in coming.[206]

As the 1990s approached, more interesting Soviet UFO cases came along. One of these, albeit in partial and truncated form, comes from the files of the Soviet state security agency, the *KGB*. It contains first-hand testimony from soldiers describing an incident near Kasputin Yar, a major rocket launch facility in the southeastern Soviet Union, on July 28-29th, 1989. The area is equivalent to America's White Sands Proving Ground, and indeed it was there in 1947 that the Soviets launched their own captured German V2 rockets.

Near midnight, according to the file, a disc-shaped object flew silently toward the area, flashing intensely bright lights from beneath it. It hovered over the weapons site less than one hundred feet above

---

206 Huneeus, Antonio, *Foreign News Tribune*, New York, NY, June 14, 1990. Stonehill, Paul & Mantle, Philip, *The Soviet UFO Files*, p. 92-95; Vallee, Jacques, *Soviet UFOs*, p. 103, 128. See also ufoarea.bravepages.com/crashes_1986_siberia.html.

the ground. It was approximately fifteen feet in diameter, and was illuminated with a dim, green, phosphorus-like color. A bright beam appeared from beneath it, and the object circled a few times, moved away, then returned. The KGB documents indicate that an order was given to scramble fighter jets to intercept the object, but the object never allowed the aircraft to come close to it. After ninety minutes or so, it flew away. The case has several corroborating witnesses to it, and reads like so many American cases.[207]

Explaining cases such as these as secret classified technology is problematic. Could this really have been a secret American flying saucer, spying on the Soviets? Or, did the Soviets have their own secret program that spied on their own facilities? Or, was there—*is there*—an off-the-grid society that was spying on both of them, and everyone else?

Another fascinating and controversial case occurred in the Soviet city of Voronezh, on September 27, 1989. It involved a landed craft, a tall, bizarre-looking entity, and a public park filled with children and a few adults. There were many witnesses, much testimony, and much ridicule in the Western press. To this day, the case is something of damaged goods, in large part because of the sensational nature of the encounter, and the supposed unreliability of Russian witnesses, at least in the opinion of Western journalists. Yet, the case retains its defenders to this day.[208]

An event much harder to dispute took place near Moscow on March 21, 1990. That night, in the hours before midnight, a number of unknown objects were seen over a wide area. Many residents contacted authorities, all describing what they saw in highly unconventional

---

207 KGB file "Communications on Observation of Anomalous Event in the District of Kasputin Yar (July 28, 1989); English translation by Dimitri Ossipov; cited in Berliner, Don, *UFO Briefing Document*, 1995, p. 134.
208 "Aliens Visit Voronezh," *Moscow News (Tass)*, Oct. 11, 1989. Vallee, Jacques, *UFO Chronicles of the Soviet Union*, p. 40-61. Stonehill, Paul & Mantle, Philip, *Soviet UFO Files*, p. 98-99. "Soviets' close encounter leaves experts skeptical," *Republican*, Waterbury, CT, 10/10/89. Jacobson, David, "Space aliens look foreign to skeptics," *Hartford Courant*, 10/11/89. "A thought provoking conversation with alien beings described," Reuters, 10/13/89. Mott, Patrick, "Galactic Glasnost," *Los Angeles Times*, 10/26/89. Mitchell, Alison, "Bizarre tales: glasnost or psychosis?" *Newsday*, 10/29/89. Shiflett, Dave, "Invasion of the Mind-Snatchers, *Wall Street Journal*, 10/30/89.

Chapter 6: High Strangeness—UFOs from 1970 to 1990

terms.

Two Soviet interceptors were dispatched. As one pilot closed in on the unknown, he saw two white flashing lights on the UFO while tracking it on his airborne radar. He ordered the target to identify itself, whereupon it changed its speed and altitude. The pilot turned and reapproached the UFO, passing it very closely this time. This time, in addition to seeing the flashing lights, the pilot briefly saw a silhouette of the object. Still, however, he could not identify it.

Ground-based personnel saw the encounter. They noticed that the UFO seemed to disappear as the aircraft approached it. They also saw it turn and approach the jet at a very high speed. It would disappear, then reappear behind and above the jet. One of the military witnesses said it maneuvered in an S-turn flight, both horizontally and vertically. Another said it looked just like a flying saucer.

The case received comment by the Soviet Minister of Defense, Ivan Tretyak, as well as the Chief of the Soviet Air Defense Forces, General Igor Maltsev. Maltsev stated there were over one hundred visual observations of the object made by military personnel, and that two photographs were taken, which have never been released. He confirmed the extraordinary capabilities of the object, including a speed that exceeded modern jet fighters by two or three times, all the while moving silently. Maltsev added that whoever was operating these craft "had somehow come to terms with gravity." He refused to speculate on the identity of the object, but added "at the present time, terrestrial machines could hardly have any such capabilities." A truly remarkable admission coming from such a high-level figure.[209]

Whatever it was, clearly this was an object that had no problem easily outperforming a Soviet military jet.

---

209 CIA Foreign Press Report: Concatenated PROD Reports, 1988-1994; Headline: USSR: UFO Sightings No. 2 – General Maltsev Comments. Report Number: FB PN 90-123. CIA document collection. Subject: UFOs reported near Moscow, April 15, 1990. "UFOs on Air Defense Radars," *Rabochaya Tribuna*, Moscow, 4/19/90; English translation by the U.S. Foreign Broadcast Information Service (FBIS). See also "Soviet Air Defenses Baffled by Huge UFOs," *MUFON UFO Journal*, 6/90. Musinsky, V. D.,"Through the Secrecy Barrier," *International UFO Reporter*, July/August 1990. Ilyin, Vadim K., "KGB's 'Blue Folder' Reveals Shootings, Landings in USSR" [www.mufon.com/znews_kgb.html]. Vallee, Jacques, *UFO Chronicles of the Soviet Union*, p. 139. Berliner, Don, *UFO Briefing Document*, p. 138. Stonehill, Paul and Mantle, Philip, *The Soviet UFO Files*, p. 50-51.

Triangles over Belgium

Through the winter of 1989 and into 1990, the nation of Belgium experienced a significant wave of UFO activity. Many of the sightings were of triangular craft, but which otherwise acted very much like traditional disc-shaped flying saucers. That is, silent maneuvering, extended loitering and low-hovering capability, and instant acceleration. Many of those reports were well-attested to, including quite a few by police officers.

The most dramatic night of this wave of sightings occurred on the night of March 30 into the 31st, 1990, only a week and a half after the Moscow sighting. A policeman contacted a NATO radar station, reporting three unusual lights forming an equilateral triangle, something which other police patrols soon confirmed. NATO radar then confirmed an unknown target moving at a very slow speed. For the next two and a half hours, a number of police officers and civilians noticed up to three sets of triangular lights, much larger in appearance than stars, often accelerating and maneuvering in unusual ways. At certain times, when the lights came down low enough, some witnesses were certain the lights were attached to a huge triangular craft.

NATO Air Defense scrambled two F-16 jets. Both jets quickly tracked unknown objects on their radar, but each time they approached one of the objects, the radar lock was broken and the object took evasive action. Ground witnesses confirmed that the lights of the UFO went out every time the F-16s approached (reminiscent of the events over Malmstrom AFB in 1975). According to a statement by the Royal Belgian Air Force, the speed of one UFO changed immediately from 150 knots to 970 knots (roughly speaking, miles per hour) and dropped its altitude from 9,000 feet to 5,000 feet—nearly one mile—in one or two seconds, a simply astonishing maneuver. For several hours, the unknown objects seemed to be toying with the interceptors.

Because the stealth fighter and stealth bomber had recently been revealed by the U.S., and because both of them had unusually angular designs for aircraft of the time, there was some speculation that people had seen some new version of stealth technology. However, this is not tenable. Neither of those aircraft, nor any other known craft, possess the maneuvering capabilities of the objects seen over Belgium (and northern Germany) that night. They remain unknown. If they are part of a clandestine but wholly terrestrial program, it still begs an array of questions: What agency was responsible? Why engage in such maneuvers? What would be the purpose or mission of these exercises? Why have such aircraft not been acknowledged for the past two decades? Why is there nothing to this day, officially speaking, that can duplicate their maneuvers?[210]

It may well be that the events over Belgium were somehow related to the events near Moscow from just over a week earlier. Today, more than twenty years later, there has been no confirmation from any agency regarding what might have caused the Belgian sightings. It is evident, however, that these UFOs did not require jet fuel to carry out their incredible aerial performance. Of course, that applies to all the UFOs covered in this book. Such performance, clearly points to another source of power, a new technology altogether. More on this later.

Summary

If one thing is glaringly obvious, it is that the UFO phenomenon is global and has included many military encounters.

The question must be asked: if UFOs are the product of a clandestine technology, something unrelated to extraterrestrials or some form of being we can describe as "other," then what agency has been responsible? Does it belong to any of the world's governments? Where is the scientific and technological infrastructure responsible for it? Are we dealing with the effects of what I have elsewhere described as a Breakaway Civilization?

---

210 Memo, "SUBJ; IIR6 807 0136 90 Belgium and the UFO Issue," Joint Chiefs of Staff, Washington, DC, 1990. For good summaries of the Belgian Triangle case, see Pratt, Bob, "The Belgium UFO Flap," *MUFON UFO Journal*, 7/90. "Remarkable military encounter in Belgium," *International UFO Reporter*, July/August 1990. de Brosses, Marie-Therese, "F-16 Radar Tracks UFO" translated by Robert Durant, *MUFON UFO Journal*, 8/90. Berliner, Don, *UFO Briefing Document*, p. 139-144. Lambrechts, Major P., "Report Concerning the Observation of UFOs During the Night of March 30-31, 1990," preliminary report dated May 31, 1990. De Brouwer, W., Preface, *Vague d'OVNI sur la Belgique - Un Dossier Exceptionnel*, Brussels: SOBEPS, 1991.

To answer this question, we must, unfortunately, speculate rather than rely on confirmed knowledge. Nevertheless, the strongest answer continues to appear that the core of the truly extraordinary UFO sightings of the period just discussed are indeed *not us*. Whether extraterrestrial or not, they do not appear to be from our civilization. This seems especially so when we explore, as we shall in the next several chapters, some of the experiences and sightings that included claims of encounters with non-human beings.

Even so, the 1980s generated enough evidence, some of which was admittedly anecdotal, indicating that the clandestine human infrastructure was developing capabilities that might begin to approximate "true" UFO characteristics. In particular, the sightings of objects near Area 51 during the late 1980s give us reason for thinking this.

But could clandestine human technology have been behind all of the truly difficult UFO sightings of the 1970s and 1980s? The aerial activity over the various nations of the world: the U.S., Soviet Union, Brazil, China, Africa, the Middle East, and elsewhere indicate that something extraordinary was going on. Something of global reach, with technology vastly beyond anything officially on the books.

Considering that the UFO phenomenon presents evidence of such advanced technology, able to outclass the world's best militaries with utter ease, it is not difficult to see why there would be secrecy enveloping the entire subject.

Chapter 7
UFOs, 1991 to the Present

Since the 1990s, perhaps the most striking feature of the UFO phenomenon has been the sheer number of incredible, inexplicable, and just plain *impossible* sightings. Doing justice to all of those which are good and genuine would fill several thick volumes. What follows here, of necessity, can convey only the essence of this explosion of activity.

There are several major repositories of UFO reports, but it has been decades since any researcher has collected and published anything that could remotely be considered a complete list for any given year. Conservatively speaking, there are no less than 10,000 UFO reports generated every year in North America alone, judging only from the top two websites that collect them.[211] Even after accounting for some probable duplication of reports, it is obvious that UFO sightings are not merely a daily, or even more often occurrence, but are plentiful and widespread.

Of course, readers should remember that ninety percent or more of all UFO sightings are explainable in more-or-less prosaic terms. However, it is also true that most people do not report their UFO sightings, and very possibly this is by a factor of ten or more.[212] In other words, there is a good chance that these two factors roughly even out.

To consider that there may well be something like 10,000 genuine UFO sightings each year, simply in one region of the world, forces us

---

211 The National UFO Reporting Center [nuforc.com] and the Mutual UFO Network [mufon.com].
212 This is my own experience based on hundreds of UFO witness interviews, and seems to be consistent with other researchers who have published or otherwise shared their research in this area with me.

to take a fresh perspective on the nature of our society, our world, and our reality. It means that there may be, on average, twenty-five to thirty genuine sightings *each day* of what we may reasonably describe as non-human technology. This seems extraordinary, and it is. Nevertheless, this is still a tiny number compared to the amount of conventional traffic traversing North American air space.[213] While UFOs are fairly widespread, their observable activity is still dwarfed by the non-stop buzz of human civilization. Yet, they are most definitely *out there*.

The Beginning of the Video Era

UFOs have been recorded on film since the 1950s. Many of these appear to have been hoaxes, although some appear to be legitimate and mystifying. It was not until the end of the 1980s, and particularly the 1990s, that the era of the portable camcorder arrived. Suddenly, a great many bizarre aerial objects were being captured on video.

One of the first great examples of this new development was during a mass sighting of UFOs over Mexico City on July 11, 1991. Because a total solar eclipse was taking place, many people had their video cameras ready and pointed toward the sky. This was no ordinary eclipse. In the first place, it was a "monster eclipse," lasting over six and a half minutes of totality at the maximum (the theoretical maximum of an eclipse is just over seven minutes, and most last less than two minutes). Moreover, there was a great build-up to this one, as many people claimed it was predicted by ancient Mayan prophecy, and that it was going to herald major Earth changes and greater cosmic awareness. These changes were believed to stem from an encounter with the "Masters of the Stars," which would occur during the eclipse.[214]

Within the context of such a build-up, Mexicans witnessed a striking aerial display. Several bright objects, all of which looked solid, even metallic, were seen by thousands. One in particular looked very

---

213 About 1/1000th of that number. There are over 25,000 commercial and military flights in the skies above the USA each day. See flightaware.com.
214 Maussan, Jaime, Elders, Britt, Elders, Lee. *Masters of the Stars* (Video), 1994.

much like a silver disc. They appeared to reflect light and seemed to move intelligently across the sky. Digital enhancements revealed them to be shaped somewhat like a hockey puck, nothing like a star or planet. The clincher for most students of the videos was how the objects moved in front of passing clouds. Whatever they were, they were nothing conventional.

Object video-recorded over Mexico City, July 11, 1991.

Interpreting this amazing display is another matter. Believing whether or not this was a sign from the Masters of the Stars will hinge upon assumptions that may forever be unprovable. However, Mexico has been the scene of a large number of UFO sightings in subsequent years, many of which were videotaped.

Another interesting piece of video evidence of UFOs was recorded on August 23, 1995, near Gulf Breeze, Florida. This area had been well known for UFO sightings since the late 1980s. However, whereas most of the photos from Gulf Breeze had been associated with Ed Walters and had come under dispute (although, in the opinion of many analysts, without justice), this video was shot by a man named Mike Hawkins. Strikingly, it showed an object that looked identical to those photographed previously by Walters. The video is compelling and lacks any reasonable conventional explanation.[215] Instead, it provides good corroboration to the Gulf Breeze UFOs of the previous eight years. As time passes, it seems increasingly clear that the attacks on Ed Walters were motivated to destroy his credibility and hence the entire wave of sightings themselves. In other words, the Gulf Breeze UFOs of the 1980s and 1990s were real.

Photographic evidence, naturally, will never be as strong as video recordings in supporting the existence of UFOs. This is especially so regarding images that are submitted anonymously. Still, a few are worth consideration. On September 16, 1996, six photos were taken in the town of Valley, Alabama, then sent to a local radio station and newspaper. The photographer claimed he was repairing a fence on his property when his dog began barking loudly. He noticed a low-flying object, shaped like a capsule, looking as though it belonged in the U.S. space program of the 1960s. It hovered and then moved slowly over one of his cow pastures. What makes the six photographs so interesting is that each one captured the object at a different angle and elevation, making a hoax a much more challenging proposition. Intriguing though the photos are, their anonymity ultimately prevents them from being considered stronger evidence.[216]

Just a month later, on October 27, 1996, a very interesting snapshot was taken in Hungary. The photographer, Lajos Kosina, took a picture of his girlfriend in front of a field. Upon having the photograph developed a few weeks later (this was before digital photography became common), he was surprised to see a disc-shaped object clearly in the sky behind her. This type of thing has happened quite frequently. But this is surely one of the best cases of a UFO being photographed without being seen at time. The photograph, in particular the negative, has been studied using optical and computer techniques. According to those analyses the object in the sky is not the result of a film fault, nor is it a small model suspended on a wire. It appears to be a genuine, flat, disc-shaped object reflecting the autumn

---

215 YouTube video at www.youtube.com/watch?v=FRDoZHr4GLk.
216 "Valley, Alabama, USA, UFO Photograph Taken, 1996" at www.ufocasebook.com/valleyalabama1996.html.

Chapter 7: UFOs, 1991 to the Present

UFO in Hungary, October 27, 1996. Enlarged object in inset.

sunshine—a flying saucer.[217]

Another interesting video was shot on July 4, 1998, in Somerset England, by man named Rod Dickinson. Unfortunately, there is a great deal of camera shake in the video, making it difficult to follow the object, or even to see it clearly at times. However, a detailed analysis by a Hollywood movie professional concluded that the shake provided good evidence for the video's authenticity. In other words, the specifics of the camera shake made fakery more difficult. The witness certainly seemed sincere to all those who interviewed him. Incidentally, on the frames of the video where it can be seen clearly, the object looks like a classic flying saucer.[218]

UFOs that Weren't

Despite some fascinating video and photographic evidence of UFOs, it is good to remember that not only are most of these things not alien craft, but there have been several cases that have gained acceptance among some researchers which are probably not legitimate. Consider the following cases to be cautionary tales, lessons in how we can be

---

217 "October 27, 1996: Erpatak, Szabolcs-Szatmar, Hungary" [www.ufoevidence.org/photographs/section/topphotos/photo315.htm.
218 See the video and analysis at YouTube www.youtube.com/watch?v=WQRMFQ80Y9g.

fooled.

One is a photograph from July 17, 1992 which aired later on Chilean television. It was taken from a Chilean satellite, about 400 kilometers (250 miles) above the Earth's surface. The image shows something that appears to be either an enormous UFO, or something very close to the camera. In fact, it is almost certainly the Moon. There are elements of this image that we still don't fully understand, but the camera from that satellite requires eighteen minutes to take a picture of the Earth. During this time, it is still in motion, as is the Moon, giving ample opportunity for distortions to occur. More than once has the Moon been mistaken for a UFO.[219]

UFO? No, the Moon. The Chilean satellite image of 1992.

Another prosaic case which is widely discussed as a genuine UFO event occurred on February 2, 1993. That evening, several people in Jefferson County, Kentucky, reported a UFO. There was indeed an object in the sky and a police helicopter even had an encounter with it. At times the object looked like a huge ball of fire, larger than the helicopter. It changed its brightness erratically, and made what the officers perceived as ramming attacks. The policemen, who were unquestionably honest and reliable, were convinced it was a genuine

---

[219] A very good discussion of this can be found on the website Above Top Secret [www.abovetopsecret.com/forum/thread756602/pg1]. For a discussion on the camera capabilities of this satellite, see https://wikispaces.psu.edu/display/RemSens597K/V.

UFO. The case later received television coverage and has been considered a strong case by some researchers. Yet, the object was certainly a lighted balloon, described in detail shortly afterwards by the man who had lit it and sent it aloft. He had not considered that his balloon would be reported as a UFO, he said. The case is instructive, showing that ordinary objects can be interpreted by intelligent people to be something other than what they really are. We always have to be careful.[220]

The last example, for now, of well-known UFO evidence that appears questionable is a series of photographs from 1993, taken at Australia's Maslin Beach. These photos, which show a UFO over a body of water have a detailed story accompanying them, at least according to the person who submitted them. A close analysis, however, reveals strong evidence that these images are hoaxes: models that were most likely suspended in front of the camera. The windows are the best giveaway, clearly looking as though they had been cut out of cardboard.[221]

Not all prosaic explanations of UFOs are the result of hoaxes. Most are simply misinterpretations by honest people of something that surprised them. However, even accounting for cases of mistaken identity, a review of the last two decades makes it evident that there is an abundance of truly mystifying cases.

The Tether Incident

Of all videos that are accepted in some circles as genuine UFO evidence, but which probably are not, perhaps the best known was from NASA's STS-75 mission, more widely known as the Tether Incident. This occurred in late February, 1996, during a mission to carry and deploy a Tethered Satellite System into orbit at around 200 miles, within the Earth's ionosphere. The purpose of this, among other things, was to demonstrate electrical power generation. The tether was

---

220 Nickel, Joe, "Flying Saucer 'Dogfight'" [www.hope144.com/flying-saucer-dogfight/]. See also Rutherford, Glenn O. "Kentucky Chopper Case," *MUFON UFO Journal* 6/93 [www.slideshare.net/mufonnexus/mufon-ufo-journal-1993-6-june].
221 A good discussion of this is available on the website Above Top Secret [www.abovetopsecret.com/forum/thread334493/pg1].

UFOs for the 21st Century Mind

12.9 miles long and nearly all of it was deployed when it broke while in orbit on February 25, 1996.

A few days later, NASA recorded what looked like a veritable armada of objects moving and maneuvering around the tether. This has been the subject of engaging debate ever since. NASA has maintained that the cameras recorded debris from a recent water dump. Others have argued that the debris in the video appears to go behind the tether, which would clearly be too far away for a water dump. In addition, the video shows so many of these objects, all appearing as pulsing, circular discs, often with a hole in the center, and what appears to be a notch cut out of the edge. Certainly, the fact that they appear to go behind the tether is suggestive that they are real. At the time of the recording the tether was approximately one hundred miles away from the camera. At that distance, any visible object behind the tether would have to be enormous.

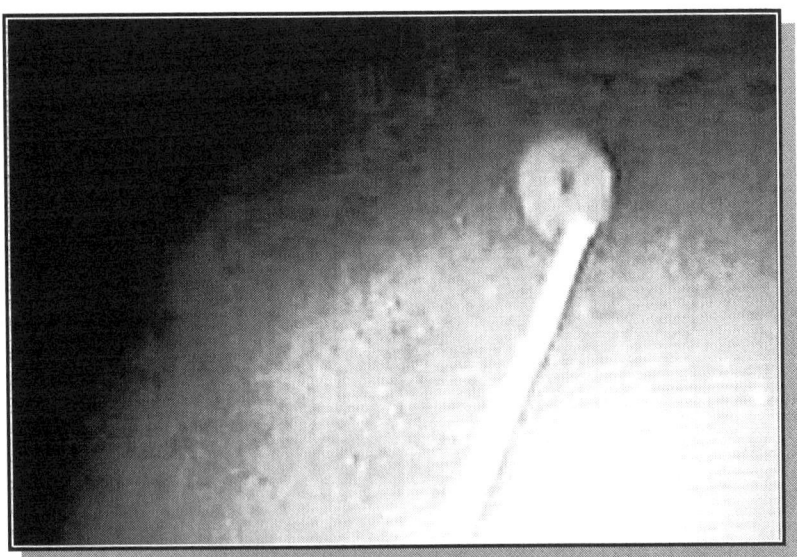

The broken NASA tether, seemingly in front of an enormous object in Earth orbit. In reality, this is an optical illusion.

This would be true, *if* the objects actually were behind the tether. In fact, the video shows a number of optical illusions. Fundamentally, the objects that appear in this video look nothing like they actually were, primarily because of effects caused by the camera's electronics, lens and sunlight.

First among these is the thickness of the tether itself. The video shows a long, illuminated tether floating away in space, which looks fairly thick to the eye. In reality, the tether was less than one centimeter thick. It looks thick in the video because of the intense reflectivity from the sunlight. The reflectivity is strong enough that a small ice particle could pass in front of the tether, but the tether's brightness would make it seem that the object is moving behind. This can easily be duplicated with any ordinary digital camera by taking a picture of the full moon behind bare tree branches. The moonlight will often appear to wash through the branches, making it seem that the entire tree is behind the Moon.

This is the basic effect one sees regarding the STS-75 video. After all, if these were truly enormous objects moving behind the tether, they would have seemed as bright as the Moon itself down on Earth's surface. This was not an event in deep space, but in the Earth's ionosphere. Yet they were never noticed, unlike the tether itself, which was noticeable for some time before it fell from orbit.

Complicating the analysis, some of the objects (or, more accurately, particles) appear to change speeds and directions. However there are a number of things that might have accounted for this, including collisions with other particles that happened not to be visible to the camera. Moreover, the particles in the video look very much like the so-called "orbs" that many people have captured on their digital cameras. Although there are those who believe such orbs are actual anomalies, even entities of some sort, it seems more likely that Occam's razor cuts differently. It is much more reasonable that the so-called photographic orbs are caused by reflection of light on dust particles, but recorded by digital technology in a way that film-based photography usually did not. Hence their proliferation in the age of digital photography.[222]

Incidentally, the objects in the tether incident look very much like an object captured on video by a British woman named Sharon

---

[222] Oberg, James, "STS-75 Shuttle 'Tether' Video Analysis" [www.rense.com/general/stsd.htm].

Rowlands in 2000. With her brand new camcorder she recorded a distant bright object that, upon zooming in, showed the exact look and texture of light seen in the objects on the tether video, as well as of standard digital photographic orbs. While one person called her video one of the top five UFO videos of all time, it is more likely the result of an optical effect. It may never be known what the source of the effect was, but the movement of the object was not unusual. Generally, it appeared to hover motionlessly, although there were times when it seemed as though it was maneuvering. What Sharon Rowlands recorded remains unknown, but the fact that her object looked precisely like the objects in the tether incident ought to provide a hint that they are the result of the same effect inside the digital camera.[223]

Although the tether incident is not good evidence of space-based anomalies, there are other cases that offer credible evidence. Some of these were published on the website of the late Jeff Challender, who assiduously recorded NASA's many shuttle mission videos and found many oddities. One that is especially intriguing is the example of a U-turn in space by an unknown *something* during the mission of STS-114, on August 6, 2005. Even more intriguing was a motion stabilizing enhancement of the object, when it became obvious that the object was maneuvering to the left and right as it moved through space. This is a truly remarkable video.[224]

Photographic and video evidence is important in the overall case for UFOs, but such evidence is not infallible. Researchers must evaluate it carefully. Indeed, this includes all types of instrument-recorded evidence. We must remember that instruments can make mistakes, can cause illusory effects, and can sometimes fool even the best and most sober of investigators.

Terror in the Air

Still, only fools ignore all evidence, and that includes the evidence

---

223 Sharon Rowland's UFO video can be seen at YouTube [www.youtube.com/watch?v=Hvl8wF9vpcI].
224 A mirror of Jeff Challender's website is available at rdolan.hostcentric.com/projectprove/index-2.html.

acquired by our own eyes. Some of the cases that follow ought to produce a chill inside any reasonable human being who spends any time in aircraft. That is because recent history has produced a number of close encounters with UFOs by aircraft, including a few that were *very* close. There appears to be a great deal of unaccounted-for activity in our skies.

On the night of April 21, 1991, for instance, a London-bound airliner flying at 22,000 feet over the coast of Kent came to within 1,000 feet of an unknown object. The incident was classed as a *near-miss*, and an official inquiry was launched by the British Civilian Aviation Authority (CAA). The official conclusion: "Extensive inquiries have failed to provide any indication of what the sighting may have been." The report did note the pilot's observation of the object, which was, "light brown, round, three meters long," and with no clear means of propulsion. While no other aircraft was supposed to have been near the airliner, the report stated that, "a faint radar trace was observed ten nautical miles behind the ... aircraft.[225]"

There are quite a few of these cases. Another occurred on June 1, 1991, when a yellow-orange, cylindrical object, ten feet long, was seen at close quarters by the crew of a Britannia Airways Boeing 737 en route from Dublin to London. Just over two weeks after that, yet another cylindrical-shaped UFO was seen, this time by a German engineer aboard a flight headed toward Hamburg, Germany.[226]

Air France had a dramatic aerial encounter on January 28, 1994. While flying over the Paris region, the crew noticed a large brown-red disc hovering on the horizon. It seemed constantly to be changing its shape. In the words of the pilot:

> This object seemed to us then absolutely abnormal by its size which seemed immense, its dark red color and of the fuzzy edges. I had the impression to observe a gigantic lens in evolution. It did not resemble anything we had seen in our flying careers.[227]

---

225 Filer, George. "UK's Civilain Aviation Files Document 30 UFO-Jetliner Near Misses" [rense.com/general11/UKs.htm].
226 ibid.
227 "Air France Flight 3532 sighting of brown-red disk-shaped object" [ufoevidence.org/cases/case1062.htm].

Another near-miss was reported by pilots of a British airliner on January 6, 1995. Captain Roger Wills and copilot Mark Stuart were beginning their descent towards Manchester Airport in a Boeing 737 with sixty passengers on board. Seventeen minutes before touchdown, a mysterious, triangular-shaped UFO flashed past the right-hand side of the aircraft at a distance described as being "very close." So close, in fact, that the crew instinctively "ducked" in their seats. Their conversation with air traffic control is on record. The encounter certainly disturbed the pilots.[228]

Later in 1995, on May 25, over the Texas panhandle, a cigar-shaped object with a row of brightly flashing lights along its length was seen by the crew of an America West airliner. The case was thoroughly investigated by the astronomer and experienced UFO researcher, Walter Webb, on behalf of the UFO Research Coalition.[229]

Again in 1995, this time on July 11, a wingless object was seen near a Norwegian plane. This was a Dash-8 passenger plane that had taken off from Oslo and was about forty miles north of Trondheim. The co-pilot caught sight of a flying object that moved to the right of the aircraft.[230]

On Feb. 28, 1996, the pilots of two airliners near Cleveland reported a very bright pulsating light below them. One pilot dropped his altitude to make certain that the lights were not ground-based. They were not, as he was then able to see them above his position. Ground control suggested the light might be a reflection in the clouds from another aircraft, but the pilots of both aircraft were adamant that the light had a distinct source of its own. A passenger on one of the flights is known to have taken photographs, but none have been publicly released. A detailed transcript of the encounter is available on the web.[231]

There are so many of these encounters. Another one occurred on

---

228 "UFO / Airplane Near Miss, Manchester Airport, UK 1995" [www.ufocasebook.com/manchester1995.html].
229 "America West Airlines Flight 564 UFO Case" [ufoevidence.org/cases/case225.htm].
230 "Wingless Object Near Norwegian Airplane" [ufoevidence.org/cases/case54.htm].
231 A transcript and audio recording of the pilots communication with air traffic control is available at www.aliensthetruth.com/UFO_sightings_famous.php?view=1&ID=31. See also National UFO Reporting Center report [www.nuforc.org/webreports/015/S15014.html].

Chapter 7: UFOs, 1991 to the Present

August 9, 1997, near New York City's Kennedy Airport, when a Swissair flight had a close encounter with an unknown object.[232] On February 3, 1999, an object described "as big as a battleship" was seen over the North Sea by the crew of a British charter jet.[233] On November 23, 2003, shortly before landing at LaGuardia in New York City, while still over New Jersey, an airliner encountered a bright red circular disk, seen clearly by one of the passengers.[234] On November 3, 2004, during a descent to San Francisco, an experienced airline pilot reported a maneuvering orange light. The pilot was very cautious and checked for any atmospheric explanation, but there simply was none. The object then just disappeared.[235]

Of course, these and many other aviation encounters do not prove that UFOs are extraterrestrial. They do not even prove that UFOs are necessarily unconventional objects. If pressed to the wall, one might find excuses for every one of these cases. But that does not mean those interpretations would be correct. Some of these encounters may have prosaic explanations, but it does appear that something important has been going on in our skies. Whether it stems from unknown *others* or secret technologies of our own civilization, it should remain important to any thinking person.

Encounters with "Them"

If close encounters in the air leave one unimpressed, perhaps we can move on to actual encounters. Not with UFOs, but with what surely appear to be nonhuman, alien beings. Again, it must be emphasized that the cases described here are a mere sprinkling of what has been reported. After studying many of these cases over the years, it appears that some form of memory manipulation and erasure has been involved on people who have had these experiences.

---

232 "1997, Swissair Jet Has Near Miss with UFO" [www.ufocasebook.com/swissair1997.html].
233 "February 3, 1999, Jet Crew Tell Of Close Encounter With UFO" [www.ufocasebook.com/1999jetcrewencounter.html].
234 "Passenger on Airliner Sees UFO over New Jersey" [ufos.about.com/od/ufossept2011/a/passengersightinglaguardia.htm].
235 "California Airline Pilot Reports UFO" [ufos.about.com/od/classicufocases/a/california110304.htm].

Yet, not all people are the same. Some people's apparent alien experiences seem to bleed through into their normal waking consciousness. They remember, or at least they seem to remember, *enough*. Also, judging from the testimonies, it seems that not all of the beings themselves are equally concerned with attempting to control human memory.

What we do have are a certain number of cases that are difficult to dismiss out of hand.

The Khoury Incident

One of these is the remarkable experience of Peter Khoury, in Sydney, Australia, on July 23, 1992.

Khoury was alone in bed at 7:30 a.m. Suddenly, he awoke very alert and sat up. Two humanoid females were sitting on his bed, both entirely naked. They looked human but, then again, not quite normal. One looked somewhat Asian, the other looked perhaps Scandinavian, with light-colored eyes and long, exotic-looking, blonde hair. They both had unusually high cheekbones and very large eyes. The blonde woman also had an unusually long face. Both had nearly blank expressions.

The blonde woman seemed to be in charge. She sat in a kneeling position on the bed directly facing Khoury, who was nearly in shock. Then she reached out with both her hands and cupped the back of his head, drawing his face toward her chest. Khoury resisted, but she pulled harder, so that his mouth was on her nipple. Who knows why, perhaps just terror, but he bit hard. A small piece of her nipple came away in his teeth.

Oddly, she did not cry out. Her expression simply conveyed the idea to Khoury that, whatever he was supposed to have done, he did it wrong. The small fragment became caught in Khoury's throat, and he went into a coughing fit. Suddenly, the two women simply disappeared.

Once he realized they were gone, he tried clearing his throat with water. It did not work. Then he had an urge to urinate and went to the bathroom. He realized that his penis felt very painful. Standing in the bathroom, he pulled back the foreskin and found two thin, blonde, strands of hair wrapped tightly around. The hairs were not easy to remove, and the process was painful. Finally, he removed them and placed them in a sealed plastic bag.

The object in Khoury's throat remained lodged there. He coughed constantly. He tried clearing his throat with water, bread, and anything else he could think of, but nothing helped. Finally, after three days, it just went away.

The hair samples became the subject of the first openly-reported DNA test on a possible alien abduction. Tests noted how extremely thin, and almost clear in color, the hairs were. Under normal circumstances, hair that clear would almost certainly have been chemically treated, but this hair was not. Had it been so, the mitochondrial DNA could not have been recovered. Analysts concluded that, even though the hair was unquestionably very light blonde, it was not from a light-skinned caucasian racial type. Instead, the hair showed five distinctive DNA markers that are characteristic of a rare sub-group of the Chinese racial type. The scientists examined a database containing tens of thousands of samples of mitochondrial DNA. Of these, only four other people had all five of those markers. All were Chinese, and each one had black hair.[236]

Mitochondrial DNA is passed only from mother to child, so this suggests that the mysterious blonde woman shares a common female ancestor with the four Chinese people in the database. But how could that be? As researcher Bill Chalker put it, it seems unlikely that any person with blonde hair and an exact DNA match to the mysterious blonde woman could be found in the city of Sydney, nor on the continent of Australia, nor probably anywhere in the world.

All of which begs the question, who were these two female beings? It would appear there had been a sexual encounter, or perhaps a close call, something which Khoury did not recall for whatever reason. How else, one wonders, would the woman's hair become wrapped around his penis? The fact that they were both fairly attractive (albeit odd and

---

[236] Additional DNA tests might show the paternal lineage as well, but this would be very expensive and has not been done in this case.

a little too exotic for comfort) and especially the fact that they were naked, makes it seem obvious that there was supposed to be a sexual encounter, or that there already had been one. The blonde woman seems to have been the instructor, and the Asian-looking woman the student, perhaps there as an observer.

Are we dealing with humans with very rare and somewhat anomalous DNA? This was Chalker's suggestion, which seems reasonable. In other words, this would suggest the existence of a clandestine human group, long distinct from the mainstream of humanity, as being behind part of, or most or all of the UFO phenomenon.[237]

The Kelly Cahill Case

Another Australian UFO encounter of the early 1990s has also gained some prominence among students of ufology. This was the August 1993 experience of Kelly Cahill and her husband, along with two other motorists who were in a separate vehicle. Although all four people seem to have experienced something, Kelly Cahill has been by far the most public of them.

Around midnight, the Cahills were driving home in the province of Victoria when they noticed lights of a rounded craft in front of them. The craft and lights appeared simply to hover silently above the road. Kelly thought she could even see people through the windows. She screamed to her husband and the craft zoomed away.

They continued driving home, shaken. Then they noticed another light, one so bright that it nearly blinded them. Immediately, they felt unusually calm and relaxed. At some point, Kelly asked, "What happened, did I black out?" Her husband said nothing, and they continued to drive home.

Upon arriving home, Kelly detected a foul odor, something like vomit, and then realized she and her husband had an hour of missing

---

237 Chalker, Bill. *Hair of the Alien: DNA and Other Forensic Evidence of Alien Abductions* (Gallery Books, 2005). Also Chalker, Bill "1988, DNA Sample From Khoury Abduction Raises Big Questions," *International UFO Reporter* Spring, 1999 [www.ufocasebook.com/khouryabduction.html]. See video at www.youtube.com/watch?v=-YL11D935Nw.

time. As she undressed for bed, she noticed a strange, new, triangular mark on her navel. For the next two weeks, she experienced severe stomach pain and was hospitalized for a uterine infection.

Without hypnosis she began remembering details of the encounter. She recalled that her husband had stopped the car, that they had both left the vehicle and had walked toward the massive craft. She remembered another car having stopped on the side of the road. As she and her husband approached the craft, they saw a strange creature, about seven feet tall. Kelly described it as black, but not the color black. Rather, she said, black as though all matter had been removed from it. She later described it as evil and lacking a soul. The eyes of this being were large, similar to the eyes of flies, and they glowed red. She then noticed that there were many more of these beings in the field beneath the immense hovering object. One group of them glided very rapidly toward Kelly and her husband, covering one hundred yards within a few seconds. Another group approached the other car. At this point, apparently, she became unconscious. Her next memory was of being back in her car.

The occupants of the other car later came forward and told a similar story, showing marks on their body and drawing pictures of the same craft and beings. For her part, Kelly later had dreams of a black alien stooping over her helpless body, as if he were kissing her navel.

The case is generally considered among the better ones. There are photographs of Kelly's triangle and the marks on Glenda, the other woman who was there. Some skeptics have wondered why the other witnesses, including Kelly's husband, have not been more forthcoming themselves. Nevertheless, most researchers of the case have considered Kelly Cahill to be sincere.[238]

Schoolchildren in Zimbabwe

As if the two preceding cases were not startling enough, another one from the early 1990s is more compelling still. This concerns an

---

238 Booth, B. J. "The Kelly Cahill Encounter" [www.ufocasebook.com/Cahill.html]. Cahill, Kelly, *Encounter* (HarperCollins, 1997). See "Kelly Cahill Encounter" on YouTube at www.youtube.com/watch?v=UeBIqChvNXw.

encounter with over sixty schoolchildren in the town of Ruwa, Zimbabwe, on September 16, 1994.

These children were outside during recess when they saw a large craft land in an adjoining field. But there was more. Three or four beings, clearly not human, were beside the craft, and one was apparently perched atop it. The children all ran into the building, to the shock of their teachers and administrators. Unfortunately, and for reasons that are unclear, there were no adults present when this event happened.

It is not unusual for a child to tell a strange UFO story, nor for an adult to dismiss it. But what makes this case so compelling is that each of these children adamantly told precisely the same story, with much detail. They were obviously sincere about their experience. These children were young, around the ages of seven and eight. South African investigator Cynthia Hind did a thorough examination of the case, and Harvard University psychologist, Dr. John Mack, interviewed many of these children personally when he visited shortly afterward.

Some of the school children of Ruwa, Zimbabwe and their drawings.

There is a powerful and compelling ten-minute video of these children on YouTube, talking to Dr. Mack about what they saw.[239] They described their experiences identically. Their drawings, too, both of the craft and beings, are remarkably consistent. The beings were short, with black wraparound eyes ending in points. Each of the children seem to have been deeply afraid, and it appears at least some of them received mental impressions from the beings.

It is easier to acknowledge that the event happened than to understand what it signifies. Did the beings simply stumble, accidentally, upon these children while engaged in other matters? Did they explicitly decide to make their appearance when there were no adults present? What would be the purpose of having such an encounter with these young children?[240]

An Entity in Varginha, Brazil

As the above cases hint, many of the most compelling "alien" encounters of the 1990s took place outside the United States. This includes a famous incident that occurred in the Brazilian town of Varginha.

According to multiple alleged (but unconfirmed) leaks from within the Brazilian military, U.S. North American Air Defense (NORAD) contacted its Brazilian counterpart at midnight on January 20, 1996. The Brazilians were told that there was a UFO coming down over the southern part of the country. The next morning (again according to the anonymous informants), the Varginha Fire Department received a phone call about a "strange creature" seen in an area known as Jardim Andere. Assuming the call was either a prank or a drunk witness, the department ignored the report. Then came a second call, then a third, and then a fourth.

At this point, the Fire Department, which in Brazil is part of the military, responded. When the firefighters arrived upon the scene, they

---

239 "Zimbabwe - UFO - 62 School Children" at YouTube www.youtube.com/watch?v=bgZE8s0hBRQ.
240 Lawhon, Loy. "The Zimbabwe School Close Encounter" [www.ufoevidence.org/Cases/CaseSubarticle.asp?ID=130].

were shocked to see that there was indeed a creature. It had three protrusions on its head, almost like small horns, and had glowing red eyes. It had long arms, short legs, and large feet. It appeared to be dazed, and the firefighters easily captured it.

Later that day, three young women were walking home after work. Taking a shortcut through a wooded area, they stumbled upon another one of these strange creatures. It appeared to be identical in appearance to the one captured by the firefighters.

There were other creature reports from that day and there are unconfirmed reports that a number of others were captured. One was said to have been taken to a small hospital before being transferred by military personnel to a larger facility. At least one of the creatures was said to have died and then taken to the University of Campinas for an autopsy. Two others were said to be taken to the University of Sao Paulo for examination. A few weeks after the event a 23 year-old military policeman named Marco Eli Cherese, who was involved in the investigation, died. Supposedly, he fell ill from the effects of contact with one of the creatures.

There is much more to the case, including an interview conducted by American researcher Dr. Roger Leir with a doctor who examined one of the beings. The case is fascinating, but nothing is confirmed, everything is alleged. It is something like Roswell, in that a great deal of witness testimony is pitted against government denials, except that in the case of Roswell, one could always fall back on the newspaper account of a crashed flying disc. In the case of Varginha, there is not even that level of confirmation. Still, the case is intriguing, and it could be true.[241]

The Washington Elk Case

Every so often, witnesses testify to seeing UFOs take livestock or wild animals. According to three witnesses who spoke to UFO researchers, one such event took place in the State of Washington on

---

241 Pratt, Bob, and Luce, Cynthia, "The Varginha ETs" [www.mufon.com/bob_pratt/varginha.html. Westman, Jorgen, "The Varginha Case" [www.ufo.se/ufofiles/english/issue_3/varginha.htm].

February 25, 1999.

During the late morning, fourteen forestry employees of a large, unnamed company were planting trees in the Cascade Mountains. Through the morning, three of the men were observing a herd of elk in the valley below them. Suddenly, to their great surprise, a flat object, curved at one end and straight at the other, shaped something like the heel of a shoe, appeared over a ridge. They noticed two stripes on its back end. At first the three men thought the object was something like a parachute. But then they noticed it closely following the contours of the terrain below it and began to think otherwise.

When the object moved toward the herd of elk, the men called out to their co-workers. Now, all fourteen men watched the silent object approach the elk. When the object got fairly close the herd bolted toward a densely wooded area.

All but one.

Oddly, one elk did not run. Instead, it trotted nonchalantly in an entirely different direction. The mysterious object floated over this elk, then appeared to lift it off the ground. While the elk slowly rotated beneath it, seemingly floating in the air, the object began to move off. It barely cleared some trees, and then glided over to the next valley and was out of sight. A few minutes later, it reappeared, with no elk in sight, and rose at high speed until it disappeared into the sky.

The case was reported to Peter Davenport of the National UFO Reporting Center. Davenport and another investigator traveled to the site and interviewed several of the witnesses. They also examined the body of a female elk that was found north of the site, although it could not be determined whether or not this was the same elk that had been lifted into the air. Many of the witnesses had been with the company for years and were deemed to be reliable, but beyond that, investigators hit a dead end. Indeed, how would one obtain additional information?[242]

---

[242] A detailed summary of the case is available at the National UFO Reporting Center [www.nuforc.org/CB990225.html]. See also "Disc-shaped object: Elk abduction: Washington State, 02-25-1999" [www.ufocasebook.com/elkabduction.html].

Who Are These Beings?

The preceding encounter cases are among the more spectacular ones of the 1990s. Clearly, they are distinct from one another, but they do share some important similarities. First of all, the beings all seemed to have an agenda of some sort.

None of them spoke, nor even showed recognizable emotions. In three of the encounters, (Peter Khoury, Kelly Cahill, and the Zimbabwe school children) the entities seemed quite formidable in their capabilities, sometimes moving from place to place with a speed that would be impossible for any human. Indeed, in the Khoury case, the two female beings appear to have simply vanished, somehow able to leave the physical space instantly. Perhaps they entered another dimension, or were beamed up, like in a *Star Trek* movie.

In the Washington elk incident, no actual beings were seen, but, this encounter also showed the UFO operators to have very powerful capabilities. Presumably, they intended to use the elk for some reason, perhaps as food, although not if the elk found by the two investigators was the same elk. Frankly, not enough information is available for a determination.

One noticeable feature of these cases is that the entities all looked different. In Khoury's case, they seemed essentially human, but very unusual. In Zimbabwe, they appeared to be classic Grays. In the Cahill case, their appearance somewhat matched descriptions of tall hooded Greys, except they were even taller and had red eyes. Then there is the Varginha case, which (if descriptions can even be credited) is an outlier in terms of physical appearance. In other words, we are left in some confusion.

Could it be that we are dealing with multiple groups? Or different looking beings which work for the same group? Are they biologically engineered, customized life forms, and as such, capable of incredible variety? Or, are these all screen memories, unrelated to the actual appearance of the beings themselves? It may be that no one truly knows, not independent researchers, nor perhaps even those in the classified world. There will be more to say on this matter in the next chapter.

The Spectacular Yukon Sighting

It seems odd that the following case is not very well known. However, it occurred in a remote area, far removed from major media centers or much of the UFO research community. This was in Canada's Yukon province and occurred on December 11, 1996, a cold, dark, wintry night in the Great White North. The main observations were near Fox Lake, roughly ten miles long and frozen at this time of year, not far from Alaska, and hundreds of miles distant from any major city or publicly known military base.

According to more than twenty witnesses, an enormous aerial object, lit up like a Christmas tree, drifted past the lake between 8 p.m. and 9 p.m. Two of the witnesses were cousins, driving in separate vehicles. Each saw it over the lake, slammed on their brakes, and got out of their vehicles. They watched the huge object as it slowly drifted towards one of them and was soon almost directly overhead. It then moved slowly across the highway and over a hill to the east, whereupon it was lost to view. Both men drew pictures of the object, and it certainly looks very impressive. One might think a huge, slow moving object such as this could be a blimp, but this seems very unlikely. The Goodyear blimp, for instance, is quite large, nearly two hundred feet long, but who cannot recognize that? Besides, this object was much, much more brightly lit than the Goodyear blimp ever was, and seems to have been much larger, rounder, and taller. Moreover, why would the Goodyear or any other blimp even be in such a remote area?

While the two cousins were observing this object, a married couple with their baby were a bit farther to the south along the same highway, driving toward them. They too saw the object. By the time they caught up with the cousins and pulled over, the object had moved off. The married couple continued driving until they arrived at a lodge farther ahead. There, they told the owner about what they had seen. He promptly recounted a sighting from an earlier witness, who had gotten very close to this object.

At the nearby village of Pelly Crossing other people described the same object. In one case it seemed to respond to a man's flashlight by accelerating toward him. When he turned off his flashlight, the object

Illustration by investigator Martin Jasek of the Yukon object of 1996, based on witness accounts.

stopped. By then, it had gotten quite close to him, filling much of the sky. It also emitted several beams of light, including one that swooped along the ground. The man ran across a clearing, perhaps to get a better view. When he turned to look for the object, it was gone.

Altogether, there are twenty-two known witnesses of this object. The event was investigated by Canadian engineer Martin Jasek, who wrote a detailed account. The sighting is extraordinary and the case includes many drawings and detailed interviews many, if not all, of which are available online. Its remote location, unfortunately, has hindered it from becoming better known.[243]

In 2012, some researchers claimed to have solved the case. It was discovered that the Russians had launched a satellite earlier that day, and that the re-entry of the second stage of the rocket occurred in the same location and at the same time as the sighting. The coincidence seems compelling. It would seem that the witness testimonies were not reliable, and that when seeing something unfamiliar they unwittingly created a spaceship out of rocket debris. However, it is not so simple as that. While the re-entry lasted just a few minutes, the sightings were

---

243 Jasek, Martin. "22+ Witnesses Observe a UFO Larger than a Football Stadium Yukon Territory, Canada" [www.ufobc.ca/yukon/22index.htm].

recorded over a series of hours. Moreover, many analysts are unconvinced that the consistent, detailed, and numerous witness descriptions square with the re-entry of a rocket into Earth's atmosphere.[244]

The Phoenix Lights

All of which brings us to the most famous UFO event of the 1990s, the extraordinary Phoenix Lights of March 13, 1997. Entire books and documentaries have been devoted to this event.[245] Actually, this was comprised of two events, and therein lies some of the confusion regarding the case.

Initially, people reported a boomerang formation of lights, first seen in Henderson, Nevada, and then as it moved south, down the state of Arizona. Some of these descriptions were not merely of lights, but of an actual craft which was reported to the National UFO Reporting Center, police, the media, and Luke Air Force Base. Among witness descriptions, there was some variation. All reported lights, but sometimes as a pattern of five lights, sometimes seven, and sometimes even more. Occasionally they were red and orange, at other times yellow and white. Sometimes they moved rapidly, sometimes slowly, and sometimes they hovered.

This object appears to have been seen just north of Phoenix where three witnesses reported it as a huge, wedge shaped, craft with five lights. It passed directly over their heads. Another nearby group of witnesses described very much the same type of object, and added that it hovered directly over them for about five minutes. As it did so, it filled a huge part of the sky. They were able to see individual features along the bottom of the object, and there was no question in their minds that they were seeing a large, solid object. There were quite a few more of these types of sightings. That, in essentials, was Phase One

---

244 A good discussion of this case is available at Above Top Secret, "Yukon UFO "Mothership" Incident: December 11th, 1996" [www.abovetopsecret.com/forum/thread487438/pg1&mem=]. See also Sheaffer, Robert, "'Top Ten' UFO Case - Yukon, Canada, 1996 - BUSTED!" [badufos.blogspot.com/2012/04/top-ten-ufo-case-yukon-canada-1996.html].
245 Kitei, Lynne D. *The Phoenix Lights: A Skeptics Discovery that We Are Not Alone* (Hampton Roads, 2010); and Kitei, Lynne, D. *The Phoenix Lights: We Are Not Alone* [DVD]. See also the Phoenix Lights Network website [www.thephoenixlights.net].

of the Phoenix Lights sightings.

Phase Two began later that evening, between 9:30 p.m. and 10 p.m., when the people of Phoenix were treated to an amazing display of hovering lights over their city. These lights appeared to be motionless and in perfect formation. They were a truly astounding sight to behold: an enormous semi-circular string of lights in the night sky. Despite being video-recorded by multiple residents, media coverage was practically absent for several months. Then, the story exploded, especially after the public affairs office at Luke Air Force Base announced that the lights were flares launched from A-10 warthog aircraft. Some video and photo experts who analyzed these lights have concluded that they are flares, despite how amazing they look. Among these is Dr. Bruce Maccabee, an optical physicist who has analyzed many UFO images and videos.

Other analysts, however, do not. One of the most prominent of these is Jim Dilettoso, who compared the lights to the thousands of images on his database, which he likened to testing fingerprints or blood samples. He tested for size, brightness, movement characteristics, and more. "I didn't get a match to flares, airplane lights, Venus, swamp gas, flashlights, whatever," he said. "That means it's unknown. Not a spacecraft necessarily, but unknown."[246]

Many years after the incident, a pilot of the Maryland Air National Guard stated he had flown one of the aircraft in question, and a history of the Maryland Air National Guard asserted that its 104th Fighter Squadron was responsible for the incident. Is this true, however? In a private communication with me, Dilettoso wrote:

> I spent much time . . . with top 2 officers of the Arizona National Guard. They dismissed the fact the lights could have been flares, and moreover, heavily dismissed the claim that the Maryland National Guard had been dropping flares that night. These 2 people I know were the commanding officers who 'trained' the Maryland National Guard. Not only were they on the ground by 6 PM, the MNG never mentioned a word about being up that night, when the news of the Phoenix Lights paraded on TV for the

---

246 Scott Craven. "Intrigue persists over lights in sky - For first time, military pilot tells of dropping flares; others say 'Phoenix Lights' were UFOs." *The Arizona Republic,* Feb. 25, 2007 [www.ufocasebook.com/intriguepersists.html].

next few days, including while the MNG was still in Arizona being trained.[247]

Perhaps pressure has been exerted to promote the flares theory. Without question, there was great pressure put upon the Phoenix City Council not to investigate the incident. It even led to the ouster of City Council member Francis Barwood, the one member who called for a genuine investigation. It also led to a press conference by Arizona Governor Fife Symington, in which a person wearing an alien costume was trotted out for the television cameras as an obvious joke. Largely overlooked, however, is Symington's public statement in 2007 about the matter. By then he was no longer governor, and was less constrained in his public statements. Symington admitted that he himself had seen the object on that day. It had upset him deeply and he organized the press conference in order to defuse media interest and the threat of public panic. "I'm a pilot, and I know just about every machine that flies," he said. "It was bigger than anything that I've ever seen. It remains a great mystery."[248]

Something important happened over Phoenix that day. It is interesting that, despite the fact that the first series of sightings lacked any video or photographic evidence, many researchers continue to consider it to be the stronger case. Still, both sightings have good reason for support.

One wonders, however, if the lights from later that night were part of the tried and true method of sowing confusion into genuine UFO sightings. During the 1980s, in New York's Hudson Valley, amid numerous reports of large boomerang and triangular objects flying low over the highway, there were a few confirmed cases of pilots flying small ultra-light aircraft in close formation. The presence of these pilots was used, and is still used, to discredit the entire wave of those sightings. Now consider Arizona, and how even the state's governor acknowledged the threat of public panic. Is it really so hard to think

---

247 Jim Dilletoso, email correspondence with the author, March 15, 2013.
248 "Former Arizona Governor Comes Forward About UFO Sighting From 10 Years Ago" *Fox News*, March 24, 2007 [www.foxnews.com/story/2007/03/24/former-arizona-governor-comes-forward-about-ufo-sighting-from-10-years-ago/].

that an order was given to drop flares over the city, an explanation that would eventually be used to disable the story? No, not at all. But, conclusions must rest solely on the evidence offered. This includes not only official statements, but also testimony from the many witnesses, as well as a close analysis of the videos themselves. On this measure, the notion of flares as the culprit remains too debatable to be considered a certainty.

If only the entire event had occurred a few hours earlier, when daylight would have left the matter in no doubt.

Triangles

Whatever the objects over Arizona may have been, the earlier one at any rate appears to have been something like a triangle. Perfectly triangular craft have been noted for quite a few decades now, despite the fact that there are still no perfectly triangular craft officially flown by the air force of any nation. In 2012, NASA and Boeing announced they had successfully demonstrated the X-48C, a "hybrid wing body" that is somewhat triangular and offers advantages in fuel efficiency. It is also extremely quiet.[249] Perhaps this is why some researchers think of triangles as somehow less exotic than spherical or disk shaped flying saucers. There is no inherent reason why this should be, since none of those shapes were aerodynamic within conventional technologies of the twentieth century. Yet, reports of triangular objects go back through the 1940s and even earlier, becoming more widely seen since the 1970s. The question arises, who has been making them? Us or . . . them?

The answer may well be both, but certainly part of the answer is *us*. One sighting in particular has always led inexorably to this conclusion. In August 1989, a world-class aircraft recognition specialist named Chris Gibson was working at a North Sea oil rig installation, when he happened to see a black triangular aircraft refueling from a KC-135, accompanied by two F-111 fighter aircraft. Gibson was explicit about

---

249 Wrenn, Eddie. "The future of Air Travel: NASA and Boeing test radical triangular plane (just don't expect a window seat)" *Daily Mail*, 8 August 2012 [www.dailymail.co.uk/sciencetech/article-2185304/NASA-Boeing-successfully-test-triangle-airplane.html].

Chapter 7: UFOs, 1991 to the Present

what he saw. He is difficult to refute.[250] There has also been a great deal of talk of the perfectly triangular TR-3A and TR-3B aircraft, sometimes known as the Black Manta. Yet there remains no confirmation. Officially, only mockups were ever built of those aircraft.[251]

Yet, sightings of perfectly triangular craft continued through the 1990s and beyond. One occurred in November, 1993, by a motorist driving along Interstate 5 in Seattle. He saw what could only be described as an immense, black triangle. It was perfect in shape, with red lights at each corner, flying low and silent over the highway. He was convinced that hundreds of motorists had to have seen it. Most intriguingly, the object flew toward the airfield at the Boeing facility. It was then lost to view.[252]

There are many of these reports. Some are of smaller triangles, and others that are simply immense. The large ones are often referred to as Big Black Deltas, or BBDs. Quite a few of these have also been seen in the Seattle area. In other words, near Boeing's manufacturing plant.

Most of these have been reported from within the United States, but not all. There was a rather good sighting from September 7, 1997, over Paris. This is from the files of the official French government UFO research program, GEIPAN. Shortly after 1 a.m., a man on his balcony saw a triangular form with three lights (two blue and one green), moving slowly. He heard nothing, but felt his body vibrate. He tried to take a picture of the object, but apparently by the time he got his camera ready, the object was blocked from view. He estimated the object to be enormous, "approximately 700 meters," presumably meaning either in diameter or one of its sides. Either way, this would be gigantic. According to the witness, the entire sighting lasted for twelve seconds, although one wonders how he could be so confidently exact.[253]

---

250 Gray, Simon, "The North Sea Aurora sighting" [www.abovetopsecret.com/forum/thread60770/pg#pid632163] and [www.secretprojects.co.uk/forum/index.php?topic=2868.0].
251 See the Wikipedia page for the "TR-3 Black Manta" [en.wikipedia.org/wiki/TR-3_Black_Manta].
252 Val Tenuta, Gary. "Close-up Sighting Of A Black Triangle UFO, " September 3, 2004 [rense.com/general57/blactri.htm].
253 "Large triangular-shaped object with lights observed in Paris, France" [www.ufoevidence.org/cases/case1124.htm].

One of the best known triangle cases occurred on January 5, 2000, and is often referred to as the Illinois cop sighting. Between 4 a.m. and 5 a.m. on that cold, dark winter morning, a number of witnesses, including quite a few police officers, saw a large, low-flying, extremely quiet triangular craft glide past above them. It was said by witnesses to be two stories high, with two rows of lights clearly visible. Most witnesses said this object was very large, several city blocks long, possibly as long as the proverbial football field, although one of the officers doubted this. Police officers fully supported the statements by civilian witnesses. One officer rushed to grab his Polaroid camera to photograph the object, but the picture unfortunately came out poorly. This is not unusual when people try to photograph a UFO. Frankly, photographing any moving object in the dark without preparation is going to be difficult at best.

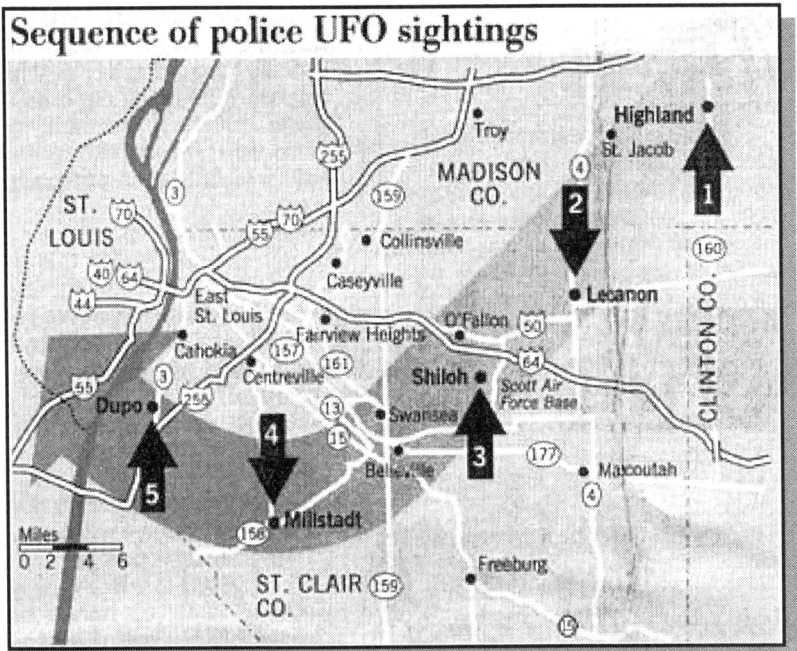

Path of the large triangular craft, from the *St. Louis Post-Dispatch*.

Perhaps the most noteworthy aspect of this sighting was how the object could pivot and accelerate so rapidly. Several officers attested to this. Such observations make it highly unlikely that the culprit was a balloon of some sort.[254]

Another interesting element of this story concerns its treatment in the American news media. After the standard chuckles and *woo-woo* allusions, some reporters suggested that the object was an experimental military craft, possibly associated with nearby Scott Air Force Base. It is perfectly reasonable to wonder about this. But left unasked was the obvious question: *how could the object fly as it did?* That is, nearly silently, and with instant acceleration? It might not be a bad idea also to ask why the U.S. military might build an aircraft of such immense proportions? Forgetting the issue of extraterrestrials, these are simply questions of great public and scientific interest. Yet such obvious questions have been unasked.

Sadly, within the establishment-oriented media, so it has always been with significant UFO cases, including the triangle cases.

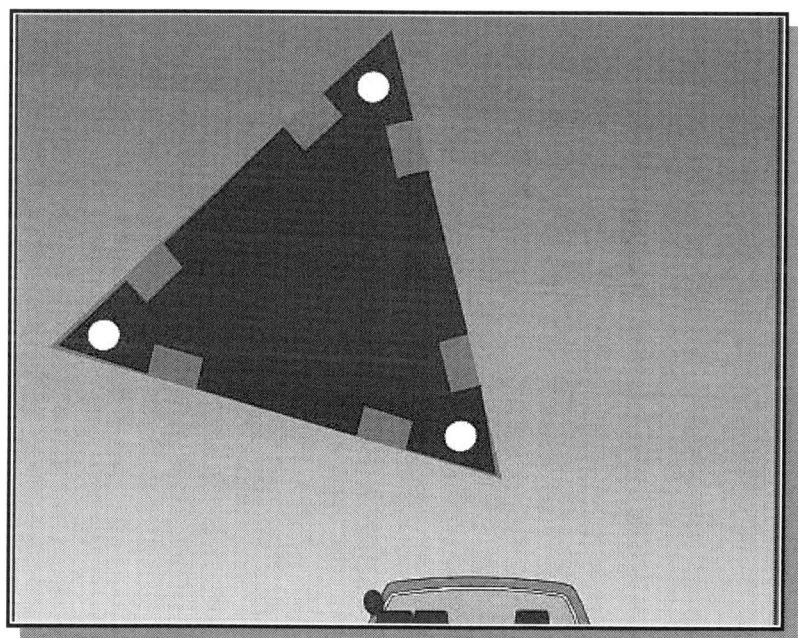

Illustration by witness of triangular object over Kingston, Ontario, January 2003.

I personally investigated an interesting triangle case that took place in Kingston, Ontario, on January 24, 2003. The case was reported

---

254 Marler, David B. *Triangular UFOs: An Estimate of the Situation.* Richard Dolan Press, 2013. See also "Illinois UFO Sighting" [www.ufoevidence.org/topics/illinoissighting.htm].

initially to the National UFO Reporting Center. The witness had seen an absolutely perfect equilateral triangular craft with sharp, not rounded, corners, and lights at each corner. She had been driving home from work and saw the object appear from behind some trees and approach her position. Rolling down her car window and slowing to a near-stop, she leaned out and looked directly above, astonished. The object then glided in the direction of the Canadian Forces Base at Kingston. Again, we have a suggestive possibility that these triangles are somehow connected with military operations.

Such a connection is probably real, but there are a number of UFO triangle sightings that are of a high strangeness nature. Some of these would seem to be beyond the capabilities even of the black budget world. This was so even during the Hudson Valley sightings of the 1980s. Even so, it must be acknowledged that the capabilities of the black budget world may be quite advanced—indeed, I have speculated about a so-called Breakaway Civilization. Thus, we are still grappling in the dark. Beyond a doubt, however, somebody is flying these triangles. Getting to the bottom of this issue could very well be an important step toward understanding the UFO issue in general.

UFOs in the 21st Century

Upon reviewing UFO sightings of the 21st century, it is striking just how many good ones there have been. Especially puzzling and fascinating is a wave of sightings in an area that is truly remote and quiet, and yet from 2002 to 2004 was among the most active UFO hotspots on Earth, not merely for sightings of craft, but also apparent encounters with beings. This is an isolated region in British Columbia centered around the town of Houston. Unlike its gigantic namesake in Texas, Houston, British Columbia has a population of roughly two thousand. There has never been much happening there. Yet, for some reason, Houston and its surrounding region had an incredibly high number of sightings of unusual and unconventional craft that have never been explained.[255]

---

[255] Houston, BC Resident Brian Vike recorded many of these events. His blogsite is hbccufo.blogspot.com.

Another wave of sightings was occurring at that time in the nation of Argentina. Sightings of enormous cigar-shaped craft, stories of large well-lit UFOs stopping cars and affecting electronics, and one from the late 1990s of UFOs stealing water from an Argentine military base.[256]

One of the most important cases of the new century took place very close to Washington, D.C., on the night of July 25-26, 2002. A number of witnesses in a nearby suburb saw what can only be described as a chase of multiple UFOs by at least two F-16 aircraft. I interviewed two of these witnesses at length. The incident was reported in the *Washington Post*, which published a tepid article discussing only the later part of the evening, when a solitary UFO was observed being chased by two F-16s. The article itself appears to have been published only because a local radio station had already reported the incident. Yet, the article did describe an interesting fact: an unnamed Air Force spokesperson stated that not only did the object outperform the F-16s, but suddenly disappeared from the radar. In other words, it had been tracked on radar, and then just disappeared.[257] According to one of the witnesses, the object at one point descended at an eighty-degree angle and then stopped, apparently waiting for the two F-16s to catch up, whereupon it zipped away. Another witness, a retired police officer, saw at least two UFOs being chased by multiple F-16s. In his opinion, the UFOs were substantially larger than the F-16s. Recall that all of this was near the nation's Capitol in post-911 America, a serious violation of airspace.

The year 2002 also offered very good photo and video UFO evidence. During October alone, three striking photographic or video images of UFOs were recorded. On October 5, one person photographed what certainly looks like a flying triangle over Las Cruces, New Mexico. The incident was filed with the National UFO Reporting Center. Actually, the photograph shows two unknown objects, one

---

256 Many of these stories were reported in the UFO news service, *UFO Roundup*, managed by Joseph Trainor from 1996 to 2005. The full archives of the site can be accessed at ufoinfo.com/roundup/.
257 Vogel, Steve. "F-16s pursue unknown craft over region," *Washington Post*, July 27, 2002.

of which is clearly triangular.[258]

On October 20, 2002, a very interesting photograph of a UFO was taken. The photo was of a saucer or disc type object clearly in the sky over some trees in the town of Tyrone, Pennsylvania. It was investigated by researcher Stan Gordon, who found the witness to be sincere and the photograph to be genuine.[259]

Meanwhile, just one state over on the same day, a good video of a UFO was recorded in the city of Albany, New York. A cameraman with the local *Fox* television station was at the Albany airport, recording stock video of aircraft taking off and landing. After the video was brought back to the station's studio, it was noticed that a strange object of some sort had flown across the frame. Such objects have been recorded many times, and are typically referred to as *rods*. The object here was very long and thin, like a needle, with four short appendages jutting out. There has been much debate over what these rods are. Many have argued, convincingly in some cases, that they are simply insects flying close to the camera.

Not everyone is convinced, however. In the case of the Albany rod, I have been able to find no insect matching its appearance. Moreover, an extended analysis of this video was done by optical physicist Dr. Bruce Maccabee. Although his analysis was inconclusive (he was unable to obtain the original digital copy of the video), he conceded the distinct possibility that the object at one point went behind a cloud. Looking at the video, this appears to be the case. Maccabee also left open the possibility that additional "noise" from the second-generation copy might have accounted for this. How much noise this generates (if any) is a fair question. And where, we may ask, is the original digital recording? It turns out that the FBI has it. Immediately after the video was shown on local television, the FBI asked for and received the original, so that only copies are available to the rest of the world. I confess I have always been baffled by the analysis conducted

---

[258] "2002-Las Cruces, New Mexico, Triangle UFO" [ufos.about.com/od/thetriangleufos/ig/trianglegallery/lascrucesnm100502.htm].
[259] Gordon, Stan. "Tyrone, PA-UFO Emits Beam Of Light - Is Photographed In Flight, 10-20-02" [www.ufocasebook.com/tyronepa2002.html].

Chapter 7: UFOs, 1991 to the Present

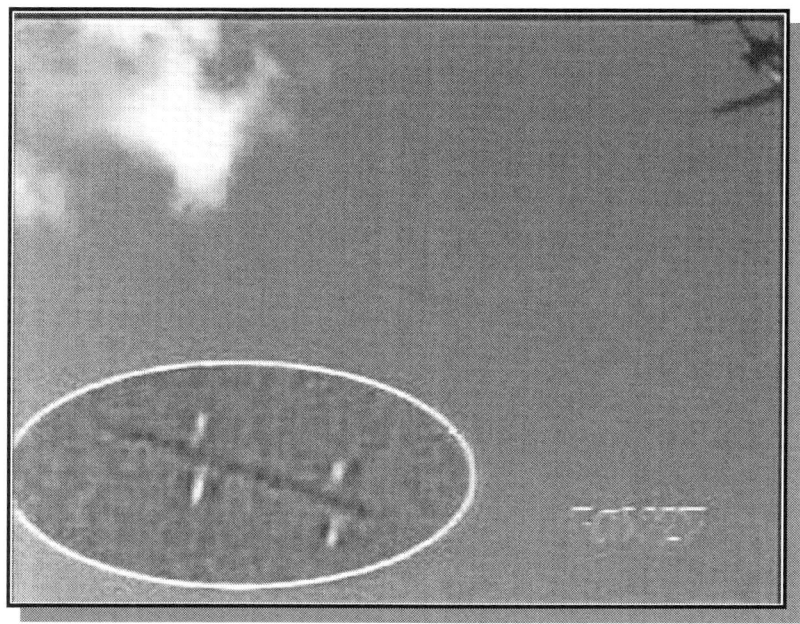

Frame from the video of the object at the Albany airport, October 2002. Object enlarged and seen more clearly in inset.

by New York's MUFON chapter, which somehow concluded the object was an insect.[260]

Quite a few interesting UFO videos have been recorded in the United Kingdom. One was shot in Lancashire on November 16, 2003, by a man named Martin H. (his last name is unavailable). The full video is more than eight minutes long, and shows a bright, golden, spherical object in the sky. Eventually, it moves behind a cloud and is lost to sight. It certainly is not any recognizable aircraft. While its shape is circular, it does not behave like a balloon. Instead, it seems to move quite deliberately and looks as though it has an internal source of light.[261]

Several excellent videos and photographs of UFOs appeared in 2004. One of my personal favorites was taken in Australia, on January 15, by a highway inspector who was photographing a railway crossing. Only later when he looked at the image on his computer monitor did

---

260 "The Albany International Airport UFO video" [www.ufocasebook.com/albany.html]. See also Maccabee, Bruce, "Preliminary Analysis of the Albany TV Object" [brumac.8k.com/AlbanyTVObject/AlbTVObjectPrelim.html].
261 See article (untitled) [www.ufowisconsin.com/outofstate/r2003_1116_leyland_lancashire_uk.html]. Unfortunately, the YouTube video appears to have become unavailable.

he notice a disc-shaped object in the upper right portion of the photograph—a common occurrence. Many people have looked at this image and all that can be said is that the photograph is genuine. Something quite unusual was captured in the sky. Why is it, we may wonder, that there are so many instances of such objects being photographed when they are not seen?[262]

Later that same year, the Mexican Air Force announced that one of its aircraft had electronically recorded something in the air that was not seen visually. That is, there appeared to be one or more aerial objects that were invisible. These were captured by two different electronic methods: airborne radar and forward looking infrared (FLIR). Something appears to been there. Skeptics immediately offered a variety of explanations, including geological stresses causing "Earth lights" and classified American craft. If the latter, the question remains how total invisibility was obtained.[263]

There are many more excellent cases from 2004 and 2005, not simply video and photo, but attempted jet interceptions of UFOs, and much else that one can imagine.

UFO Over O'Hare Airport

Certainly, one of the most important UFO sightings of the 21st century so far has been the Chicago O'Hare Airport incident of November 7, 2006. Indeed, this particular sighting can claim a great deal of responsibility for kickstarting increased UFO media coverage which, as of this writing years later, has not abated.

On that day, about a dozen employees of United Airlines saw an oval or disc-shaped object hovering in the sky below the level of the clouds. The object was visible for roughly 15 minutes before it instantly accelerated and departed. According to the witnesses, it flew through the clouds so quickly that it punched a hole in them that was visible for some time afterward.

---

262 "UFO Caught by Oz City Worker's Digital Camera" [www.ufoevidence.org/cases/case236.htm].
263 Booth, Billy. "2004: The Mexican Military Video" [ufos.about.com/od/visualproofphotosvideo/p/mexicanvideo.htm].

Chapter 7: UFOs, 1991 to the Present

The employees at United were told not to discuss the matter. One of them, however, reported it to the National UFO Reporting Center. From there, the story made it to the *Chicago Tribune*, which in turn led to the interview of about a half dozen other witnesses. Initially, United and the Federal Aviation Administration denied any knowledge of the incident, but each was forced to recant after it was clearly shown that they had been lying, following a Freedom of Information Act request by the *Tribune*.[264]

So, what object might hover over one of the busiest airports in the world? Could this have been a military test of some sort? This seems unlikely, but again this is one reason we still use the phrase *UFO*. After all, the object was unidentified. Unidentified, and certainly quite extraordinary. The National Aviation Reporting Center on Anomalous Phenomena (NARCAP), which specializes in analyzing UFO encounters by aviation professionals, soberly concluded that:

> ... a potentially significant air safety problem existed at O'Hare International Airport on the afternoon of November 7, 2006. Anytime an airborne object can hover for several minutes over a busy airport but not be registered on radar or seen visually from the control tower, constitutes a potential threat to flight safety.[265]

And Over Stephenville, Texas

The last spectacular American UFO account, at least which has received substantial media attention, took place on January 8, 2008 over central Texas, near the town of Stephenville. This may well be the most extraordinary of all American cases from the 21st century, at least so far. Much evidence is available, both in witness testimony and in FAA radar records, indicating that an extraordinary and large object was pursued by American F-16 fighter jets. The object was so large

---

264 Hilkevitch, Jon. "In the Sky! A Bird? A Plane? A UFO!" *Chicago Tribune*, January 1, 2007 [web.archive.org/web/20071117073414/www.chicagotribune.com/classified/automotive/columnists/chi-0701010141jan01,0,5874175.column?page=1&coll=chi-newsnationworldiraq-hed].

265 *Report of an Unidentified Aerial Phenomenon and its Safety Implications at O'Hare International Airport on November 7, 2006. Case 18.* By Richard F. Haines, Ph.D. Senior Editor Chief Scientist with K. Efishoff, D. Ledger, L. Lemke, S. Maranto, W. Puckett, T. Roe, M. Shough, R. Uriarte. March 9, 2007. Report can be read in full at narcap.org/reports/TR10_Case_18a.pdf. Summary available at www.ufocasebook.com/narcapohare.html.

that one witness described it as a "flying Walmart." The object came in at a very high speed, and then just stopped. One witness said it stopped directly above him, where it blocked out the entire sky. He saw a great amount of detail of its underside. It then took off and was gone, pursued by fighter jets.[266]

There are quite a few witnesses to this case. One of the extraordinary things about it is that MUFON obtained FAA radar records for at least the initial portion of the event. These confirmed the presence of not simply one, but several unknown aerial objects in the area at that time. The radar records did not indicate that U.S. jets attempted to intercept these objects, despite being in their proximity. Even more interesting is that the records indicated that the object's last direction indicated it was moving toward the Crawford ranch. This is where President George W. Bush was residing at the time. Incredibly, the FAA said it had no additional records to offer.[267]

Incidentally, the Air Force, as it had always done, initially denied that anything unusual had occurred. Not only did it deny any knowledge of UFOs near Stephenville, it denied that there were any F-16s in the area, as well. Eventually, however, it was forced to admit that there were some F-16s in the area, but then claimed it was solely for a scheduled training exercise. The MUFON investigation and files on this case are very good. They still await a proper documentary treatment and retelling that would do the case justice.

Northern Canadian Military Encounter

The following encounter came to me via an active duty Canadian soldier in 2013. It is as-yet officially unconfirmed, but my interview with him was extensive and I consider this a good case that has a likelihood of further confirmation in the future.

The event in question occurred in mid-January 2008 (precise date undetermined), the same month as the UFO encounter at

---

[266] A good site containing many of the original news articles on the event is stephenvillelights.com.
[267] "Special Research Report: Stephenville, Texas," *Mutual UFO Network* (MUFON) [www.ufocasebook.com/pdf/mufonstephenvilleradarreport.pdf].

Chapter 7: UFOs, 1991 to the Present

Stephenville, Texas, except that this event happened in one of the most remote places on Earth: the Canadian military base, CFS Alert. This is the most northern human habitation on the planet, directly west of the northwest tip of Greenland, on the shoreline of the Arctic Ocean. The base was established during the 1950s as an electronic listening post directed against Moscow and remains active today, particularly as a communications station for NATO's nuclear submarines that patrol the area. It is manned year-round by roughly fifty personnel. The closest habitation to it is America's Thule Air Base, 400 miles to the south, and the tiny village of Grise Fiord (pop. 130) about 460 miles to the southwest. Beyond that, there is nothing in any direction for a thousand miles or more.

Location of CFS Alert (circled).

During the winter months, it is dark twenty-four hours a day. Weather is often treacherous. For several days before the encounter, weather had been bad, and the men stayed inside. Finally, the weather cleared enough that the base commander took ten or fifteen men outside for a constitutional hike and to get some fresh air. The witness who related this event did not go outside, but stayed at the base and was in the cafeteria getting a meal. Large windows showed a black sky outside.

Suddenly, outside the windows a bright light turned on, brighter than daylight. The witness, and the other few men in the cafeteria at the time, assumed that someone had turned on floodlights for some reason, although it seemed very odd that lights would be on. For about ten minutes or so, it remained extremely bright, and then the light suddenly was gone. The men continued to eat their meal.

A short while later, the men who had been outside returned to the base. Their faces expressed shock and bewilderment. Upon questioning several of them, it was learned that when the men were less than a hundred yards from the base, they saw a metallic-looking cigar-shaped object silently glide from the south to a position directly over the base, where it stopped. The object then shone an intensely bright beam of light onto the station. The men were astonished. They had a very good view of it, seeing it clearly against the background of known structures and landscape, agreeing that its size was roughly 200 feet long. The light lasted for about ten minutes. Then the object began moving off to the northwest, directly over the ocean and was soon lost to view.

The following day, the station received an unscheduled visit from a U.S. Air Force Colonel. The witness, who was good friends with the base commander, saw the two of them talking in the cafeteria. He approached, said hello, and then brashly said, "You must be here because of our UFO sighting yesterday." In front of everyone present, and using some strong language, the colonel reprimanded the soldier, tersely informing him that he was completely out of line and had no need to know about any of this. Turning to the base commander he said, "get control of your men," and then walked out of the room.

The colonel did not even spend the night, but flew out shortly afterwards. A few days later, the base commander had the occasion to speak privately with the witness, saying only that he was told by the colonel that the UFO event was "the most serious air space violation in the history of CFS Alert."

Several long conversations and much research by myself and the witness caused us to rule out any conventional explanation for this event. The range would be daunting, nearly impossible, for any helicopter, and Thule would be the only possible candidate, although a helicopter flight from there would be little more than a suicide mission, considering a range of 400 miles in blackness and questionable weather. In any case, the object's silence, shape, and continued flight over the frozen Arctic sea clearly ruled out "helicopter." Its ability to hover ruled out anything else we could think of.

Whatever the origin of this craft, it appeared to show a definite interest in the station, and may well have had a connection to the nuclear submarines with which the station regularly communicates.

The Turkish UFO Videos

For anyone interested in UFO videos, a quick search on YouTube will not disappoint, at least in terms of quantity. Every week, someone asks me for my opinion about some UFO video. It is difficult to know which are legitimate. One case, however, that I have come to believe is genuine is actually a series of videos that were recorded at the coast of Turkey in 2007, 2008, and 2009.

One still image (of many) of the object over the Sea of Marmara, Turkey.

The videos look too good to be true, but the man who recorded them has been interviewed extensively, and a number of other people have confirmed the UFOs, including the respected American researcher, Dr. Roger Leir. This is an object that is not readily visible except as a moving light over the water. However, upon zooming in, a very definite shape of craft becomes evident. The quality of video is excellent. A skeptical argument claims that it is nothing more than the reflection of lights from distant yachts on the water. However, no skeptical argument has been provided with any true technical or photometric analysis, while conversely supporting arguments have persuasively demonstrated that the altitude of the light is far too high to be from any waterborne craft. In addition, the video is so clear that the argument of reflections of any waterborne object surpasses the boundaries of even the most slavish credulity to the established dogma: that UFOs cannot possibly exist.[268]

I think the Turkish videos are legitimate and I do not believe the craft is one of "ours." Nevertheless, responsible researchers must leave the case open for further research.

How Deep Does This Go?

Without question, the last twenty years have been full of UFO activity. When we examine the sum total of what has been going on, it is mind-boggling. In terms of quality as well as quantity, the 21st century has seen an unrelenting wave of UFO activity and encounters with the extraordinary.

The cases recounted in this chapter consist of a mere scratching of the surface. There remains much more to discuss, and many more questions to ask. Who are we dealing with? How strange does this phenomenon *really* get? Are people actually being taken and, if so, *why?* and *how?* Are they also having telepathic and even spiritual encounters with some of the beings from, shall we say, *elsewhere?* If so, what does it all mean? And, how do we hope to investigate this phenomenon in a way that is both scientific and creative, in a way that productively grapples with this mystery? And what of the future? Will we be forever stuck in this netherworld of ignorance and cover-up? What happens if, and when, and after the secret comes out?

The good news is that these are questions that will be treated for the remainder of this book.

---

[268] See "Turkey UFO Incident" [turkeyufocase.blogspot.com].

Chapter 8
Contact and Abduction

Studying UFO history and politics only begins the process of grappling with some of the complex, mystifying, and at times disturbing elements of the phenomenon. When we really think about it, the fundamental issue is one of *contact*. That is, between us and them, whoever *they* happen to be.

There is, of course, a school of thought arguing that the most credible UFO sightings are not extraterrestrial, but rather the product of secret terrestrial technology. From this perspective, the UFO phenomenon does not equal contact with some variety of *Other*. Yet, I suggest that the idea of human contact with Others has much logic to it, and good evidence as well.

Where the Rubber Meets the Road

Over the decades, or even centuries, the claims of contact have been many. People have described their experiences with beings that are not human and surely do not appear to come from *here*. Frequently, although not always, these have been in connection with UFO sightings. Evaluating these claims is tricky. Yet, if we are to have any understanding of this critically important phenomenon, we must consider them carefully.

Some are easier to study than others. Cases that involve clear witness testimony, especially including multiple witnesses, are nice to have. Physical evidence, whether in the form of marks on the body, implants, or other types of trace evidence, are obviously helpful. These are some of the classic hallmarks of what we would call alien abduction.

Also quite prevalent, although even more difficult to assess, are claims of communication with extraterrestrial intelligences, sometimes while in the physical presence of actual beings, and sometimes purely telepathic with no apparent beings present.[269] Often this has been seamlessly integrated with other forms of channeling, involving entities from other dimensions, other periods of time, and various distant places. Such claims have spiked significantly since around 1990.

Several questions naturally arise. First, are the claims and encounters consistent? If they are, then to what extent is any consistency explainable as a cultural phenomenon and essentially a situation of people copying from each other? Is there evidence that some of these channelers are sincere? Or hoaxing? If sincere, is there evidence that they are correct or accurate? Not everyone who follows such channelers seems to care about such things as scientific evidence. There is, in fact, a powerful philosophical divide within the UFO research community reflected in these questions. More on this later.

Therefore, let us explore both sides of contact: abductions on the one hand, intentional contact on the other. In many ways, perhaps fundamentally, these are entirely different phenomena. Still, we shall consider the possibility that they may be two sides of the same coin.

What follows is a brief historical overview of how some of these encounters evolved over time. But it is important to stress that encounters continue to this day. Many researchers are actively investigating them, trying to untangle the threads of reality from those of dream and fantasy.

Contact vs. Abduction

Contact and abduction have each been described as physical and non-physical events. Generally speaking, however, claims of alien abduction are most often perceived and described as physical events. That is, in most cases, a person seems to be taken physically from one place, is brought to another place whereupon things are done to that person, and then he or she is returned at the end. It may well be that

---

[269] Indeed, telepathic communication is reported so consistently, that if self-proclaimed abductees report seeing an alien's lips moving and hearing a spoken voice, they are usually seen as less credible.

Chapter 8: Contact and Abduction

what we think of as physical abductions are more complicated than mere "physical" events. Essentially, however, most alleged alien abductions seem to be physical events, and have to do, at least in part, with our physical bodies.

Such is not always the case regarding alleged contactees. During the 1950s and 1960s, it was fairly common for people to claim physical contact with benevolent extraterrestrial races. Nearly all of these claims involved extraterrestrials that looked entirely human, and who were mostly concerned with protecting mankind and the universe from the danger of atomic weapons. Later, the concerns shifted to the threat posed to Earth's ecosystem by mankind.

Such claims of physical contact continue to this day. More recently, however, and roughly parallel to the rise of the New Age movement from the 1970s onward, there has an additional emphasis on claims of nonphysical, channeled contact with extraterrestrials, or sometimes even humans of the future. Of all such cases, none have risen to the level of scientific evidence (more generously, we add that the scientific community has not made an effort to investigate these claims). However, there is certainly no shortage of detail, often very rich, in the statements of some of these channelers. That makes them very interesting, and for some people, quite compelling.

There is another difference between abduction and contact encounters. This is in the perceived motivations and actions of these other beings. Overall (emphasizing that I am painting with rather broad strokes here), people who have experienced apparent alien abductions have been more likely to see the event as a negative or disturbing experience. Not always, but in general.

Typically, people with apparent abduction experiences feel traumatized by their memories. Whatever else we say about the UFO/ET phenomenon, there is a great deal of pain and suffering associated with abduction. This is made worse than many other types of trauma, simply because the victim feels constrained from discussing it openly, often not even with family members. Such men and women go through their lives doing their best simply to put this piece of their life in as remote and tiny a corner of their minds as possible.

On the other side of the coin, those who claim to be channelers of extraterrestrial intelligences nearly always interpret those entities in a positive or benevolent light. The beings, whether they be the Pleiadians, Ashtar Command, Bashar, or the plentitude of other allegedly channeled entities, are nearly always interpreted as helpers of humanity. Typically, they seek to elevate human consciousness enough so that we might enter the greater galactic community. This idea has gone through its own evolution during the last few decades.

The result is that we have, in a sense, two political parties within the community of people interested in UFOs. One might see them as the *Good ET* and the *Bad ET* parties. A bit simplistic, perhaps, but a fair generalization when looking at the big picture.

Alien Abductions: Birth of an Idea

One interesting point historically is that, for quite some time, alien abductions were not believed to be real. Indeed, with few exceptions, no form of extraterrestrial contact was accepted by either the general public or UFO researchers during the entire decade of the 1950s, and most of the 1960s. A few researchers began to consider the possibility more seriously during the 1970s, but it was not until Budd Hopkins published his first book, *Missing Time*, in 1981, that the phenomenon came to prominence, first among researchers and then around the world.

Upon reflection, this lag in acceptance should not surprise us. All important ideas need time to be accepted. Usually they meet with some resistance along the way, sometimes a great deal of resistance. In the case of abductions, it was not so much that researchers changed their opinions as that they died off and a new generation of researchers replaced them. This is the pattern with all important new ideas.

The UFO phenomenon is so complex, representing technologies and realities so far beyond our normal understanding, that it was not possible for the generation of the 1950s to dive into that ocean and swim in the depths, not without first learning to swim. For the more we learn, the more complex this subject becomes.

Chapter 8: Contact and Abduction

There were, in fact, a few encounter cases during the 1950s that came to the attention of researchers. A few of them even appear to have been genuine abductions. However, little to no investigation was done. Such cases just seemed too fantastic to merit study, but one also suspects that researchers simply did not know how to proceed.

The best known of those cases, and most interesting of that decade, is that of the Brazilian farmer, Antonio Villas Boas. He claimed to have been taken aboard a craft on October 16th 1957 where he was forced to have sex with a somewhat human-looking female, and then to have been deposited back on his farm afterward. It was implied by his alien lover that the purpose of their tryst was for her to become pregnant and to raise their child in space. His story has certain similarities to later abduction cases. The forced sexual encounter is a bit more rare, although the Peter Khoury encounter, discussed in the last chapter, may have been similar. As interesting as the Boas story is, all we have is his detailed written testimony and statements over the following years. While some have doubted his veracity, he may well have been telling the truth. The problem is that he was the sole witness to this extraordinary event and no research for trace physical evidence, or anything else, was done at the time. As such, the case will always be considered problematic.[270]

The Hill Abduction Case

The most important abduction case, in terms of its historical impact, was the 1961 encounter of American New Hampshire residents Betty and Barney Hill. It was the first abduction to receive an investigation not only by UFO researchers, but also by an internationally respected psychiatrist. That man, Dr. Benjamin Simon, conducted many hypnotic regression sessions on each of them. There is a great deal to work here to enable researchers to reconstruct what appears to have

---

270 Melanson, Terry, "Antonio Villas Boas: Abduction Episode Ground Zero" [www.conspiracyarchive.com/UFOs/boas-abduction.htm]. Watson, Nigel, "Alien Sex 101" *Fortean Times*, March 23, 1999 [www.ufocasebook.com/aliensex101.html]. For a skeptical account, see Rogerson, Peter, "Notes Towards a Revisionist History of Abductions, Part One," *Magonia* 2/6/1993 [magonia.haaan.com/1993/notes-towards-a-revisionist-history-of-abductions-part-one/].

happened. The case is also important because it was the true pioneer case for this topic. The Hill abduction was the first to gain widespread media attention. It enabled other researchers to follow up and investigate other apparent abduction cases.

On the night of September 19, 1961, the Hills were driving back from a vacation to Canada. Their route took them through New Hampshire along US Route 3. They expected to get home by around 2:30 a.m., perhaps 3 a.m. at the latest. Along the way, they were puzzled by an object in the sky. It seemed to move unpredictably towards them. Barney, always a strict rationalist and non-believer in UFOs, assumed it was a satellite, then perhaps a star, and then a commercial aircraft. Betty was not persuaded. Through binoculars, she saw the object silhouetted against the moon. It seemed to be a UFO.

Barney continued driving. All the while, the object almost seemed to be tracking them, several times changing speed. When their dog in the back seat began to whine, they looked up and realized the object had descended to just a few hundred feet away from them. What they saw was a large structured craft with double rows of windows. Both of them now had no question of what they were seeing. Both were terrified.

Barney stopped the car in the middle of the road and got out. He walked toward the craft, possibly to within one hundred feet of it. Betty screamed after him, but he did not hear her. When he got close enough, he saw a double row of windows and at least six figures inside. They seemed to be wearing uniforms and staring directly at him.

At this point, the memories of both became blurred. All Barney could remember was running back to the car, screaming. Now driving again, the two heard a strange beeping sound, and they seemed to become drowsy. After more time had passed, the beeping repeated itself and they were fully alert. The car was still moving. Finally, at 5 a.m., they arrived home.

For quite a while, a great deal of anxiety affected both of them. Barney, who was an impeccable dresser, noticed that the tops of his shoes were scuffed. That had never happened before. There were also strange circular marks on their car. For the next few nights, Betty was haunted by intense, exceptionally vivid dreams of non-human beings taking them away. Eventually, she wrote to Donald Keyhoe of the National Investigation Committee on Aerial Phenomena (NICAP). Still, the case did not gain much traction until several years later when, at church meetings, they began discussing their incident. Two attendees, who happened to be in the U.S. Air Force, subtly encouraged the Hills to undergo hypnotic regression. Eventually, the couple began seeing Dr. Benjamin Simon, one of the world's leading experts in hypnotic regression and, interestingly, a leading doctor and officer at the U.S. Army's chief psychiatric center during World War II. This military connection to the case remains very interesting. It certainly leads one to wonder if what really had happened to the Hills was a military abduction, and not an alien one.

Betty and Barney Hill.

Simon's sessions with the Hills lasted from January to June, 1964. During most of this time not only did each not know what the other's session had revealed, but neither patient was even aware of their own regressions. Not until they were nearing the end of treatment did Simon stop inducing amnesia following each session. The extraordinary transcripts are readily available through various books and websites. This even includes the audio recordings themselves.[271]

In short, Betty and Barney both independently recalled being taken out of their car by a small group of beings that did not look human, but were humanoid. The beings even wore clothing and uniforms. Barney recalled a physical examination, one that was rather intrusive: he was made to lie down on a table, a cup was placed over his groin, and his semen seems to have been extracted. Skin scrapings were taken, his ears and throat were examined, and a device was inserted into his rectum.

Betty recalled comparable elements. Her skin was scraped, a sample of her hair was taken, as were fingernail clippings. Her mouth, throat, ears, and hands were studied. She laid down on an exam table, and one of the procedures involved a needle being inserted into her navel, something, although she was not pregnant at the time, like amniocentesis. Before leaving, she communicated with the leader, later believing that this was done telepathically. She asked if she could bring something back to prove her experience, and the leader seemed to agree. She picked up a large book with strange symbols, but was forced to return it when other crew members objected. Then she asked the leader where he was from. He went to a wall and pulled down a strange map of space, showing many stars connected by broken or solid lines, all curved. The lines, he said, represented expeditions. Then he told her she was going to forget all about this encounter.

It was not until 1966 that the Hill case was written about in the form of a book, called *Interrupted Journey*, by journalist John Fuller. From this point, the case began to receive attention not only from UFO researchers, but the general public at large. Without a doubt, Betty and Barney both presented themselves in a very positive and credible manner. No one ever seriously considered them to have been hoaxing. The question comes down to whether or not their memories were accurate. Dr. Benjamin Simon, for his part, did not believe in UFOs or extraterrestrials, and suggested that Betty's initial dreams had

---

271 Forty minutes of audio is available YouTube [www.youtube.com/watch?v=TNGOaSGVwDg]. For extensive transcripts, see Fuller, John G. *The Interrupted Journey: Two Lost Hours Aboard a Flying Saucer*, Dial, 1966.

inspired Barney's account, which was simply a confabulated fantasy. The Hills never believed this. Barney said that he wished the whole thing had been nothing more than a hallucination.

To this day, arguments over alleged alien abduction boil down to this matter. Are the memories accurate or not?

The Herb Schirmer Abduction

Another interesting early case, one which has been somewhat forgotten, took place on December 3, 1967 to a young police officer named Herb Schirmer, of Ashland, Nebraska. On the job at 2:30 a.m., he noticed an object on the road with flickering lights. Thinking it was a truck, he flashed his high beams. To his surprise, the object took off. His police report read: "saw a flying saucer at the junction of highways 6 and 63. Believe it or not." He could not sleep that night; a strong headache and buzzing noise in his head kept him awake. The next day, he noticed a red welt just below his left ear.

Schirmer also realized that there was twenty minutes of time that he could not account for. He soon met with Wyoming psychologist, Dr. Leo Sprinkle, to undergo hypnotic regression. That was when Schirmer recalled some missing details of his encounter. First, his radio and car engine had died. Then, some sort of white object came out of the UFO. Then it communicated with him telepathically. Schirmer was unable to draw his gun. Somehow he had gotten the information that the craft belonged to a sister ship and that the occupants were based in our solar system but originated from another galaxy. They were here to prevent humans from destroying the Earth.

Later, Schirmer underwent a second hypnosis, which gave more information. He now described the object as metallic, football shaped, and glowing. He wanted to leave, but something in his mind stopped him. Beings came out of the craft wearing coveralls with an image of a winged serpent. They shot a greenish gas toward the car, flashed a bright light at him and then he passed out.

When he woke up, one of the beings asked him, "Are you the watchman over this place?" They pointed to the power plant and asked if that was the only source of power. They took him aboard and he saw control panels and computer-like machines. They told him they came from a nearby galaxy, had bases in the United States, that the aircraft was operated by electromagnetism, that they drew power from large water reservoirs, and that radar and ionization disrupted the functioning of their ships. They told him they had been observing Earth for a long time and would contact more people. Then they said, "You will not speak wisely about this night. We will return to see you two more times."

Schirmer drew a picture of the Being he best remembered, which may have looked slightly odd, but entirely human, although about a foot shorter than most adult males. Yet, this was no gray alien. Although Leo Sprinkle believed in the basic truthfulness of Schirmer's account, the story was still too far out for most researchers, who dismissed it at the time as a fantasy. What strikes one today is how comparatively tame it is compared with many more recent abduction stories.[272]

The Charles Moody Abduction

During the summer and fall of 1975, a great deal of UFO activity was reported in the Western United States. It was a time of many violations of airspace around U.S. bases, numerous sightings of unidentified black helicopters, reports of cattle mutilation, and a few fascinating abduction cases.

One concerned an Air Force sergeant named Charles Moody. On the night of August 12/13, 1975, Moody was working his shift at Holloman Air Force Base in Alamogordo, New Mexico. When his shift ended, he decided he would view the Perseid meteor shower. Just after midnight he drove a short way out of town, into the quiet night country of the American southwest.

The meteor shower was not especially captivating, but Moody saw something else. An object about fifty feet in diameter descended from the sky and hovered just off the ground. He watched it glow, wobble,

---

272 "Police Officer Herbert Schirmer Abduction"
[www.ufoevidence.org/cases/case659.htm]. "1967: The Abduction of Patrolman Herb Schirmer" [www.ufocasebook.com/herbertschirmer.html].

Chapter 8: Contact and Abduction

then make a buzzing sound, a mere three hundred feet away. Through a window in the craft, he saw humanoid forms moving around. Frightened, he returned to his car, but the battery was dead. Then the buzzing stopped and he felt an odd sense of calm as he watched the object ascend into the sky. The only problem was that he had lost eighty-five minutes, and could not understand how he arrived home as late as 3 a.m., where his wife was waiting for him.

The next day, Moody experienced lower back pain. He wondered what had happened. Over the next week this pain worsened and he developed a rash on his lower body. Eventually, local UFO researchers interviewed him, including former Air Force Colonel Wendell Stevens, and James and Coral Lorenzen, leaders of APRO, a major UFO organization at the time. Before Moody even met with any psychiatrist, a physician friend of his suggested a method of self-hypnosis, and this appeared to uncover more memories. Moody began to remember his captors. They were, as he put it, "very much like us."

Perhaps like humans, but then again, not exactly. Their heads were larger and hairless, the ears and nose were very small, their eyes somewhat larger, and the mouth had very thin lips. Moody said they were very patient with him, as he remembered fighting with the beings before being taken, which might account for his soreness. They used a kind of light or sound frequency to disable him, and then he found himself on a table in a very clean environment. They also seemed to communicate with him telepathically.

Moody even gained some information from his captors. Their main craft, they said, was four hundred miles above the Earth, and this ship was used for observing. He was told that several races from different places were working together. Radar was a problem for their craft, as it sometimes jammed their navigation. Apparently, they also told him that in the near future, there would be contact made with humanity on a limited basis. This might be roughly twenty years in the future: only then, after deep consideration by them, perhaps humanity would be accepted.

Of course, this would have been around 1995. Perhaps they changed their plans. Or, perhaps they did make limited, quiet contact. Or somehow Charles Moody got it all wrong. Or perhaps the beings purposely gave theatrically misleading information.[273]

Fire In the Sky: Travis Walton

The abduction of Travis Walton, often known as the *Fire in the Sky* case,[274] may be the single most famous alien abduction event ever. Like the Betty and Barney Hill case, there is much to digest. Also like that case, we find ourselves wanting to know more about the captors themselves. Still, what information we have is certainly intriguing.

Like the Moody case three months earlier, this incident occurred amid a wave of truly awe-inspiring and serious violations of U.S. airspace by unknown objects. It happened on November 5, 1975, in a national forest northeast of Phoenix, Arizona. Travis was a member of a six-man logging crew that was finishing up a day of work. He was just 22 years old at the time.

Around 6:15 p.m., the men left the worksite and began the drive down the logging road toward home. Then, all seven saw a glowing, silver object hovering not far above the ground. No one saw the object move—it simply was there. It was not especially large, they estimated perhaps fifteen feet in diameter and about eight feet high. It had complicated markings on it, and it seemed to light up the area. Walton was riding in the front passenger seat, and impulsively left the truck to walk toward the craft. It wobbled a bit, then struck him directly on the chest with a beam of bluish white light. According to men in the truck, the beam lifted him into the air. Then he was knocked back and fell to the ground.

His friends panicked and drove off in terror. They assumed Travis was dead and that they were going to be next. After a few minutes, however, they regained enough composure to drive back. Travis was gone, and so was the object. The men headed back to town and

---

273 Lorenzen, Coral and Jim, *Abducted! Confrontations with Beings from Outer Space* (Berkley Medallion Books, 1977), p. 38-51. Booth, Billy, "1975: Abduction of Sergeant Moody" [ufos.about.com/od/aliensalienabduction/p/moody.htm].
274 After the book and movie of that name.

Chapter 8: Contact and Abduction

immediately reported this to the police, who brought a search party and tracking dogs. No physical evidence was found. Police wondered if Travis Walton had been murdered by his coworkers.

Illustration of the Walton abduction experience.

For five days, Travis Walton was nowhere to be seen, despite police helicopters, mounted police, jeeps, and tracking dogs combing through the area. Under suspicion of murder, the crew members took polygraph examinations. The men all passed, with the exception of one man whose result was "inconclusive" and who later admitted hiding an unrelated criminal record. Still, the examiner stated the results were conclusive, proving that these men did see an object they believed to be a UFO, and that they did not injure or murder Travis.

Consider what it means that each of these men passed a polygraph test attesting to a UFO striking Travis Walton. Then consider the likelihood that all six could fool the test, and the most reasonable conclusion is that these men saw what they claimed to have seen.

Late on the night of November 10, Travis Walton reappeared. He made a phone call from a phone booth, and when his brother and a friend came to him, he was still in the booth, looking exhausted, confused, and with a heavy growth of beard. He still wore the same clothing from the night he had disappeared.

What followed upon Walton's return was nothing short of a circus, characterized by tremendous press coverage and the inevitable debate between skeptics and believers. Walton took two polygraph tests. On the first one, the polygraph examiner said he failed. However, in the interest of fairness, it must be said that it was an incompetent and antagonistic polygraph examination. The questioner interrupted Walton twenty-eight times during the questioning, and at one point berated him when Walton was confused about dates, actually saying to him, "Where have you been, in a vacuum?" It certainly appeared that he intentionally asked Walton embarrassing and irrelevant questions in order to create conditions more likely to produce a negative result. This is especially disturbing if we consider that, if Walton's story was true, he had just gone through the most harrowing experience of his life.

Years later, an investigator who had been skeptical of the abduction arranged for another polygraph test for Walton and two of his co-workers (including the one who had originally tested inconclusively). All three passed.

What exactly did Travis Walton remember?

His recollections involved two kinds of beings. One of these looked human, the other did not. First, he was examined in a white room by hairless, non-human beings in tight-fitting blue clothing. They made no sound. They held him down when he tried to get up, and he even took a swing at one of them, although in his weakened state this did not amount to much. After this, the creatures simply left the room. Travis then got up and went into another room which contained a chair. He sat in it and pressed some buttons on the arms of the chair, at which point the ceiling slid back and he saw stars going by. A human-looking being, wearing a helmet, entered the room. He smiled and silently escorted Travis to a large room where he saw a parked spacecraft. Other people were there, all of them with long hair. They

Chapter 8: Contact and Abduction

placed an oxygen mask on Travis's face and, the next thing he knew, he was lying on the pavement on the highway. He saw the UFO above him, hovering. Then it shot away, and he made his telephone call.

Considering that he was gone for five days, it is remarkable how little Travis Walton remembered. What exactly happened to him?

It might very well be that Walton was unconscious for most of that time. After all, he was struck with an intense blue beam in the chest and knocked out. Years later, Travis offered his own opinion that he was struck unintentionally or by accident and may well have been near-death. He would then have been taken aboard so that his life could be saved and the awful mistake rectified.[275]

It is also interesting that Travis recalled both human and nonhuman entities. How could it be, one might ask, that humans would be working alongside aliens in the operation of UFOs? Perhaps it would not be so unusual if we consider that other beings had taken to breeding their own stock of humans, presumably enhancing and tweaking them as they like. After enough generations over centuries or millennia, it would be obvious that the humans working with another civilization would seem nearly as incomprehensible to us as the aliens themselves. While this is pure speculation, with a phenomenon as strange as UFOs, perhaps it is not so outrageous, after all.[276]

The Andreasson Affair

By the late 1970s, more and more alleged abductees were describing small aliens with large heads and eyes and no hair, who communicated by telepathy. Some of these beings looked rather human, sometimes entirely so. Exactly what the so-called alien agenda might have been was still a matter of debate, but it appeared at the least to be some sort of information gathering effort, with abductions being part of that. Overall, the aliens seemed to be lacking in what most of us would consider an upbeat personality, but they also did not appear to be

---

275 Personal conversation with the author, October 2012.
276 Walton, Travis, *Fire in the Sky: The Walton Experience*, Marlowe and Company, 1996. On the Internet, the reader is directed to the balanced description in Wikipedia, at en.wikipedia.org/wiki/Travis_Walton.

especially dangerous. Some even appeared to be somewhat benevolent.

In 1979, Raymond Fowler, a serious and experienced UFO researcher, published a book about the experiences of a woman named Betty Andreasson. He organized a series of hypnotic regressions for Betty, a deeply religious woman who had been experiencing abductions since at least the 1960s. These sessions produced a detailed story of interaction with creatures with gray skin, large heads, cat-like eyes, tiny mouths, three fingered hands, and dark blue uniforms.[277] They moved by gliding and communicated telepathically. In 1967, several of these beings entered her home through a solid door. They "switched off" all of the family members except for Betty and her daughter. Then, they took Betty to their ship, leaving her daughter behind but somehow "frozen."

Betty was examined. A needle was inserted into her nose and head, but without any physical pain. Somehow, she was transported to an alien realm, whether physically or by means of mind control. She went through tunnels, saw a red and then green atmosphere, strange creatures and plants, and pyramid-like structures.

She also encountered other types of beings, including golden-haired, robed figures, perfectly human looking. She was given a message focusing on love and nature. Humans were destroying the Earth, she was told. The beings could not let humanity go down its current path. They gave her a vision of a Phoenix rising from the ashes of its own destruction, which seemed to symbolize humanity's ability to survive the dangerous times ahead. They also indicated to her that they shared her belief in the sacredness of Jesus Christ. He was coming soon, they said.

Interpreting this has been extremely difficult. This event took place nearly fifty years ago at the time of this writing. There is certainly no evidence that its prediction has come to pass. Of course, the word "soon" is subject to interpretation. It seems that Betty Andreasson and Ray Fowler were sharing this information honestly. Yet we may ask to what extent her recollections, and Fowler's retelling of them, were

---

277 Blue uniforms seem to be a recurring observation among abductees.

influenced by their pre-existing belief system, as both were very devout Christians? To what extent were those recollections clouded or managed by the aliens themselves? Can we expect alien entities to be entirely, or even mainly, truthful? None of these questions are easily answered.

Enter Budd Hopkins

Consider the field of UFO and ET research in 1980. The UFO phenomenon had been out in the open for more than thirty years. And yet, abductions, something that may well be at the heart of whatever this phenomenon is all about, was only just beginning to be investigated, much less understood. That is a great deal of activity occurring in a nearly completely clandestine manner, which is one reason why the work of Budd Hopkins is so important.

In 1981, he published *Missing Time*, probably the single most important book in all of abduction research. That is because Hopkins, after many one-on-one meetings with abductees, argued that the abduction phenomenon was not simply a random occurrence. It was not simply a case of being in the wrong place at the wrong time, at least not normally. Instead, his research pointed to something quite disturbing: that most abductees were taken multiple times for years and years, starting in their youth, if not infancy. Abduction was a recurrent, albeit largely hidden, feature of their lives. Even more upsetting still, the phenomenon appeared to run in families. Hopkins speculated that there was something important to these beings about certain genetic lines.

He did not express these ideas cavalierly. Hopkins was a careful interviewer of people. In the early years, he did not lead the hypnotic regression sessions, but instead relied on certified hypnotherapists, most prominently Dr. Aphrodite Clamar, under whom he trained for seven years. Hopkins himself developed outstanding skills at conducting hypnotic regressions, and even trained Harvard Psychologist, Dr. John Mack (who stated that Hopkins' skills in hypnotherapy exceeded his own). Everyone fortunate enough to have known Hopkins, as I did, agreed that his kindness and bravery brought comfort to many distraught people. More to the point, Hopkins was careful, conscientious, and explicitly avoided leading his clients into preconceived conclusions. Many transcripts of his sessions are available in his books.

Hopkins' work implied that abductions are a widespread operation involving significant resources, presumably for something considered to be of great importance to these other beings. That gives the phenomenon an ominous feeling, even if not necessarily evil. After all, no matter how extensive and potentially important abductions may be, it is easy to see why alien entities would wish to conceal what was going on from humanity.

If abductions were or are as widespread as Hopkins believed, we have a phenomenon that, if revealed publicly, could shatter millions of people. If it is true, and of the dimensions believed by Hopkins, it could easily become the most politically explosive topic not only in the US, but globally.

Into the Darkness

Budd Hopkins was not the only important abduction researcher of the last few decades of the twentieth century. In the early 1990s, Temple University historian Dr. David Jacobs become deeply involved in abduction research. He has made several important contributions.

His book, *Secret Life*, published in 1992, was the first attempt to organize the abduction process into distinct episodes. He did this based on a close analysis of three hundred hypnotic regression sessions he conducted from sixty individuals. Jacobs uncovered many consistencies, both broad and arcane, among people who had not shared their information before, many of whom were ignorant of abduction research.

The abductors were typically less than four feet tall, with large bald heads, huge dark eyes, no ears, and a slit-like mouth—in other words, Grays. These abductors took great care to take their subjects in a covert manner, when they would not be missed. Frequently, they would place a screen memory into the mind of the abductee, often an unusual owl, deer, or other type of animal. The person would be under complete neurological control, unable to move a muscle unless the abductors

Chapter 8: Contact and Abduction

allowed it. They would often be floated through closed doors and windows, or even walls and ceilings. Jacobs admitted that this seemed impossible. Yet, he argued, somehow these beings had figured out a way of doing it, while also rendering themselves and the abductees invisible.

Abductees would typically be brought into rooms that seemed designed for the purpose of studying humans. They would be undressed and made to lie down on a central table. A physical examination would follow, lasting no more than twenty minutes. If the person had been previously abducted, any changes in the body, such as scars or even braces on teeth, would be examined by the aliens. Near the end of the experience, the beings would implant a small, metallic object into the abductee through the nose or ear, or else remove a previously implanted object.

Communication between abductees and these aliens was always telepathic. Throughout the process a being slightly taller than the others would calm the abductee by staring into his or her eyes. Jacobs coined the term "Mindscan" to describe how the tall alien would peer into the mind of the abductee. Through the various recollections, it almost seemed as if the procedure were sucking thoughts and memories out of the abductee's consciousness. Frequently, the abductee would be given reassuring statements, such as, "You are very special to us." Sperm would be collected from men, eggs and fetuses from women. Many female abductees reported having fertilized eggs inserted into them, while others who were already pregnant had their implanted embryo extracted. It also appeared that abductees were targeted in their childhood and mined of genetic and reproductive material throughout their lives.

All this information, drawn with consistency from abductees, led Jacobs to conclude that these abductees were living "a secret life," one that was being exploited by a secret alien group operating on Earth. These beings, he concluded, are not here to help us, nor are they here for scientific inquiry. They are pursuing their own agenda, which is the creation of a human-alien hybrid species. As Jacobs put it: "We have been invaded. This is not an occupation, but it is an invasion. At present we can do little or nothing to stop it."[278]

Unsurprisingly, there have been critics. Several countered that, despite his well-put together study, Jacobs did not give much attention to earth-bound explanations for abductions, such as "hysterical contagion, psychogenic fugue states, temporal-lobe dysfunction, and the like."[279] More fundamental are criticisms about the value of hypnotic regression at all. Many times, careful regression, which is often no more than a state of deep relaxation, can indeed help to recover genuine memories. But there does remain the danger of unintentional confabulation: the creation of a detailed scenario that never happened. Human memory is powerful and often accurate, but not always. After all, even without any leading questions, it is possible that the consciousness of the hypnotherapist can influence at least some patients. Therein lies the problem. Are *these* uncovered memories accurate? On the other side of it, however, can we really believe that Jacobs was so able to influence his sixty hypnotic subjects that all of them reported fundamentally the same type of scenario? Granted, a hypnotherapist might possess some influence over what the subject recalls, but . . . *that much?*

A few years after writing *A Secret Life*, Jacobs wrote an even more disturbing analysis, appropriately titled, *The Threat*.[280] Here, he delved more deeply into the apparent alien plans to infiltrate humanity by creating a hybrid race and replacing humans as Earth's dominant species. By now, his research pointed to decidedly psychopathic personalities held by many of these hybrids. Again, all of this is drawn from the individual recollections of interaction with aliens through regressive hypnosis. The book is disturbing, and indeed Jacobs himself was disturbed by it. Understandably, the most normal human reaction upon reading it would be to hope that he is wrong.

Once again, much of the issue comes down to the reliability of

---

278 Jacobs, David. *Secret Life: Firsthand, Documented Accounts of Ufo Abductions*, Simon and Schuster, 1993.
279 *Kirkus Reviews* [www.amazon.com/Secret-Life-Firsthand-Documented-Abductions/dp/product-description/0671797204].
280 Jacobs, David. *The Threat: Revealing the Secret Alien Agenda*, Simon & Schuster, 1999.

hypnotic regression. We know that regression can cut both ways: to help someone find repressed truth and inadvertently create false memories. The latter can happen not merely through direct mind manipulation techniques, something that has been studied in detail for many years, but also simply during the course of ordinary life. People do misremember things. The pertinent question here is whether the practitioners of hypnotic regression have been guilty, whether intentionally or not, of influencing the memories of the people they have regressed.

It may be impossible at present to give a clear, quantifiable, answer to that question. On a personal level, having known Budd Hopkins, David Jacobs, and other individuals who have practiced hypnotic regression, as well as having seen a number of regressions occur, I believe that the best practitioners are professional and do not unduly influence their subjects. But no one knows with complete certainty where the actual memory ends and confabulation begins.

It is helpful, however, to remember that many people do not need hypnosis to recall their apparent alien encounters. There have always been a certain number of experiences that are remembered spontaneously, sometimes immediately, sometimes a bit later. For most of these people, there is no question of the strength of their conviction, and often of the clarity of the memory itself. So we have a phenomenon that, despite all efforts of skeptics to debunk and dismiss it, is more complex than any single explanation, or even several explanations can provide.

Alien Implants

One criticism leveled by skeptics of alien abduction is the lack of evidence to examine. In fact, there are claims of evidence, in the form of body marks and extracted implants. Quite a few people have described seeing odd marks on their bodies following either an evening of disturbing UFO-related dreams, or other signs like waking up with drops of blood on the pillow. There are a great many photographs of such body marks, many of which are in an equilateral triangle pattern of red dots on the wrist or near the ankle. Also common are "scoop marks," in which it appears as if a small amount of tissue was removed from beneath the skin, leaving an indentation. When I visited Budd Hopkins on one occasion, he showed me a large collection of photographs he had received from people showing him such marks on their bodies.

In some cases people have gone missing, and concerned friends or relatives have called the police, especially in cases when the missing person was very young. At some point, the person would simply reappear from a room that had been thoroughly searched. There are police records that verify these events, some of which were discussed in Hopkins' book, *Sight Unseen*[281]

More interesting still are extracted implants. Implants are widely reported by abductees, especially via regressive hypnosis. According to the memories of the individuals, these tiny devices are usually inserted through the nose into the sinus cavity, or behind the eye, or in some other part of the body, such as the foot. There has been much speculation about the purpose of these implants. Clearly, they could be useful for tracking a subject, or even serving as storehouses of information, much as veterinarians today retrieve medical data on tagged animals. Could they even be used as a form of behavioral or mental modification?

There are a number of alleged alien implants that have been extracted from people. The person best known for this has been Dr. Roger Leir. Over the years, he has performed more than fifteen surgeries that removed sixteen separate and distinct objects. These have been investigated by several prestigious laboratories, including Los Alamos National Laboratories, New Mexico Tech, and others.

At the National Press Club in Washington, D.C. on April 20, 2009, Roger Leir gave an update on his work. He described the various implants he had extracted from people, all roughly the same size, and seven of which were so identical to each other that, as he said: "You could line them up on a surgical drape . . . [and] not be able to tell one from the other." The objects were typically just a few millimeters long

---

281 Hopkins, Budd and Rainey. Carol. *Sight Unseen: Science, UFO Invisibility, and Transgenic Beings*, Atria Books, 2003.

to as long as a centimeter, and as thin as pencil lead. Leir was amazed during each surgery by the lack of inflammation or rejection reaction in any of the subjects. In his view, this is impossible with our current, known technology. No point of entry was visible, nor was any scarring. Each implant had a very tough, biological type of coating, which presumably accounted for the lack of inflammation. This coating, said Leir, was so tough that a surgical blade could not cut through it.[282]

But Leir, a medical doctor, was not qualified to comment on the metallic objects inside these implants. For this press conference, he was accompanied by Dr. Alex Mosier, whose Ph.D. is in physical chemistry. Mosier and Lier studied one implant in great detail, using a battery of tests. Several fascinating features stood out.

First, the object had certain things in common with meteorite fragments, but also interesting differences. It had certain metals common to meteorites, such as Gallium, Germanium, Platinum, Ruthenium, Rhodium, and Iridium. But, of course, why would identical-looking meteor fragments be embedded inside so many different people, without having caused pain or inflammation? Mosier also saw something very interesting. He noted "a deviation of nickel from terrestrial ratios that the analysis lab couldn't explain." In other words, he was suggesting that the implant contained nickel with an isotopic ratio not found on Earth.

Second, the object contained nanofibers very similar in appearance to carbon nanotubes. This is something no meteoric sample has ever been observed to have. This suggests engineering and manufacture. As Mosier put it, "You don't find these things in nature. They have to be processed, engineered, and they're not easy to make."

Third, sodium chloride—that is, salt crystals—were detected, but in a very unusual shape and configuration. Mosier believed that this also suggested engineering.

Finally, and very striking, the object was magnetic. It gave off a radio frequency in the range of 14.7 MHz.

---

282 See "Press Conference - National Press Club - X-Conference 2009 - Washington DC - Part 2 of 2 (Full HD)," Exopolitics Denmark, beginning at 18:45 minutes [www.youtube.com/watch?v=hfrvzXlK92U].

To Mosier: "the combination of all this data indicates some kind of unusual engineering within this object. Elemental analysis indicates it's likely non-terrestrial. It could be meteoric, possibly. It could be something else."

Something else seems more likely, especially considering the presence of what appear to be carbon nanotubes and electromagnetic emissions. To Mosier, this suggested the possibility of what he called "a functional device that may serve to monitor or control."

Incidentally, the frequency of the object, 14.749 MHz, is, in the United States, assigned by the FCC for low-power, short range-use, mostly for objects known as data tags. These typically track objects or transfer digital information within a very short range, for instance inside a large room or warehouse for purposes of tracking inventory with a handheld device.[283]

Leir's battery of tests were done with a barebones budget. He and Mosier both emphasized the need for more and better testing. Clearly, to be considered scientifically valid, the results need to be replicated by other laboratories. Not to fault Leir and Mosier, who did everything within their capability, but the demands of scientific proof are very high. The next step is obvious: significant research money allocated to the study of these implants.

However, we are obligated to state what seems to be obvious: the objects had elements that appeared to be extraterrestrial and of extraordinary technology. It produced a radio transmission. It had nanofibers similar in appearance to carbon nanotubes. It was contained within a type of cocoon that prevented the body from creating an inflammatory response. And the subject, as all of Leir's subjects, had UFO sightings and apparent abduction experiences.

Consider how often human beings tag other creatures. Perhaps advanced life forms treat humanity in the same way. Of course, we must also consider the likelihood that these implants could be a black budget or classified military operation. After all, it might strike some as a bit "old school" for an advanced extraterrestrial race to use RF

---

[283] It is worth mentioning, however, that there is no reason one cannot have high-powered transmissions at 14.75 MHz, aside from FCC regulations and international treaties.

Chapter 8: Contact and Abduction

emitting magnetic chips. The technology behind these devices is clearly very sophisticated, but if we consider the possible advances made in secret by a breakaway civilization, or something along those lines, probably not beyond their capability.

These implants are important, they are real, and they could be at the cusp of gaining scientific credibility. But we are still not any closer to answering the question: who is making and implanting them? Human, alien, both, or something different entirely?

John Mack

During the early 1990s, John Mack, Harvard professor, psychiatrist, and Pulitzer Prize recipient, became very interested in the topic of alien abduction. Within a few years, he had personally interviewed over one hundred abductees, which formed the basis for his important book, *Abduction*, published in 1994.[284]

As a medical professional, Mack's first responsibility was to the health and well-being of his patients. Even so, he did not regard abductees as patients in the usual sense. With a few exceptions, he considered them normal and healthy people who had experienced something disturbing and mysterious. In fact, he considered it remarkable that, despite the obvious trauma they had undergone, most of these people were not medically or psychiatrically disturbed.

The three key pioneers of abduction research: Budd Hopkins (l), David Jacobs (c), and John Mack (r).

Whereas Hopkins and Jacobs tended to view abductions as an assault by extraterrestrial beings upon humanity, Mack did not. He

---

284 Mack, John, E., M.D. *Abduction: Human Encounters with Aliens*, Scribner, 1994.

observed that many abductees believed that they had gained greater spiritual awareness or insights as a result of their experiences, which benefit humanity's continued evolution. In other words, contact between human and non-human extraterrestrial intelligences could have positive outcomes.

Like other abduction researchers, Mack noted the apparent telepathic communication between aliens and abductees. But out of this, he drew a new conclusion: this communication appeared to be instrumental in altering human consciousness. This direct mind-to-mind communication was not especially pleasant. It involved implanting horrible images such as environmental disasters, earthquakes, or other catastrophes. The aliens seemed to be monitoring the response of the abductee and sometimes provided information about when a future disaster would occur. The mental connection was not always about disasters, though. It could simply be the transmission of some piece of information that spurred the abductee to grow in some way.

As an example, Scott, one of the subjects in Mack's book *Abduction*, had been a skeptic on the matter of extraterrestrials, but then was humiliated to recall how beings had laid him on a table and used various wires to stimulate sexual arousal and ejaculation. In his words, all of this was in order to "make babies."[285] He felt violated and angry that the beings were controlling his memories and "messing with his head." On another occasion, he was shown cylinders with tiny babies, presumably from his sperm. He was also taken to an underground facility, where he saw that the alien beings were something like an extended family to him, in the sense that they knew everything about him. Indeed, they knew more about him than any human family would have known.

Scott learned, somehow, that these beings were in the process of changing themselves physically so that they could breathe on Earth. This is a key part of the hybridization process, he said. He also observed that they think much faster than humans do. During telepathic communication, he said, they need to slow down in order

---

[285] Barney Hill had reported this same type of procedure years before.

not to overwhelm us. Scott believed that their intention was to live on Earth, but possibly without humanity—unless humanity were to change, in which case we might live together. Scott contrasted human and alien existence. Human beings, he said, are alone. They do not share their thoughts, or much of anything. Among the aliens, conversely, nobody is alone, there are no secrets. Everybody knows everything. Based on his recalled experiences, Scott concluded that if humanity does not change, our world will change for us.

Disturbing though these recalled memories were, they spurred Scott to become more aware of the need to protect the Earth, of finding ways to explore and expand his own thinking and consciousness, and of fundamentally becoming a better person.

Thus, while Mack agreed with other researchers that abduction experiences are often traumatic, and even appear cruel at times, he believed it could still be spiritually transformative. He saw no inconsistency in this, "unless," as he put it, "one reserves spirituality for realms of the sublime that are free of pain and struggle." Going on, he wrote, "sometimes our most useful spiritual learning and growth comes at the hands of rough teachers who have little respect for our conceits, psychological defenses, or established points of view."

In effect, suggested Mack, the abduction process has the potential to free our minds. In the first place, acknowledging the very existence of these other beings, after the initial shock, may be "the first step in the opening of consciousness to a universe that is no longer simply material. Abductees come to appreciate that the universe is filled with intelligences and is itself intelligent."

This was why Mack often used the less value-laden term, *experiencer*, instead of *abductee*, to describe these individuals. His impression was that the abduction process is not evil, "and that the intelligences at work do not wish us ill." He came to the belief that the phenomenon is fundamentally about the "preservation of life on earth, at a time when the planet's life is profoundly threatened." Throughout his life, Mack kept his mind open to the possibilities of what humanity is facing, and even questioned whether these beings were actually extraterrestrial. He never made the extraterrestrial hypothesis (ETH) his definite conclusion. He wrote that they come "from a source that remains unknown to us."

The Other Side of Contact

From here we move to the other side of contact. It is a side with a much longer pedigree than alien abduction, at least insofar as how long it has been discussed. This is intentional contact by humans with nonhuman entities, whether they be conceived as extraterrestrial or otherwise.

The idea is ancient. What is a shaman, after all, but someone who makes contact with entities from another realm in order to provide guidance or protection for their own society? Even the neighborhood priest comes from a long history of spiritual masters and adepts whose job was to serve as the receptacle for the divine or holy spirit in order to bring enlightenment, or at least guidance, to the people. In essence, such endeavors are no different from contemporary claims of channeling extraterrestrial beings. Whatever it may be that is happening during such an experience, no answer is going to satisfy everyone.

The idea of communicating in this manner with extraterrestrials (as specific from other types of entities such as ghosts or divine beings) seems to date to the 18th century, when the philosopher Emanuel Swedenborg claimed to have done this telepathically. Then, during the 1870s, the mystic Helena Blavatsky claimed to have done the same. A few decades later, Aleister Crowley, after performing sexual rituals and taking opium, engaged in a state of meditation something like self-induced hypnosis. He also claimed to have contacted an extraterrestrial being, although in this case not merely in a spiritual manner, but physically. In fact, he drew a picture of this being, whom he said was named Lam. Lam had a large head and bears a passing resemblance to large-headed alien grays.

Blavatsky and Crowley were two key figures in the creation of today's New Age philosophy. Blavatsky in fact created a new movement based on an ancient term, *theosophy*, which means "divine wisdom." It is a philosophy of mysticism, fundamentally at odds with

Chapter 8: Contact and Abduction

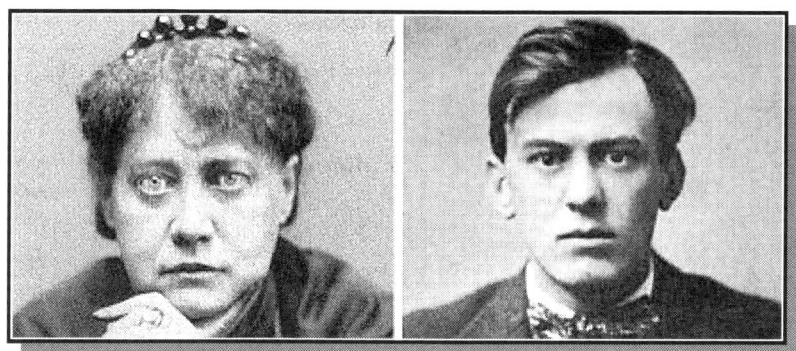

Helena Blavatsky (l) and Aleister Crowley (r).

the scientific method. That is because it is premised on the idea that knowledge comes from both external *and* internal sources. In theosophy, internal truths have equal validity as scientific truths. In other words, if something 'feels' true to oneself, it is just as valid as a scientifically observable fact. This may seem outrageous or simplistic to some, but it is in fact a core tenet of theosophy.

The obvious reply is that such a philosophy is quite convenient for hoaxers and delusional people, since internally intuited or heartfelt truths—or, for our purposes, nearly all channeled ET communications—are not falsifiable, not verifiable, and therefore could easily be fabricated.

But from a theosophical point of view, this is missing the point, which is that by going "inside" to one's truth, one delves into esoteric, internal, divine realms not accessible by normal waking or upper consciousness. That is the claim. Essentially, theosophy continues the ancient, mystical, esoteric traditions. In this respect, it is also not very different from standard Christian, Muslim, or Hindu religious beliefs, or the beliefs of many other traditional cultures around the world.[286]

But it is not merely the methods of theosophy that have influenced modern New Age culture, including alleged channelers and contactees of extraterrestrials. It is the very content of belief itself. A key part of theosophy has to do with the "Ascended Masters," sometimes called

---

[286] Except perhaps with the caveat that theosophy and New Age beliefs (in theory) do not require a priest or authority figure to lead the flock. In practice, that tradition is replete with self-styled gurus who are all-too-content to lead their followers to Ascension.

the Mahatmas. These beings, it is said, once lived on Earth. Through their various lives, they learned the many lessons they needed to learn, balanced at least 51% of their karma, and gained mastery over the limitations of the material planes of existence. Thus, they fulfilled their Divine Plan, or dharma. As a result, they are considered God-like and a source of divine love.

Claims of channeling Ascended Masters have become fairly common. During the 1920s, and well into the 1940s, the theosophist Alice Bailey channeled an ascended Tibetan master who relayed information on such topics as ancient wisdom, philosophy, science, contemporary events, and more. In later years, people have claimed Ascended Masters to be part of various interdimensional, or transcendent organizations, such as the *Spiritual Hierarchy of Earth*, the *Great Brotherhood of Light*, or *Great White Brotherhood,* and similar names. From here, we easily arrive at such groups as the *Galactic Federation of Light,* one of the commonly alleged extraterrestrial organizations that channelers discuss today.

One idea that has become part of New Age culture is that people will eventually attain "Ascension," moving forward in spiritual evolution beyond Planet Earth. In this formulation, the Ascended Masters (or the Extraterrestrials) are here to help people do that. In the years leading up to December 21, 2012 (the end of the Mayan Calendar and a date many thought the world might end), there was an incredible build-up about the Ascension, and some believed it would elevate humanity into the next "density," or level of consciousness, particularly for those who had 51% positive karma. The connections with 19th century Theosophy are obvious.

This philosophy is an important foundation of the ideas espoused by people who claim to have had intentional contact with extraterrestrials, either physically or spiritually. Clearly, we are still wanting to answer the all-important question: is any of this for real? Or is it all nonsense? Does it even belong in a study of the UFO phenomenon?

Before trying to answer this, let us explore a bit more.

Chapter 8: Contact and Abduction

Adamski and the 1950s

As soon as flying saucers became a media sensation, there were those who came forward claiming to have had contact with the operators of those craft, not as abductees or merely observers, but as people who had actual communication. Typically, they relayed the philosophies of these beings, most of which followed from the principles of Theosophy.

The most prominent of these early contactees was George Adamski. Adamski was a Polish-born amateur astronomer who had moved to California and then claimed to have had multiple contacts with human-looking extraterrestrials throughout the 1950s and early 1960s.

On November 20, 1952, accompanied by a small group of friends Adamski set out to an area of the California desert where, he said, his intuition told him he needed to go. He told his friends that he believed he was going to have an extraterrestrial encounter. Arriving at the spot, he walked far ahead of his friends. There, alone, he claimed to have met a completely human-looking extraterrestrial pilot, dressed in a kind of jumpsuit. The person hardly spoke a word, but Adamski claimed that, through telepathy and hand gestures, he was able to understand most of the conversation. The pilot, whose name he later learned was Orthon, told him many things. First, that he came from the planet Venus. Also, that all the other planets in the Solar System are inhabited, that all extraterrestrials essentially look human, and that a nuclear war on Earth would cause serious disruption in the cosmos. This last statement explained their current interest in humanity.[287]

The problem with this is that, although Adamski claimed his companions were able to see the extraterrestrial, all of them later admitted they had not. They had not even seen the spacecraft. Adamski had simply gone off on his own and then returned to tell them what had happened.

This was not the only time Adamski pulled such a stunt. He did precisely the same thing in 1963 at the Vatican, when he claimed to have met with the Pope and to have received a medallion. Accompa-

---

[287] Leslie, Desmond; Adamski, George. *Flying Saucers Have Landed*, British Book Centre, 1953.

George Adamski next to a painting of Orthon.

nied by two friends, he went off ahead of them in the crowded Vatican Square and was gone for thirty minutes. He then came back, claiming he had met with the Pontiff. Research into this matter has proven conclusively that this was a lie. Adamski's medallion was merely a tourist trinket. He did not even enter the Vatican through the area where the Pope was at the time. Nobody ever saw him with the Pope, and his two friends were forced to take him at his word. This is not how to build a solid case, but it was Adamski's typical *modus operandi*. Incidentally, he told his friends that the Pope's health was very good when, in reality, the Pope was gravely ill and would be dead within two weeks.

It is hard to avoid the conclusion that Adamski was a hoaxer. In my own journeys through this field, I have met a number of people who believed in him, and a few who knew him personally and supported him. Yet, too many facts get in the way.[288]

In addition to Adamski, there were many other individuals of the 1950s who claimed similar types of contact: Daniel Frye, Howard and Connie Menger, George Van Tassell, Cedric Allingham, Orfeo Angelucci, Truman Bethurum, Elizabeth Klarer, and many others.

---

288 For a good critical analysis of Adamski, see Hallet, Marc, "Why I can say that Adamski was a Liar" [www.marc-hallet.be/Adamski.htm].

Chapter 8: Contact and Abduction

Each of these people claimed to have had personal contact with human looking extraterrestrials, and all of the extraterrestrials had messages for humanity. In the 1950s, that message was almost exclusively geared toward the dangers of atomic power and weaponry.

Over time, the messages evolved somewhat, but still retained the basic concept that the beings from elsewhere had knowledge that could be used for the betterment of both humanity and the individual. This, too, has always been a central tenet of theosophy. During the 1970s, for instance, Italian contactee, Giorgio Dibitonto had a number of alleged contacts with "space brothers," including rides in starships. These beings were claimed to be the angels of the Bible, still charged with revealing spiritual truths to humanity and with guiding us on the path toward higher development. They told Dibitonto:

> You have set matter and spirit against each other.... If you could free your mind from its presumptuous arrogance, and become meek and simple, pure and good... Then you would solve the whole problem of evil and your unhappiness. The intellect becomes ensnared if it represses or subverts [the wisdom of the heart]. Then the heart and the mind become enemies of each other, and the result is all manner of misfortune and sickness.[289]

This is a classic presentation of theosophical thought, and a perfect encapsulation of most messages from the "space brothers," whether received in person, or via channeled or telepathic communications. Indeed, since the 1990s, the message from the space brothers has become almost exclusively spiritual. Even nuclear weapons and the environment have taken a back seat to the need for humanity to ascend to a higher level of consciousness in its ongoing process of spiritual evolution. In such a way, we can peacefully join the greater galactic community.

I would suggest that it shows how the Theosophical influence has had a damaging effect on the UFO subculture, just as it has done more generally within our broader society. Focusing on love over hatred is a good thing, of course, just as seeing the ultimate unity of all life forms. But the emphasis, again and again, on the "heart" over the

---

[289] Debitonto, George. *Angels in Starships* [galactic.no/rune/Angels%20in%20spaceships.htm].

intellect, on intuition over rational thought, on cleansing one's own spirit before working together in a communal, political matter to effect change, take away our most important tools to function in a world filled with gross injustice, government secrecy, and the loss of human rights around the world. That is, the New Age movement, insofar as it has become a force in our world, has never been a force for fighting real injustice, has never worked for political change, and has arguably only caused people to spin their wheels in a self-indulgent yet ultimately fruitless path toward "enlightenment."

Like early Christianity, it is a religion of the powerless. But whereas the powerless adherents of early Christianity included many women and slaves who were clearly attracted to a better world in the afterlife, in the case of the New Age movement today, the powerlessness of our society is of a different sort. That is, people have understood more and more through the twentieth century and beyond that the problems in our world in terms of environmental degradation, warfare, injustice, and more are so bad that we often despair of being able to fix them at all. Therefore, the Escape into Self has become very appealing to some. If the world is going to hell, why not make your private life a little more beautiful while you can? Why not keep out all "negativity" and essentially pretend it doesn't exist?

Living in a bubble can be attractive for a while. It is like living in a wonderful dream while your house is burning down around you. What's better: dying while you dream, or waking up and trying to deal with the fire?

But the political dangers of New Age thought are separate from the truth or non-truth of the alleged communications with extraterrestrials. On this matter, there is more to say.

Telepathic Contact: The Affa Case

Generally speaking, there has been a trend over the decades, moving from physical to non-physical forms of alleged contact with extraterrestrials. But even during the 1950s, communications with extraterrestrials via Ouija board, spirit mediums, and channeling was fairly common.

Chapter 8: Contact and Abduction

One especially interesting case was that of Affa. According to UFO researcher and historian, Jerome Clark, Affa first appeared in 1952 to a small group in Prescott, Arizona, headed by George Hunt Williamson. These communications were mainly through automatic writing, identifying Affa as from the planet Uranus and living above Earth's atmosphere in a very large space ship.

Then, in 1954, Affa appeared in the automatic writing of Mrs. Frances Swan of Eliot, Maine. Here, too, Affa said he was from Uranus and in a huge ship above the Earth. What is hard to reconcile are the many conflicting elements of what Swan transcribed. On the one hand, there was a great amount of detail, including technical knowledge that surely seemed beyond her education. On the other, there are passages in her transcription that certainly do not strike one as from an extraterrestrial source. For instance, here is a description by Affa of his ship. He described it as over two hundred miles long, essentially the size of a small nation, and said:

> We have recreational centers and swimming pools here. There are no women on this ship because the nature of the work is for the strong ones. We have to keep in training at all times as the work is most strenuous… My favorite sport is fencing. I like swimming and hiking also. Many of the sons box and wrestle with the exception that no one ever gets hurt. We do this on a point system only. I also ride horseback and do some target shooting. We have rifles much the same as your own but we use them only for sports of which we have several.

Extraterrestrial? If there was ever a smell test to detect such a thing, the preceding passage would cause Affa to flunk it. But the Affa story does not end here.

Swan happened to live next door to retired U.S. Navy Rear Admiral, Herbert B. Knowles. Knowles believed Swan was legitimate. He tried to interest the U.S. military as a way to establish useful communication with these extraterrestrials and arranged for two officers from the Office of Naval Intelligence (ONI) to meet her on June 8, 1954. They asked questions of Affa, the answers of which were presumably unknown to Swan, such as, "What is the length of Uranus' day?" and "What is the distance between Jupiter and the sun at Jupiter's apogee?"

According to her investigators, the answers were correct. But Affa also promised a radio transmission on June 10. When this did not happen, ONI apparently lost interest. This is a curious pattern, incidentally. Often, one hears of channelers and people claiming contact with aliens who may have some initial accuracy in their more mundane claims. Yet, their grandiose proclamations fall flat.

Matters did not end here, however. Although there are somewhat conflicting accounts of what happened next, Affa was a subject of interest at the CIA's National Photographic Interpretation Center (NPIC). During the summer of 1959, Navy Commander Junius Larsen learned of the incident at Swan's home from the previous month. He had a strong interest in spiritualism, and was also an ONI liaison officer with NPIC. Larsen met with Swan, whereupon she taught him automatic writing. Larsen believed that he, too, had communicated with Affa, although Clark related that Swan was skeptical.

Larsen returned to Washington and met with the head of NPIC, Art Lundahl, as well as Lundahl's assistant, Navy Lieutenant Commander Robert Neasham. Larsen entered a trance and believed he contacted Affa. When the men asked Affa to prove that he was there, Affa told them to go to the window. Neasham saw what he believed was a craft among the clouds, although clearly it could not have been the enormous craft Affa previously described to Swan. In any case, Lundahl claimed he never saw any craft. Neasham described the event to Air Force Major Robert Friend, head of Project Blue Book. For Friend's benet, Larsen related telepathic messages from Affa and other space people, but on this occasion the aliens refused to appear. An alternate version has it that Lundahl was not present during the first session, in which the craft was clearly visible, and when he was present for a second session, Affa did not appear.[290]

---

290 Gourley, Jay, "The Day the Navy Established 'Contact'," Second Look, May 1979 [presidentialufo.com/old_site/affa_cia.htm]. Clark, Jerome, *Extraordinary Encounters: An Encyclopedia of Extraterrestrials and Otherworldly Beings*, ABC-Clio, 2000, p. 12-13. Cameron, Grant, "Eisenhower and his alien contacts, part 2" [www.presidentialufo.com/dwight-d-eisenhower/473-eisenhower-and-his-alien-contacts-part-2#_edn3].

What exactly was going on during Francis Swan's automatic writing? Or, for that matter, in the communications with Larsen and George Hunt Williamson? Was this just a facet of the mind of the person engaged in the act of automatic writing, disconnected somehow from one's ordinary consciousness but still entirely one's own? Or was it really true? Was it some form of gentle deception by these other beings? Or worse?

Towards Assessing the Claims

Regarding channeling, or automatic writing, or any other form of communication like this, there appear to be sincere people who mean well but are deluded, and there are also hoaxers. But perhaps there are a few cases that are legitimate. If so, what was Affa?

The question is important because, starting in the late 1960s, such alleged communication with extraterrestrials became more prevalent, not so much via automatic writing as through channeling. Today, along with people who claim to have telepathic "downloads," this is easily the dominant form of "talking" with aliens.

Setting aside the obvious theosophical content of most of these communications for the moment, it is important to ask whether or not there is something to it? And if so, how might it work?

For example, is there something to the practice of deep meditation and channeling that allows a human being to reach into a certain inner "place" and contact a higher intelligence, perhaps one that is extraterrestrial?

I will return to this issue in more depth later in the book. But I may suggest that the answer is, at least partially, *yes*.

The question is really not much different in substance from questions over the power of prayer. Does prayer work? There are people trying to prove this, with results that everyone continues to debate.

Regarding UFO contact, we would do well to recall that most contactees and abductees have claimed some form of telepathic connection with these other beings. In fact, such connections are often felt by people who have UFO sightings, without even experiencing the extra level of abduction or contact. In other words, these beings appear, somehow, to connect to us telepathically.

Anecdotally, there are many interesting examples of people who have meditated or engaged in some other esoteric practice which seemed directly related to their encounter. Even the previously mentioned 1927 UFO sighting by explorer Nicholas Roerich falls into this category. The event occurred in the ultra-remote Altai Himalaya region of Tibet. It turns out that Roerich and his wife, Helena Ivanovna Roerich, who was also there, happened to be active Theosophists. Both were brilliant. Nicholas was probably a genius: a first-rank painter and visionary philosopher who wrote essays about the cosmic evolution of mankind, the spiritual factor in the development of humanity, the need for international peace and brotherly love, and the need to protect the Earth. He received several nominations for the Nobel Prize. Helena Roerich was his partner in everything. In fact, shortly after the sighting, she would translate two volumes of the writings of Helena Blavatsky. And there, in the middle of nowhere, they saw a truly intriguing UFO. What are the odds?

Ultimately, the problem with all esoteric information and communications is that they are almost always unverifiable. When predictions have been made, they have invariably been wrong, or else a big, obvious, *so what?* In the current crop of channeled information, allegedly from extraterrestrials, there is an abundance of theosophical platitudes concerning the need to raise humanity's "vibrational frequency" to achieve higher consciousness and open portals to the next dimension. There is little to nothing, however, that is verifiable or amenable to scientific testing.

Regarding both basic forms of contact with extraterrestrials, whether by abduction or intention, we have a great deal in the way of claims, and a great deal that has not met contemporary standards of scientific validity. The most promising avenue for research at this point seems to be into alleged alien implants. Still, neither abductions, nor contact have impressed many scientists.

But both have, arguably, made changes in what we call human

consciousness. Within the human mind, they exist. And, it is not the worst bet in the world that both have some correspondence with an external reality. Unfortunately, both are littered with junk claims that must be discarded. It is a bit like searching for treasure in a landfill. There is something valuable hidden within, but we may need to hold our noses while searching.

The matter of contact provides endless fascination, leading to many questions. Perhaps the most important of all is, Who are these entities? We may not be able to answer that question to everyone's satisfaction, but we shall certainly explore the rabbit hole.

Chapter 9
The Growth of Ufology

Ufology in 1970 was a field in need of a facelift. The 1960s had seen a crescendo of tension amounting to a crisis. It developed and festered until the release of the *Scientific Study of Unidentified Flying Objects* by the Condon Committee in early 1969. This report, conducted through the University of Colorado, was meant to be a legitimate scientific analysis that would determine the validity of the UFO phenomenon, or at least to decide whether it was something truly unusual and extraordinary, or unworthy of scientific interest.

The Committee's verdict was definitive, and very much negative. UFOs, concluded Edward Condon, were of "no probative value" to science, meaning that the study of them did not promise to advance scientific knowledge. Condon recommended that the Air Force drop Project Blue Book, its office devoted to UFOs, which the Air Force promptly did.

It was as though a balloon had been inflated, and inflated again, and inflated still more, only to be popped.

From the Ashes of the Condon Committee

Granted, the Condon Committee study had been a rigged game, with a preordained negative conclusion. Nevertheless, the study of UFOs became a serious twofold problem: first, how to study the topic scientifically and second, how to earn respect from the public?

It did not help that UFO sightings appeared to have subsided at that time. Throughout much of the 1960s, there had been many sightings and a fair amount of public attention brought upon on the subject. Indeed, there would again be more activity later on in the 1970s. But for now, it seemed, not much was happening. Perhaps, some wondered, the skeptics were right, that the UFO phenomenon had been nothing more than a passing fancy of popular culture and hysteria. Perhaps science had shone its light upon the subject. It had opened the vault and found it empty.

American Ufology: The Big Four

Naturally, UFO research did not cease. Within a few years of the Condon Report, there were four research groups in the United States that, small though they were, had some claim to being "national" organizations.

One was the National Investigative Committee on Aerial Phenomena (NICAP), based out of Washington, D.C. For years, NICAP had challenged the Air Force position on UFOs and tried to initiate open congressional hearings on the matter. But NICAP in the 1970s was circling the drain. Its longtime director, retired Marine Corps Major Donald E. Keyhoe, had been ousted in 1969 by Colonel Joseph J. Bryan III, a man later discovered to have once headed the CIA's Psychological Warfare division. Leadership of NICAP passed to John Acuff, who had been the head of another military and CIA-affiliated group. Acuff ended NICAP's criticism of government UFO policy. More significantly, he destroyed its investigative and reporting network. Acuff also plundered the organization personally and essentially destroyed it. Through the 1970s, NICAP was a mere shell of its former self. By 1980, it was no more.[291]

For years, NICAP's main rival had been the Aerial Phenomena Research Organization, (APRO) based out of Tucson, Arizona. Founded in 1952 by James and Coral Lorenzen, it had developed an impressive structure. A typical *APRO Bulletin* of the late 1960s listed some 40 or more Ph.D.s or M.D.s as consultants, covering a wide range of disciplines. The organization had representatives from forty to fifty nations. It was a worldwide network, subsisting on memberships of less than $10 per year.

Thus, with NICAP's willfully incompetent leadership, one would

---

291 Fawcett & Greenwood, *Clear Intent*, p. 207. Hall, Richard, "NICAP: The Bitter Truth," *MUFON UFO Journal*, 3/80.

think that APRO was primed to lead American ufology. But APRO received its own unwelcome shock in 1969, when one of its regional officers, Walter Andrus, took many members with him to form the Midwest UFO Network based out of Seguin, Texas. Many NICAP members also joined. Soon renamed the Mutual UFO Network, MUFON quickly became a leading UFO research group. Andrus focused on building a grassroots investigative organization. It is interesting to note that he was formerly in the U.S. Navy, and many of MUFON's board members had Navy and intelligence community backgrounds. Among the most prominent was Thomas Deuley, a former Lieutenant Commander in the U.S. Navy and former employee of the National Security Agency. In time, a great deal of speculation and suspicion would develop on the matter of MUFON's relationship to the U.S. intelligence community. It is worth noting, too, that MUFON's grassroots efforts never succeeded past membership levels of a few thousand.

In 1973, yet another American UFO organization was founded. This was the Center for UFO Studies (CUFOS) near Chicago, created around the astronomer Dr. J. Allen Hynek. Hynek was the most famous name in ufology at the time, having formerly been consultant to the Air Force for Project Blue Book. However, Hynek was not the founder, but co-founder of the organization. The other co-founder, Sherman J. Larsen, was quite obscure. Although UFO researcher and CUFOS member, Jerome Clark, once described Larsen as little more than "a retired ... businessman," as naive and not very intelligent, Larsen almost certainly had been in the U.S. Army Counter Intelligence Corps (CIC). During World War Two and afterwards, the CIC was an elite intelligence agency, essentially the spy-catchers of the U.S. military. The great researcher Leonard Stringfield, who had been a friend of Larsen's, mentioned that Larsen had worked for CIC, and had even told him where CIC's Chicago-area headquarters were. Larsen also had contacts with the RAND Corporation—a major Defense think tank—and claimed to have obtained UFO documents via that agency.[292]

Then there was Hynek. Because of his longtime connection with Blue Book, other researchers often held a certain amount of suspicion against him. Coral Lorenzen, for her part, never forgot that Hynek was comfortably paid as an Air Force consultant, often in a skeptical or even debunking role, during the 1950s and 1960s. For years, she and her husband had believed (correctly) that the government was spying on them. They also knew that the CIA-sponsored Robertson Panel of 1953, of which Hynek was a member, had recommended monitoring their organization. Granted, Hynek was a junior member of that panel, but he had been a member nonetheless. Nor was Coral Lorenzen the only one with a problem about Hynek: many MUFON members also distrusted him.[293]

Leaders of 1970s Ufology: James and Coral Lorenzen (l), J. Allen Hynek (c), Walter Andrus (r).

These were the four major American groups receiving UFO reports, conducting investigations, and trying to understand the mystery. Memberships were low for all of them. APRO and MUFON had no more than two or three thousand members each, CUFOS and NICAP hardly anything. All had prominent members with connections to the U.S. military and intelligence community. Maybe some of this was because people in those fields developed a genuine interest in the subject. Still, given that surveillance of the UFO research community

---

292 Larsen, Sherman J., "Documentation: Evidence of Government Concern," Sherman J. Larsen and Bill Laub, Co-Investigators. *1971 Midwest UFO Conference*, June 12, 1971, St. Louis, Missouri, Holiday Inn-North. "News 'n' Views," *MUFON UFO Journal*, 7/86. Stringfield, Leonard H. *Situation Red: The UFO Siege!*, Doubleday, 1977.
293 Lorenzen, Coral. "Hynek: UFO Movement Basically Amateurs," *APRO Bulletin*, Vol. 33, No. 2, Jan. 1986.

had been going on for years, it would not be especially paranoid to wonder if something else was going on.

Scientific Ufology

All of these groups promoted "scientific ufology." This was in direct response to the rejection of UFOs by the Condon Committee. Hence the term "Ufology" came into use, along with the perception that the study needed to be conducted scientifically. All of this effort was toward the eventual goal of attaining social respectability. MUFON for its part began developing an investigative methodology and a network of trained investigators. Of course, that was the ideal; reality often lagged behind. But, there were MUFON investigators who investigated baffling UFO cases: doing the legwork, interviewing witnesses, analyzing possible landing sites, preparing reports.

The goal of scientific ufology is surely laudable, and considering the state of affairs after the Condon Committee, understandable. It also served to de-politicize the issue to a large extent. Cover-ups and conspiracies were definitely *out* during the first few years of the 1970s.

The main problem with implementing scientific ufology is that real science requires real money. One can employ scientific principles in an investigation; one can create methodologies and protocols with which to conduct investigations. But without funding, investigators must work on their own time and money, doing the best they can to investigate reports.

In practice, to this day this means that investigators seldom arrive at the scene of a sighting quickly enough, and often only after driving long distances. Then they interview whatever witnesses they can, doing their best to check with local airports and meteorologists and other experts for conventional explanations. They also need to check the background of the witnesses, if possible. If they are very lucky to find physical evidence of some sort, they must find a way to have it analyzed scientifically. This is when things can become expensive. Furthermore, what laboratories would even dare to be associated with helping to analyze alleged UFO-related evidence?

That is a best-case scenario. Groups like APRO or MUFON were fortunate to have investigators at all. The vast majority of sightings of necessity remain, years ago as well as today, as little more than raw reports awaiting a competent investigation to determine whether they constitute a genuine mystery.

Intelligence Community Penetration

And yet, the problems of investigating UFOs go deeper still. Over the years, there have been many direct connections between the U.S. intelligence community, especially the CIA, and UFO research. This is not paranoid conspiracy theory. Ever since UFO research has been conducted, people from the military and intelligence community have been involved in it, and indeed have monitored it. We must ask whether they have also influenced it and, if so, has it been for a covert agenda?

The 1953 Robertson Panel mentioned APRO as a UFO research group that needed to be monitored. APRO's leaders described several instances from the 1950s and 1960s that strongly appeared to be attempts at infiltration by covert operatives into their group. During the 1970s and 1980s, one of APRO's most prominent members, William Moore, worked closely with Air Force Intelligence and, apparently, the CIA. It is known that Moore passed on information to his intelligence handlers and also knowingly disseminated at least one tampered document into the UFO research community, as well as the still-disputed MJ-12 documents. He did much of his work in conjunction with Richard Doty, a member of the Air Force Office of Special Investigation, (AFOSI) who has regularly been accused of spreading disinformation into the UFO field. In fact, Doty admitted more than once to having done so.

Then there was NICAP, dominated throughout its history by prominent military and intelligence figures. Many members of its founding Board of Governors and leaders in the 1950s were senior members of the Navy or CIA. Roscoe Hillenkoetter was a Navy Vice Admiral and former head of the CIA. Nicolas de Rochefort (NICAP's first Vice Chairman) was a scriptwriter for the CIA-controlled Voice of America, and was also a member of the CIA's psychological warfare staff, something unknown to the public at the time. De Rochefort's boss at that department was Colonel Joseph Bryan, who joined NICAPs board in 1960. Bryan's CIA pedigree was unknown at the time. During the early 1960s, Karl Pflock, a CIA briefing officer, joined NICAP and chaired its Washington, D.C. subcommittee. In 1969, after Bryan led the ouster of Keyhoe from leadership of NICAP, the organization was essentially destroyed by one CIA-connected leader after another: Alan Hall, Stuart Nixon, and Jack Acuff. It is interesting that, throughout NICAPs history, the organization focused on the Air Force as the source of the UFO cover-up. When Keyhoe began focusing on the CIA by the late 1960s, he was gone. Certainly, the organization had financial troubles, and Keyhoe was getting older, but it surely appears that NICAP was managed, and then deliberately mismanaged, by the U.S. intelligence community.[294]

The same issues pervaded MUFON from its inception. The organization's Navy connection have already been mentioned. But there was also Richard Hall, who had previously worked closely with Keyhoe in NICAP, and who was prominent for years in MUFON. Hall had been former Air Force officer, and even as a young man in his twenties had shocked Keyhoe by how much he knew about UFOs. Now, with MUFON, Hall was a leading light, and consistently downplayed the government cover-up angle of UFOs, just as the entire organization did for years and years.

A review of MUFON's leadership through the years shows a remarkably high number of figures with government and intelligence community connections, scattered throughout the organization. During the 21st century, MUFON developed a brief relationship with the billionaire Robert Bigelow, an important figure in the U.S. defense and aerospace community. For about a year, Bigelow poured money into MUFON's investigative capabilities, with the proviso that his own team had up to date access to all MUFON investigations. The matter ended acrimoniously, with each side claiming the other reneged on its

---

294 Zechel, Todd, "NI-CIA-AP OR NICAP?", *MUFON UFO Journal*, 1-2/79. Good, Timothy, *Above Top Secret: The Worldwide UFO Cover-up*, p, 348.

Chapter 9: The Growth of Ufology

agreement. There remain members of MUFON who believe the organization gave Bigelow's group much more access to its files than it should have.

By itself, that is not necessarily a disturbing situation, except when one considers that MUFON's cases are almost never publicly reported, other than brief summaries that appear temporarily on the public website. Over the years, MUFON has been accused of being an organization in which all data goes in, and very little comes out, unless it is going to the appropriate intelligence channels.

Whether this is true, or to what extent it is true, is still a matter of speculation. Regardless of the answer, MUFON is in need of a public relations facelift. Unlike real-life plastic surgery, however, its changes need to be more than cosmetic.

CUFOS fits the same pattern. For years, the organization published a newsletter of good quality. Beyond that, however, its tiny membership prevented it from doing much else. Philosophically, it has taken the most conservative of positions regarding the phenomenon without actually debunking it. Yes, says its leadership, there is indeed a UFO reality of some sort, but has been non-committal over what it signifies. Nor has the organization ever supported the idea of a cover-up.

It is among the mainstream media where CUFOS for years has been prominent, all out of proportion to its numbers in the UFO research community. During the 1970s and 1980s, it elicited suspicions from observers such as Jacques Vallée and Timothy Good that it had a relationship to the U.S. intelligence community.[295] Whether these suspicions are valid today is another question. Yet, looking at the matter from the process of "manufacturing consent," the phrase and title from Noam Chomsky's most classic work, the role of CUFOS can be seen as one in which it has drawn a line demarcating the edge of respectable ufology. Beyond such a line lies the fringe.

If some or all of these UFO groups were infiltrated by intelligence community operatives, it would fit a broader history. The FBI's infamous Cointelpro program was an infiltration program during the

---

[295] It may mean nothing or something that, after NICAP was run into the ground by its CIA-connected leadership, its files all went to CUFOS through the efforts of Sherman Larsen.

1960s to destroy progressive and radical organizations promoting social change. It was very effective. We know of the CIA's infiltration and influence during the cold war over such nominally independent organizations as the Voice of America and the Congress for Cultural Freedom.[296] Today, infiltration and control has achieved a higher art form still. Intelligence and government agencies cannot openly be connected to most organizations, which requires that relationships exist behind the scenes. This is true of mainstream media and the academic community, where there are significant numbers of CIA and intelligence-connected people. Looking at UFO organizations, which research a matter of profound national and international security, the reasonable assumption is that they too have been affected.

Along these lines, I recall a private conversation I had with a respected UFO researcher, as well as a trusted friend, who told me of a conversation he once had during the 1990s with an acquaintance who was a CIA employee. This acquaintance told him that the CIA regularly attended all major UFO conferences, just to monitor what was going on and who was saying what.

Entering the Weird

Looking at the situation in the early 1970s, the growth of American UFO organizations was far from the only interesting development. Without question, researchers slowly began to appreciate just how strange the phenomenon is.

The extraterrestrial hypothesis (ETH) had dominated most thinking on flying saucers and UFOs during the 1950 and 1960s. This should not be surprising, considering that this era marked the beginning of the space age, and the fact that many of the objects looked like extremely advanced mechanical objects. They also operated throughout the atmosphere, including the upper atmosphere and space. In this context, the ETH was logical.

---

296 A good overview of this is in Saunders, Frances Stonor, *The Cultural Cold War: The CIA and the World of Arts and Letters*, The New Press, 2001.

However, probably in part from the slapdown by the Condon Committee, there was a reaction against the ETH. To some people, the theory began to seem simplistic. Perhaps it was. Certainly, there was an abundance of truly bizarre reports which did not easily lead to a "nuts and bolts" explanation of alien creatures inside space ships coming from another planet.

Much of the influence behind this new perspective came from Jacques Vallée and John Keel. Both argued that UFOs could not possibly be extraterrestrial spacecraft.

Through the late 1960s and 1970s, Vallée expressed his dissatisfaction with the ETH, culminating with his "Five Arguments against the ETH." Not all of the arguments are especially compelling, but some remain intriguing.[297]

In the first place, he argued, there seemed to be too many UFO sightings and close encounters to explain them as extraterrestrial craft. If they are from another planet, there sure are a lot of them flying around.

Then there is the problem of the body structure of these so-called "aliens." If they evolved on another planet, or another part of the universe, why would they look humanoid, with two arms, two legs, and a head with eyes, ears, nose, and mouth? Could human-looking creatures really have evolved elsewhere? Moreover, such biological designs do not appear biologically adapted to space travel.

Vallée thought of other oddities mitigating against the ETH. The phenomenon, whatever it is, seems to have been recorded throughout human history. If these other beings are from another planet, they seem to have been here for ages, and probably live here by now. Moreover, the ability of UFOs, at least on occasions, seemingly to manipulate space and time suggested different and perhaps richer alternatives to mere extraterrestrials.

John Keel, who investigated the Mothman case in West Virginia and wrote *The Mothman Prophecies*, had a similar perspective. He coined the term *ultraterrestrials*. These beings, he suggested, were not living

---

[297] Vallee, Jacques F. "Five Arguments Against the Extraterrestrial Origin of Unidentified Flying Objects," *Journal of Scientific Exploration*, V. 4, N. 1, 1990.

here in our reality, but in another version of reality, perhaps another dimension. Some of Keel's thought connected UFOs to what we would call the paranormal, and he linked poltergeists and other paranormal events to many UFO sightings. Thus, he suggested, not aliens in flying saucers, but intelligences from other dimensions, were interacting with humanity.[298]

By the early 1970s, such alternative ideas as offered by Vallée, Keel, and others were spreading among researchers. Since then, they have continued and deepened into a significant school of thought. In general, UFO research was reinventing itself during the 1970s. At the same time, it was trying to establish itself on a firm intellectual footing and gain some measure of respectability.

Psychosocial Explanations

Across the Atlantic Ocean, the ETH fell even further from grace. During the 1970s and later, many prominent write in the United Kingdom and France supported a psychosocial or psychocultural hypothesis to explain UFOs. Researchers such as Hilary Evans, the editors of *Magonia* magazine, and many of the contributors to *Fortean Times* magazine argued that the truly interesting UFO reports are best explained by psychological or social means.

This is not to say that they have believed all sightings and encounters to be in the head. Instead, their position recognizes that human beings have always had encounters with anomalous and strange things, but that these encounters are filtered through the cultural values and expectations of each person. According to this hypothesis, when one reviews the many strange events and encounters that have occurred throughout all of human history, it becomes apparent that most are not about aliens from space, but rather reflect deep-seated thoughts, fears, and beliefs.

Of course, we may still wonder about what types of anomalous events might have caused people to react and believe the way they did. What kind of fireball in ancient Egypt, or 17th Century southern

---

[298] Keel, John A., *Operation Trojan Horse: The Classic Breakthrough Study of UFOs*, Anomalist Books, 2013. Originally Published as *Operation Trojan Horse* (1970).

Chapter 9: The Growth of Ufology

Russia, could convince the people that they were encountering an intelligently maneuvering apparition? What kind of anomaly would convince a twenty-five year-old surveyor in the Canadian Northwest Territories in 1936 that he was seeing "the most perfect configuration of an airship" one could imagine, which then instantly accelerated to the edge of the horizon?

Proponents of the psychosocial perspective claim that they are not the same as debunkers, because they feel UFOs are still an interesting subject worthy of serious study, even if it is approached in a skeptical way. Fair enough, one supposes, and it is certainly true that human psychology is one of several key areas with which a serious ufologist must be familiar. But to those people who, after careful study of the phenomenon, have concluded that UFOs pose a serious anomaly in our reality, such theorists may certainly seem very close to debunkers.

FOIA and the Crash Retrieval Syndrome

Despite the new approaches to ufology that developed during the 1970s, the ETH never receded completely. This became especially so by the latter part of the decade, when the U.S. Freedom of Information Act (FOIA) became an important tool for researchers. During the 1940s, 1950s, and 1960s, those individuals in the military and intelligence communities who created classified documents about UFOs did not expect that they would ever become public. By the late 1970s, however, after much effort by researchers, some of them did. Not an especially large percentage, but several thousand pages worth.

The bounty of FOIA was manifold. First, it reinforced the idea that at least some UFOs were reported by military sources as solid, mechanical objects of unusual design and incredible performance. They were not always ephemeral apparitions, distant lights in the night sky, but material objects that were up-close-and-personal, sometimes even tracked and pursued by military agencies. Extraterrestrial? Indeed, perhaps so after all.

FOIA also made it clear that there really was some sort of 'cover-up' on UFOs. The documents showed beyond any doubt that, at the same time the U.S. military was telling the public that flying saucers and

UFOs were either imaginary objects or misunderstood natural phenomena, these same agencies were very concerned about UFOs, and that jets had been scrambled to chase after them.

As a result of such revelations, UFO researchers were energized into thinking that they might possibly get lucky. Perhaps they might find the *one* document that would unambiguously prove the reality of UFOs and of the cover-up, once and for all. A document making it crystal-clear that the President of the United States knows about the extraterrestrial nature of UFOs, or something equally powerful.

At the same time, another prong in the attack on secrecy was developing. This was in the collection of stories that supported the idea that there had been secret retrievals of crashed UFOs, including the acquisition of dead alien bodies. The most famous of these stories is the crash of a UFO near Roswell, New Mexico, but quite a few accounts surfaced during the late 1970s and after. Most were uncorroborated and unsubstantiated claims, sometimes not even from the direct witness, but his or her spouse if that person were no longer alive. Nevertheless, the cumulative effect was that, by the end of the decade, there were at least fifty accounts that had been collected, each detailing some incredible aspect of this phenomenon.

Like FOIA, the crash retrieval stories were also pursued by some researchers as a possible key toward unlocking the door of secrecy. Foremost among these were Leonard Stringfield, William Moore, and Stanton Friedman, although there were others. Within just a few years, ufology had developed a potentially dangerous one-two punch.

The Intelligence Empire Strikes Back: The Early 1980s

For those on the other side of secrecy's wall, concerned about keeping the terrible UFO secret away from the public, the developments of the late 1970s would appear to be problems that required active counter-measures. What followed during the early 1980s certainly appears to have been exactly that.

What happened was that a known U.S. Air Force military intelligence specialist named Richard Doty began to communicate with certain researchers in the field, giving deep information that could not be verified and which was sometimes shown to be false. One of Doty's connections was researcher William Moore, who in 1980 co-authored the first book on Roswell. Clearly, Moore was an important connection. Throughout the 1980s, Doty (or those connected to him) fed Moore what appeared to be inside information. One item came to be known as the Aquarius document, which described a UFO-related briefing given to President Jimmy Carter. Another contained classified commentary on a UFO incident, but in which the acronym NSA (for National Security Agency) was changed to NASA (National Aeronautics and Space Administration). Although it appears that the rest of the document might be legitimate, researchers still do not know.

Doty also fed information to other researchers at this time, including Linda Moulton Howe, who had recently produced a powerful documentary on cattle mutilations. In 1983, Doty showed her what appeared to be explosive, Presidential-level documents, that confirmed the UFO-extraterrestrial reality, and then some. Although Howe was clearly impressed by them, she did not go public until long after the moment had passed.

The following year, Doty (or, again, someone connected to him) mailed the infamous MJ-12 documents to a research associate of Moore. This was Jamie Shandera, a man with his own involvement in the world of U.S. intelligence. Like the documents Doty had previously shown Linda Moulton Howe, these described highest-level policy in containing and dealing with the UFO issue. For several years, Moore hesitated to publish them. Then, in 1987, Doty tired of waiting and arranged for U.K. researcher Timothy Good to get a copy. Now realizing that Good was about to publish them in his own book, Moore decided to publicize them first. After that, all hell broke lose. Supporters and debunkers lined up for battle, and indeed have continued to do so to this day, now more than a quarter of a century later.

The result was that what had initially seemed like a straightforward proposition—getting hold of the right document that would *prove* UFOs and the cover-up—became much more complicated. For now

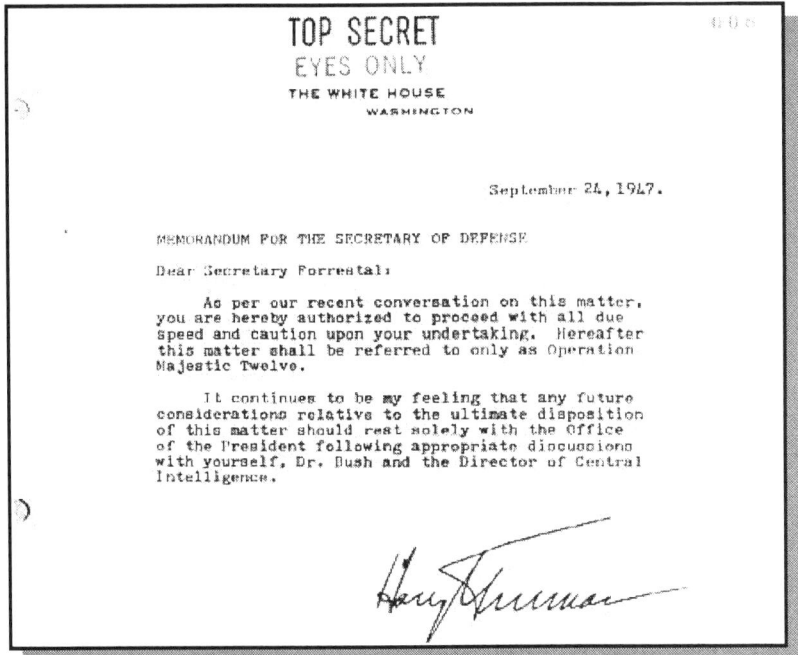

Cropped page of the MJ-12 documents, which have remained divisive in ufology to the present day.

researchers were dealing with documents that *looked* real but which had been tampered with, or which might be completely fake, or which might be real. Not only that, but the entire crash retrieval phenomenon had become tied into this, similarly splashed with mud.

What was real? What was not? Suddenly, nothing seemed certain any more.

The Eve of the Internet and the State of Ufology

Such was ufology in the 1980s, all before the birth of the Internet. It was a field that seemed rife with dissension and distrust. Many wondered, whatever happened to scientific ufology? Whatever happened to the idea of gaining some level of consensus over the meaning of this phenomenon, or the attempt to gain social respectability? By the late 1980s, such goals seemed like a fond, distant memory.

Yet, looking back on those years, one thing does stand out: an identifiable community of UFO researchers. These were people who were immersed in the field, who researched, who investigated, and who wrote articles and books. They may have disagreed with each other on many matters, but they all spoke the same language, as it were. That is, most of them supported the idea of scientific ufology, and most of them believed the subject needed more intellectual rigor. Even those who were beginning to believe in a conspiracy of some sort were tame by standards of later years. No one spoke of the Illuminati, the Bilderbergers, or Bohemian Grove. If there was any belief in a conspiracy or cover-up, researchers confined their analysis to the U.S. Government.

Such relative collegiality was even in evidence regarding the matter of alien abductions. Budd Hopkins and others had brought the subject to prominence during the 1980s. Not everyone agreed that abductions were taking place at all, much less on the scale that Hopkins was suggesting. Yet, although the debate was spirited, it remained a reasoned one.

But all of this was contained within a very narrow circle; that is, primarily within the few printed UFO-related journals of the time. Circulation was never high. The outside world hardly noticed at all.

By the late 1980s, all that started to change.

The First Bulletin Boards

The birth of the Internet did not come at once, but gradually and piecemeal. Yet, a key year in its maturation, perhaps *the* key year, was 1986. This was when the collection of connected newsgroups, known as Usenet, began to expand beyond discussions about computers and programming and other matters of geeky interest. In 1986, for the first time, a non-computer-related bulletin board entered the scene: Paranet, which focused on UFOs. Indeed, and perhaps to the surprise of many, the UFO phenomenon was one of the first non-technically-oriented subjects to thrive on the Internet. From the beginning, UFOs were a key part of the Internet.

Still, 1986 was a long time before there was a world wide web, before there was a graphical user interface, before visuals of any type could be displayed. There were bulletin boards, newsgroups, and a new thing called electronic mail, used by very few people. From the mid-

1980s until the mid-1990s, the Internet consisted essentially of white or green letters on a black screen.

Yet even in those early years, it was immediately obvious that this was something very, very different than anything that had ever existed before. Comparing it to the invention of Gutenberg's printing press is not an overstatement. Indeed, it may be an understatement.

Like everything else, the UFO field was affected and transformed by the Internet. Previously, anyone wanting to share their thoughts on UFOs with the rest of the world typically submitted articles to one of the journals, all of which had editorial policies of some sort. This might reach a thousand readers if the author were fortunate. Certainly, one could research and write a book on the subject, but realistically this is not something most people would do, then or today.

With Paranet, however, anyone with a computer and an Internet connection could find an audience. Believers, skeptics, geniuses, cranks, people with the best motives, people who were hoaxing, and everyone else came out of the woodwork. Almost immediately, they created a wild and thriving online community.

Out Come the Leaks

There is no question that Usenet enabled the explosion of leaks that followed. Three early sources were Bill English, John Lear, and William Cooper. All three surfaced in 1987 and 1988, all three told various stories of allegedly inside knowledge concerning some aspect of extraterrestrials or the UFO phenomenon. The stories have been compelling to many, but after all these years, none have been substantiated.

In essentials, the accounts painted a picture of human-alien collaboration gone horribly awry. One of the main features of the scenario concerned a meeting between President Eisenhower and a group of extraterrestrials. This involved an exchange of sorts: technology going to humans while the ETs were permitted a peaceful and unobstructed presence on Earth, as well as permission to take a small number of humans on occasion for their own purposes, to be brought safely back without their knowledge. According to Lear, however, his sources told him that the deal went wrong, and the aliens were now doing whatever they wanted. The human control group was powerless to stop it.

Cooper followed up on Lear's claims with even more grandiose and dark statements, reflecting his own growing megalomania and disconnection from reality. Essentially, Cooper had a gift for claiming as his own information that came from other sources. Perhaps he had the ability to believe his own lies. To give just one example, in 1988 Lear had sent Cooper a package containing a number of documents and items, one of which was a poor quality copy of the Zapruder film, depicting the assassination of President John F. Kennedy. The video showed the driver, William Greer, turning around briefly toward the President as he was shot. At that moment, there appeared to be a flash emanating from Greer's position. In reality, the flash was a reflection of sunlight on the hair of Greer's supervisor, Roy Kellerman, who sat next to him. But Cooper became obsessed by the video. For ever after, he claimed that while in the U.S. Navy during the early 1970s, he had seen Top Secret documents stating that Greer had been Kennedy's shooter using a specially prepared gun by the CIA. To those who disagreed with him, he typically resorted to shouts and bully tactics. It was for reasons like this that veteran UFO researcher Don Ecker referred to Cooper as "the most blatant B.S. artist I have ever run into."[299]

It did not take long for serious researchers to spot problems with what Cooper was saying. By then, however, he had already become an iconic figure, a status entrenched after his death in a shootout with police in October, 2001. Regarding this shootout (lest one think he was targeted for assassination) Cooper had for years been involved in local altercations, always carrying his gun, and had long been wanted for tax evasion. He had vowed never to be taken alive. Before he was gunned down, he had shot one of the police officers in the head.

---

[299] An excellent analysis of Cooper's deception on this matter, and which includes Ecker's quote on Cooper, is "Bill Cooper Debunked: The William Greer JFK Hoax" [www.youtube.com/watch?v=bExUM0kGIa8]. For a longer analysis of Cooper, see Dolan, Richard M., *UFOs and the National Security State: The Cover-Up Exposed, 1973-1991*, p. 443-447, 450-454.

One lasting effect of Cooper, however, was an emphasis on the power structure that existed behind-the-scenes, as it were, and the relationship of that power structure to the UFO cover-up. He wrote about the Illuminati, the Bilderbergers, the Jasons, and other groups which he said were instrumental in the cover-up of the UFO reality. Some of this information was useful insofar as he acquired it from credible sources, while much was just plain wrong.[300] Many researchers have followed up and similarly concluded that there is indeed a cover-up on UFOs that exists beyond the formal reaches of governments, whether American or otherwise.

Bob Lazar and Area 51

As the field of ufology exploded during the late 1980s and early 1990s, the field was overwhelmed with conflict and debate over each new claim that appeared. Among the most heated of all arguments centered around Robert Lazar, who claimed to have been employed briefly to study the propulsion system of an alien craft. Once again, as with the MJ-12 controversy and so much else since, to this day there are those who believe his account while others claim to have debunked it.

Lazar went public at the end of 1989 through a series of interviews with Las Vegas journalist George Knapp. These described his experiences working at a place most Americans had never heard of: a facility known as S-4, at a dry lake bed in Nevada called Papoose Lake. He claimed this was about ten miles south of Groom Dry Lake, site of another obscure place (at least in 1989). That is, Area 51.

Today, people have access to tools such as Google Earth to look for evidence of S-4. If one were to do so, they would essentially see nothing more than a few narrow dirt roads leading to and around it from Area 51. Nearby is the Nellis bombing range. Yet, it is true that Google Earth sometimes hides locations that are sensitive for national

---

300 See, Cooper, Milton William, "The Secret Government: The Origin, Identity, and Purpose of MJ-12," (May 23, 1989), which is available at many sites on the web. A good analysis of some of Cooper's mistakes, particularly regarding the Jason Group, is in Cameron, Grant and Crain, Scott T., *UFOs, Area 51, and Government Informants: A Report on Government Involvement in UFO Crash Retrievals*, Keyhole Publishing Co., 2013.

security purposes. A number of places around the world are intentionally blurred, blacked out, or blocked out in some way, including the famous NSA site at Pine Gap, Australia, a mile-square area near the Trinity Site in New Mexico, and quite a few others. Regarding S-4, there is simply no easy way to confirm its existence.

While Lazar has retained many detractors over the years, others continue to support him strongly. It is worth mentioning, too, that even if his claims are untrue in part or whole, there have been quite a few other Area 51 insiders who have made similar statements about alien technology being near there, many of whom were interviewed by George Knapp under conditions of anonymity.

Thus, more than twenty years after Lazar, his claims continue to be controversial, unconfirmed, and debated. Welcome to the world of ufology.

Rumors of Disclosure Around 1990

In retrospect, it should not be surprising that around 1990 or so, there were discussions and rumors among researchers of an announcement that would reveal the existence and reality of UFOs.

First of all, such rumors have circulated among UFO researchers since the 1950s. Every decade has seen the rise and fall of anticipation about extraterrestrial "Disclosure." It is hard to know how reliable most of these rumors were, but it does appear that there have been periodic discussions behind the scenes about the pros and cons of doing so. I discussed this once with a prominent, publicly known scientist with a longtime association to the intelligence community. This man told me that such sorts of discussions occur every five to ten years at high levels, presumably in government, although the specifics were not made precisely clear.

This individual, along with a colleague of his, also told me there were discussions within the Bush White House in 1990 as to whether or not to announce the UFO reality. As the Cold War withered away, so too it seemed one of the original reasons for UFO secrecy. Yet, no announcement came. As it happens, the claim of an aborted 1990 disclosure was also advanced by ex-U.S. Air Force Captain, Robert

Collins, in his book, *Exempt from Disclosure*. Did it really happen? We still do not have enough information yet.

The Web and the First Wave of Research

Disclosure from a Presidential announcement did not happen in 1990. But something else did begin at around that time, and it rapidly accelerated as the decade progressed. This was the sharing of information via the ever-expanding, ever-transforming Internet. The bulletin board system of the 1980s exploded during the early 1990s. By the middle of the decade, the Internet grew wings. A World Wide Web was spreading, one with an easy-to-use graphical user interface.

The basic, revolutionary fact was that people were sharing more information—much, much more information. News reports about UFOs were being distributed to a vastly wider and more engaged readership than in the past because people who had an interest in this topic finally had found a way to reach each other, no matter where they lived in their country, or indeed the world.

At this time, there were several UFO-related news gathering services. Among these were Michael Lindemann's *CNI*, which ran for five years and was quite valuable during the early 1990s. Other useful sources were *Filer's Files* by retired USAF Major George Filer, *UFO Roundup* by Joseph Trainor, and quite a few others. After 1996 and 1997, when the Web truly exploded, this type of information grew even more. By the late 1990s, the amount of available information was orders of magnitude beyond what had been available a mere decade earlier, to say nothing of the decade prior to that.

As more people gained access to the Internet, they became astonished at what they could find. As a way of tracking current events, the Internet quickly became essential. Even prior to the Web itself, email lists were becoming common, and allowed researchers to follow up on leads much more quickly than could have happened earlier.

Even so, the Internet was not fully mature by the late 1990s. While researching my first UFO book at this time, the Internet was valuable to me, but even so it was no substitute for printed books and journal articles. Yet, it was invaluable for helping to track down sources that would have been daunting to find otherwise. It was a research tool of great value, a value which only increased with each passing year. The Internet enabled people finally to escape the heavy-handed censorship of UFO information that had predominated in the mainstream media for so many years.

21st Century: Explosion

The information highway of the 1990s expanded into a superhighway during the first few years of the 21st century. It is easy to forget that the year 2000 was not so long ago. Although it feels to us that the modern Internet has been with us forever, it is still so very young.

What has happened is an explosion not merely of information but of ways to get it. The development of search engines alone has been revolutionary. Their near-omniscience is taken for granted by most people, but they are purely a 21st century phenomenon. Through Google, Yahoo, Bing, or other engines, UFO data of any sort is instantly available, and relevant news can be sent to one's mailbox every day.

There are an abundance of research-oriented websites. For sightings, at least in North America, there is the National UFO Reporting Center, which records over 5,000 sightings each year. The Black Vault, another valuable resource, is a large repository of released government files on UFOs and a host of other relevant topics. These offer a mere sprinkling of what is out there.

Of course, more information also means more mistakes. It also means more disinformation or, at least, misleading information. The Internet has allowed millions upon millions of people to contribute to the global conversation on UFOs, but that also means that there are effectively no standards necessary for joining it. In all places at all times, making unsupported claims is the easiest thing to do in the world. In the world of today, unfortunately, many people do not care about providing valid evidence to support their claims. Indeed, it is obvious that many do not really understand how to go about such a thing. Worse still are those who use the Internet to create false data and persona, and yet others who use sensationalism to make a name themselves, and sometimes money.

YouTube and Facebook

It is startling to remember that YouTube did not exist until 2005. And yet it immediately became the video showcase of human civilization and culture.

For years, UFO researchers assumed that with the proliferation of more and better quality video cameras, at some point there would be a breakthrough. Someone would record *something* that would be considered undeniable proof of the reality of UFOs. Today, hundreds of new UFO videos uploaded each year to YouTube. Some of these videos seem extraordinary, others boring and inconsequential. Generally speaking, however, the quality of video is irrelevant. This is because, as we have discovered, video alone is no longer enough to count as evidence of UFOs.

Which brings us to the great irony of the YouTube era. The current flood of UFO videos, even many of which are apparently excellent in quality, has not brought the definitive proof researchers had expected. This is because without a proper investigation of a case, without vetting witnesses, and indeed without preparing some sort of professional report, these videos can never be anything more than intriguing entertainment or at best fodder for speculation. The fact remains that most objects seen in the sky can be explained in conventional terms, given enough time and energy to do the investigation.

Nevertheless, there is no question that YouTube has provided an outlet for some truly extraordinary videos, many of which I do think are valid captures of what can only be called UFOs. In other words, YouTube is valuable, but it is only one tool. Without being supplemented by responsible investigation, it will never be enough for moving this issue forward.

Of course, there is more to YouTube than UFO videos. The site is complete with thousands of lectures, interviews, documentaries, and insights from researchers worldwide. On that basis alone, it is of inestimable value as an educational tool. It was not long ago that easy access to such information was simply not possible for most people.

Chapter 9: The Growth of Ufology

Alleged UFOs (circled) over London, 2011. One of many such fake videos to be found on YouTube.

Like YouTube, Facebook is a young institution that has redefined the way that people interact with the world, and especially how they share information. The benefits and pitfalls are obvious. A flood of news passes through, much of which educates and inspires, much of which confuses and distracts. It spreads legitimate news as easily as it spreads unfounded rumors from spurious sources. Facebook has become the headquarters of "copy and paste reporting."

There are always people who thrive on drama. In a world that is filled with genuine conspiracies and subterranean machinations, such people find it easy to latch onto stories that confirm their darkest fears, even if they lack proper attribution or means of verification. For such people, the craving for sensationalism is like a drug. Unfortunately, there are always people willing to promote such stories, sometimes for fame, sometimes for money.

So much more information is available. But the need for sober and dispassionate investigation of claims has never left us. Today, it is arguably more necessary than ever before.

The Decline of Professional Journalism

Unfortunately, just when more than ever we need professional journalists with bravery and integrity, they have become an endangered species. Free, professional journalists have long been understood as the backbone of a functioning representational government. Yet, the past generation witnessed the steady decline of the journalistic profession.

Mergers of once-independent newspapers have left people with fewer and fewer independent voices. In particular, the integration of media conglomerates with other corporate entities, such as the ownership of NBC by NBC Universal, which is simply a holding company for GE and Comcast. That matters because GE has been, year in and year out, one of the largest defense contractors in the United States. MSNBC is co-owned by NBC and Microsoft. Such types of arrangements are the case with all major media. The other very few major owners of media are Disney, News Corporation, Time Warner, Viacom, and CBS. These huge entities own most of the dominant voices in American television, radio, newspapers, magazines, motion pictures. They also have a dominant presence throughout much of the world. Realistically, their interlocking partnerships with each other essentially make them the same mega-corporation. It would be interesting to learn how much overlap exists among the dominant shareholders of these corporations, although this type of information is proprietary and therefore off-limits.

At the same time that media mergers have created such bloated giants, genuine journalism and investigation have been determined to be too expensive. Much cheaper, it turns out, is spouting mere opinion. Thus, we see everywhere that opinion is masked as news.

The result is the most corporate-friendly brand of journalism ever seen in history. We are faced with a mainstream news media that is completely in bed with powerful corporate and private interests, and is closely connected to national security interests.

Such an outcome is toxic to real journalism, to say nothing of liberty itself, which depends in part upon a free press. All the more difficult, too, for engaged citizens who care about UFOs to find a piece of solid ground upon which to stand. It is all the more reason that such citizens must do it themselves.

Whistleblowers, Real and Alleged

The world has become wide open. We are near the point where anyone can speak to anyone, anyone can say anything—with the important proviso that they not violate the ever-expanding definition of what constitutes national security. A generation ago, alleged whistleblowers such as Bob Lazar were relatively rare. Now, new claims appear seemingly every week. Project Camelot, managed for years by Kerry Cassidy and Bill Ryan, has interviewed many of these individuals. Some of them interviews are fascinating and provide valuable information. Some have claimed to be insiders with sensitive information that has proven difficult or impossible to prove. Others have been roundly criticized as disinformants.

It is not hard to see why we might be drawn to such sources. We realize that the mainstream system of news reporting is not merely woefully inadequate, but irremediably unreliable, self-serving, and corrupt. We know, instinctively and factually, that we are being lied to every day by a structure of power that wants to control and pacify the great masses of humanity. So, when we hear someone who claims to have inside information about the *true* situation, we want to listen, and maybe believe.

Still, many of these alleged whistleblowers have failed to confirm their claims, or even their own credentials. You don't get to be a whistleblower if you can't reach that first step of verification. Some have been investigated and shown to be frauds. The rest just seem to come and go. They make their allegations, then they disappear never to be heard from again, like the anonymous Norwegian politician who in 2008 who claimed there were massive underground facilities for the global elite to use when "Planet X" arrived not later than 2012. Mass death would ensue.[301] This is not to single out Project Camelot, because it remains important for private efforts like theirs and others to keep searching for legitimate information about our world. Such information certainly won't fall like ripe fruit from the national security establishment. Yet, unverifiable and even alarmist claims are

---

301 "A Letter from a Norwegian Politician," [http://projectcamelot.org/norway.html]

everywhere. Today, they typically arrive as a new Facebook rumor to steal our attention and then move on. They are a distraction to genuine research, and students of our world's unseemly underbelly need rigor and caution when dealing with them.

Beyond legitimate investigators who are simply out on the fringe and taking chances, there are certain public individuals, connected however loosely to UFO research, who make prediction after prediction, often based on unverifiable "inside sources." Such predictions are never of trivial matters, but of major, globally transformative events. Whether predicting the so-called Project Blue Beam event, the approach of the comets Elenin or ISON, mythical secret wars, destructions of the secret bases operated by the so-called "black hats," or the incessant claims of imminent Disclosure of UFOs and extraterrestrials by the U.S. President, these so-called researchers have nothing to do with the proper study of UFOs. They merely pile on to the rumor mill, gaining notoriety and website hits while providing endless distractions from real work.

This is unfortunate because undoubtedly there are real, actual people out there who are trying to be whistleblowers. Such people may well fear that their signal will be lost amid the noise that permeates the alternative research community.

Increase of Sightings

As if all this extra noise did not pose enough of a challenge, we have something else to consider. UFO reports have been on a dramatic increase since the 1990s.

Here are the numbers from the National UFO Reporting Center (NUFORC):[302]

1990: 277	2003: 4366	2008: 5188
1995: 1422	2004: 4693	2009: 4868
2000: 3031	2005: 4446	2010: 4542
2001: 3477	2006: 4076	2011: 5226
2002: 3624	2007: 4652	2012: 7774
		2013: 7086

302 National UFO Reporting Center, Report Index by Month [www.nuforc.org/webreports/ndxevent.html].

Perhaps people are genuinely seeing more UFOs than in prior years. After all, we might theorize that the beings responsible for the phenomenon would be more interested in us now than previously. But realistically, most of this increase is due to the ease of reporting. The NUFORC website began accepting live reports from the public during the late 1990s. Before that, people needed to call in by phone, which meant they needed to obtain the phone number somehow, or else they reached the center via other organizations. As emailing submissions became standard, and especially as more and more people became connected to the web, reports skyrocketed. This explains the ten-fold rise of UFO reports during the 1990s, from less than 300 per year to 3,000 per year. The growth has continued, spiking sharply in 2003 to well over 4,000 sightings, to more than 5,000 in 2008, and over 7,000 in 2012 and 2013!

The contrast with earlier decades is stark. During the days of Project Blue Book, the largest number of reports in one year, by far, was during 1952 when the Air Force received just over 1,500. That was considered an incredible amount at the time, but would have amounted to roughly two months of sightings during 2012.

With NUFORC accepting anywhere from 5,000 to perhaps 8,000 sightings during a given year, we are talking about an average of fifteen to twenty UFOs being reported to that site each day. Consider, too, NUFORC is devoted nearly exclusively to North American sightings. Not only this, but NUFORC is not even the only major website that records UFO sightings in North America. There is, after all, the Mutual UFO Network (MUFON), which publishes roughly 6,000 or more sightings per year, in other words, about the same number as NUFORC. Undoubtedly, there is some overlap, although researchers really have no idea how much since no one has done the work to find out. But, it would seem conservative to state there are over 10,000 UFO reports made in North America each year from these two websites alone. That might translate to perhaps thirty or more each day.

As messy as the data collection system is in North America, it is vastly better than what exists elsewhere. There are outstanding UFO researchers living in all parts of the world, but much greater organization is needed. At a bare minimum, there need to be civilian-based organizations that can accept UFO reports from the public, and then have some ability to follow-up, at least on some of the more promising cases.

One thing ufology needs to do—certainly not the only thing—is to develop an annual compendium of UFO reports from around the world. The capability now exists. Imagine how useful it would be if research groups from North America, Europe, the Middle East, Asia, and Africa all collaborated and shared their data. Now, well into the 21st century, there is no reason for this not to happen.

Of course, other problems will remain. After all, how can can these thousands of reports ever receive proper investigations? With what money? What resources?

The Need for Proper Investigations

With the foregoing in mind, it is easy to appreciate the value of the few organizations that do any systematic and rational investigation of UFO reports. Of these, MUFON is the most prominent in the western hemisphere, perhaps the world. If this is so, and with no intended disparagement of MUFON, then global ufology is in a sad state of affairs.

MUFON exists on a threadbare budget. It has roughly two thousand members, and perhaps a few hundred investigators. Of these, there are a mere handful of truly dedicated, active investigators who can be relied upon to follow through with solid investigations, research, analysis, and reporting. After all, they do this on their own money and time. Yet, it must be said, that despite the many obstacles in their way, MUFON's investigators have made an irreplaceable contribution to ufology. Without someone to investigate a report, we are left only with claims and counter-claims, but no progress in obtaining reliable knowledge.

MUFON's greatest assets are its investigators who do the work and strive to adhere to scientific ufology. As long as the organization can retain people like that, it can have a future.

But it has never grown. Since its foundation in the 1960s, MUFON's membership has hovered at around two or three thousand. Considering the immense popularity of the UFO subject around the world, how can this be?

A key reason is a historical failure of leadership, and ultimately a lack of vision and imagination. Looking back at nearly half a century of activity, what has MUFON really done? The answer is: it has collected reports, investigated what it could, published a small journal for its members, and held annual symposia. That is about it.

Amid all of its data collection, MUFON has consistently failed to provide a clear message to the rest of the world. How much more effective its research and data collection would have been had it taken the effort to compile and publish something like an annual report. The U.S. Air Force did this during its operation of Project Blue Book, but of course, what MUFON could do would be so much better. It could create something along the lines of a twenty to fifty page report, prepared by competent writers. It could include a statistical analysis of the annual sightings, along with the number of true unidentifieds for the year, something researchers have not seen on a large scale since Blue Book closed in 1969. Such an annual report might also include brief summaries of the top ten or twenty reports of the year.

MUFON has never attempted even this basic piece of public relations. By itself, it would go very far to establish it as the "go to" organization in the eyes of the media, and would improve its credibility with the general public, perhaps even the academic and scientific community. I should add here that in 2013 I had a conversation with MUFON's new International Director, Jan Harzan. He told me that this now is indeed a goal of the organization, which surely would be a positive step.

But this longstanding failure is only part of a larger symptom of MUFON's basic problem. Because, although it possesses more of a grassroots history than other American UFO organizations, it has still generally failed to engage or inspire its own members. For years, members have complained about data going into MUFON and never coming out. Hand in hand with such complaints have been suspicions about the national security and intelligence community connections that have always dominated MUFON's Board of Directors. Certainly, it is a Board that selects its own members, allowing minimal input from the rank and file membership.

In other words, MUFON has not demonstrated that it is anything more than a closed, *old-boy* network that takes time and resources from its members, but gives little in return to its members or the world. If the organization does not reform, it will only be a matter of time before another organization, one which resonates with the public, will make MUFON irrelevant. Such a turn of events can easily happen quickly and unexpectedly, and MUFON will be no more.

To prevent such an eventuality, its path is clear: it must institute truly democratic change that will allow its members to feel that they have a stake in it. Such things are always possible. Whether or not MUFON can actually do this is less clear, not while its current structure remains in place. More than anything else, it needs a cool, fresh breeze and a great deal of sunshine pouring in. We should sincerely hope this happens, because someone needs to be doing proper UFO investigations.

The Modern Armchair Researcher

Although we need responsible organizations to conduct proper investigations of UFO sightings and create public reports of their activities, ultimately it comes down to each person doing all he or she can.

Unlike during earlier eras, most of our interaction with the UFO topic today comes through the Internet. Whether via Facebook, YouTube, or a website, people learn almost everything online. The amount of information can be overwhelming, and is certainly not always true. This means that each person must become his or her own best investigator. What we need, before anything else, is a proper philosophy. We need principles by which we can create order out of chaos.

Chapter 9: The Growth of Ufology

The first principle is a commitment to check facts and sources. Any claim, whether by a well-known researcher or someone previously unknown, needs to be questioned and investigated. We must be in the habit of asking certain basic questions. On what basis is the claim being made? What is the evidence brought forth? Can the evidence be examined independently, whether by other researchers or even by ourselves? Can we determine whether the author has an unnamed agenda?

In conducting such research, it is important to find the original source of the allegation. There are a number of ways to do this. As an example, we may consider the claims around the notorious Project "Blue Beam." Today, there are countless websites and YouTube videos discussing this alleged plan. It has many variations, but in essentials it revolves around a clandestine group creating a "false flag" scenario (whether as a staged alien invasion, a second coming of Christ, or some similarly terrifying event) which would then frighten people into submitting to a totalitarian New World Order. Each day, new people are exposed to this claim. Naturally, they wonder if it might be true.

The first thing to do is subject it to a web search. A Google entry on "Blue Beam" quickly leads to the site "Rational Wiki," a well-known skeptical website. There, one finds a description of the origins of the idea: one Serge Monast, a deceased French Quebecois who first discussed it publicly in 1994. We learn further that the likely origin of that idea was a 1991 episode of *Star Trek: The Next Generation*, which in turn derived from a script written by Gene Roddenberry during the 1970s. While the tone of Rational Wiki is sarcastic and unprofessional (the site stridently debunks conspiracies and claims of the paranormal), information is provided that one can further examine and verify.[303]

Obviously, relying on one source is not a good idea, but it is a start. Our next step is to locate the very first instance the phrase "Blue Beam" to appear on the Internet. Since web searches can locate sites going back to the early 1990s, they now cover a sizable portion of our recent history.

---

303 "Project Blue Beam" [rationalwiki.org/wiki/Project_Blue_Beam].

The good news is that such a search is possible via Google's search engine, by typing in "blue beam" and selecting "Search tools." A drop down menu appears, and one selection allows for searching by date. Unfortunately, the capability does not yet exist to obtain all results in complete chronological order, but the next-best-thing is that one can perform discrete searches, for instance year by year.

We quickly learn that an "Operation Blue Beam" was used by French and Belgian paratroopers in the nation of Zaire in 1991. Clearly, not the Blue Beam we are seeking. Also, unfortunately, the method is not perfect, as a number of apparent "hits" from early years actually lead to sites of later years—the original website may have been from 1992, but it may also have been updated. Researchers need to check each link to confirm the actual date of the site. But diligence does pay off with Google's date search feature. *Lo and behold!* We find that the earliest reference to Project Blue Beam appeared on June 14, 1994, in an issue of a small American journal, *Contact: The Phoenix Project.* This was a journal with an idiosyncratic, religious agenda, which discussed many conspiracies, real and alleged. It also seemed to have a great love of the all-caps feature. Incidentally, the publisher of that journal later claimed credit for averting the Blue Beam catastrophe by his exposure of the plot.[304]

We find that the initial formulation of Blue Beam was a purely evangelical Christian formulation, which promised a false rapture and many other false "signs" that would cause people to turn away from the true faith and make way for the Anti-Christ. Serge Monast predicted Blue Beam for several occasions, most notably the Year 2000. After nothing happened at that time, the idea morphed increasingly into an ET-invasion scenario.

This is the value of date search: it can allow researchers to find, fairly quickly, the history of an idea or claim over the past several decades. This is an excellent way to see how various themes, memes, tropes, and claims have entered our society. Very often, when seeing the original instance of a piece of information, a researcher can make a better

---

304 *Contact: The Phoenix Project*, V. 5. N. 12, June 14, 1994. [www.phoenixarchives.com/contact/1994/0694/061494.pdf]

Chapter 9: The Growth of Ufology

determination of its validity. Not always, but often. It is also interesting, up to a certain point, to see how many websites simply copy and paste their information from each other. One quickly learns that such behavior is endemic.

Another tool that any armchair researcher should know is the reverse-image search. Like the Date Search feature, it is powerful and underutilized. The idea of reverse image search is simple: a jpeg file is uploaded or dragged into the Image Search bar. Then, through image identification software, all examples of that image which exist on the web are displayed. The first company to offer this was TinEye, which debuted its search engine in May 2008. Yet, it was not comprehensive or especially well-known. Matters were different when Google rolled out its very powerful version of reverse image searching in June 2011. In a short period of time, reverse image searches have exposed many alleged images of UFOs or alien bodies as hoaxes, either from movie stills or other sources.

Using Google reverse image search in 3 steps: a powerful tool.

YouTube is another place where UFO researchers spend a lot of their time. As previously discussed, it is important to remember that a video alone does not constitute sufficient evidence for the reality of a UFO. Yet, some videos undoubtedly are worth follow-up effort. In such cases, probably the first order of business is simply watching the video carefully and reading the comments below. In all likelihood, someone has already provided a useful insight. But for real followup, a researcher will want to contact the uploader of the video. Doing this is essential for several reasons. First of all, for genuine video analysis to be done, the original, highest-resolution copy must be available, and this can only be obtained from the uploader. Also, however, the uploader may be able to answer key questions, (assuming he or she recorded the video) or may be able to discuss the incident, or perhaps produce other witnesses, and in general help find a way for independent researchers to investigate further. All of this is basic follow-up investigation, and well within the capabilities of most researchers and students of UFOs.

It should be added that researchers who spend any time with UFO videos should take the time to study video editing software, such as Adobe After Effects. One need not become an expert. But anyone can learn via some basic web searching and tutorials about techniques and capabilities for spotting video manipulation.

Another important policy for serious researchers is to become familiar with websites that host active bulletin boards relating to UFOs. It is true that there are always a number of people at these sites who are simply trolls and obstructionists. Nevertheless, such sites, such as abovetopsecret.com, alienscientist.com, and many others, usually have contributors with genuine insights. They are useful because no one is an island. No one alone has the time or resources to unravel and answer every nagging question they encounter. Others have frequently done the work before us, and there is no point in letting their hard work go to waste.

Researchers must also remember that skepticism is a good thing. UFOs are elusive. Whatever they represent does not readily reveal itself to us. Mistaken assumptions and false conclusions are common and

Chapter 9: The Growth of Ufology

understandable. It is therefore wise and appropriate to hold our own conclusions at bay until we gain as much information as possible, and at all times we must be willing to change our minds. For this reason, serious researchers must always seek out skeptical perspectives. Those who believe in the reality of UFOs may disagree with skeptics on many important matters. Indeed, many skeptics turn their positions into a religion of sorts, in the process combining a relentless ignorance of the topic with insufferable arrogance. But skeptics are essential to helping ufology move forward.

First of all, on many specific cases, skepticism is entirely justified. History shows that the large majority of raw UFO reports are explainable in conventional terms. Responsible research must search for ways to debunk UFO cases, not because of an ideology that says such things are impossible, but because we must adhere to high standards of evidence before making strong claims. Pragmatically speaking, it is worth remembering that understanding the skeptical position on a particular case can save a researcher embarrassment later on, especially when they discover that a case they have supported for years turns out to be entirely prosaic. Such things happen, after all. Moreover, when we encounter a good skeptical argument, but are still able to see why it falls short, we have strengthened our understanding of the case under examination. Any time we assume we have all the answers, and that the so-called enemy has nothing to contribute, we become victims of our own limited worldview.

In general, researchers and students of UFOs should cultivate a calm attitude and an unwillingness to become overly stressed when encountering new claims and information. Rather than rendering snap judgments, give time for new information and perspectives to sink in. In an era as volatile as our own, we would do well to be more prudent in our judgment and statements.

So, when the latest and greatest UFO sighting comes your way, take your time. Read through comments and analyses offered by other people, and not merely those already inclined to agree with you.

Most of all, beware of people who make grandiose claims of any sort. They are never to be trusted. If you doubt this, go back through history at the many great and grand predictions which never passed.[305] Talk is cheap. In such matters, I recall the wise and true words of my father, a veteran New York City police officer. He always told me: *money talks, bullshit walks.*

The Philosophical Divide

Over the last generation, we have seen several transformations in what we may call the alternative community. One element is political, in which it has become ever more radicalized, particularly since September 11, 2001. But, there has been a philosophical shift as well. Lacking a perfect label for it, perhaps we can simply call it the arrival of New Age thinking. The overall result of this has been mixed.

In the first place, old fashioned materialistic ufology has limitations. As far back as the 1960s and 1970s, researchers had been pointing out that the UFO phenomenon is *strange*, and seemed to be beyond our conventional understanding of science. At the same time, contemporary science, especially physics, has opened up new vistas of thought, such as quantum entanglement, non-locality, and other concepts that seem in line to some degree at least with some ancient beliefs about the power of the mind, even mind over matter. In other words, everything we encounter in New Age culture.

Consider quantum entanglement (which will be discussed at greater length in a later chapter). This is something physicists have noted and discussed since the 1930s. Entanglement happens when certain tiny particles, such as photons and electrons, interact physically, then become separated, but then continue to act as a pair in terms of their position, momentum, spin, polarization and more, even across great distances. How does this happen? In other words, they seem to be connected or in some sort of communication. Especially odd is that the effects appear to transcend the speed limit of transmitting information; that is, faster than light. Small wonder that Einstein once called it

---

305 For a list of failed apocalyptic predictions, see "List of dates predicted for apocalyptic events," From *Wikipedia, the free encyclopedia*.[en.wikipedia.org/wiki/List_of_dates_predicted_for_apocalyptic_events].

"spooky action at a distance."

There has also been work done on remote viewing, much of which has been within the U.S. intelligence community. Despite what the propaganda has said, remote viewing works. That is, human beings have indeed been able to "see" things remotely, not merely across space but seemingly across time. What does this mean regarding the fabric of our reality? How is it possible that someone can see something on the other side of the world, or something that has not yet happened in our time stream? Doubly so with claims of remote influencing, even remote killing, as in the real story behind *The Men Who Stare at Goats*.

There are several reasons why this relates to ufology. One is the apparent capability of these objects to violate our known laws of physics by appearing or disappearing, accelerating instantly, floating people through walls and ceilings and so on. Another is the apparent capability of these beings to enter our minds. We see this again and again in the research.

In other words, the mind is important to this field in ways that earlier generations of researchers did not understand. We need to explore this in ways that make sense scientifically.

Our problem is that we are still at a point where confirming mind to mind communication is difficult, if not impossible. Still more problematic are claims by people—a growing number each year, it seems—to have received telepathic communications, or channeled transmissions, from other entities, many of whom are said to be extraterrestrial.

It is not that such claims are necessarily false. After all, if we allow for some level of remote viewing in ourselves, this is something that may well be part of human nature itself. It should not be ruled out *a priori* that unusual types of communication are impossible.

Instead, the problem is that until we find a way to understand channeled communications more scientifically, and more importantly to find a way to verify or disprove them, they cannot be considered valid types of evidence. They may be true, or not. Yet, unless outsiders can test such claims in some manner, it is an unfair burden placed on others when asking for their belief.

As an aside, my own conclusion is that the large majority of claimed channeled transmissions and telepathic "downloads" are false. Sadly, there is a prevalence among too many to disregard the concepts of science when reviewing such claims.

During the buildup to the "Great Event" of December 21, 2012, the Internet was flooded with sites that discussed the coming transformation of humanity, almost always referred to as humanity's ascension or awakening. The attitude among many was so strident, so certain, that it was frequently considered an unarguable fact. Logic was absent. One statement from a typical blog expressed the mindset very well:

> If you don't understand or feel the concept of transformation of self, ascension, awakening, then, really, what do you know? It means you haven't experienced the awakening which, by the way, it is not scientifically proven... and in that case, you are a rationalist with no faith or contact with the divine, and the age of rationalism has passed, thank God. I hope you will get to a point when you will use the reason of the heart and not focus so exclusively on the physical mind that can only perceive illusion.[306]

This is a perspective with a long history. It differs not a bit from the perspective of the earliest Christians, and indeed of most of the world's spiritual traditions. It states that truth must be perceived. It must be felt. That what we call objective reality is an illusion, and not the true reality. This belief usually includes the idea that humanity's power of mind is very great, perhaps infinite, and that after we achieve a transformation, or awakening, or ascension, we will become as gods, with power to control our world through the mind.

This type of thinking is not part of ufology, as such, in that it is not directly concerned with the study of UFOs. Yet, it is in the air, permeating the alternative field to a greater or lesser degree. In many cases, as in the above statement, it constitutes a direct refutation of science. Elsewhere, it tries to merge the science of non-locality with New Age mysticism, nearly all of which derives from the Theosophy of individuals like Helena Blavatsky, Alice Bailey, and even Aleister

---

306 Comment from "Oana," at nibiruchallenge.blogspot.com/2009/05/word-on-david-wilcocks-2012-enigma-or.html.

Crowley.

We would be foolish to reject such attempts out of hand. All new ideas, especially those that have sprung from deep-seated human needs, and which are so widespread, should be studied for what they can offer. But we should remember that all new philosophical developments contain much that is eventually discarded.

The best course is to react with deliberation while we incorporate the science of the mind into ufology. While we do so, channelers and others who make unverifiable predictions must be held accountable for their claims. That includes seeking out skeptical arguments that debunk their claims, for there is no question that some of these individuals are fakes through and through. Simply because it may be possible in theory that a person can "hear" an extraterrestrial in his or her mind does not mean that some other person is telling the truth when they claim to communicate with beings from Andromeda. Or that they time traveled, or went to Mars, or that on December 21, 2012 (or now some future date), you will transform into a crystalline entity without the need to eat food, and that all the nasty problems humanity currently faces will be solved.

Only fools discard the tried and true rules of evidence for a pile of magic beans.

Ufology's Future

Whether the current leaders and thinkers in UFO research recognize this or not, this discipline must remain up-to-date. It must be based on sound scientific principles, but with the ability to embrace fresh ideas and new technologies. What is needed is leadership. Not merely from the head of whatever organizations may exist, but true leaders wherever they may be.

Until the secrets are all disclosed, or until these other beings announce themselves to us, we will remain at the stage of trying to record, understand, and explain this mystery. In the coming years and decades, we will be seeing new technologies introduced that will help us to do this. As recently as the dawn of the 21st century, few people could have foreseen that cell phones would be capable of sharing so much information, or indeed that they would surpass computers as the dominant form of Internet connectivity. Who knows what the next few decades will bring.

Today, you can search databases of UFO sightings that were not available even recently. You can download an app on your smartphone that keeps you informed on new UFO sightings in your area, or any area. MUFON has such an app, and it certainly does not perform as intended, but the idea is excellent and eventually such an app will be perfected.

Phones will continue to evolve and acquire new capabilities, perhaps detecting infrared signals or electromagnetic disturbances. The possibilities seem endless. It is essential for researchers to remain aware of these developments and use them.

Of course, we need the technology in order to communicate and learn from each other. The value of YouTube has already been discussed, but beyond this, we face a future of ubiquitous video conferencing and live streaming. Already, these technologies are both starting to make a difference in ufology. They need to be pushed further.

Ultimately, however, no matter how far into the future ufology goes, it must continue to rely upon sound investigations and proper reporting of results that actually reach the public. Scientific ufology, but with modern leadership, political savvy, and a commitment to the people.

Ufology: Getting Personal

One thing I have learned in my two decades of studying the UFO phenomenon is that it has the power to captivate someone's attention and become an obsession. I will never forget my first year of true attention and research into this field, and the many nights of lying in my bed, staring at the ceiling, trying to reconfigure my worldview in a way that made sense with the new facts I had learned. For myself, the feeling was more akin to an intense intellectual curiosity than anything else, a "splinter in the mind" (in the words of the character Morpheus from the movie, *The Matrix*). For some, however, the effect goes deeper still. I have seen personalities become nearly destabilized by the effect of having their once-stable worldview shaken or even shattered by the subject of UFOs.

I don't know of a sure-fire method to prevent this from happening to certain people. We are all different. There are some people, who knows why, who seem to roll with this transformation more easily than others. In some cases, however, there are those who become convinced that they have had experiences of some sort with this phenomenon, including direct contact with these other intelligences. Such people may be correct or not, but there is no question that their new information affects them deeply. They become obsessed by this subject in a way that consumes their lives, sometimes in an unhealthy way. It is a difficult thing for any person to reinvent their basic understanding of the world, especially after they reach a mature age. No one wants to go through that process, because it is an implicit recognition that their many prior years were spent living in a kind of illusory world.

Ironically, it is often those with a higher level of formal education who seem to have a hard time with this. After all, they have spent those years convinced that they were ahead of the game, that they were more knowledgeable than the average person about how the world works, and invested much of their self-esteem and identity into that understanding. But it can happen to anyone.

All of this is made harder by the fact by their belief that most of their friends, family, and colleagues would either not believe them, or might even ridicule them. And so while they go through this difficult transformation, there are often very few people they can talk to about it.

Added to this is another problem. Once someone decides that this is a subject worth their attention, they usually realize that there is an overabundance of information and literature. It can feel overwhelming, especially if one is starting not only with a limited knowledge of the subject, but often a relatively limited knowledge of science, history, philosophy, politics, psychology, or any number of other subjects that are certainly helpful in navigating one's way through this tangled field.

But the challenge is harder still when we remember that most people have other responsibilities in their lives: family, jobs, social obligations and the rest. If they work long hours, as many do, they are tired when they come home and are probably not in the mood to do hours of research, day after day, to help recreate some semblance of an ordered reality, especially when that new reality is much less congenial and reassuring than what they had once known. Moreover, they probably don't want to fight the machine, they don't want to be heroes; they just want a good life.

Ufology is not a subject for the faint of heart. Like all great questions of which the human mind is capable—*Does the soul exist? Is all of reality explainable by science? Is there a God? Do all people have inalienable rights? Is it possible for human beings to create a just civilization?*—the question, *Is there another advanced intelligence operating covertly on Planet Earth?* is one that demands many qualities. One is patience. Another is persistence. Yet another is courage. The act of exploring this subject in the depth it deserves exacts a transformation not merely of our previous worldview, which is hard enough. It changes ourselves, deeply and truly.

Chapter 10

Who Are They? What Do They Want?

Perhaps this is the most difficult of all subjects within ufology. Unfortunately for us, it is also the most important. No matter how many facets we explore of this endlessly fascinating subject, we ultimately arrive at *The Question*: who or what are we dealing with? It is a question that has engaged every mind that has ever approached the subject of UFOs, and a definitive answer has eluded its most brilliant thinkers.

The Problem of Human Perception

In a subject as cloudy as determining who these beings are, we must be aware of the quality of evidence. In every case, the specifics come down to witness testimony. Skeptics rightly point out that, given the fallibility of human perception and memory, witness testimony by itself is problematic as evidence.

Of course, UFO skeptics go further, asserting that anyone who claims to remember an alien abduction is not remembering a real event in any objective sense. Instead, it is usually asserted, there is some level of confabulation involved. That is not to say that the alleged abductee is lying, but that some level of faulty memory is at work. Indeed, there are a number of cases where this has clearly been so. It is true that a person can remember something that did not actually happen, particularly while under hypnotic regression, and especially when that session is conducted by someone who is leading their imagination. In the first place, the human mind has the ability to create vivid scenarios. In the second place, we all have some ability to fool ourselves, and everyone has at some point in their life misremembered something important. Even if alien abductions are real, confabulation is always a possibility.

Suppose an alien abduction has taken place. How likely would it be that the abductee had a perfect memory of the event? Management of human memory is real. Intelligence and military agencies have been working on this problem since the 1940s. Even the psychiatric profession quite openly has published a great amount of research on human memory management.[307] We have strong evidence that this has been of importance to the CIA, KGB, and other intelligence agencies.[308] I once interviewed a former U.S. Air Force intelligence specialist who had what strongly appeared to be a memory erasure process upon discharge from her service at Okinawa in 1982. This was done to her by the U.S. military, or some group in the U.S. intelligence system, using a combination of counseling, drugs, and electronic stimulation of the brain (ESB).

Let us assume, for the sake of argument, that some people are having encounters with entities, or an advanced species. Let us further assume that these beings may not want the abductees to have a meaningful recollection of the event. It seems quite possible, even likely, that they would take their own steps to thwart that person's memory. For this reason alone, abduction memories should be accepted with caution.

Having said this, it seems unreasonable to adopt an ultra-skeptical position that human perception and memory are inherently unreliable. Granted, our memories are incomplete and sometimes faulty, but all of us have memories, and most of our memories are generally accurate. For example, I distinctly recall being on a roller coaster ride as a boy one summer, feeling absolutely petrified. I remember the feeling of desperately wanting to get off, and of being in tears. I remember my mother greeting me when the ride was over, but I don't remember the exact year. Was I six or seven years old? Where exactly was I? What did I do for the rest of that day? These are things I do not remember, but

---

307 A good starting point is the work of Elizabeth Loftus, Ph.D., through numerous books and published papers, for example, "Make-Believe Memories," *American Psychologist*, November 2003 [homepage.psy.utexas.edu/HomePage/Class/Psy394U/Bower/07%20False%20Memories/Loftus%20Make-believe.pdf]. See also en.wikipedia.org/wiki/Elizabeth_Loftus.
308 Of the many books on this subject, a good starting point is Marks, John, *The Search for the Manchurian Candidate: The CIA and Mind Control*, Crown Publishing Group, 1979.

I know I had the experience. To doubt all witness testimony or recollections simply because they are held to be inherently unreliable is irrational. It is an attitude not supported by human experience.

Therefore, if we accept the validity of witness testimony and recollections, we may well be inclined to believe that these beings are alien in some way or another, and that they are interested in us.

It is helpful at this point to remember that the UFO phenomenon itself rests on a more solid foundation than simply witness recollection. It also includes recorded instrumentation, military documents, and more. This is important because such sightings and encounters clearly beg the question of who or what is behind the phenomenon. When we encounter something that is more advanced than anything that is supposed to exist, along with claims of some people to have encountered advanced non-human intelligences, then we are at least justified in making some provisional or hypothetical conclusions.

All of which means that the thoughts that follow in this chapter are more speculative than most other aspects of the UFO phenomenon. They do not always possess the certainty one would like. Such is life. Sometimes, all we can do is to make the best hypothesis we can at the time, and move on.

So. Who. Are. They?

After his book, *Communion,* was published in 1987, Whitley Strieber received nearly 140,000 letters from people around the world over the next seven years, all claiming to have had alien encounters.[309]

Aside from the staggering number of letters and claims, several things stand out. In the first place, most of the writers reported experiencing a lifetime of strange encounters and experiences, many of which involved other family members. In addition, a large portion of these people reported experiencing the kind of abduction scenario that has become so widely recognized, in which small gray beings took them aboard a UFO and subjected them to intrusive medical procedures.

---

309 Strieber, Whitley, *The Communion Letters.* Anne Strieber, Editor. Harper Prism, 1997.

Even more interesting, however, is that a larger number did not describe such an abduction experience. Instead, they described encounters with other types of beings: insect-like beings, reptoids, and several different human types such as Asian-Orientals, Nordics, and robed beings in the manner of Greek gods. There were even descriptions of beings of pure light.

A large majority, roughly eighty percent, described having a positive experience in one way or another. But it seemed obvious that most of these interactions were at a very high level of strangeness. These letters made it clear that encounters with these non-human beings was a complex phenomenon, and beings themselves seemed to be highly complex.

Of course, it certainly would have been nice had someone taken a reliable photograph of any of these beings. Such elusiveness continues to make this topic so difficult. Yet the accounts keep coming.

What do we make of these varied beings? Do they represent different groups? If so, what might their own relationships be among each other? Do they cooperate with one another, or do they compete?

There is yet another type of being that many people claim to have encountered. These are entities said to be channeled by certain individuals, or somehow reached telepathically. Here, we are dealing with experiences that would appear to have nothing to do with UFOs or ufology. Except for one thing: many of these communications are alleged to originate from advanced beings from elsewhere in the universe. As a result, this has become a large part of the UFO community, if we can call it that. These messages can be appealing to people, but that is a separate matter from whether or not they come from extraterrestrials. Regarding that point, It should be obvious that channeled communications are not valid evidence unless they can provide information that is clearly unknown to the channeler and can be verified independently. We will return to this idea.

First, let us look at the other types of alien beings people claim to encounter.

The Grays

The Grays became ubiquitous in popular culture for a simple reason: they were easily the most commonly described entity among people who spoke to UFO researchers. They seemed to be everywhere. Moreover, it does not make sense to suggest they are a screen memory for some sort of covert human activity. In the first place, the memories of these beings are often submerged within a person's memory for a long time. Secondly, when such memories are recovered, the actions of these beings, their movements, sounds, and behaviors scream *not human!* This is not a case of human abductors wearing alien masks.

Variations of the Grays have appeared in reports for many decades. True, the descriptions of extraterrestrials from the 1950s and 1960s describe beings rather different from the typical Gray. Even so, such descriptions, from Europe and South America, as well as some of the earliest American abduction cases of the 1960s, portray beings with basic similarities: very short in height and (often) large, roundish heads.

Even today, however, multiple types of Gray are reported. Not all witness recollections describe them as having solid black eyes. Some accounts describe large, almond-shaped eyes, but with vertical slits for pupils, giving a cat-like or reptile-like effect. Moreover, some Grays are nearly as tall as a human male, while others are two or three feet tall. Some are extremely thin while others more stoutly built. There are a number of other variations, as well.

Despite the variations, there are enough consistent accounts that we can try to give a picture of the Grays. If anything stands out, it is that they are conducting a widespread and secret abduction program. They take their targeted people usually when they are easiest to take, either at home, usually in the middle of the night, or sometimes while driving. Secretiveness is key for them. It is absolutely essential for them to maintain cover over their program.

Their capabilities are extremely formidable, far beyond our own. They can induce physical paralysis or unconsciousness in their target with ease. They can completely control one's physical movements, or even float a person through solid barriers. They use highly advanced

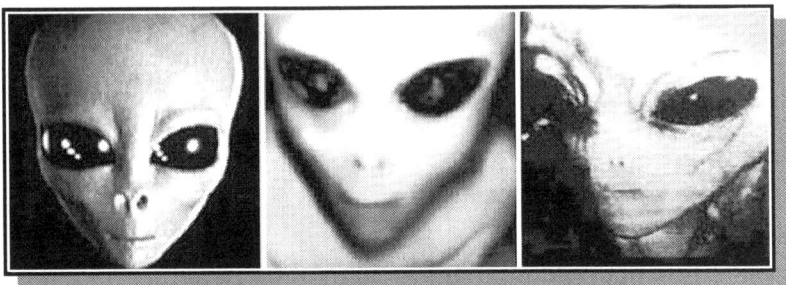

Common depictions of Gray aliens.

technologies such as brilliant wands or other exotic equipment to examine individuals and monitor their bodies. They are able to insert and remove tiny implants, whether these be in the sinus cavity, behind the eye, or even in the brain. They collect human sperm, eggs, and fetuses regularly.

Two capabilities are of paramount importance. One is their apparent mastery over our space-time reality. Floating people through walls is one manifestation of that ability. Invisibility is another. But most significant (at least in the recollections of many abductees) is their knowledge of a person's life path. That is, of their future. In the example of abductee Betty Andreasson Luca, one of the most detailed and well-known cases, we get this sense very strongly, that these beings exist beyond our localized experience of time. Not only do they know our future, but they can influence it to some extent.

Their mental capabilities are equally important. Throughout abduction research, this stands out. These beings have extraordinary intelligence and are intensely telepathic—something worth long consideration. They communicate by entering one's mind, a capability that ought to warrant great caution on our part. For anyone who can enter your thoughts can most assuredly influence them. Indeed, this is undoubtedly how they induce screen memories of their encounters, making proper recall so much more difficult.

Then there the matter of memory control and erasure. It does happen that people may, over time, recover some of their memories. That is because not everyone is the same. Some people's memories are able to bleed through, as it were, more readily than others. But the fact remains that most of the memories of these experiences have been blocked and tampered with. In other words, the first line of defense for the Grays is to block one's memory; the second line of defense is to tamper with the recollection itself.

They seem to do this by inducing a fear-based command in people for them never to think about the event, much less discuss it. I have interviewed several of these people. Most have had an overpowering feeling that they were never supposed to discuss their experience. When they finally did so, usually after many years had elapsed, they experienced severe anxiety. Other researchers have gotten similar results.

These beings demand absolute secrecy. But what are they hiding from us?

Everything points to the likelihood that these Grays are involved in a long-term program, one involving a much longer trajectory than typical human plans and programs. This appears to have been going on for several generations, perhaps longer. Clearly, they are interested in human sexuality and reproduction. Many female abductees have reported being taken back to a craft to be shown hybrid-type babies that were supposed to be their offspring. This would point to a breeding program for the creation of human-alien hybrids.

Such a thesis has been discussed for some time by now. But although it has become something of a cultural cliché, it has become one for a reason: there are many witness recollections that point to this conclusion.

So, if the Grays are creating a human-alien hybrid species, is this with a view to have such beings integrate into our own society? Or even to replace us? David Jacobs, who has looked at this possibility perhaps more than anyone else, thinks *yes,* that they seek to replace us in one form or another.

With respects to Dr. Jacobs, this scenario strikes me as implausible. Over the years, there have been a few, sporadic, claims of encounters with hybrid beings. Every one of them points to the need of these beings for seclusion from human society. One instructive account is in the book, *Raechel's Eyes*. Raechel, an apparent hybrid, seemed to have tried to go so far as to take university classes and even have a roommate. Needless to say, she did not fit in, and also did not last long in the system.[310]

Assuming a breeding program is in fact happening, we should be cautious in developing conclusions on its purpose. It could be that it is simply to allow future generations of Grays or aliens to live on Earth more comfortably in some manner, not necessarily to integrate. Or, simply for them to acquire something of value in human DNA and continue to live in a separate world of their own.

In any case, there is more than breeding going on. The Grays seem to be monitoring us actively. The implants, for example, point to a monitoring program, and it appears that many abductees are monitored throughout their lives.

One of the key messages people report from the Grays is that they are concerned over humanity's destruction and poisoning of Earth's natural environment. Several abductees have reported that they are stationed here, and have been testing our water, soil, vegetation, and animal life for quite some time. If it is also true, as some evidence suggests, that the Grays have also taken animals from around the world, it could be to track changes to reproductive systems and therefore to the Earth's environment. The Grays often tell abductees what they are doing is necessary and important, even for the betterment or preservation of mankind or life on Earth. In particular, a number of abductees have reported the Grays are concerned about nuclear technology and weapons. Indeed, the message is that they are watching out for us.

This is reasonable enough. If we humans arrived at another world and saw the most advanced species there in the process of destroying that planet's ecosystem, we too might be concerned.

Still, we are not in a position to know if the Grays are truthful. There is nothing to stop them from lying to us. Is it impossible to think that humans would lie to natives of another planet in order to

---

310 Littrell, Helen. *Raechel's Eyes: The Strange but True Case of a Human-Alien Hybrid*. Granite Publishing, 2006.

gain their trust for our own ulterior purposes, whatever those might be? Such a scenario was portrayed in James Cameron's movie, *Avatar*. The idea could be to convince the inhabitants that their planet is in danger and the newcomers want to help. The human race could not possibly be the first *marks*, the first suckers, in the history of the universe.

We may ask, are the Grays evil? Putting aside the question of what would constitute interstellar evil, we suppose they might be, but this is probably the wrong way to look at the matter.

If they are here to help humanity, then at best they are doing their job with great subtlety, since there is no clear evidence that they have done anything significant in that regard. Maybe they cannot. Humanity may be beyond their control. Of course, if they really wanted to shake us up and help us change our ways, one supposes they could make a formal appearance. So they either will not or cannot. That is a bit distressing, since at this point we are technologically outclassed by these creatures.

In reviewing the research and claims about these beings, one seldom hears much speculation about what their psychology, personalities, and social relations might be like. Obviously, we can only guess about these things, and yet judging by the alleged interactions, they seem cold-blooded by our standards. Abductees generally report that these beings do not express emotions, although a few felt hostility coming from them, and a few have also reported feelings of benevolence. On the more grisly side, it has happened more than once that abductees have linked Grays to animal mutilations. For this, Linda Moulton Howe's *Glimpses of Other Realities, Volume 1* provides a good deal of information. As several individuals recalled, these creatures cold-bloodedly removed blood and organs from cattle while those animals were still alive.[311]

In such instances, we might see the Grays as acting toward other life forms just as humanity has done throughout its history. In reality, these beings are still much more humane than we are. Any doubters

---

311 Howe, Linda Moulton. *Glimpses of Other Realities. Volume I: Facts and Eyewitnesses.* LMH Productions, 1994.

need only consider our beef and poultry industries, for starters.

Still, it is unsettling that the Grays do not treat humanity as equals. We are very much the Junior partner in this relationship. They deal with us on their terms. They do to us what they want to do.

It is interesting, also, to consider the likelihood that they are the product of genetic engineering, and may well have strong components of artificial (or at least artificially designed) intelligence. We ourselves are on the cusp of redesigning our own genetic code, and of developing what is known as strong artificial intelligence (AI). That is, AI that may become self-aware. From there, it is an easy matter of having that AI interacting in some way with our own brains, perhaps through the implantation of nano chips, or perhaps some other way. In other words, a century from now, human beings may look and act very differently than we do today. A typical human IQ might be 300 or 500 or more, for all we can tell. All of that difference would be due to genetic and technological enhancements.

Perhaps we will not journey down that road. But we might. It could be that the Grays were designed for a specific purpose. After all, their enormous heads and spindly bodies are unlikely to have evolved naturally. A brain so large would require too much of the body's resources, too much nutrition, all at the expense of other bodily functions. Yet, one could design such a creature. With a brain so formidable, there would be no need for a powerful body. Humans are not as powerful as lions or elephants, but we can control them. With access to higher thinking and technology, physical strength is irrelevant.

It is possible that the Grays were designed specifically to interact here on Earth. After all, a truly extraterrestrial race would be unsuited to interact with Earth's environment. There would be problems with everything here, from the solar radiation, to the strength of gravity, to the microscopic organisms and more. To remain here, an advanced race from elsewhere would at least consider modifying themselves genetically. One supposes they could simply walk around in protective suits, like we do when we are away from Earth's protective environ-

Chapter 10: Who Are They? What Do They Want?

ment, but if they want a long-term presence, then modifying themselves seems most logical. And what would make more sense then to extract native DNA and adapt it for their purposes?

Perhaps this is the reason why many of the so-called aliens that have been reported are humanoid, reptoid, and insectoid. We have humans here, we have reptiles, we have insects.[312] Perhaps the Grays are partly related to one or more of Earth's native species.

Therefore, when we speak of alien-human hybrids, it is equally valid to suppose that the aliens themselves are already hybrids. Not long ago, scientists routinely dismissed talk of genetic manipulation on such a scale. We have come a long way, however, in the last ten years, with much more to learn in the coming decades.

Even if the Grays were genetically designed to function on Earth, they clearly have not reached the point where they can walk around easily. Or perhaps they have, but simply need secrecy. Either way, it would seem that they need a secure environment in which to work and live. Maybe their solution is a vessel in upper orbit, or perhaps farther away, parked on the far side of the Moon. Perhaps, too, they have created bases here on Earth, deep underground. We ourselves have the technology for this, including the ability to go deep beneath the ocean floor.[313] In essentials, all one needs is oxygen and energy. The oxygen can be extracted from the water, while the energy can be geothermal, or even a small nuclear generator. Certainly not impossible at all.

Why could not the Grays be able to live and work here on Earth without interruption or annoyance? What would prevent them from going deep underground without our knowledge, especially if they did so in prior generations, long before we developed our current technologies? There have certainly been no shortage of sightings of UFOs going

---

312 Although an interesting alternative view was expressed by the late Mac Tonnies, in *The Cryptoterrestrials: A Meditation on Indigenous Humanoids and the Aliens Among Us*, Anomalist Books, 2010. He suggested that the recollection of humanoid, insectoid, and reptoid beings has more to do with human memory constructing such creatures because these are what we are familiar with.
313 Sauder, Richard, Ph.D., *Hidden in Plain Sight: Beyond the X-Files*. Foreword by Richard M. Dolan. Keyhole Publishing, 2010.

into and coming out of large bodies of water.[314]

These last few points are applicable to any alien creature, not simply the Grays. Let us now discuss certain beings that often get overlooked, perhaps because they simply do not seem that exotic. These are beings that look perfectly human, except that they are something different from perfectly human.

Human-Looking Aliens

There are several distinct types of human-looking beings involved in the UFO/ET/abduction phenomenon.

Some appear to be involved in the abduction process. Budd Hopkins collected several odd cases like this, which he eventually included in his final abduction-related book, *Sight Unseen*.[315] Over the years, people approached him with cases so strange that for a long time he did not know what to do with them. They involved encounters with ordinary-looking people, but who seemed somehow to work as "helpers" of some sort during abductions. He had one case, for instance, of family members who recalled a very strange long-term house guest from years before. This was someone with very odd behaviors, no known means of support, and, when they began to reflect upon the situation, apparent connections to abduction experiences they recalled. In other cases, as well, there seemed to be human helpers or facilitators to an alien abduction experience. These individuals all seemed to lack the basic social skills one would acquire from living in normal human society. It would seem that they were raised by other means.

There are also stories of odd humans of a different sort, who may be working on a different agenda.

I will relate a story I was given by a woman I met at a conference in 2010. She and her husband seemed perfectly ordinary. The woman

---

314 Sanderson, Ivan T. *Invisible Residents: A Disquisition upon Certain Matters Maritime, and the Possibility of Intelligent Life under the Waters of This Earth*. The World Publishing Company, 1970. See also Feindt, Carl W. *UFOs and Water:Physical Effects of UFOs on Water Through Accounts by Eyewitnesses*. Xlibris Corporation, 2010.
315 Hopkins, Budd and Rainey, Carol. *Sight Unseen: Science, UFO Invisibility, and Transgenic Beings*. Atria Books, 2003.

was in her late 50s, friendly, and seemed to be a stable individual. She related a very strange event that happened to her when she was an early teen during the mid-1960s. She lived in a small town in Western Pennsylvania, and was attending church with her mother. Although in such a small town, most of the church attendees were familiar to each other, she now noticed two new people in the row directly in front of her. Not only had she never seen them before, but they were clearly and obviously different from everyone else. To start, both of them were physically very beautiful. Both had blond hair, both looked to be in their twenties, and both were wearing extremely beautiful blue suits. To the witness, a young teen girl who was quite aware of clothing and fashion, the fabric of their clothing was unlike anything she had ever seen: incredibly fine, perfectly put together, and vastly beyond the quality of anyone else's clothing.

Throughout the service, she was obsessed by the couple, and could not understand why no one else seemed to observe them. She noticed that they were not familiar with when to stand, sit, kneel, or sing—the activities during a typical Roman Catholic mass.

What was truly disconcerting, though, was that she heard them telepathically. They never looked back to her, they never seemed to speak, but somehow, she said to me, she heard them in her mind. They seemed to be discussing whether or not they were fitting in. They appeared to believe they were successful, when the young witness heard the female think to the male, "she can hear us." For the rest of the mass, the frightened and fascinated teenager heard no other thoughts coming from them. When the service ended, the two strangers very abruptly and efficiently left, somehow getting out ahead of the rest of the crowd.

The young girl decided to pursue them. She bolted out, pressing through the crowd. She heard her mother calling after her, but she kept going. Out of the church, she saw the couple walking very quickly past the parking lot, toward a grassy hill. Then they went behind the hill and were momentarily lost to view. She hurried up after them. When she got to the top of the hill, she saw them again. By now, they were in a clearing and walking fast toward a wooded area.

The intrepid young witness began to race down after them. But then she saw another figure. There, at the edge of the woods, stood an unusually tall figure dressed in a black suit, wearing a black hat. He reminded her of the character "Lurch," from the 1960s television show, *The Addams Family*. His appearance was frightening to her, and she stopped dead in her tracks. Glued to her spot, she saw the two blond people approach the tall person and scurry behind him into the woods. The tall man then turned and followed them in.

Although there was no UFO sighting in this story, it is clearly of interest to ufology. What kinds of people were these two blond individuals, and who was the very tall person? One supposes they could have been part of a study group using psychics to test how well they could read thoughts in a public setting. Perhaps they were even Russian spies, although this seems like a stretch. Everything about them seemed not to fit in. They were not like anybody else: not in their behavior, not in their physical appearance, and not in their mental capabilities.

This is similar to another account I was given by a retired U.S. Air Force Colonel, a man with a Ph.D., and who worked in sensitive classified programs from the 1970s through the 1990s. This man also had a strong interest in UFOs and extraterrestrials and, in the presence of his wife, told me of an encounter the two of them (plus a friend who was psychically gifted) had with two individuals at a Las Vegas casino. The three were walking through an upper level area when the psychic grabbed the Colonel's arm. They all stopped.

As the Colonel related the story, all three saw a strikingly beautiful blonde-haired woman. Of course, Las Vegas has many beautiful men and women, but somehow this woman seemed different. The psychic was convinced that this woman was not a normal human being. When the psychic and the Colonel's wife took a nearby escalator down to the next level, the Colonel remained behind, watching the woman. Then he heard her in his mind: "Don't bother with me, you have no business here." That, in essentials, was the message from her. The force

Chapter 10: Who Are They? What Do They Want?

of this statement hit him hard.

Just then, the woman's male companion, also blond, approached her. Together, they walked toward the escalator, and for this they needed to walk by the Colonel. He was determined to stop them. His idea was to say something that would start a conversation. Instead, they walked right by him.

He followed. Down the escalator they all went—the couple in front, and the Colonel right behind. While they descended, he stared at the backs of their heads. Like the teen girl who sat in a Pennsylvania church in the 1960s, the Colonel could "hear" their thoughts. From what he could remember, the conversation was essentially a statement that "he has no need to know about us, he will not know." Looking down, he saw his wife and their friend watching them from behind a slot machine (his wife laughed when he recounted this part, confirming how nervous she had been). When they reached the floor level, the telepathic blond couple simply walked away. None of the three pursued them.

There are many more of such accounts. Ingo Swann, the famous remote viewer, had a frightening encounter with an extraordinarily beautiful woman in a Los Angeles supermarket during the 1970s. He became convinced him that she was intensely telepathic and not human, at least not like the rest of us. At that time, he encountered two mysterious "agents" whom he had met previously, and who were observing the scene. Shortly afterward, he was warned by their boss that this woman was not human and was very dangerous.[316]

If we are concerned about alien-human hybrids infiltrating our society, as the first generation of abduction researchers (particularly Hopkins and Jacobs) have claimed, what do we make of stories like this? Because it would seem that these beings have already infiltrated, and they look much more normal than the wispy haired, delicate hybrids that one often hears about.

Based on such accounts, it seems that these beings have a strong ability to read our minds. They know when we are listening to them.

---

316 Swann, Ingo. *Penetration: The Question of Extraterrestrial and Human Telepathy.* Ingo Swann Books, 1998.

In addition, these stories hint at something else about us: that we ourselves have a telepathic faculty that can activate at certain times, perhaps in their presence, or at other moments as well.

Other questions arise. Are they exactly like us biologically? It would seem logical to think that they came from Earth. If so, how did they become so different? Is it wrong to think of them as aliens? Should we simply see them as human beings who, at some point in the past, reached a faster track of development, leaving the rest of us behind? Is this the answer to the entire UFO mystery: an ancient breakaway civilization? And are memories of alleged Grays and other alien beings simply screen memories themselves? Then again, if that is true, why do they need to conceal themselves from us? What do they have to fear?

One possibility is that they use human society, or somehow seek to manage it, or perhaps benefit from it in some way. Of course, all this is speculation. We are in a subject that generates ever more questions, and not enough answers.

In addition to stories like the preceding, there have been claims by some people to have encountered benevolent human-looking extraterrestrials. These come to us primarily via so-called *contactees*, that is, people who have claimed repeated contacts with extraterrestrial beings. Typically, we are told that such beings have used that person to deliver their message to mankind.

Such stories ought to elicit an instinctual skepticism. Previously, I addressed my skepticism concerning the claims of George Adamski. Yet, there are many other such claims. None should be dismissed *a priori*, and all are (at least in theory) worthy of investigation. Unquestionably, most of the claims are outlandish, and one must wonder why the beings would select some of these people to spread their message. Most of the so-called contactees over the years have seemed entirely ordinary, lacking any social leverage or literary skill. Yet, for all we know, there could be something unusual about them, something significant.

The key feature of the most intriguing of these types of cases is the combination of outlandish claims and strong evident sincerity. In this regard, the "Friendship Case" from Italy is typical. Until recently, the story was kept quiet, known only to a few Italian researchers. When one of the main contactees involved in the meetings died, some of the others decided to talk.

The meetings were said to have taken place over many decades, starting in 1956, and to have continued through the 1980s. It involved several men who had been contacted—quite physically, not via channeling—by a group of extraterrestrials. These beings were human looking, although some were extremely large (nine to ten feet tall), while others were only three feet tall or so.

On the face of it, it sounds utterly unbelievable. But the witnesses all seemed intelligent, cultured, and sincere. A few were highly regarded in their community. There is a collection of testimonials from them, and alleged videos and photographs. The beings themselves claimed to have come from planets elsewhere in our galaxy and beyond. There were only a small number of them living on Earth, in bases under the ground and sea, some of which were said to be along the Adriatic coast.

In the words of the witnesses, "the Friends are our elder brothers. They are human. Indeed, in comparison it's we terrestrials who are less than human." This is the reason given why they generally would not show themselves. In the many alleged meetings, the "Friends" gave a distinct message of Good versus Evil, stating that they have love and goodwill for mankind.[317]

There is one other fascinating tidbit that came out of the Friendship case. A documentary about it briefly showed a letter written by the great French philosopher Voltaire to the Count of St. Germain on 6 June 1761. This had been shown to one of the Italian contactees as an example of a possible extraterrestrial contact in the 18th century. The letter is authentic, and (translated in English) reads:

> I reply, sir, to your letter you sent me in April, in which you reveal frightening secrets, among which the most terrible for an old man like me, the hour of my death. Thank you, Germain; your long journey through

---

317 A documentary on the Friendship Case is available on YouTube. See "The Friendship Case - Alien UFO Documentary" [www.youtube.com/watch?v=iD1EufflceA].

time will be illuminated by the friendship I have for you, until the day your revelations will come true in the middle of the twentieth century. The *talking pictures* are a gift to the time I have left to live, your *mechanized flying machine* could one day bring you back to me. Farewell, my friend. Voltaire.

The documentary offers the possibility that Germain was in contact with extraterrestrials. Without doubt, he is one of the most mysterious figures in world history. Voltaire once said that Germain was "a man who knows everything and who never dies." Germain was a brilliant European courtier and diplomat and never directly answered questions about his origins. He also never seemed to age and would often tell others that he was several centuries old.[318] As the commentator Doug Webber pointed out, Germain is considered to be the possible author of an esoteric French book entitled *La Très Sainte Trinosophie* (The Most Holy Trinosophia), described as an "allegorical initiation, detailing many kabbalistic, alchemical and masonic mysteries."[319] However, there are passages in this book that seem as though they were written by a contactee from the 1950s, including this passage:

> Scarcely had I risen to the surface of the earth, when my unseen guide led me still more swiftly. The velocity with which we sped through space can be compared with naught but itself. In an instant I had lost sight of the plains below. I noticed with astonishment that I had emerged from the bowels of the earth far from the country about Naples. A desert and some triangular masses were the only objects I could see.[320]

Perhaps St. Germain was just a very clever trickster. If so, he held the most brilliant minds of Europe under his sway. We may well wonder, was he somehow in possession of esoteric knowledge that itself came from *others* who have lived here in this planet for a very long time?[321]

---

318 "Count of St. Germain," in *Wikipedia, the Free Encylopedia* [en.wikipedia.org/wiki/Count_of_St._Germain]
319 "The Most Holy Trinosophia," From *Wikipedia, the free encyclopedia* [en.wikipedia.org/wiki/The_Most_Holy_Trinosophia].
320 Comte de St. Germain, "The Most Holy Trinosophia." Adapted from Manly P. Hall, *The Most Holy Trinosophia of the Comte de St. Germain*. Philosophical Research Society, 1963. [www.rexresearch.com/germain/germain.htm]
321 See the very interesting analysis of the Voltaire-St. Germain connection by Doug Webber, "UFO Secret: The Friendship Case, Voltaire, and Germain" at dream-prophecy.blogspot.com/2013/06/ufo-secret-friendship-case-and-count-of.html.

Regarding St. Germain, as with the Friendship case, we must be guided by the quality of evidence, and clearly neither story can be offered as proof of human contact with extraterrestrials. Yet, there are so many other such stories. Moreover, if it there are human-looking but highly extraordinary beings occasionally interacting with us, then why not the Friendship case, or some others?

There is yet another variant of human-looking "aliens," if we can call them that. They are sometimes another type of "Nordic" or "Blonde" being who appear almost like angels. One such appeared to the abductee Betty Andreasson, whose stories were described at length by the researcher Raymond Fowler. In one instance, Betty was abducted by Gray-like entities, then taken to an exotic base apparently off the planet. There were small beings similar to Grays, but there were also golden robed, shining beings, who were entirely human-looking.[322]

Such descriptions occur frequently enough, although they are complicated by the fact that many of these encounters are not connected with actual UFO sightings. They are simply claims of contact. Still, if we are considering possible aliens or extraterrestrials, must we ignore them just because they are not part of a UFO sighting? That seems arbitrary and silly.

But caution is always necessary. Many of these encounters are dreamlike, or even dreams. That does not mean they are not necessarily real. After all, when someone has unusually vivid dreams with profound messages from robed, shining beings, one might well conclude they are worth a consideration. Nevertheless, there is an element of the surreal to some of these encounters. This must give our rational minds pause. Ultimately, the power of our conclusions must be related in some manner to the strength of our evidence.

Other Types of Beings

People have reported other types of beings, including those resembling insects and reptiles. The reptoids, in particular, have

---

322 Fowler, Raymond E. *The Andreasson Affair: The Documented Investigation of a Woman's Abduction Aboard a UFO.* Introduction by J. Allen Hynek. Prentice Hall, 1979.

become famous via David Icke and his assertion that some members of the human power elite are actually reptilian shape-shifters.

Whether or not one believes that the extreme claims that the British Royal Family and others are secretly shape-shifting reptoids who drink human blood, a number of abductees have reported seeing reptilian captors. Some have alleged sexual assault, even rape, by these beings. There is a belief among some people that these entities live off human fears and other emotions, something like psychic vampires, and meanwhile helping to keep the population in mental slavery. Whether such a claim is true or not is impossible to prove and arguably pointless to try.

But are there reptilians? Yes, if we accept the substantial number of abductees who claim to recall them. I will add that one of my colleagues, a seasoned UFO investigator, told me of an interview this person conducted with a senior retired U.S. Defense official. The official discussed his professional knowledge of three major types of extraterrestrials living on Earth. According to him, all three types (the Grays, the Nordic-Humans, and the Reptoids) were being actively monitored by the black budget military. While this is just another story, it resonates with me because it comes from a source I know and respect. I take it as a possibility.

This is even a greater alleged assortment of beings than what has been discussed here. Undoubtedly, they cannot all be true, especially when considering that human memory itself can be managed and manipulated. What some people report as a specific alien type, or as variations of a particular type, may well be a screen memory.

It seems safe to say, however, that all of these beings possess capabilities we lack, whether these be technological, mental, or by control over the very spacetime fabric itself.

We may ask, if even we cannot answer, what is the most likely explanation that accounts for all of these beings? All we can do for now is speculate. But, clearly, humanity is on the fast track, wherever it is leading. For millennia, we existed with limited technology. Then, overnight, we shot into space. Any intelligence with the ability to monitor us can see that we are transforming ourselves in a fundamental way. Right now, we are probably putting on the best show in this portion of the universe.

Will we complete our transformation into whatever it is we are becoming? Or will we crash and burn? Do *they* have an opinion one way or the other? Do they have conflicting opinions?

Getting probable answers to any of these questions is daunting enough. Dealing with it in strictly scientific terms seems impossible at present. Researchers of UFOs, abductions, and contact are in a quandary because none of the current evidence is acceptable to the world of science. None of the evidence offered can be studied independently. Everything mentioned in this chapter derives strictly from testimony and claims from people. Certainly, many of these people seem perfectly normal, and many sound persuasive. Moreover, if we allow that there is a UFO reality of some sort, their claims have some logic. But that is not the same as proof. No matter how strongly we may believe that one or more of these types of beings are here, we would do well to remind ourselves of the persnickety little fact that no claims of contact have been proven scientifically. Someone's experience may count as proof to that person, but personal experiences clearly cannot count as proof to other people.

The foregoing applies even more to the following class of alleged extraterrestrial beings: those said to be channeled or somehow in mental or spiritual communication with certain people who claim to speak for them.

Channeled Beings

The first thing to acknowledge about channeling is that it has not received scientific corroboration or support. Even among its supporters, few if any are so bold as to assert that it has strong, genuine, scientific evidence to support it.

And yet, if we submit for a moment to examining the subject in a non-scientific, purely anecdotal manner, there have been certain instances in which, at least to some reasonable people, there may be something to it. At this point, many skeptics undoubtedly would consign this position to the *woo* camp, but there just seem to be too many individuals who are sincere about channeling. Whatever they are doing, it is not hoaxing. They are tapping into something, whether an actual entity or a deep part of their subconscious mind. A number of channelers have described their feelings while they channeled, and they certainly believe they were connecting with another entity.

Is it outrageous to consider that human consciousness has certain capabilities to transcend what we perceive as our ordinary spacetime reality? Although the scientific support may be thin, it is not absent, as the modern history of remote viewing demonstrates.[323] In addition, as the next chapter shows, there may be a valid scientific structure to allow for it. If this is so, why not channeling?

Nevertheless, it is always good policy to start from a position of skepticism when it comes to channelers, especially those who claim to have been in contact with extraterrestrials. After all, channelers have been with us forever, but only in the last few generations have they claimed to have any communications from extraterrestrials. Surely, this seems like a cultural phenomenon.

Moreover, the track record of channelers fails to inspire confidence. Believing the claims of all of their contradictory and often mutually exclusive predictions would leave one extremely confused, to say the least. The memory of the failed 2012 Ascension predictions by many channelers and psychics also left a bad taste. Finally, insights or wisdom provided by a channeler is one thing; concluding therefore that they must be accurate when claiming it comes from an extraterrestrial being is quite another.

New Age Aliens

Channeling extraterrestrials goes right to the beginning of the modern UFO phenomenon. As early as 1952, a contactee named

---

[323] There is a huge literature on remote viewing. The reader is encouraged to read Marrs, Jim, *Psi Spies*, Alienzoo, 2000; Schnabel, Jim, *Remote Viewers: The Secret History of America's Psychic Spies*, Dell, 1997; Targ, Russell and Puthoff, Harold E., *Mind-Reach: Scientists Look at Psychic Abilities*, Hampton Roads, 2005; McMoneagle, Joseph, *Mind Trek: Exploring Consciousness, Time, and Space Through Remote Viewing*, Hampton Roads, 1997.

George Van Tassell claimed to be in telepathic communication with extraterrestrials. He made no paranormal claims, but stated that they used advanced technology to connect with natural human abilities. The name of the being who contacted him, he said, was named Ashtar.

Ashtar's earliest messages focused on the dangers from nuclear weapons. They also described an extraterrestrial "government" that monitored Earth and wanted to improve life for humanity. This was the origin of the idea of Ashtar Command

Soon, Ashtar Command was being channeled by others. The messages did not always agree, and rivalries developed. Many predictions followed, often centering on the imminent arrival of an Ashtar-led armada to guide and protect mankind.

During the 1970s, a person known as Tuella began channeling Ashtar Command. Rather than emphasize technology or politics, she focused on inner spiritual development and achieving "higher dimensions." This, of course, coincided with the beginnings of the modern New Age movement. Other Ashtar channelers continued to emphasize apocalyptic themes, even stating that Ashtar Command's ships would soon arrive to help people evacuate the planet. One such channeler predicted this would happen in 1994.

The Internet gave Ashtar Command a new life. It appears that no matter how many failed predictions exist in one's track record, there are always people who will find a way to believe the next one. Today, after more than half a century of existence, Ashtar Command (now known as Ashtar Galactic Command) seems to work as a kind of committee that keeps control over its messages. Apocalypses are definitely *out*.[324]

But Ashtar Command is just one small part of the modern channeling of alleged extraterrestrials, which exploded into ufology during the 1980s. Barbara Marciniak, for example, began channeling the Pleiadians at that time and gained an influence that is difficult to

---

324 Partridge, Christopher (Ed.), *UFO Religions*, Routledge, 2003. Tuella/Ashtar Command, *Project World Evacuation,* Guardian Action International, 1982. See the Ashtar Command website at www.ashtarcommand.org.

overstate.[325] Her sessions provided a virtually complete statement of modern New Age philosophy. She was not the first channeler to give such messages, but she was the first popular channeler who explicitly communicated with extraterrestrials and incorporated such a philosophy. Earlier channelers, such as J. Z. Knight, the channeler of Ramtha, essentially offered the same ideas, but Ramtha is Lemurian, not extraterrestrial.

And what is that message? In the case of the Pleiadians, they speak to Marciniak from the future. They claim to be one of many extraterrestrial life forms interacting with Earth, not all of which are benevolent. They claim that Earth will experience a major event, beginning in 2012, during which the battle for dominion of our world will take place. Indeed, the original prediction was not for 2012. When it was in made in the early 1990s, it was set for the year 2000. Now that the 2012 prediction seems to have failed, too, perhaps a new date will be set.

Or, perhaps it has happened on schedule, since most of us cannot perceive this battle, which is said to occur in the "fourth and fifth" dimensions, and most of humanity perceives only three dimensions. According to Marciniak's sources, this is because 300,000 years ago, in an earlier struggle for Earth, human DNA was disassembled by malevolent beings from twelve strands to a double helix structure. These beings wanted to keep humanity ignorant so as to feed from our fear, anger, and doubt. The fundamental message is that Reptilians are really in charge of this planet and keep humanity for their own sustenance.

In this context, the Pleiadian message via Marciniak is to remind humanity of its divine origins, to trigger its DNA reconstruction, to help people re-assimilate "light" into their bodies, and raise their "frequency." All of this will enable them to travel in higher dimensions and survive the coming upheaval. This is the core of what has been called the Ascension process.

It has also become the foundation of the New Age belief system

---

325 Marciniak, Barbara. *Bringers of the Dawn: Teachings from the Pleiadians*. Bear & Co., 1992.

insofar as it is connected to UFO studies. But it is more likely the message, and not the cosmology, that has attracted most adherents. The message, in essentials, is one that has been channeled for a long time, including in the *Seth* books by Jane Roberts, and even before: that each person creates his or her own reality by their thoughts and intentions. You create your reality by your thoughts. Some people take this notion further than others. Ramtha, for instance, says literally that "you are God," and that consciousness and energy create the nature of reality.

This is a philosophy that has a great attraction to many people, although most of us might draw the line at the presumption (and narcissism) of calling ourselves God. Just as questionable is the idea that one *literally* creates one's own reality. The contention is that there is no actual reality separate from one's thoughts. Everyone can agree that our thoughts are critical in the success or failure of our life's endeavors, and many even acknowledge that one's thoughts can affect the body's health and healing processes. Yet, this is different from stating that thoughts literally *create* reality. Taken to an extreme, it would mean that if you don't think it, it's not happening. Particularly if you are convinced you are God.

There are more obviously attractive features to the philosophy, particularly when it coincides with the existentialist idea that there are no excuses in life. Most of us can appreciate that each of us is ultimately responsible for creating our "world." Ditto a spirituality that emphasizes having the proper intention in all matters, and promoting "Christ consciousness."

But that is another topic altogether, and beyond the scope of this book. Our question is not whether or not someone likes the philosophy. Rather, we want to know how likely it is that extraterrestrial beings actually are being channeled?

My personal conclusion is, *not very*. The statements that come to us purporting to be scientific have not found corroboration, or have been plainly disproven. And most of the statements, it has to be said, show little to no appreciation of science.

One example of many is that the Earth was going to come into full contact with a so-called Photon Band in 2012. When that happened, we were told, the planet would be covered with purifying energy. Those who had cleansed and restored their Lightbodies would be ready. Those who had neither integrated nor made amends would apparently perish. The Earth would experience darkness, and then eternal light. A new Earth would come into being.

Aside from the fact that 2012 came and went with nothing of the sort, there is no evidence for the existence of a Photon Band. A claim that it was discovered by satellites in 1981 is baseless. Nor is there logic to the statement that Earth can pass through it, since believers state that it surrounds the Pleiades—a very long distance away, aside from the fact that Earth is moving away from the Pleiades, not toward it. Despite being devoid of logic or evidence, ideas such as this one have been stated as unarguable facts.[326]

There is a great deal of this type of thinking. It is certainly not scientific. Most of it is nearly impossible to test. How does one test the idea that humans have twelve etheric strands of DNA?

Of course, channelers are invited to make predictions that are meaningful and correct. If they were to do this, they might begin convincing more people that they are truly tapping into something. Providing some genuine confirmable information and scientific insights would be preferred, perhaps a proper explanation for gravity, or a detailed (and verifiable) information about secret political or financial activities.

Yet, it may be premature to dismiss all alleged communications of this type. As discussed earlier, there is reason to believe the beings involved with UFO phenomena are telepathic. There have also been a select number of historical channelers (such as Edgar Cayce) and several remote viewers of more recent years who appeared to have a remarkable record.

With each passing year, physics demonstrates the reality of non-locality, sending to oblivion our conventional notions of time and

---

[326] A detailed analysis of the foregoing is: Hudson, Bill, "New Age Ascension" [2012hoax.wikidot.com/oldstart].

Chapter 10: Who Are They? What Do They Want?

space, and suggesting that consciousness is a key part of the structure of our reality. Does that mean it is the underlying aspect of all existence, as some people claim? The world's leading quantum physicists and neuroscientists do not seem to be saying this. But it does appear that consciousness *matters* in a way not fully appreciated by current science.

Conceding this, may we not theorize that some extraterrestrials might speak through selected human beings?

There will be more to say about this in the next chapter. The bottom line about channelers, however, is that they cannot be considered valid sources of information regarding extraterrestrials. One may choose to believe them and appreciate the messages. But there is no genuine evidence that any channelers are actually communicating with extraterrestrial entities. That said, stranger things have happened, so we may keep the door open.

A Word on Crop Circles

The relationship of crop circles to the UFO phenomenon is not always straightforward, but I believe there is a relationship. There have been some credible claims of people seeing balls of light in connection with these, but that is rare. And there are no proven, credible sightings of actual UFOs in connection to the formation of these amazing patterns.

The real connection is in the fact that these formations appear to be unexplained, judging from our contemporary technology. There are indeed circle hoaxers. In fact, they often consider themselves to be artists and many of them do excellent work. It is not true to claim, as some do, that all so-called hoaxed circles are easy to identify. Some of them are very well done, and are easily found on YouTube. Overnight, such circle makers can make well-done, complex patterns.[327]

But some of these formations are so immense and complex as to defy reason. And after all these decades, none of the perpetrators have

---

327 As an aside, it's interesting to note that some of them report experiencing unusual phenomena and general strangeness when they are creating their circles. Perhaps there's something else going on there.

been caught in the act of making any of the truly extraordinary formations. Moreover, several oddities have been recorded. Some formations, for example, have had stalks that were pushed down without having been broken, bent sometimes six or more inches above the ground, clearly indicating they were not pressed down with a wooden plank. While the known circle artists all use planks, it is clear that at least some of the formations were not done this way. All with a complexity that is truly astonishing.

Laboratory studies have indicated that the nodes of some of the stalks were blasted out on one side. It is not known for sure how this happened, but the effect has been replicated by highly localized microwave heating. This causes the water inside to vaporize and be expelled. The stalk then flops over to one side. If something like this caused the formations, then we are clearly talking about a highly sophisticated agency behind the phenomenon.[328]

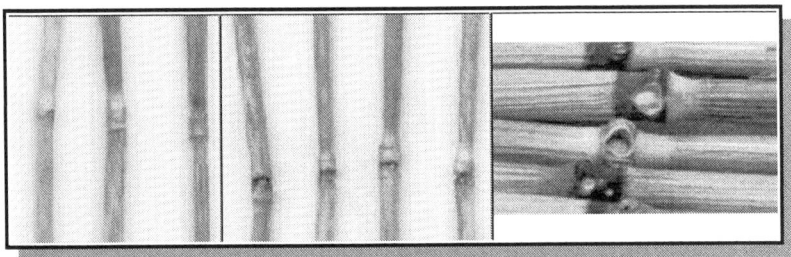

Normal stalk nodes (l) compared with blown nodes (c, r)

The patterns of the formations themselves have been studied endlessly. Aside from being supremely beautiful, many seem to be messages in one form or another, often with cosmological implications. None seem ominous or evil. If one receives any sense or feeling from them, it is benevolence.

If were to be the case that these formations are created by an extraterrestrial or non-human intelligence, we may conclude that at least one of the groups here might in fact care about us and wish to help us.

---

328 See Talbott, Nancy. "Plant Abnormalities." BLT Research [www.bltresearch.com/plantab.php].

Chapter 10: Who Are They? What Do They Want?

Getting to the Bottom Line

If there is something regarding the UFO phenomenon about which we need to exercise caution, it is over who or what we are dealing with. It is not that nothing is going on. Quite the opposite: it is clearly the center of the phenomenon, something of critical importance. For that reason, caution is most important.

And caution reminds us that the evidence of contact is not strong scientifically. Yet, if we approach this phenomenon with as much common sense as possible, we can see that there is too much smoke to ignore the likelihood of fire. Too many people have had too many experiences, so many of them traumatic, so many that have caused their hearts to race upon recall, so many others of deeply positive significance. Something important is happening, something profound, something secret.

Whoever these beings are, we are not dealing with them on equal terms. How we can get to a position of equality or parity may not be something we can easily learn. It may not be possible.

But there is every reason to believe that they are well aware of our path. Just one hundred and fifty years ago, our society was dominated by horse power and wooden carts. In the blink of a cosmic eye, we have created a world that, even to our recent ancestors, is unimaginable. Global communications, connectivity, information immediately available wherever we go, with more revolutions on the way: nanotechnology, artificial intelligence, 3-D printing, quantum computing, genetic manipulation, and more.

If they have ever observed us, must now understand that we are on the verge of entering their world.

The recent buildup toward the failed Ascension has underscored our inability to predict the future with any precision, and has certainly emphasized the shortcomings, to say the least, of channeled information. Nevertheless, it will no doubt be true that a century from now, if there are humans looking back upon their history, they are likely to see our current era as a singularly transformative one. Our society, our civilization, and indeed our species is undergoing the most rapid and fundamental change of all time. Intuitively, we realize this, but our daily routines cause us to forget. And it is not literally overnight. Today is like yesterday, this year only slightly different from the last.

But then we step back just enough, and we see the incredible blur of change that has taken place. Our world today is fundamentally different from the world of fifty years ago, even thirty years ago. Despite the adventures and struggles of people who lived in earlier eras, they never experienced the kind of dramatic, fundamental change that we now see. Moreover, this change is happening without the impetus of a major global war. It is happening because our society appears to have reached a stage of permanent revolution. It is a revolution that affects everything: our science and technology, our politics, our economics, our social customs, our intellectual endeavors, and indeed our consciousness. Everything is changing.

Will we join a galactic community, if there is one? Will we instead reach a point where we understand that such a community is dominated by interstellar economic hitmen, bent on little more than exploitation of our own and perhaps other species of life, much as humanity behaves toward other life forms on our planet?

Perhaps we will need more time to find out. When we do, we will probably have a bit more information to refer to when we decide with whom or what we are dealing.

Chapter 11
Weird Science: Propulsion, Energy, Spacetime, and Consciousness

The UFO phenomenon represents science far in advance of what we currently have and know. The deeper we explore, the more radical, the more profound, that science becomes. For many years, students of UFOs have wondered whether these objects, if that is even what they are, are explainable within our current understanding of physics.

The Radical Science of UFOs

Take propulsion technology, for starters. What is it, after all, that can allow a craft to loiter indefinitely, accelerate instantly, make right angle turns, and do the many incredible things UFOs have been observed to do? And to do these things silently?

But this is only one area in which UFOs pose a scientific challenge. There is the related but distinct issue of energy. After all, these objects certainly do not seem to run on gasoline or jet fuel. Do they have something better?

Even questions like these, important though they are, are pedestrian compared with other questions we might raise. So many encounters with UFOs seem to indicate that the beings, whether they be extraterrestrial or otherwise, possess some sort of mastery over spacetime, itself. Over and over in the literature, we encounter the so-called *Oz Factor*. These are moments of high strangeness in connection to UFOs and the beings that control them. Objects may appear or disappear suddenly; sometimes witnesses will have the sense, not only of missing time, but of time distortion. Does the UFO phenomenon represent a breakthrough in our understanding of spacetime? Another spacetime related question concerns *how did they get here?* If any of these UFOs derive from civilizations elsewhere in the universe, then it is quite possible they have learned to distort spacetime in order to reach us, even if they come from another dimension of reality itself, whatever that might even mean.

Finally, we might ask about consciousness itself. There are cases of people reporting telepathic communication with these other beings within a wide variety of contexts. This has happened not simply during recollections of abductions, in which telepathic communication seem to be the norm, but also in connection with sightings of the objects themselves, whether they look like actual craft or orbs. More than once, a person has reported waking in the middle of the night with an urge to look outside their bedroom window, only to see an orange orb. What is going on there?

We also find, time and again, that UFO witnesses react to their experience in ways that seem inexplicable to them afterwards. Sometimes they react to their encounter with an uncharacteristic sense of calm, or sometimes with hysterical panic. Perhaps that is due to a deep psychological process, but it might be that these beings have an advanced understanding of the human mind, enabling them some level of control. That is, somehow to get inside our heads.

But the importance of consciousness does not end there. There is some anecdotal evidence indicating that meditation can trigger more encounters. Is it possible that *they* become more interested in us when we refine and elevate our own thought processes? Does that make us more interesting to them? Or does that allow us to reach them somehow, or reach their reality, wherever that is?

This is a question that can lead us to explore a fundamental philosophical issue, one that has existed for thousands of years. Essentially, the matter comes down to the materialist versus the non-materialist outlook. Is there a dimension of reality that is not easily amenable to our traditional scientific methods of measurement? Moreover, does human consciousness, or consciousness in general, have the ability to affect reality? These are two separate questions, but clearly they bear a relationship to each other. To what extent do thoughts create or affect what we perceive as material reality? Is such an idea nonsense, or is there something to it? What is the science that supports it? I broached this subject in the previous chapter, and would like to explore it further in this one.

In general, a proper understanding of UFOs and everything related to them promises to bring humanity into a new series of scientific paradigms. But we should remind ourselves that science, properly done, requires the scientific method. It has worked exceptionally well for the past five centuries, and we would be fools to discard it. It involves testing, testing, and more testing. But even more than this, the test data itself must be open and available for others to comprehend and repeat. Repeatability is key.

So is open availability to the data. It is one thing to conduct an experiment and state that such and such an effect has occurred. It is quite another to describe the protocols, equations, parameters, and conditions of that experiment in such a way that someone else can follow the instructions and duplicate the result. This is the foundation of peer review: independent, qualified people must be able to check the work.

Within the UFO literature, we often hear the word "pseudoscience" bandied about. Pseudoscience is not simply a derogatory term directed against subjects that professional scientists disdain. It has certainly become a slur often enough, but what we call pseudoscience can accurately be described as conjecture only, without any ties to scientific experimentation, experimental physics, or mathematics. Fundamentally, pseudoscience represents a claim without the scientific method supporting it.

In addition to pseudoscience, there is fringe science, something different yet again. We can best understand fringe science as hypotheses that are loosely connected to proven mathematics, experimental physics, or some other form of scientific experimentation, but which have not yet been submitted for peer review. This does not mean that something currently considered pseudoscience or fringe science is necessarily false. Of course, it *might* be false, and often enough, it is.

But it might also be that the phenomenon under study has so far eluded our attempts to subject it to a classical scientific analysis.

Scientifically speaking, then, this is the best reason to remain open-minded about subjects that are currently considered fringe science or even pseudoscience. Sometimes, we simply have to wait for our science to catch up with a phenomenon. This does not invalidate science as a tool, nor the phenomenon itself as worthy of study. Science is not the bad guy here, and neither are UFOs.

Propulsion

Paul Hill was a senior NASA scientist during the 1950s and 1960s. He was Professor of Aeronautics and was an original member of the National Advisory Committee of Aeronautics (NACA) in 1939. In other words, Paul Hill was involved in America's aerospace program right from its birth. He had an impressive career and received many awards.

Paul Hill was also a UFO witness. His experience convinced him that the phenomenon was real. Over the years, despite NASA's formal position that dismissed UFOs, Hill became known within NASA as their resident expert on the subject. As a result, many UFO reports ended up on his desk—informally, not officially.

During the 1960s, Hill worked quietly on a book. He completed it in the mid-1970s, after he had retired, and it remained unpublished until 1995, five years after his death. His book, *Unconventional Flying Objects: A Scientific Study*, is still considered today to be the single best scientific treatment of UFOs.[329]

As Hill put it, his goal was to show that "UFOs obey, not defy, the laws of physics." When we think about the behavior of many reported UFOs, this may not be readily apparent.

Our currently accepted physics is founded on the conservation of energy and momentum. And yet, UFOs appear to accelerate without ejecting any material behind them. Both Newton's law of gravity and Einstein's theory of General Relativity require the existence of

---

[329] Hill, Paul R. *Unconventional Flying Objects: A Scientific Analysis*. Hampton Roads, 1995.

"negative mass" (or negative energy) for something like antigravity to be possible. This has been a major hurdle to the study of UFOs by many physicists.[330]

Hill wondered about this, as well as other observed features of UFOs: the lack of a sonic boom despite reaching supersonic speeds, their incredible accelerations, presumably without killing their occupants, and much more. He concluded that although these types of motions are not consistent with aerodynamics, they *are* consistent with some form of repulsive force-field propulsion. In other words, UFOs make sense if they are using some sort of "antigravity," just as we produce magnetism with electric currents. He added that the occasional changes in color noticed by some witnesses make sense if we assume that one side effect of this force would be a plasma field. This would be caused by ionization of the surrounding air, which in turn could alter the apparent color of the craft.

Hill studied cases in which UFOs appeared to demonstrate this force field. These included instances in which a person or a vehicle was affected, tree branches moved apart or broken, roof tiles knocked out, ground or water disturbed, and so on. He concluded that these interactions pointed to a repulsive force field surrounding the craft, and definitely not propulsion involving jets, nor pure electric or magnetic effects, nor radiation (although radiation was in evidence sometimes as a secondary effect).

This force field is gravitational-like, and in fact is gravity-canceling. One result of this is that living beings inside it can cope with the incredible accelerations of hundreds of g-forces. That is because, as reviewer Dr. Harold Puthoff pointed out, by manipulating the acceleration-type force field, even at supersonic speeds, occupants would be in a "constant-pressure, compression-free zone," and their craft would be surrounded by a flow of air that is subsonic. In other words, *not* supersonic, meaning no sonic boom. A nice bonus would be that rain, moisture, dust, insects, or other low velocity objects would follow streamlined paths around the craft, rather than hit it.

---

330 Markowitz, W. "The Physics and Metaphysics of Unidentified Flying Objects", *Science*, Vol. 157, 1967.

Another benefit is that the surface of the craft would not heat excessively, which one would expect from ordinary aircraft moving at extremely high speeds. The space shuttle and other high-tech aircraft, for instance, require sophisticated heat shielding to allow them safely to re-enter Earth's atmosphere. Not so, when the craft can benefit from a force field. Essentially, the airflow approaches the craft and then moves away, depositing no energy in the process.

Puthoff concluded that Hill:

> . . . assembled as good a case as can be made on the basis of presently available data that the observation of some 'unconventional flying objects' is compatible with the presence of engineered platforms weighing in at something around 30 tons, which are capable of 100-g accelerations and 9000-mph speeds in the atmosphere.

More important for the technical reader, added Puthoff, was Hill's supporting argumentation that "these platforms, although exhibiting the application of physics and engineering principles clearly beyond our present-day capabilities, do not appear to defy these principles in any fundamental way."[331]

Hill did not explain how to generate such a repulsive, gravity-canceling force. Of course, he can hardly be faulted for this. Within the open scientific literature, no one else has figured it out, either. Antigravity remains a Holy Grail. For this reason, some UFO skeptics have dismissed Hill's work. Supporters respond that his work shows that UFOs do not involve half a dozen or more inexplicable phenomena. Instead, there is essentially *one* inexplicable phenomenon. Surely, this is no reason to discard his work. After all, the physics of a typical cell phone would have baffled any genius of the 19th century.

Electrogravitics

Paul Hill showed, within reason, that the creation of a gravity-canceling field, or force field of some sort, goes a long way to explain the otherwise inexplicable performance capabilities of UFOs. This has

---

331 Puthoff, Harold E., Ph.D. "Review of Unconventional Flying Objects, by Paul Hill." *Journal of Scientific Exploration*, Vol 10, No.4, 1996. For a more recent analysis on the problem of space travel, see Puthoff, Harold E. "Advanced Space Propulsion Based On Vacuum (Spacetime Metric) Engineering," *JBIS*, Vol. 63, Pp.82-89, 2010.

Chapter 11: Weird Science

led researchers into the field of electrogravitics. Some of the pioneering work in this field was done by none other than Nikola Tesla. Other important figures include Thomas Townsend Brown, Paul Biefeld, Paul LaViolette, Thomas Valone, and Yevgeny Podkletnov.

Within the world of officially established conclusions and truth, the prevailing assessment is that electrogravitics does not generate a significant effect.[332]

However, it seems that a good case can be made for electrogravitics.

Tesla's connection to the subject has captured a great deal of attention and remains a puzzle. This is not surprising when we consider not only his prodigious genius, but the fact that many of his papers were confiscated by U.S. government officials at his death in 1943. While some were released in 1952, many others have disappeared.[333] There is more than enough room enough to wonder what classified research was carried out based on them.

Especially during his later years, Tesla made several scientifically radical remarks about matter and energy. He was roundly criticized for this, but they are fascinating nevertheless. In 1930, for instance, he had this to say:

> . . . all perceptible matter comes from a primary substance, of a tenuity beyond conception and filling all space—the Akasha or luminiferous ether, which is acted upon by the life-giving Prana or creative force, calling into existence, in never ending cycles, all things and phenomena. . . . Can Man control this grandest, most awe-inspiring of all processes in nature?[334]

Among some UFO and non-mainstream researchers, Tesla's work implies a form of free energy and beyond, including the ability to "precipitate matter from the ether" and even create life "in infinite forms."[335] Nothing in the published papers of physics appears to support this claim, and it would certainly be the basis of a scientific

---

332 The Wikipedia entry on electrogravitics quotes an unnamed source that "no conclusive evidence of electrogravitic signatures has been found." Unfortunately, the statement is not linked to the source and could not be found after a thorough search by the author.
333 "The Missing Papers," *Tesla:Master of Lightning*, Video Documentary. New Voyage Communications/PBS, 2004. [www.pbs.org/tesla/ll/ll_mispapers.html]
334 Tesla, Nikola. "Man's Greatest Achievement" *New York American*, July 6, 1930.
335 Swartz, Tim. *The Lost Journals of Nikola Tesla*. Global Communications, 2000. [www.bibliotecapleyades.net/tesla/lostjournals/lostjournals06.htm].

revolution if it is. However, we may grant that within the world of classified scientific research, it may be another story.

It is also sometimes asserted that Tesla pioneered ideas relative to electrogravitics. What is definitely known is that work in this area began no later than the early 1920's. Dr. Paul Biefeld, a physicist and acquaintance of Albert Einstein, discovered that a highly charged capacitor possesses an odd tendency to move in the direction of its positive pole. Biefeld assigned his student, Thomas Townsend Brown, to research the phenomenon. Brown was able to document what appeared to be a gravity-reducing effect, which became known as the Biefeld-Brown Effect. It is the foundation of electrogravitics.

Fundamentally, electrogravitics uses an electric field to charge or polarize an object that has a specially-constructed shape—typically a disc-shaped object works best. When such a charge is applied to the edge of a surface of an object or craft, the result is a propulsive effect. In other words, the disc moves. According to an important article in 1956 from the aviation publication, *Interavia*, by an anonymous author who spent two years researching the matter, Brown demonstrated this effect on discs charged with roughly 150,000 volts. They were tethered and reportedly flew "with results so impressive as to be highly classified. Variations of this work done under a vacuum have produced much greater efficiencies that can only be described as startling."[336]

There are certain known, conventional, possibilities that could cause a propulsive effect. One was that of ion wind. Brown, however, ruled that out, since he conducted some of these tests in a vacuum, where such an effect is impossible. There is another effect, known as electrostatic levitation, that could conceivably cause motion to the disc, but this, too, seems to be different from what Brown achieved. Electrostatic levitation is a real phenomenon under certain conditions, although it has never been shown to levitate an object in a stable manner. Conceivably, one might be able to design a feedback control system that constantly changes the electric fields to hold an object in

---

[336] "Towards Flight - Without Stress or Strain or Weight, " *Interavia*, March 23, 1956 [No author attribution].

Chapter 11: Weird Science

position, perhaps an equivalent of fly-by-wire in modern aircraft. There is no indication, however, that it can achieve the kind of force or acceleration that Brown obtained in his tethered-disc experiments. He seemed to be on to something entirely different. The Biefeld-Brown effect appears to involve a different kind of physics altogether.

Consider that some of these experiments were done in a vacuum, the application to space travel is evident. It would indicate that electrogravitics could be used as a means of propulsion for spacecraft as well as aircraft.

This work by Brown, and apparently others, seeped out to the public in 1956, when *Interavia* and a few other publications printed stories about imminent breakthroughs in antigravity. But then, nothing. The stories ended almost as quickly as they began. One possible scenario is that the research went black. Could it be that a few advances were made since that time within the classified world?

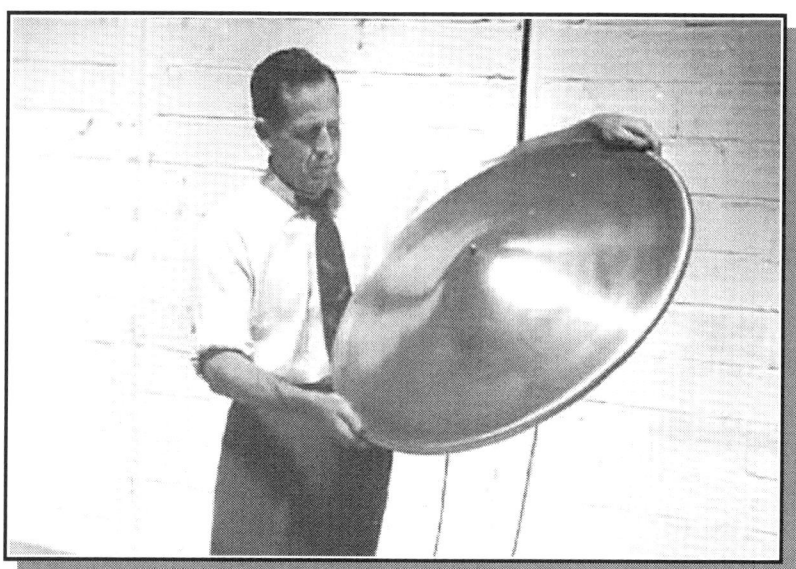

T. Townsend Brown with a disc from his electrogravitics experiments.

Some public discussion of electrogravitics has continued. In 1991, the U.S. Air Force published a report on a study of electrogravitics concluding that, although there did seem to be some anomalous forces produced via electrogravitics, it was not very much, and not significant enough for propulsion. The report did say, "these may warrant further consideration in the future."[337] Such a conclusion might make someone wonder if quiet research has continued since 1991.

More recently, Bernard Haisch, Harold Puthoff, and several other physicists have demonstrated connections between the electromagnetic zero-point energy field and inertia. They have speculated about possible further connections with gravity.[338]

The American physicist Ning Li also provided theoretical support for anomalous gravitational effects from a superconducting spinning disc in a strong magnetic field. In other words, gravity-weakening effects. According to her research, rotating ions create a gravitomagnetic field perpendicular to their spin axis. If a large number of ions can be aligned, a strong gravitomagnetic field can be achieved, which in turn produces a strong repulsive force. This might be done by trapping superconductor ions in a lattice structure in a high-temperature superconducting disc.[339]

The engineer Yevgeny Podkletnov has reportedly done experiments demonstrating something like this, with rotating superconductors in a magnetic field. He claimed to have achieved some gravity reduction effect, although a number of technical reasons some physicists question whether the results can be taken at face value.[340]

Probably the most detailed arguments for electrogravitics come from Dr. Paul LaViolette and Dr. Thomas Valone, both of whom have written extensively about field propulsion (i.e. antigravity) technologies and the cover-up of their reality. Both argue that there

---

337 Talley, R.L, "Twenty First Century Propulsion Concept," Veritay Technology Inc, East Amherst NY. Prepared for the Phillips Laboratory, Air Force Systems Command, Propulsion Directorate, Edwards AFB. May 1991. PL-TR-91-3009.
338 "Review of Experimental Concepts for Studying the Quantum Vacuum Field." E. W. Davis, V. L. Teofilo, B. Haisch, H. E. Puthoff, L. J. Nickisch, A. Rueda, and D. C. Cole. *Space Technology and Applications International Forum*. STAIF 2006. American Institute of Physics. p. 1390-1401.
339 "Static test for a gravitational force coupled to type II YBCO superconductors." Ning Li, David Noever, Tony Robertson, Ron Koczor, Whitt Brantley. *Physica C: Superconductivity*. V. 281, Issues 2–3, 1 August 1997, p. 260–267. [www.sciencedirect.com/science/article/pii/S0921453497014627#]
340 Podkletnov, Evgeny. "Weak gravitation shielding properties of composite bulk Y Ba2Cu3O7-x superconductor below 70 K under e.m. field," Submitted on 10 Jan 1997 (v1), last revised 16 Sep 1997. Cornell University Library. [arxiv.org/abs/cond-mat/9701074]

are advanced aerospace technologies that can control gravity and would obviously revolutionize air travel and energy production. They discuss different field propulsion devices with thrust-to-power ratios thousands of times greater than any jet engine. They argue that NASA has been involved in a cover-up to block these advanced technologies from public knowledge and use, although of course such technologies remain under military development.[341]

Obviously, if this technology is real, it would revolutionize transportation technologies, merely for starters. It could also expose deeply classified and sensitive programs. As early as 1993, LaViolette argued that the B-2 Advanced Technology Bomber—the stealth bomber—used electrogravitics to provide some amount of gravity control.[342]

It is interesting that, despite the fact that electrogravitics has not been debunked, and even enjoys some mainstream scientific support, it has received so little formal research funding. Perhaps we should not be surprised. Clearly, it is revolutionary in every way. If it is being developed within a classified setting, all the more reason to suppress it publicly. Yet, the question arises: would it be possible to suppress public funding of it on an international scale? On a purely scientific basis, why would it receive so little institutional support worldwide? Two reasonable answers come to mind. First, there may be the perception that there are no short-term or medium-term prospects for financial success. Second, that it is being suppressed by major powers in the areas of national security and energy.

Energy

Speaking of energy, if UFOs are producing such intense magnetic fields, are able to perform with such incredible capabilities, have physical effects on the environment around them (including sources

---

341 LaViolette, Paul A. Ph.D. *Secrets of Antigravity Propulsion: Tesla, UFOs, and Classified Aerospace Technology.* Bear & Company, 2008. Valone, Thomas, Ph.D. *Electrogravitics Systems: Reports on a New Propulsion Methodology*, Integrity Research Institute, 1995. Valone, Thomas, Ph.D. *Electrogravitics II: Validating Reports on a New Propulsion Methodology.* Integrity Research Institute. 2005.
342 LaViolette, Paul A. Ph.D. "The U.S. Antigravity Squadron." Published to the Internet, 1993. [www.bibliotecapleyades.net/ciencia/ciencia_flyingobjects44.htm].

of power such as the engine of a car or the power grid of an entire community), then they must be using a tremendous amount of energy. What is their source of power?

There is no consensus on this, other than it is likely to be far better than high-octane gasoline. However, a few ideas have been proposed. One is that gravity is "somehow" converted to usable energy, but how precisely is not clear. Another is that UFOs utilize remote transmission of power, that is, a wireless energy transfer. But, from where?

Probably the one most within current capabilities (although still not officially attained), would be through clean nuclear fusion. This is a definite Holy Grail in energy generation.

Nuclear power plants employ fission, which tears atoms apart, releasing energy and radioactive by-products. Fusion is different. It occurs inside every star, and has been replicated by humankind in the form of the hydrogen bomb. A nuclear fusion reactor would duplicate this process, but in a controlled way. It involves fusing together two "heavy" hydrogen atoms, known as deuterium and tritium, to produce helium, which is inert and harmless, without radioactive waste, along with vast amounts of energy.

Actually, *vast* does not begin to capture the magnitude of this energy. The amount of energy would be well beyond anything achievable through nuclear fission, which is itself a tremendous source of power. After all, fission powers nuclear submarines and aircraft carriers for years at at time. It powers large cities with ease. But fusion is far beyond this, beyond anything human civilization has yet harnessed. Surely, the amount of power in a controlled fusion reaction would easily suffice for any electrogravitic flying saucer. Or any large fleet of them.

Researchers are working on controlled nuclear fusion, and many people believe it can be achieved. Physicist Michio Kaku has predicted a fusion breakthrough by around the year 2030, or perhaps 2040.[343]

A nuclear solution may be the answer to the question of "what powers flying saucers?" It is curious, incidentally, that Bob Lazar, who

---

343 "Michio Kaku: Fusion Really Is 20 Years Away," YouTube video. [www.youtube.com/watch?v=4gRnezJNFro]

Chapter 11: Weird Science

claimed in 1990 to have worked at the S-4 Facility in Groom Lake, near Area 51, stated that the atomic Element 115 served as a nuclear fuel. This element reportedly provided an energy source that can produce antigravity effects under proton bombardment, along with antimatter for energy production. As Lazar put it, as the intense strong nuclear force field of Element 115's nucleus was properly amplified, the gravitational effect would distort the surrounding spacetime continuum. In effect, this would greatly shorten the distance and travel time to a charted destination. Essentially, Lazar was saying this would bend the spacetime fabric itself.[344]

Aside from fusion, another possibility that has received attention as a breakthrough source of energy is the proposed utilization of ambient energy, most commonly referred to as Zero Point Energy, or ZPE.

It is referred to as "zero point" because it is energy that exists at zero degrees Kelvin, otherwise known as absolute zero. Even at that temperature, the coldest possible in the universe, a state lacking all thermal energy, nothing can be frozen so solidly that its molecules become absolutely still, because the atoms of the molecules would still be in motion. One experiment conducted by scientists involved cooling helium to within one degree of absolute zero. Even at that temperature, helium's molecules retained enough kinetic energy to keep it in a liquid state instead of freezing solid. Apparently, only ZPE could account for the energy that prevented the helium from freezing.[345]

Therefore, if one were to pump all matter and all heat energy out of a container, as one approaches absolute zero, all that would be left in the container would be a vacuum and zero point energy. In other words, some source of energy exists all the time.

It is like a sea of energy that exists everywhere. It is all around us, and is in the emptiness of space. Some claim that the energy density of ZPE exceeds that of nuclear energy, but there is no consensus. In

---

344 Huff, Gene. "The Lazar Synopsis." As posted to alt.conspiracy.area51, 12 Mar 1995. [web.archive.org/web/20070607032357/www.serve.com/mahood/lazar/synopsis.htm].
345 Valone, Thomas, Ph.D. *Zero Point Energy: The Fuel of the Future*. Integrity Research Institute, 2007.

this context, ufologist and nuclear physicist Stanton T. Friedman makes a salient point:

> I have often been fascinated by the simple fact that when one goes from the 'huge' atom to the 10,000-times smaller nucleus, one goes up in energy per particle by millions of times. So what will happen when we are able to dig into the quarks that make up neutrons and protons? Will a huge new source of energy be found? What new sources have already been found by civilizations only thousands of years ahead of us, rather than the much more likely millions or billions of years ahead of us that some places in the local neighborhood must be? We know that matter-antimatter annihilation is an efficient process, even if we don't know how to store antimatter.[346]

A point well worth consideration as we get down to the smallest fabric of existence.

The real question is, can we get ZPE to do useful work for us? Part of this depends on whether there truly is a great amount of energy to be extracted, and whether a device can be built to do it. It does appear possible in theory to obtain heat and energy out of the vacuum. This could mean free energy devices that are carbon-free and use no fuel. Dr. Thomas Valone, who once worked at the U.S. patent office, described losing his job because he advocated for precisely these types of suppressed systems.

What is lacking is a proven ZPE device. Some people have made vigorous ZPE claims, such as Colonel Tom Bearden. However, Bearden has been persuasively critiqued and rejected for bad mathematics and even delusions.[347] There are others, too, who have claimed success in creating a ZPE device, or other types of "free energy" devices which may or may not be related to the energy systems of UFOs. John Searl of the U.K. is one such inventor. For all we know, one or more of these devices may indeed work. The problem is that none as yet have been shown conclusively to work. Moreover, all lack peer reviewed analysis and study.

Again, as with electrogravitics, we need to understand why this is so. Is it because the science is just not strong enough? Is it because of the

---

346 Friedman, Stanton T. *Flying Saucers and Science: A Scientist Investigates the Mysteries of UFOs*. New Page Books, 2008. p. 85.
347 Jadczyk, Arkadiusz, "Bearden and Hoagland," *Quantum Future* [quantumfuture.net/quantum_future/bearden.htm].

bureaucracy of the world of science and academia, combined with a terror of sticking one's neck out? Or it is related to the lack of government funding because this is a classified subject and the real work is done in secrecy?

One thing is evident. Whatever the source of energy behind the UFO phenomenon, it is a revolutionary step beyond what human civilization is currently utilizing.

Spacetime

Our common sense is Newtonian, our universe is not. Like the physics of Isaac Newton, our common sense is logical, comforting, and much simpler than the actual fabric of reality. Particularly as it is understood by theoretical physicists today, reality is far more complex.

In Newton's formulation of reality, time and space continue indefinitely. Neither has a beginning, nor end. Both are constant. If the clock says 2:45 p.m. somewhere on Earth, and it is 2:45 p.m. somewhere on a rock circling Alpha Centauri four light-years away, then in one hour it will be exactly 3:45 p.m. in both places, and essentially everywhere else. This is because in a Newtonian world, nothing affects the passage of time. It moves at a constant rate everywhere. What goes for time also goes for space. It continues on and on infinitely. Time and space, moreover, are entirely distinct and separate, fundamentally unrelated to each other. This, at least, is what Newtonian physics and our common sense both tell us.

However, starting with Einstein, we began to understand space and time not as separate from each other, but as an interwoven fabric—the spacetime fabric. We began to understand gravity as something that curves space, and time as something that is affected by gravity, just as it is affected by the motion of objects that move through space. In other words, time is relative. It does not pass at the same rate everywhere.

We also now understand that our universe has an origin, not only in time, but in space. In other words, what we call the Big Bang was not merely some big explosion in space. It was, rather, the creation of space and the creation of time. As difficult as it is for our minds to

UFOs for the 21st Century Mind

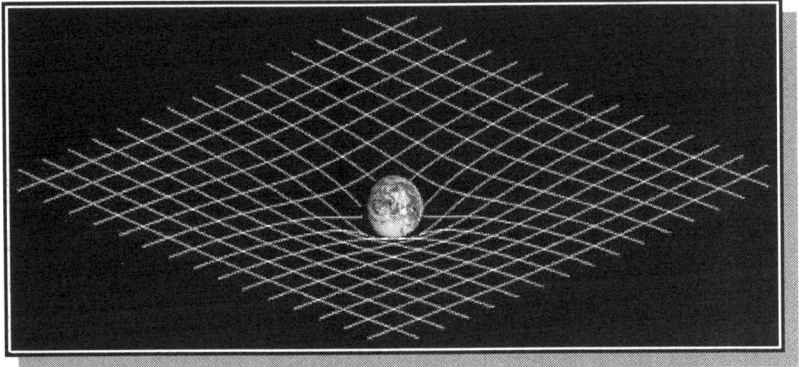

A standard depiction of spacetime curvature in relation to gravity.

visualize and truly grasp this concept, not only was there no time prior to the Big Bang, but there was *no space* in which the universe could exist prior to that moment. How is such a thing possible? Such is one of the many mysteries of modern theoretical physics.

It is not that the UFO phenomenon leads us necessarily to grapple with some of the leading issues of physics and cosmology. Rather, those leading issues help to inform ufology, just as they inform many other areas of intellectual endeavor. However, it is also true that ufology does eventually bump into some of these questions. After all, UFOs constitute a truly puzzling mystery on so many levels. Should it surprise us that, at some point, there would be a connection to leading edge physics? Perhaps at several points?

Miguel Alcubierre

Consider faster than light (FTL) travel, for instance. Everyone who has ever heard of $E=mc^2$ *knows* that it is impossible to exceed the speed of light. How many times have astronomers and physicists discussed the virtual impossibility of interstellar travel, all due to the, shall we say, *astronomical* distances involved? To travel even from a relatively near star of fifty light years distance (which in the grand scheme of things is essentially next door) would take fifty years at the speed of light. With such an obstacle in place, how can beings from anywhere else even know about us, much less get here? The electronic signals from the beginning of our Age of Television would only now be reaching places of that distance. Anyone farther away will have to wait much longer still. In the opinion of many physicists, to expect any other beings to reach us is a fantasy.

Except for those, of course, who have been thinking along the fringes, and who seem to have made some progress.

Miguel Alcubierre, a physicist at the University of Wales, described a space-travel scenario that seems rather like *Star Trek*. With Alcubierre's warp drive, one could in theory reach other places in the universe as easily as we drive to the nearest city. Longer journeys perhaps might feel like driving across the country.[348]

According to Einstein, spacetime twists, changes, and essentially distorts under the influence of concentrations of energy. Alcubierre suggested that it might be possible to use this phenomenon to travel from one star to another, faster than the speed of light. This could be done by creating a disturbance in spacetime so that the region directly in front is contracted, while the region directly behind is expanded. This distortion of spacetime would therefore propel the object forward, something like a surfer riding a wave.

At first glance, this seems to violate Einstein's special theory of relativity, which says that no object can exceed the speed of light. Alcubierre, however, showed that his warp drive does not violate it. Instead, the light also travels within spacetime and is carried along, just like the spaceship. Relative to the spaceship, the light beam is still traveling at the speed of light. Moreover, the spaceship is not moving at the speed of light relative to its immediate vicinity. Instead, it is moving along with the warping of spacetime around it. As it turns out, this is compatible with Bob Lazar's description of how spacecraft travel, which Lazar discussed prior to Alcubierre's theory.

To those of us on Earth watching a spacecraft accelerate away as Alcubierre hypothesized, it would seem incredibly fast. However, to those inside the craft, it would seem normal. An important feature to Alcubierre's theory is that the warp drive would not cause time

---

348 Alcubierre, Miguel. "The warp drive: Hyper-fast travel within general relativity." *Class. Quantum Grav.* 11-5, L73-L77 (1994) [members.shaw.ca/mike.anderton/WarpDrive.pdf]. Puthoff, H. E. (March 1996). "SETI, the Velocity-of-Light Limitation, and the Alcubierre Warp Drive: An Integrating Overview." *Physics Essays* 9 (1): 156–158.

dilation. In other words, one could travel to the Andromeda Galaxy, two million light years away, be back in time for supper. The reason is because the traveller would not be traveling at or near the speed of light through spacetime. Rather, spacetime itself would have warped for the traveler.

The idea of warp drive is eminently attractive, and the mathematics appear to be sound. Is there anything stopping us from achieving it?

Not surprisingly, yes. The key is something Alcubierre called *exotic matter*. This would power the warp drive. It possesses negative energy density, whereas normal matter (which is everything that makes up our world and universe), has positive energy density. Two pieces of matter with the same energy density are attracted to each other by gravity. Two positives are attracted, and two negatives are attracted. Positive and negative energy matter, however, are repelled by gravity.

Exotic matter is not fantasy, at least probably not. In 1948, the Dutch physicist Hendrik Casimir predicted that the effects of negative energy densities are observable. He reasoned that if negative energy densities existed, two closely spaced parallel conducting plates in a vacuum would be attracted to one another. This phenomenon, now called the Casimir effect, was measured in 1958, and is usually taken to be a confirmation that negative energy densities are possible.[349]

At least in theory, then, warp drive is possible. Of course, that does not prove it is feasible, even for a more advanced species, but it is probably foolish to discount the possibility. At least it does not seem to violate the laws of physics. Clearly, certain technical details must be resolved before aerospace firms start building starships. The first order of business would be to learn how to produce such exotic matter. That may take awhile.

Dimensions and Strings

Let us proceed further now, and ask a question or two about the fundamental structure of the universe, or, more accurately, of the

---

[349] H. B. G. Casimir, and D. Polder, "The Influence of Retardation on the London-van der Waals Forces", *Phys. Rev.* 73, 360–372 (1948). Casimir, H. B. G. (1948). "On the attraction between two perfectly conducting plates". *Proc. Kon. Nederland. Akad. Wetensch.* B51: 793.

multiverse and multiple dimensions. That, and string theory.

At first glance, one might think string theory has nothing to do with this idea of extra dimensions. But as some physicists argue, they are closely related.

String theory, or superstring theory, tries to answer the question of what constitute the fundamental, indivisible building blocks that make up our universe. There are, of course, atoms, which contain electrons, neutrons, and protons. Inside neutrons and protons are even smaller particles, *much* smaller, known as quarks. Within conventional physics, that is essentially it. But string theory suggests that deep inside any of these particles, there is something else.

According to string theorist Brian Greene, that something else is "a dancing filament of energy, a vibrating string," that vibrates in different patterns, producing different particles that make up the world around us.[350] The universe, as string theory conceptualizes it, is built up of an enormous number of tiny filaments of vibrating energy, vibrating at different frequencies. Different frequencies produce different particles.

There are several Holy Grails in our world; string theory offers one of them. In this case, it is a Grand Unified Theory of Physics. String theory states that matter (electrons and quarks) and radiation (photons and gravitons) derive from one entity, and that these all exist within the rubric of vibrating strings. This is what is meant by a unified theory.[351]

As there always is with anything, there is a catch. String theorists such as Greene, Michio Kaku, and others point out that the mathematics of string theory do not work in a universe that has just three dimensions of space. Nor does it work in a universe of four, five, or six dimensions. They assert, however, that it does work in a universe with ten dimensions of space and one dimension of time. That is, eleven

---

350 Greene, Brian. "Making Sense of String Theory." YouTube video [www.youtube.com/watch?v=YtdE662eY_M} and Kaku, Michio. "The Multiverse Has 11 Dimensions." YouTube video [www.youtube.com/watch?v=jI50HN0Kshg].
351 For more information on this, see Greene, Brian, *The Elegant Universe: Superstrings, Hidden Dimensions, and the Quest for the Ultimate Theory* (Vintage Books, 2000), and *The Fabric of the Cosmos: Space, Time, and the Texture of Reality* (A.A. Knopf, 2004).

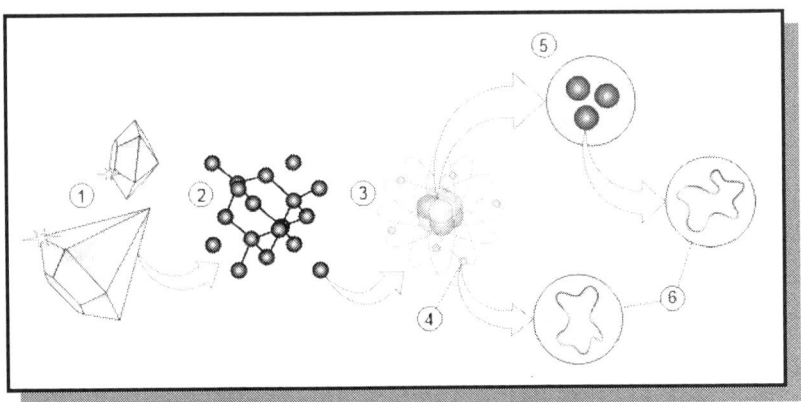

Levels of magnification (From the Wikipedia page on String Theory): (1) Macroscopic level: Matter; (2) Molecular level; (3) Atomic level: Protons, neutrons, and electrons; (4) Subatomic level: Electron; (5) Subatomic level: Quarks; (6) String level.

dimensions.

Kaku suggests we think not of a universe, but a multiverse filled with bubbles. The skin of each bubble represents an entire universe. Thus, he says, we are on the skin of a bubble, like flies on flypaper. Ours is an expanding three-dimensional bubble. Sometimes, these bubbles may bump into each other, or sometimes split into two or more bubbles. In string theory, he argues, there can be bubbles of different dimensions, but never more than eleven. Each of the bubbles—universes—floats in a much larger area, which is the hyperspace. Each bubble also vibrates and, as Kaku poetically puts it, creates music. This cosmic music resonates throughout eleven dimensions in hyperspace. It is a good candidate, he suggests, for the mind of God that Einstein wrote about.

String theory and multidimensional theory do not make predictions about civilizations existing in those other dimensions. They see these dimensions as tiny and curled up inside themselves somehow in a way that, frankly, most of us strain to understand.

An interesting aspect to string theory is that it does seem possible, mathematically, to make a case for it. Perhaps strong enough that it conceivably attains the level of scientific proof. As Brian Greene described it, there are in modern physics roughly twenty different numbers that describe our universe. Such numbers include the mass of particles such as electrons and quarks, the strength of gravity, the strength of the electromagnetic force, and others. They have been measured to great precision, and they *must* have the values they do, otherwise the universe would not exist. Greene's image was of twenty dials of a complex machine: turning any one of those dials would cause the universe to vanish.

But there is one thing no one knows, which is why each of these numbers possess their particular value. String theorists reason, however, that since the manner in which the strings vibrate is affected by the geometry of the extra dimensions, if they knew exactly what the extra dimensions looked like, they should be able to calculate the allowed vibrational patterns. Therefore, they should be able to calculate those twenty numbers. If their results agree with the actual values of those numbers, this could be the first fundamental explanation for why the structure of the universe is the way it is.

There are a few reasons why this matters from a ufological perspective.

Most fundamentally, it is clear that there are deep mysteries about certain aspects of UFOs, certain things about the phenomenon that simply do not make sense. At the same time, our most advanced physicists still lack a grand unified theory of physics: a single, unified set of equations from which all of reality *can* make sense. If it turns out that string theory provides that foundation, we may eventually be able to make better sense of the UFO phenomenon in ways that currently elude us scientifically.

There is another reason string theory and theoretical physics in general matters to the study of UFOs. For while string theorists tend to discount the idea of alien civilizations existing in other dimensions of reality, to say nothing of other universes, serious UFO researchers are usually not willing to do so. Surely, it is much easier for such researchers to offer such an opinion, since deep knowledge of physics (to say nothing of string theory) is comparatively rare. It is always easy for newcomers to jump in and make crazy statements. Nevertheless, we may permit our innocence to express itself here, if only to come down on the side of wonder and possibility, and ultimately a belief that, given enough time and knowledge, we may indeed be able to find a way to cross boundaries that currently seem impenetrable.

Time

Trying to understand the nature of time is one of those issues that can keep you pondering for days, weeks, years, and lifetimes.

As with space, time isn't exactly what our brains and common sense tell us. Newton wrote of it as an arrow that goes in one direction only: forward. But gravity affects time, so that in fact time moves more slowly at the Earth's surface than in the upper atmosphere. The difference is nothing that a human being could ever notice, but experiments with atomic clocks have proven it to be true. The effect is pronounced at the singularity of a black hole, a place where gravity exerts such a power that time actually stops.

Speed also affects time. We know that the faster one travels, especially when approaching the speed of light, the more time slows down. Hence the phenomenon known as time dilation, in which a person inside a spaceship traveling at 99.999 percent of the speed of light will age only one year in transit while 223 years would pass back home on Earth. This is not an illusion, but an actual effect of time dilation. Time does not move at the same rate throughout the universe.

According to Einstein's $E=mc^2$, faster than light speeds are impossible. Nevertheless, if you were to exceed the speed of light, then in theory you might be going back in time. Perhaps surprisingly, there is no law of physics preventing time travel. And by time travel, I do mean travel into the past.

The mathematician Kurt Gödel was the first person, in 1949, to find a solution to Einstein's equations that allowed for time travel.[352] If the universe rotates, and you were to go around the universe, you would come back before you left. Einstein admitted this seemed possible, but was unconcerned, since he knew the universe did not

---

352 See "Gödel metric," at *Wikipedia, the free encyclopedia* [en.wikipedia.org/wiki/G%C3%B6del_metric].

rotate, but expanded. "Since then," said Michio Kaku, "physicists and mathematicians have discovered hundreds of other types of solutions of Einstein's equations which allow for time travel."

One such way is to have a wormhole. As the universe can bend and contort, it can also in theory fold up on itself, something like taking a sheet of paper and folding it. If you were to draw two dots on the paper and fold the paper until the dots met, it would be like the idea of a wormhole. Recall that if we could fold space in such a manner, we would not merely be bending space, but bending spacetime. Therefore, according to a number of physicists, it may be possible using wormholes to travel back in time.[353]

Physicist and cosmologist Paul Davies believes so. "If a wormhole could exist and could be traversable," he stated, "then it would provide a means of going back in time. So it all hinges on whether stable wormholes are a reality or if there's some aspect of physics ... [that] might intercede and prevent the wormhole from forming. That's an open question."[354]

Not surprisingly, there is a catch. According to Davies, "Using Einstein's equations you can show that the energy needed to bend space and time into a pretzel is comparable to an exploding star. A black hole."

Obviously, we currently lack the capability to harness this much energy. But is it possible that our future civilization, or another civilization somewhere else, will have, or does have, such a capability?

Of course, even though no known law of physics prevents time travel, it may be impossible all the same. Actually going back in time would not only involve going back to a specific time and place, which is daunting enough. But in fact, truly to go back to a specific moment in time means going back to a particular moment in spacetime. Think of it this way. This moment you are currently experiencing—if you could extract one precise, incredibly specific moment—is not simply

---

353 Kaku, Michio. "Is Time Travel Possible?" YouTube video [www.youtube.com/watch?v=X02WMNoHSm8].
354 Lamb, Robert. "Is Time Travel Possible?" *Discovery News*, April 22, 2010, [news.discovery.com/space/is-time-travel-possible.html].

a moment in which you are sitting in your chair, in your room, or wherever you happen to be, it is a moment in which the Earth is in a particular position relative to the Sun, galaxy, and universe; in which the Earth, Sun, planets, galaxies, particles, and packets of energy everywhere are in a precise relationship with each other throughout all of existence. In fact, that is probably the best definition of a "moment" imaginable: the relative position of all particles to all other particles in all of existence, since that is always changing.

Therefore, when we talk about time travel into the past, we are not merely talking about going back to some place on Earth to meet your grandfather or observe the dinosaurs. We are talking about rewinding the entire universe—all the particles, all of everything.[355]

One possible loophole to this problem might be the existence of multiple or parallel worlds. This would eliminate the paradoxes that bother all the physicists. (e.g. If you go back in time and kill your grandfather, you can't be born, which means you can't go back in time to kill your grandfather.) Perhaps multiple universes is a way out, except that there is no physical theory that actually predicts this. As far as anyone can tell, such an idea has only existed in the realm of science fiction.

Such conundrums might be circumvented by referring to universes of greater dimensions. Because we live in a three-dimensional reality (plus the dimension of Time), it means that we perceive time as forever moving ahead in a straight line. Perhaps, however, to a fourth-dimensional being, time might not seem like that. Instead, time might seem like a sphere. Both perspectives are correct from their points of reference. A fourth-dimensional being could traverse this time continuum simply by going from point A to point B, because such a being can perceive that dimension. The third-dimensional being cannot perceive that dimension.[356]

Interesting, but again we might ask how this is relevant to ufology?

---

[355] A good examination of this is Rubak, Josh. "Is Time Travel Possible?" [www.rubak.com/article.cfm?ID=16].
[356] A more sophisticated discussion of this idea can be found at uforesearchnetwork.proboards.com/thread/793.

Chapter 11: Weird Science

One reason is that it helps us to explore one of the fundamental questions we face: who are these "others" and where do they come from? Is it possible that visitors in UFOs are traveling from the future? This is a claim, a theme, a meme that has gained a fair amount of attention. Personally, I remain doubtful that time travel is part of the answer to the UFO mystery. However, as long as leading physicists and mathematicians keep the possibility of time travel alive, closing that door is probably unwise.

Entanglement, Consciousness, and the "Others"

Our science gets stranger still. There is the matter of quantum entanglement, which Einstein never liked, but could not debunk (he called it "spooky action at a distance"). We will also explore to what extent consciousness itself is a key to understanding the presence of "other beings" here in our reality. Beyond that, we can inquire whether our thoughts manifest, activate, or otherwise create the "physical" world around us. Among other things, this includes communicating with extraterrestrials, interdimensionals, or whatever these beings are.

First, entanglement. This is a real thing, and remains difficult for physicists to understand. Rather than try to explain it, most simply observe and measure the effect. Kaku, who so often explains complex ideas in physics with such ease, described entanglement in one of his many YouTube videos. Visualize two electrons, he said, which are very close together and vibrating in unison. If, however, you separate them, it can happen that there is something like an invisible umbilical cord that continues to connect them, such that if you "wiggle" one particle, its partner is aware of this. Something is connecting them, even at a distance. Now, separate these particles by the spacial dimension of a galaxy, one hundred thousand light years. Even at this incredible distance, if you "wiggle" that electron from one end of the galaxy, the electron at the other end of the galaxy is instantly aware of the fact that its twin is wiggling. The communication is therefore much, much faster than the speed of light, which is supposed to be impossible.

This effect has been measured, not at the distance of a galaxy of course, but across hundreds of miles. The calculations are said to be solid.

One wonders whether entanglement could be used to send messages that are faster than the speed of light. In Kaku's judgement, probably not. What is actually traveling from one electron to the other, he argued, is random information. "It's not morse code," he said. "You can't send a love letter instantly from one part of the universe to another part of the universe faster than the speed of light." In this view, while Einstein was wrong about nothing being able to exceed the speed of light, "no usable information" can exceed it.[357]

Living with Uncertainty

In 1931, Kurt Gödel developed a fascinating set of mathematical theorems about logic which he called his "incompleteness theorums." Recall that a theorem, unlike a theory, is proven to be true.

Gödel's theorems state that any given set of logical rules, except for the most simple, will always contain statements that are undecidable. They can neither be proven nor disproven. This is because any logical system with even the slightest complexity will inevitably become self-referential.

This suggests that no grand mathematical system can ever prove or disprove all statements. All logical systems will have statements that cannot be proven or disproven; therefore, all logical systems must be "incomplete." It also implies that physics will never be able to develop a theory of everything, since no set of rules can explain every possible event or outcome.

More relevant for the study of UFOs, it also indicates that logically, "proof" is a weaker concept than "true." In other words, there will always be things that, despite being true, cannot be proven to be true. That is not only unsettling to scientists, it is frustrating to UFO researchers.

There may very well be things our minds can never know. One of Gödel's incompleteness theorems states that no system can prove its

---

357 Kaku, Michio. "Why Einstein Gets the Last Laugh." YouTube video [www.youtube.com/watch?v=QErwOK3S5IE].

own consistency. Thus, no sane mind can prove its own sanity. Also, since that same law states that any system able to prove its consistency to itself must be inconsistent, any mind that believes it can prove its own sanity is, therefore, insane.[358]

We may never get to a point in our understanding, and specifically in our science, where we can prove everything that is true. Some things may be true, but may forever be unable to prove. Perhaps this may give us a fresh perspective to the idea of taking certain matters on faith.

Consciousness

The questions about consciousness are many. One that has been raised earlier in this book is whether or not people have the ability, by the power of mind, to communicate with entities from elsewhere. More generally, we wonder, what are the limits of the powers of the mind? What are the limits of consciousness? Can consciousness *create* reality, as some have claimed?

To this last question, there are at least two meanings, and two answers.

In the first meaning, the answer is *yes*. Right now, there are roughly two million bits of sensory data trying to make their way into your mind. Unfortunately, or maybe fortunately, your mind can only process about 40,000 bits of incoming data per second. This means that your mind is constantly sorting data into two categories: what matters and what does not. Only two percent of the data reaches your consciousness.

Clearly, the data that you select creates your reality. Or, perhaps more accurately, *how you perceive* reality. It follows that you have an ability to decide what matters, and what does not, at least to a greater or lesser extent. The things you tell yourself about yourself, and the

---

[358] There is an immense literature on Gödel's theorems, but the Wikipedia entry is a good starting point. See "Gödel's incompleteness theorems," From *Wikipedia, the free encyclopedia* [en.wikipedia.org/wiki/Gödel's_incompleteness_theorems]. A fascinating article on this theorem, along with a number of other puzzling problems of modern physics, is Johnson, Jeff. "10 Strange Things About the Universe" [listverse.com/2010/11/04/10-strange-things-about-the-universe/].

things you tell yourself about others, such things matter a great deal. They shape your mental world, your personality, and your future perceptions. It is like creating roadways in your mind, and in fact this is literally true in the sense that you train certain neurons and pathways in your mind. Certain connections become powerful, other connections weaken, all due to the habits of your thinking. You can, at any moment, choose to create pathways in your mind. In that sense, you can choose to create yourself however you desire.

To the second meaning of the question, "do our thoughts create reality," we are asking whether our thoughts shape *external* reality, to the extent that there are things external to our mind and our bodies. To that, I have to say yes and no. Whether more yes than no is something I personally have not yet decided. But that our thoughts can shape external reality is one of those annoying, persistent possibilities that fly in the face of materialistic scientific thinking.

One of the most famous experiments in physics is the double slit experiment. If you shoot photons at a wall, blocked by a barrier with a single vertical slit, the result is a spray pattern in which the electrons hit the wall, but nevertheless in a definite vertical arrangement.[359] The photons, in other words, behave just as particles would be expected to behave.

When you create a second vertical slit for them to pass through, so that you have two vertical slits side-by-side, the resulting pattern on the wall behind shows an interference pattern. In this instance, the photons behave more like a wave than particles. More accurately, they travel as waves, but are detected as particles.

When you fire one photon at a time, things become more strange. When they go through a single slit, the result is still a particle pattern. When they go through one at a time through the double slits, the result is *still* a wave pattern, even though there appears to be no way they could be interfering with each other. This holds true even if you shoot one photon at a time through one slit, then one photon at a

---

[359] Photons, incidentally, are distinguished from electrons primarily because they lack mass and therefore aren't particles. They are created when an electron falls from a higher energy orbit to an orbit lower in energy. The energy lost is emitted as a photon.

time through the other. The result is still a wave pattern.

Is it possible that the photons pass through both slits at once? To detect which slit the individual photons pass through, detection devices can be installed at each slit. Each photon can then be observed to go through either one slit or the other, but never both. So far, so good. However, when they do this, the resulting pattern is a uniform distribution with no interference. The photons are now behaving as particles.

How it appears is that the act of observation has caused the photons to lose their wave nature and act as ordinary particles.

But matters get stranger still. The great physicist, John Wheeler, once proposed something called the delayed choice experiment, which has since been replicated. Incredibly, it confirms that the thought of the observer not only determines the result of how the light behaves, but even does so retroactively.

Imagine a configuration in which two telescopes are positioned behind the detection screen, each telescope aimed precisely at one of the slits. After the individual photon passes through one of the slits, the detection screen can be removed very quickly to reveal the telescopes, allowing the photon to pass through one of the telescopes. The scientist decides whether or not to remove the screen.

When the screen remains in place, the result is a standard interference pattern, with the photons acting as waves. However, if the experimenter chooses to remove the screen, the distribution of the photons is an exact particle distribution, with no interference pattern whatsoever. It appears solely upon the choice of the experimenter as to whether the photons act as waves or particles. This choice happens after the photons have passed through the slits. The experimenter's choice in the present has somehow affected the behavior of the photon in the past.[360]

---

360 For a good overview and many useful links, see "Double-slit experiment," From *Wikipedia, the free encyclopedia* [en.wikipedia.org/wiki/Double-slit_experiment].

Entanglement

Based on the double slit experiment, there would seem to be a scientific foundation to the idea that consciousness, or mind, has some sort of relationship to light, and perhaps even to time. If we also accept that there is such a thing as telepathy, or some form of mind-to-mind communication such as clairvoyance or remote viewing, we may wonder if there is something that can tie them all together. Ultimately, are there any scientifically promising concepts of *psi* phenomena?

There are indeed. One that is especially promising comes from physicist Dean Radin, a member of the Institute of Noetic Sciences, founded by Apollo astronaut Edgar Mitchell. Radin's book, *Entangled Minds*, suggests that what we call *psi* phenomena is in fact a result of quantum entanglement of the mind.[361]

While physicists accept entanglement, they generally see it as a delicate relationship among individual particles, or at most a few atoms. Kaku, for instance, does not believe quantum entanglement can achieve telepathy. He discusses the problem of decoherence. That is, while the particles (electrons) are in phase, they are 'coherent.' This is quantum entanglement. However, each person is comprised of trillions upon trillions of atoms. Thus, to get two minds to vibrate in unison "would be impossible. The world's record for making objects entangled is only just a few atoms. Imagine trying to entangle two minds together." If you want to read someone's mind, he suggests, you would be better off taking MRI and EEG scans of the brain, then decipher them via computers, what is known as radio-enhanced telepathy.[362]

Yet, Radin suggests that entanglement is a widespread fact of reality, and also the best explanation for why people experience what we call paranormal events, except that they are not paranormal. They are entirely normal.

---

361 Radin, Dean, Ph.D. *Entangled Minds: Extrasensory Experiences in a Quantum Reality*. Paraview Pocket Books 2006.
362 Kaku, Michio. "Telepathy Is Easier Than You Think." YouTube video [www.youtube.com/watch?v=Fl8GvPRvikM&feature=relmfu].

There are several implications of this thesis. First, everything in the universe is ultimately energy, and energy is influenced by mind. Second, quantum physicists suggest that electrons, or events, are potential, rather than actual physical entities. Indeed, all of existence may be fundamentally an unlimited quantum field of energy, a sea of infinite possibilities waiting to happen. Thus, there are various potentials, essentially until somebody looks. It is as though we force the universe to make a determination about which potential is going to be actualized. Third, consciousness collapses the wave function into actual particles that exist in space and time. Another way to put it would be to say that consciousness experiences energy as matter. Things only appear as matter when they are being observed.

Ultimately, the observer is not separate from the observation; the experimenter is not separate from the experiment. The observer plays a part in creating the reality that is being observed. The Heisenberg Uncertainty Principle of consciousness states that no pure measurement is possible without creation. Physicists who deal in quantum mechanics state: "You cannot (objectively) observe something without changing it in the process."[363]

Such ideas have circulated in one way or another in scientific circles for much of the twentieth century, but great ideas sometimes take time to make their impact fully felt. Our physics remains in the midst of an intellectual revolution. This revolution is not complete, but the implications look increasingly clear that humankind is in a new stage of scientific understanding. Classical physics—the physics of locality and causation within an unchanging playing arena of space, with time that shoots in one direction like an arrow—no longer fully applies.

Evidence of data from phenomena such as remote viewing or other types of psi phenomena indicate that something is going on that classical physics does not explain. Radin's concept of entanglement, or some variation thereof, may provide an explanation of this. Consciousness seems to be a key.

Yet, as biologist Rupert Sheldrake pointed out, "we don't know how

---

[363] "The Observer Creates Reality Simply By Observing," posted by Enoch Tan. [www.mindreality.com/observer-creates-reality-simply-by-observing]

consciousness works, or what it does. This is one of the things which in science is called 'the hard problem,' because there is no known reason why we should be conscious at all, or exactly how the mind works." His suggestion is that "our minds are field-like, that they are not confined to the inside of the head, that they spread out into the environment around us. And because our minds are extended beyond our brains, they can have effects at a distance."[364]

Perhaps this is it: consciousness is a force of nature. If this is so, it might explain the claim that we sometimes encounter, that the occupants of alien craft are themselves part of the propulsion and control systems. Perhaps it could explain the radical movements of the craft, as well. Of course, that is alien consciousness. Will we ever find out if human consciousness is up to that task?

Connecting to Ufology

For ufology to accept the idea of mental connections between *us* and *them*, we still need to be careful. Claims continue to require evidence. We can listen to claims, but we are fools if we discard the scientific method in examining them. Nevertheless, it seems evident that consciousness does matter within ufology. Claims of mind-to-mind contact abound. Since contemporary science does not appear to rule out that such things are impossible, we might feel confident that real progress can be made in the coming years.

This can be said of all the scientific subjects we have looked at in this chapter. For years, observed UFO phenomena have seemed to present sheer impossibilities to many scientists. Naturally, this has been one of the major stumbling blocks preventing its wider public acceptance. Reported observations of craft that zigzag, or instantly accelerate, or of people being floated through solid walls, stagger our common sense. It is a common sense that still relies largely on a slightly souped-up version of 19th century scientific materialism.

If the particulars of UFO reports were to seem as impossible today

---

[364] Sheldrake, Rupert. "The Extended Mind: Recent Experimental Evidence, Rupert Sheldrake September 2, 2008." YouTube video [https://www.youtube.com/watch?v=JnA8GUtXpXY].

as they did in prior generations, then we might be justified in dismissing many of the observations as misidentification, confabulation, or some other kind of mistake. Instead, as the years go by, it appears that science is catching up to the phenomenon. Slowly but surely, we are finding our way toward making scientific sense of this greatest of mysteries.

It is as if the UFO phenomenon were teaching us something very important, not merely about the nature of the cosmos, but about ourselves.

Chapter 12
Into the Future, Into Ourselves

Given the nature of UFO secrecy, we might ask if it will ever end? After all, this is a situation that has been going on since the 1940s, a full human lifetime. Despite the constant activity recorded by people year after year, there has been no official disclosure of the UFO reality. It is obvious that those in possession of this great secret, whether human or non-human, have no intention of revealing it. For that reason, there are a number of commentators who conclude that Disclosure will never occur. This, however, is a mistaken conclusion, caused by too narrow a viewpoint.

We must remind ourselves that the secret keepers are not the only factor in the grand equation. There are three great factors. There are the human elites, who in all likelihood are the primary caretakers of the secrecy program. In addition to them, of course, there are the other beings—the *Others*, as I have sometimes called them. They, too, have declined to reveal themselves openly, even after all these years, and perhaps even centuries and millennia. We might therefore conclude, very logically, that they too will never willingly announce themselves to us. Of course, we should allow for the possibility that they may yet decide to end the secrecy at some point. The likelihood seems small, but it is possible at least in theory.

The dynamic part of the secrecy equation, however, is *us*, the people of the world. Human civilization is currently undergoing its most dramatic transformation in history. It is sometimes easy for us to forget just how astonishing our journey is.

Humanity's Trajectory

We have never been where we are now. For hundreds of thousands

Chapter 12: Into The Future, Into Ourselves

of years, human beings have lived and walked on Planet Earth, and the hominids prior to us for millions more. Yet, our recorded history, since the invention of writing, goes back a mere 6,000 years. Even if we accept the idea of a great, lost, ancient human civilization—call it the Atlantis theory—that would have been only ten to twelve thousand years ago, according to most scholars who have studied the matter. This is still not long ago in the grand scheme of things. During all of that time and before, for thousands upon thousands of years we have been, technologically, at the simplest levels. Only within the last five to ten thousand years did we even get to the level of animals pulling wooden carts.

Then, just a few centuries ago, we discovered science. Francis Bacon, Galileo, René Descartes, Isaac Newton, and the rest. They introduced a completely new way of thinking and began the process of transforming all of us. Even so, it wasn't until roughly one hundred and fifty years ago that humanity really began to develop its science and technology in earnest. Advanced metallurgy, petroleum, instant communications in the form of telegraph and telephone, the automobile, the electric light bulb, radio, flight, the development of atomic weapons, computers, the Internet, handheld devices, and everything else that is now part of our world today. No one could have foreseen this journey, neither the transformation itself, nor the speed with which it has occurred. The Internet has existed for roughly twenty years, in which time it has completely changed our world, and in ways that nobody predicted even during the early 1990s. As if anyone needs to be reminded: smart phones, YouTube, and Facebook, all of which are ubiquitous and integral elements in the daily lives of billions of people, did not make their appearance until the first decade of the 21st century.

We are not done with this journey. There is a future, and it will offer many surprises. Those who are inclined to skepticism about UFOs, who think the idea just too strange to believe, might want to study current developments in a few of our own technologies. Experts in artificial intelligence, for example, many of whom are quite mainstream, make predictions for the next twenty to forty years that boggle the mind. They are talking about computers of the near future that will be able to converse with you easily and fluently, with an intelligence that appears to match or exceed human intelligence. They won't need sleep or coffee, they will simply *go*. Futurist Ray Kurzweil sees a future in which machines achieve a "godlike" level of intelligence.[365]

Then factor in likely advances in nanotechnology, biotechnology, and perhaps quantum computing, all of which portend radical changes in the next generation. With mastery and manipulation of the human genome, what if scientists can enhance human brains via genetics or some combination of genetics and nanotechnology, that supplements the work of neurons? What if basic human intelligence can be radically enhanced, and even possess the ability wirelessly to interface with the web?

This is only the beginning. Developments in 3-D printing may be more revolutionary in the near term. This will bring the information revolution of the web and peer-to-peer transfers directly to the manufacturing process, enabling creative people around the world to design radically new products that can be downloaded and "printed" (e.g. manufactured) in one's home. More on this later in this chapter.

Within the blink of a cosmic eye, we are not simply elevating ourselves to a new type of society, nor even a new civilization, but possibly a new species of humanity itself. This is not like the transformation that medieval Europe went through during the Renaissance. It's more like the difference between *homo sapiens neanderthalis* and *homo sapiens sapiens*. There is the real possibility that human beings even a mere century from now will live in a society so vastly different, with mental tools so far beyond what we currently have, that they may look at our society as having little to offer them in terms of the problems and realities that they will be facing.

There is the obvious danger that such a technological utopia becomes a dystopian nightmare. One way would be through ever

---

[365] See especially Kurzweil, Ray. *The Age of Spiritual Machines: When Computers Exceed Human Intelligence*. Penguin Books, 2000.

Chapter 12: Into The Future, Into Ourselves

greater surveillance and control over the Internet, already everywhere. Surveillance may not always equal repression, but it does intimidate people, which has the same effect. Censorship, however does equal repression, and is also widespread. The Egyptian government famously closed off its internet during the Arab Spring of 2011, China has its Great Firewall, and many nations have censorship embedded in the fabric of their web. In 2012, privacy groups initiated lawsuits against the U.S. Department of Homeland Security over its plans for an "Internet Kill Switch," a legal wrangle that has continued as of this writing.[366]

Possibly a greater threat than this, however, are the distractions and dumbing down of our culture. For instance, new developments in gaming, will soon be virtual reality immersion. Why bother trying to solve real-world problems (or even learning about them) when you can become a virtual James Bond or date your favorite movie star in a near-real-life immersive setting? The western world long ago mastered the art of public relations in the service of political conformity and corporate profits. Clearly, the lessons of the past will be applied to our brave new world. The result may well be a zombie world of people drugged up on pharmaceuticals, ingesting processed and unhealthy GMO foods, uneducated in the history of their society, and living in an illusory world designed to distract and deflect. In other words, what modern America and much of the world already looks like, only more so, with people detached from their true selves, spinning out fantasies and simply running out the clock. Granted, alarmists have made such claims for years about the impact of magazines, comic books, radio dramas and more. However, we might remind ourselves that some of those criticisms were probably valid. More to the point, the power of our current system of distractions is much greater than anything human culture has experienced before.

In such a world, there could even be a danger of specific classes and even subspecies of humanity being developed. There could be, quite

---

366 Ciaramella, C. J. "Homeland Security must disclose 'Internet Kill Switch,' court rules," *Washington Times*, Nov 13, 2013. [http://www.washingtontimes.com/news/2013/nov/13/homeland-security-must-disclose-internet-kill-swit/]

literally, a "master race" with greater strength and intelligence, and with longer lifespans, presiding over a world of human drones, kept suitably stupid for a life of service and distraction. We already have clear and distinct classes of humanity; what is to prevent such a nightmare from entering our very biology?

If such a future comes to fruition, perhaps it will be possible to keep the end of UFO secrecy at bay for a much longer time. Perhaps. But for how long? A century? Two centuries? At some point, even in such an awful future, the secrecy program would merely be an exercise in staving off the inevitable. Even under the worst circumstances, the end of secrecy will come.

Besides, the situation is unlikely to deteriorate quite that rapidly before, say, 2035 or so, roughly twenty years from this writing. The relevance of all this for Disclosure is that because we are changing so rapidly, it seems very likely that we will develop the capability, openly and finally, to prove the matter of UFO reality to ourselves without need for official government acknowledgment. Once we get to that point, once this reality is rapidly and widely understood, governments around the world will have no choice but to acknowledge the obvious.[367]

What Can Cause Disclosure?

Regarding possible triggers that may force Disclosure, a few candidates come to mind.

One is a mass sighting. Of course, there have been mass sightings of UFOs in the past, and none have made that breakthrough. Yet, it may still happen. It is only a matter of time until multiple witnesses record a mass UFO event, each with their own camera, from multiple simultaneous angles. The quality of photography and videography for smartphones is now very good. One wonders what other capabilities these devices will soon have, to say nothing of surveillance cameras, police dashboard cameras, and other recording devices that are filling

---

[367] For a more detailed discussion of everything connected to Disclosure and its aftermath, see Dolan, Richard M. and Zabel, Bryce. *A.D. After Disclosure: When the Government Finally Reveals the Truth About Alien Contact.* New Page Books, 2012.

our world. Perhaps we will gain a widespread ability to capture infrared or night vision, or the ability to capture other types of signals, such as electromagnetic? The possibilities are there and will grow.

It is obvious that, along with better detection and recording techniques, comes better ability to create fake videos for YouTube. However, the situation is in a constant state of flux. Although video fakery has become sophisticated, faking an infrared signal may not be as easy to do, at least for a little while. The fundamental reality is that, with everyone becoming a potential videographer at any given moment, the potential for a mass, recorded sighting becomes greater and greater. Indeed, this is already happening, although there has yet to be that "perfect" sighting which gains worldwide attention, and develops enough momentum to force an admission that all of this is real. But it would be foolish to rule it out, and it may come soon. At any rate, it seems like an inevitability.

Another possibility that can force Disclosure would be a Wikileaks type of event. Like advanced smart phones, Wikileaks did not exist at the turn of the century because the global technological infrastructure was not ready for it. But now it is, and now it's here. Consider the radical releases of information that Wikileaks, groups like Anonymous, and individuals like Bradley Manning, Edward Snowden, and others have been responsible for in the first decade of the 21st century. The release of thousands of classified pages from the U.S. as well as other countries around the world, all sensitive, all detailing secret (and often illegal) activities that those parties wanted to keep hidden indefinitely. All of these releases were, strictly speaking, illegal of course, but that does not stop them from happening. The leaks are here, and the Wikileaks phenomenon is part of our world, part of our lives. It will not go away. How long will it be until explosive UFO-related material is released? Such data is probably available somewhere, ready to see the light of day. Indeed, in late 2010, Wikileaks leader Julian Assange hinted as much, but nothing substantial has yet been released.

Certainly, the release of sensitive UFO information, whether legal or not, could be a major problem to contain for those managing the secret. Could it be enough to force an admission of the reality of the UFO phenomenon? I believe so.

The universality of personal recording devices (such as smartphones) and Wikileaks are merely two aspects of the changes going on in our world today. They are symptoms and results of deeper changes that cannot be stopped. We are changing dramatically and rapidly. We cannot possibly think that in another decade, we will not have gone through more changes. What will another twenty years bring? Another century? Like the old song says, "Something's Gotta Give."

What Happens After Disclosure?

Let us assume that something forces the hand of the U.S. President or another world leader. A major sighting, a major leak; something. He or she, after a buildup of several weeks of speculation following the event, finally holds a press conference and makes that bombshell understatement: "I have been advised by the National Security Council and heads of our intelligence community that there is a reality to some of the UFO phenomenon, in that some UFOs are real physical anomalous craft, not manufactured by any known civilization on Earth."

Or words to that effect. It is the kind of statement that many proponents of UFO Disclosure would like to hear. The real question, however, is what next? I might think that any President would want to say, "Well, that's all for now, I'll be taking a vacation for a few months. See you all later." Unfortunately for the President, people will be asking a few follow-up questions.

Such as who are these beings? What is their agenda? Do we have anything to fear?

These will be very difficult to answer. There is every reason to believe that even the leaders of the black budget/breakaway society, those groups that have been studying this for years, may be outmatched by what they are dealing with. They probably have their own questions and even fears.

And what if they do know what they are dealing with? Although it is probably impossible to know the full intentions of non-human visitors (or permanent residents), it is entirely possible, judging from the data we do have, that some of them care little for humanity. What if an "alien agenda" has been determined within the intelligence community, and this agenda includes an eventual replacement of humanity by some sort of hybrid species? This is what abduction researcher David Jacobs has argued. And even if that is not true, does any President honestly believe he or she can contain rampant speculation along these lines? Panic is an easy outcome to foresee.

Even if the intentions of these other beings are said to be neutral or positive, there will clearly be tremendous suspicion by large swaths of humanity. An alien presence of any sort will not be an easy sell. There will already be a sizable number of people predisposed to interpreting such beings as nothing less than demonic. Short of dragging one of these beings to a podium and subjecting it to hours and days and weeks of questions by an insatiable public, it is unlikely that any "Disclosure" will satisfy the public regarding alien motivations.

That is only the beginning of the problems. There is a basic political question that people will ask, one with profound implications:

How have you managed to keep this secret all these years?

For years and years, we have been told that UFOs are mundane objects or natural effects, that ETs or aliens are definitely not here on Earth, not interacting with us in any way, that UFO believers may be well-meaning but have been mistaken about all of that. Such has been the mindset embedded within all of our major institutions. It is a given within our educational institutions, from primary schools, through universities and postdoctoral levels. It pervades our major news organizations, in which an open belief in UFOs is a definite third rail for one's career. (As one example, I learned from a personal source connected to America's National Public Radio that it is an explicit policy never to give the UFO topic a serious tone in any of its broadcasts. This policy is certainly the case in all major American media.) It pervades our scientific establishment, for sure, and also our political system. Political careers have been destroyed, or at least severely undermined, by the UFO taint. Such was the case with Presidential candidate Dennis Kucinich in 2008, after it became known that, many years before, he had seen a UFO. Never mind the fact that two witnesses who had been there with him also confirmed the sighting.

All of these institutions and others have treated the UFO topic as nothing more than a joke, something suitable for immature minds. But can it really be that professors, scientists, politicians, and media executives throughout America have uniformly dismissed this phenomenon without any influence from or even cooperation from the U.S. intelligence community?

The answer is no. Even the most modest amount of research into the subject has demonstrated a strong intelligence community influence over all of those institutions.

In other words, when Disclosure comes, people will clearly see that the national security apparatus has created a global culture that has suffocated the truth. Researchers will begin to investigate, in a serious way, just how these relationships have undermined the credibility of all of those institutions, as well as our apprehension of truth. There will be a major cultural and institutional housecleaning.

But it will not stop there. Citizens will want to know specifics about the structure of secrecy itself. They will want to know how much the U.S. Presidents have known. Have they been in the loop all these years, or out of it? Who has been running the UFO cover-up?

If the answer is anything along the lines of my own research, it will show that the cover-up long ago shifted away from formal Presidential authority into international and private hands. It is not that the U.S. President is irrelevant, but that the presidency serves as the public face of the power elite that stands behind. Most people have come to understand that this is the case regarding power in general, and it is more than likely the case regarding UFO secrecy.

In other words, the moment of Disclosure will trigger an intellectual revolution worldwide, and will cause us to reexamine the true structure of power on Planet Earth. Disclosure will be a moment in which the world sees and acknowledges that the Emperor is wearing nothing at all.

The lies will not stop, however. Instead, we will participate in a great new battle. For the necessity of a Presidential announcement does not mean that the CIA, and the other intelligence groups that have managed this secret for years, will simply walk away from the table. There has been a concerted effort spanning an entire human lifetime to control this topic. A great deal has been invested in it, and mere Disclosure will not alter that. The real issue in the immediate post-Disclosure world will be: who controls the spin to the story? What will Disclosure mean?

Once the UFO reality becomes a topic for public discussion, a great divide will open. People around the world will demand answers while governments parse out information as sparingly as possible. As always, spin doctors will try to manage the situation according to national security policy, but this time independent UFO researchers may get a public hearing that they had never before received. If the official spokespersons make misleading or false statements, it will be easier, post-Disclosure, for independent researchers to point this out. That is because this time, the world will be more likely to listen. There will also be many more independent journalists investigating this topic. How all that will turn out only time will tell, but the government/intelligence/corporate spin machine will certainly be working overtime to maintain control. It will be up to the people to make enough noise to force admissions from their political leaders.

Energy

If there were a true free market in our world, we would have broken the petroleum paradigm long ago. Instead, there have been three main obstacles to a source of clean, free energy. First has been the fact that so many patents relating to revolutionary technology have been classified and kept within the black budget world, in effect holding our future hostage. Second, and closely related to the first, has been the lack of institutional support to fund the research. The effect of these first two obstacles has lead to a third: skepticism that such a thing is even possible. But once it is widely understood that there is a solution, then we have overcome obstacle number three. That will probably be enough to do the job.

Following Disclosure, energy will be a central issue. As discussed previously, people will immediately understand that, whatever the source of energy UFOs are using, it surpasses petroleum. Whether quickly or not, a solution will be found. Meanwhile, uncertainties will be rampant relating to petroleum futures, and the global financial markets will roil. Fortunes will be won and lost.

A post-petroleum energy paradigm will be discovered. Perhaps it will be revealed through inquiries into the black budget world, which may well have made great strides into the matter. Leak after leak has emerged from that world, all indicating deep interest and research into these types of problems. If the story of the so-called Alien Reproduction Vehicle (ARV) is true (and I believe it is), then at least some answers to revolutionary energy and propulsion have been known for several decades. How long will it take after Disclosure before something along these lines is openly acknowledged? Moreover, when it is, what happens to the valuation of the trillions of dollars worth of petroleum and natural gas reserves around the world? What happens to stability in the Middle East, and everywhere else?

Looking to the black budget world (or the aliens, or any other source) for answers, however, will probably not be necessary. New answers will be found, if for no other reason than the realization that they are *possible*. In all likelihood, it will not take long for scientists, many of whom will work independently, to devise solutions themselves.

Whether by one way or another, the petroleum industry (along with natural gas, coal, solar, wind, and nuclear fission power) will become obsolescent.

Assume that the energy solution to UFOs involves some form of energy that we would consider free and clean. This would be the ideal solution, something that could truly usher in a new era for humanity. It would allow us to solve many of the problems we have created:

something as basic as toxic remediation, for example. Other than political will and commitment, the biggest obstacle currently preventing a cleanup of the global environment is, oddly enough, a lack of energy. Scientists have developed a startling array of microbes and bacteria that can neutralize various types of toxic contamination, but economics and energy considerations inhibit implementing these on a wide scale. Free and clean energy solutions ought to overcome such limitations. Ditto regarding cleanup of our polluted oceans, or desalination of water, or a host of other pressing needs for the sustainable support of human, animal, and plant life on Earth.

Clean and cheap energy would also trigger explosive economic growth. Throughout history there has been a remarkable correlation between the cost of energy and the rate of economic growth. The more abundant the source of energy, the cheaper it is, and the healthier the economy. When sources of energy become scarce, they become expensive, and the economy slows down. In the second decade of the 21st century, the global economy has failed to keep energy costs low enough to ensure widespread and equitable growth. A new source of energy, something implicit within the UFO phenomenon, would assure significant economic growth for a long time to come.

No oil, hence no oil wars. No energy pollution, hence a real possibility to enable the global environment to heal. Cheap energy, hence less human suffering and fewer reasons to go to war. These are very significant outcomes to be considered as a result of Disclosure. But there is more still.

Ultimately, cheap energy will transform human society itself, just as cheap petroleum did during the 19th century. But this new source of energy may be more abundant than petroleum. Will it be possible, post-Disclosure, for people to own their personal flying saucers? On the face of it, it seems a fantastic question. But is it really so outrageous? If such technology ever became widespread, it would enable a new mobility that, all by itself, would transform society. Not only would someone be able to zip off to any part of the world nearly instantly, but they might, in theory, be able to leave Earth's atmosphere. The Moon or beyond ... *why not?*

There are yet more considerations. With clean and abundant energy, it would become practical to develop a device that could generate oxygen easily and cheaply on planetary surfaces that have water, whether in liquid or frozen form. We now know there are several places in our solar system that have water, and where there is water, there is oxygen. Where there is oxygen, people can live. Indeed, with enough energy, people can manipulate their environment to their heart's content and find a way to live. It all comes down to sufficient availability of energy.

The above is a mere scratching of the surface, but already it is evident that Disclosure would quickly revolutionize human society. Consider how rapidly our digital revolution has been, and how dramatically it has transformed our world within a mere twenty years. Disclosure would be more dramatic still.

There are other sides to free energy. First, we can assume that the so-called *powers that be* may not be especially happy with such a mass democratization of energy. If everyone has enough energy, then everyone becomes more difficult to manage. From the point of view of those interests at the top of the human pyramid, this is a problem. We can assume they will undertake whatever measures possible to prevent this from happening. But the real question will be, can they succeed? This is something no one can know at present, but my own feeling is that any attempt to stop history from moving forward will inevitably fail.

There is another problem to be considered regarding free energy, no matter how clean it may be. Clean energy may not result in climate change or other types of environmental degradation. It may not be toxic to the environment the way that wood, coal, oil, and even natural gas have been. Yet, it is helpful to remember that a large portion of our global environmental crisis is not so much related to pollution as it is simply with the destruction of the natural habitat by human beings. As of this writing, there are more than seven billion people on Earth, swarming about the planet like so many locusts, devouring everything in our wake. We cannot help ourselves. More real estate development, more sprawl, less room for other creatures. This seems to be our way, but has only become a significant problem in the last few centuries, especially once humanity's population began its steep incline into the billions. Free energy may well accelerate that process. It may enable humanity to devour the planet's resources even faster, to depopulate the ocean's fishes, and to push out all other species of life that happen to be in the way of our expansion.

There is, of course, the problem of weaponry that may be developed from such sources of incredible energy. Any technology that can heat one's home indefinitely can likely be adapted to create a dangerous weapon, perhaps something that could evaporate a nation or an ocean. Unless by some miracle we all immediately become the better angels of our nature, it is frightening to consider that some of the sociopaths among us would have access to such technology. Perhaps you trust yourself with it, but can you trust all of your neighbors? Or everyone who lives in your city? Or your nation? Or the world? In the words of Spiderman's Uncle Ben, "with great power comes great responsibility."

Whether humanity finds a way to handle its great new power will be another of the critically important themes in our post-Disclosure world. More on this shortly.

A Cultural Revolution

We live in a world that is bound together by a web of interwoven lies. As the years pass, more people understand this. They see that our political and economic infrastructure rests upon grotesque exploitation of the great masses of people around the world for the benefit of an infinitesimally small group. The Occupy Movement gave them a name: The One Percent, although the true percentage is much smaller than that. Thus, the Emperor is wearing no clothes, and a few people are seeing this. It is entirely possible that Disclosure will force us openly to confront this inequality.

For Disclosure will usher in a cultural revolution not seen since the 1960s. Except that a post-Disclosure cultural revolution will be deeper, more widespread, and more threatening to the established structure of power. Millions, and possibly billions, of young people will emotionally opt out of a system and ideology that, for as long as they have lived, has been been based on lies. Along the way, they will question and expose many other officially sanctioned lies. Conspiracies and claims of cover-up will be unearthed yet again, this time with much more force. Not merely 9/11, but the false pretenses underlying all of America's recent wars, the growth of the global police and citizen espionage complex, the meaning of chemtrails, the existence of enormous secret underground bases and tunnel complexes, and even the global banking and private debt-based system that has created worldwide financial enslavement. And onward.

It is impossible to know where such a line of questioning will end, and what amount of political change will come as a result of such questions and revelations. But we will see a widespread, massive disaffection by much of humanity from the previous dominant ideology. And there will be, inevitably, a coherent political critique that encompasses total opposition to the established system, and which will be implemented on a global scale. Someone will give it a name, but for now I call it simply: The Opposition.

It will go far beyond occupying Wall Street. The Opposition will have factions, some of which will be peaceful, some of which may not be. Some may seek to occupy Area 51, or Wright-Patterson Air Force Base, or the Federal Reserve building, or the next meeting of the Bilderberg Group. It will employ sophisticated hacking and leaks to disrupt the operations of those select few who have been manipulating human destiny.

This will be enhanced or exacerbated by many people identifying explicitly with these other beings, whatever they may be. Like all revolutions, it will beat with the heart of libertarian anarchy. After all, all people fundamentally want the freedom, privacy, and dignity that is the birthright of every human soul. And like all revolutions, certain leaders will emerge who will symbolize the movement, others who will guide it behind the scenes, others still who will seek to co-opt and

Chapter 12: Into The Future, Into Ourselves

Disclosure is likely to spark protest movements greater than Occupy or the Arab Spring.

betray it, or else steer it into what they feel are safer pathways. No revolution ever delivers all of its promises. The Disclosure Revolution will succeed or fail based on the courage, foresight, and humanity of those leading it, and the passion of those pushing up from below.

The new era will see new types of utopian ideas arise, as well as a new millennialism. In other words, new ideas on how to create paradise on Earth, as well as those that predict the end of the world. Some of this will be enhanced by a more widespread use of hallucinogenic drugs, something that is already growing within the alternative community. Use of DMT through ayahuasca and other drugs is believed by many of its practitioners to enable them to open the doors of perception and experience other dimensions of reality, including the beings that are responsible for the UFO phenomenon.[368] Such is the belief held by many, and whatever its truth value, we can be sure many people will accept it. As was the case during the 1960s, there will be a great cultural divide separating the conservatives on one end from those who decide to turn on, tune in, and drop out.

Our attitudes toward spirituality and science likewise will be affected. When I researched *A.D. After Disclosure* with Bryce Zabel, one of our conclusions regarding religion was that, at least in the near-

---

368 See for example McKenna, Dennis. *The Brotherhood of the Screaming Abyss. My Life with Terence McKenna.* North Star Press, 2012.

term, religions might fare reasonably well. Although many pundits, mostly religious skeptics, typically predict the collapse of organized religion in the event of Disclosure, Bryce and I disagreed. First of all, there are a wide range of religions on this planet. Many of the Eastern religions, such as Buddhism or Hinduism, are well adapted to deal with an extraterrestrial or interdimensional reality. Mormonism, which teaches a plurality of worlds, is also well-positioned. But even the three Desert Sky God religions—Judaism, Christianity, and Islam—are unlikely to collapse in the event of Disclosure. At least not right away.

In Islam, for instance, belief in extraterrestrial life is not against its creed. Allah is said to have created many worlds. Nor is it a problem to believe in interdimensional spirits, since Islam has a number of references to the *Jinn,* what non-Muslims have often called genies. Judaism has little to say about belief in other worlds, and (excepting special, esoteric threads such as Qabalistic study) cosmology is not a major aspect of contemporary Judaic belief. An ET presence is unlikely to damage Judaic beliefs.

Christianity is a bit different, and there are obvious, identifiable rifts within it. The Roman Catholic church, on the one hand, has for the past few decades gone out of its way to promote the idea of extraterrestrial life. Quite a few statements have issued from the Vatican supporting the notion of an abundance of life in the universe as part of God's great plan. On the other hand, many evangelical Christians will interpret any alleged extraterrestrial presence as demonic. Several passages from the New Testament have been used to support this position.

New Age beliefs are different still. Most self-described New Agers are inclined to look at these other beings in a positive light, as humanity's benefactors and even space brothers. Since the 1970s, such beliefs have spread throughout the world, and certainly into the UFO subculture.

There is no bridge long enough to join this viewpoint with that of the evangelicals. The rift is irreconcilable and only two things can resolve it. One is an overwhelming amount of new information that will satisfy people to form an opinion. The other is time: time for new generations to arise, with new perspectives that cannot now even be predicted. People can change, but deep changes that affect entire societies can come only from new generations.

Although the world's major religions aren't likely to collapse in the short term, they do face dangers in the short and long term. The immediate danger would come if there is a credible claim that the great religious leaders of history were extraterrestrial. Or, if it becomes widely believed that humanity itself was the creation of extraterrestrials, and that the aliens themselves were the gods of ancient times. In essence, the idea that Jesus, Moses, Buddha, Mohammed, Zeus, or any other spiritual icon of the past was an extraterrestrial. One hears this line of speculation so much these days that it is a major subtext of the UFO belief set. Of course that does not make it true, and it seems unlikely that the truth on this matter could ever be known. Yet, if such claims are made convincingly, and enough people believe them, it would certainly cause some sort of transformation, or even great damage, to those religions. Most likely, though, devout adherents of these faiths will consider any deviations to be lies. No matter what happens, there will be major fissures among religious beliefs in the post-Disclosure world.

Regardless of the short-term effects, the long term changes affecting religion and spirituality will be very great. If Lady Fortune smiles on humanity, then our spirituality will develop into something more than the cartoon variety of children's stories and moral imperatives that make up most of the major religions today. Future generations, raised with the open knowledge of a nonhuman presence on Planet Earth, and throughout the universe, will not be satisfied with such simple stories. They will need something more relevant. Christianity, Islam, and Judaism will either have to adapt to this new reality, or they will be replaced. The old storybook versions of these religions could easily feel irrelevant to future generations.

One hopes that a future spirituality will focus on how to live ethical lives, perhaps with a focus on prayer and meditation, just as some people believe and practice today. Whether the new spirituality will be a continuation of new age beliefs or develop into something different altogether, only time will tell. In all likelihood, the non-physical and nonlocal realities of the UFO phenomenon will reinforce the idea among some people that meditation, Christ consciousness, pineal gland activation and more can help them achieve higher "frequencies," or become proper "light vessels" for their spiritual journey, or achieve DNA activation or Ascension. These phrases basically mean nothing to scientists, but they mean a lot to those who believe in them. This, too, will signify a growing split in belief and worldview between New Age spirituality and science. Or will it?

Science and the Scientists

The disclosure of a nonhuman presence behind the UFO phenomenon will discredit many scientists. After all, not only have they been skeptical about UFOs, most have been openly hostile to the idea. But science is different from scientists, and Disclosure will usher in new breakthroughs in both thought and technology.

Genetics, for starters. Assuming we gain access to alien physiology and genetics, we will gain greater insights into ways of improving human health, increasing mental capacity, understanding what controls cellular and organ regeneration, and extending the human lifespan. Ditto with other areas of biotechnology. Will we learn of effective vaccines or cures for any of the major diseases in our world today? It is entirely possible. Indeed, Dr. Robert Wood has recently argued, based on the leaked and controversial Majestic Documents, that a good portion of the science of biowarfare has derived from a secret study of alien biology and viruses.[369] Whatever the truth on this matter, black world advances in biotechnology are probably substantial, and there will probably be greater pressure applied on that black world to share what it knows.

I have already touched upon the future transportation revolution in

---

[369] Wood, Robert M., Ph.D. *Alien Viruses: UFOs, MJ-12, and Biowarfare*. Richard Dolan Press, 2013.

the form of new energy and electrogravitics. But consider the possibilities of developing a true understanding of gravity. It might enable our scientists to develop a unified theory of everything, tying gravity together with electromagnetism, and the strong and weak forces inside the atom. The implications of such a development might be difficult to predict in the near-term, but more likely than not would have dramatic long-term results.

Perhaps the most profound effect may be in how we understand the human mind. Not simply pertaining to human cognition and memory, although these are fascinating and clearly related to the subject. After all, we will want to know how human memory is affected during the abduction process. But more challenging would be questions of consciousness. Our science is already exploring whether or not consciousness exists independently of the body, although this is decidedly fringe at present. But the acknowledgement of an intelligent non-human presence would throw this investigation into high gear.

Current research into abductions and other forms of contact hint not only that space and time have somehow been mastered by these other beings, but that the mind is a critical element in their relationship to us. In this case, by consciousness we mean something that is nonlocal, something like psi phenomena. A series of well-funded scientific studies of the telepathic elements of contact, for instance, could be valuable additions to our knowledge of the mind and of the fabric of our reality. It would also allow science possibly to catch up with what many psychics and intuitives already believe, and even provide a useful framework to help us understand why psi phenomena occurs.

Belief in psi is not just a *woo woo* belief, but supported by research into remote viewing, and goes back through all human religions via the power of prayer and meditation. Ultimately, we want to know if consciousness is more than just our brain chemistry, and whether or not we have a spirit or soul.

Some might argue that a study of UFO data does not necessarily warrant that belief. I think, however, there is a case to be made that it does. If so, then human consciousness studies will become more widespread, and many new discoveries will await us. Such sciences, anything from remote viewing to out of body travel and space-time manipulation, are probably being explored now within the black budget world and breakaway civilization.

Computing and Technology

We have had a global internet for just over twenty years, during which time it has completely changed our world. Whether or not there is a disclosure about UFOs, it will continue to do so.

I discussed this earlier. Among computing experts, certain trends are a given. First, the moment will come when artificial intelligence will match and then surpass human intelligence. This event, dubbed *the Singularity*, is predicted to occur anywhere between 2030 and 2080, although some predictions are sooner than 2030, and a few are later than 2080.[370]

Second, nanotechnology will develop to a point in which nanochips and nanobots will enter the human body to kill diseases, enhance health, improve intelligence, and even make us interactive with the web. Humans may well become cybernetic to some degree, and the human mind may go wireless, so to speak.

Third, advanced computing will support biotechnology and gene therapy, enabling people and other living creatures to be customized to a degree that was never before possible. Whereas we can expect important knowledge on this to come from disclosure by the black budget world, especially via access to its work in alien biology and physiology, there can be little doubt that advances in computing will be more significant still.

The positive side of this is that it might mean enhancing certain positive traits for all people, including health, intelligence, and longevity. But it can also mean customizing different types of people for different capabilities and tasks. It's all possible, and there is

---

[370] See for example, Kurzweil, Ray. *The Singularity Is Near: When Humans Transcend Biology*, Penguin Books 2006, and www.singularity.com.

certainly no reason to assume that future governments or private groups will act according to our rules of fairness, justice, or decency.

A fourth outcome from future computing is a real chance that quantum computing will become practical and widespread. If so, this will revolutionize computing in ways that are nearly impossible to imagine. All we can say for sure is that quantum computing would be orders of magnitude more powerful than our most advanced computing today. One possibility would be a single quantum computer, or a restricted number of them, controlling our world in the interest of a small few. A quantum computer, for instance, could easily control an army of nano-drones that could be the ultimate surveillance and police force, a perfect totalitarian nightmare. But widespread quantum computing might also work in favor of greater freedom for people.

There is yet another development in our digital age that is primed to change the world: 3-D printing. Bringing the ability to recreate three-dimensional products, layer by layer, into the homes of people from downloaded CAD designs, this technology will revolutionize manufacturing. So far, most applications of 3-D printing are extruded polymers of either simple items like coffee cups, novelty items, or small objects of art that would be too complex for most human artists. Soon, however, it will involve multiple types of materials, including metals for printed circuit boards and even biological material. Major hospitals are already talking about future capabilities of 3-D printing a replacement heart.

All of this is exciting, but the key outcome of future 3-D printing is that it will allow brilliant minds from around the world to upload their designs of all kinds of products to the web, making them available to download by everyone else. Consider the bottleneck caused by an inability of inventors from getting their revolutionary creations to the market because of legal or corporate obstructions. Soon, it will be easy for anyone to download a CAD drawing of engines that run on water, or some other incredible variation of energy harvesting devices, and test it out after printing it at home. No doubt many of the so-called free energy (or "over unity") devices of the past were false starts, but the new market will enable a free flow of ideas that can be instantly tested by the rest of the world. 3-D printing will help to bring a true free market to the world, and that can be a factor in undermining the hierarchical system of control, a system which is reinforced by the narrow restrictions of our global manufacturing infrastructure, based as it is on profit and intellectual property rights. Whether these things are "good" or "bad" is irrelevant.

In effect, *The Pirate Bay* will come to the world of manufacturing, and the result will be an explosion of ideas and innovation. By 2020, this explosion will be well underway, and there will be a serious struggle by the established powers to contain it. But controlling 3-D printing, just like controlling other elements of the web, will be like fighting the mythical Hydra. Cut off one head, and two others will appear.

These five developments and many others make it is clear that we are primed to leap into the world of these other beings, with or without UFO Disclosure. We are not simply advancing in the way that humanity has done in the past. We are seeing a transformation not merely of our civilization, but of our species. Imagining our world a century from now is probably beyond even the most visionary thinker of today. After all, none from a century ago captured more than the barest smattering of our own world today.

Regarding computers and Disclosure, the real question is, how will these two things affect each other? Disclosure promises to accelerate our progress in computing science and would almost certainly bring us closer to the Singularity and everything associated with it. Of course, it could very well be that the breakneck speed of our developments in computing will bring us to Disclosure. After all, if computing intelligence does begin to surpass human intelligence, as AI experts predict, it is not hard to imagine a rapid Disclosure as a result–which will in turn accelerate future computing. Either way, we are in for a dizzying future.

Geopolitics

Before we start nanochipping ourselves, or achieving IQs of 500, or

Chapter 12: Into The Future, Into Ourselves

becoming ruled by a totalitarian quantum computer, let us reflect on political challenges that will be posed by Disclosure, not merely within the United States but worldwide.

Clearly, the United States will be strongly affected by Disclosure, and many of the most dramatic developments will take place there. The reason is simply that the cover-up has been more closely connected to the United States than any of the other major nations, excepting perhaps Russia and China. The United States intelligence community straddles the globe, with close relationships to the intelligence communities of most other nations. It is at the heart of the UFO cover-up.

There will be pressure on the U.S. President to shine the light of truth into the black budget/breakaway civilization connected with the cover up. It won't be long for people to realize that the President has also been out of the loop.

We have no way of knowing how things will turn out. Conceivably, however, there will be a moment of decision by the President. Will Disclosure simply be the pretext to create an openly totalitarian, fascist state? Today, we see creeping fascism everywhere we look. It may happen that Disclosure leads directly to a suffocating oppression in which dissent is equated with terrorism, and citizens are monitored 24/7 by every means necessary to ensure their compliance.

The White House will be a key player in the politics following Disclosure, but by no means the only important one.

This trend is all-too-evident today and will continue unless it is fought squarely by the people of the world. That is, people marching in the streets, demanding positive change, and accepting nothing else. The power of an energized and angry people is formidable, especially when they are reminded that freedom is never granted, but taken. Only action by great masses will prevent the complete loss of our freedoms and privacy, and so far there has not been enough public action.

But Disclosure will be a shock to the system, and it may be enough to awaken and energize people. It is certainly likely to spark a general confrontation. It can bring us fascism, or something approaching freedom.

There will be other practical matters of consideration. International cooperation, for one thing. For instance, what if Disclosure results in some sort of open presence by these other beings? Might it not be possible, after all? What if that presence is perceived as hostile to some degree? Whatever our desires may be regarding these other beings, we would be fools to discount hostilities entirely. And, for sure, we can count on those people who manage national security for their various countries to be thinking along the same lines.

Obviously, if there is a military confrontation, things would not look hopeful for humanity. If we have learned anything about the history of UFO confrontations, it is that the militaries of the world are outclassed. The technology controlled by these entities has been able to disable fighter jets and nuclear installations. Their craft can easily outmaneuver our own. As far as we can tell, they simply do what they want. Of course, they do appear to have crashed every now and then, and they are probably greatly outnumbered by us. Even so, humanity would not want to fight against such technologies as possessed by these other beings.

Some people have expressed concern about a *false flag* operation in which an alien invasion is faked by use of high-tech holographic displays, black budget technology, and a massive dose of global propaganda. The reason would be to frighten people into volunteering

Chapter 12: Into The Future, Into Ourselves

away their rights to a global police state that presumably would protect them from the alien menace. The operation has even supposedly been given a name: Project Blue Beam. While such an outcome is not impossible, it seems improbable, given the incredible logistical hurdles.

A false flag operation is something in which one agency (usually a government or military group) secretly undertakes some act of terrorism, which it then blames on another party, usually in order to justify a war or some other repressive measure. False Flag operations happen, as do actions by provocateurs (which is something similar but generally smaller scale). In our era, both of these happen a great deal and are nearly never openly acknowledged. After all, the global intelligence community operates with so little government oversight, so little analysis from major media outlets, and has so much money to work with, it effectively has near *carte blanche* in many, if not most, of its operations. The connection between intelligence agencies and narcotrafficking has been demonstrated many times, with no effect in our broader public discourse. Ditto the myriad behind-the-scenes political coups orchestrated by CIA and other groups, and the connections to financial corruption. The same applies to assassinations, from the 1960s-era hits against JFK, MLK, and RFK to the countless mysterious deaths of political leaders, scientists, journalists, and whistleblowers in our own time.

Then, of course, we have the events of September 11, 2001, the hinge upon which our entire era turns. It is likely that certain details of that day will forever be covered in fog, but enough information has surfaced to show any reasonable mind that, at the very least, the official version of events as stated by the U.S. government are laughably, tragically, and obviously wrong. Whether elements of the U.S. and global intelligence agency willfully allowed 9/11 to occur, or actively made it happen, can be argued elsewhere. But that 9/11 (followed immediately by the Anthrax Attack, in which the use of weaponized anthrax from Fort Detrick, home of U.S. biological warfare, was initially blamed on foreign terrorists) was *some kind of inside job* is an argument that will only continue to gain ground as the years pass. Rightfully so. It shows that elements of the U.S. intelligence community have gone to great lengths to commit atrocities in order to promote a specific political agenda, and will likely do so again in the future.

Nevertheless, there are real problems with a false flag operation like Blue Beam. As I mentioned earlier in this book, the originator of the idea, Serge Monast, was essentially a religious zealot with no evidence of any connection to insiders at NASA or elsewhere, as he claimed. Moreover, he appears to have gotten his idea from an episode of the television show, *Star Trek: The Next Generation*. His death in 1996, preceded by obvious poor physical health, made him into an instant, if peripheral, martyr.[371]

But it is the logistics of a Blue Beam operation that truly boggle the mind. The alien invasion scenario alone is a tall order. Presumably this would be done with a fleet of black triangles, although getting them to blanket the world seems a stretch. And even if they did, how to convince a world of scientists who are not merely skeptical of UFOs, but completely hostile to the idea, that these are actual alien spacecraft, seems doomed to failure. Current proponents of Blue Beam offer nothing in the way of actual research to show how such an operation could possibly succeed, other than through vague references of terrifying the world population. Besides, it is clearly unnecessary to use a false alien invasion to implement a global police state. It is happening by degrees, via a range of disinformation and smaller false flags that are doing the job perfectly well.

The alien threat card will be played only if it *must* be played. That is, in the event of a forced, genuine, disclosure of some sort. It is certainly possible that there will be pressures to emphasize the Threat of the Other, simply in order to gain acquiescence among the people. Whether that will be the dominant motif or not is something that nobody knows at present. From my perspective, it is a policy that

---

[371] An excellent analysis of Monast and Blue Beam was written by Christopher Knowles, "Project Blue Beam Exposed!" [secretsun.blogspot.com/2010/11/project-blue-beam-exposed.html]. See also Richard M. Dolan, "Project Blue Beam? Don't Count on It" [richarddolanpress.com/34-project-blue-beam-countdown-dont-bet-on-it/]

appears to be fraught with danger.

One thing is definitely clear about Disclosure: there will be a need for global cooperation. After all, this is a matter that affects everybody, not simply one nation. There are issues that will need to be handled internationally. This is because Disclosure will accelerate our already tight global integration and raise the stakes considerably. Any new source of energy that will surpass petroleum can conceivably be used for destructive purposes, and there will be a genuine need for a measure of global regulation or control over it. Clearly there will be legitimate concerns about this, but the alternative could be the obliteration of large regions of the Earth due to irresponsible use of new dangerous technologies.

There will be a need for a global response, if not to the threat, then to the challenge posed by these Others. The philosopher and genius Goethe once wrote, "Divide and conquer, a good motto. Unite and lead, a better one." Globalization is something that many people support, and many others oppose. But it is a fact, and has been developing inexorably for five hundred years, ever since Columbus set foot upon the New World. Since then, and indeed even prior, the separate civilizations on Earth have become increasingly intertwined through trade, financial relationships, merging of cultures, communications, and transportation. Within the last few generations we have moved into a world where nearly anyone can have a video conversation with nearly anyone else, any place in the world. It is a world in which news and information travel at the speed of light globally. International transactions of trillions of dollars every day traverse the globe, and it has become plainly obvious that the age of the nation state will soon be a thing of the past.

Regarding globalization, then, the question is not whether people should oppose or allow it. Rather, what form will it take? The question is entwined with the question of a post-Disclosure society: will globalization look like freedom or fascism? It can go either way.

The moment of Disclosure will present the political leaders of our world with an opportunity. That opportunity will be to take the path of light, not darkness. A path promoting freedom and truth, not one of oppression and lies. This is not to say that such a wonderful outcome will happen. We must not lapse into naïve utopianism. But Disclosure, and the months and years following it, will present humanity with a challenge not merely of how to deal with these other beings, whatever they are, and whatever their agenda happens to be. It will present us with a challenge of how to live with each other, how to graduate to the next phase of our existence. Will we do so in a spirit of global cooperation and freedom, moving truly into our adulthood as a species? Or will the dark road be taken, one of manipulation and oppression on a scale even greater than that of today? These are choices, real choices that will present themselves to all thinking people after Disclosure.

The Future

In the course of my investigations, I encountered what I feel is a credible account concerning a senior U.S. Air Force officer who had held a high-level command position at NORAD's Cheyenne Mountain facility some time ago. It so happened that I was friends with a relation of this man. Through various hints and indirect references to family and relations, this senior officer seemed to know a great deal about UFOs. On one occasion, I was told, he let his guard down. He was in a small fishing boat with the older brother of my friend, when the young man raised the topic of UFOs. The officer looked very seriously at him. His only words in reply were: "they are eons and eons beyond us."

This conversation happened some decades ago, and humanity's rapid technological development might now reduce *eons* to mere *centuries*. Still, the story resonates with me, simply because I know the source, as well as a few things about the career of this officer. Consider what eons and eons might mean. After Disclosure, these other beings are still likely to be so far ahead of us that open contact between us and them, open communication of any sort, might well remain inconceivable.

The irony of Disclosure could well be that we will continue to have many unanswered questions about exactly who and what we are dealing with. We will have gotten to a point where we can prove to ourselves openly as a society that they are here, yes. But that is different from being able to grab hold of a live one for open study. Fighting the black budget world would probably offer the most hope on this matter, but it may well take an extended struggle to make that happen, perhaps many years. It is also quite possible that whatever bodies are being held make up only a small piece of the grand puzzle of what constitutes these *Others*. Very likely, the real action after Disclosure will be dealing with issues internal to our own society.

It may well be that at least some of these beings have established a residence on our world. There is certainly reason to believe, gained from countless insider leaks and claims, that there is communication of some sort between them and the black budget community. There are also claims, and good reason to consider, that some of them have insinuated themselves into our society, perhaps even our power structure. Why would that be so illogical? On the contrary, it would seem to be entirely logical. They would know that humanity is on the *fast track*, and that when we get to the point where we might prove to be a genuine annoyance, all the more reason for them to have their own people on the inside. In the post-Disclosure world, this question will be raised more than once. There will be no easy way around it.

Disclosure of the UFO reality will force our civilization to resolve many longstanding challenges and problems. Looking at only a few of these, it is easy to see why secrecy on this matter has been paramount for so long. Uncovering it will be the most revolutionary act in human history.

The Long View

Looking further ahead into the future, we can discern some contours of that distant shore. It will be a world with an open recognition of the presence of other, *alien* intelligences here on Earth, interacting with this planet and humanity. That will be out in the open. Whether *they* will be out in the open is another matter altogether. But its open acknowledgement will be a great spur to our intellectual development. The dominant technologies a century from now will be difficult, perhaps impossible, for us to recognize today. Computing power and artificial intelligence will be orders of magnitude greater.

Human beings themselves are likely to be different in many ways. Placing a value judgement on this is probably pointless. For better or worse, we are on the cusp of a great change. We will see changes not merely to our technological infrastructure, but probably to our own species via gene therapy and other forms of biotech. The basic intelligence of at least a portion of humanity (the very well-to-do) is likely to increase greatly. Envisioning the future in such a world is difficult. In all likelihood, we will still have families, love relationships, and a physical need for food, sleep, and sex. On that basis, we may assume that humans a century from now will share basic traits with us. Yet, how much do we have in common today with a medieval peasant or a paleolithic hunter-gatherer? Certain things, yes, but we also inhabit a vastly different mental universe. It seems likely that our great-great grandchildren, at least some of them, will be that far ahead of us.

Any Disclosure of an ET/UFO reality will accelerate humanity's development in that direction. Ultimately, nothing will stop that development, Disclosure or no. It seems likely, too, that the further and further we move into this bizarre future, the less dramatic and revolutionary UFO Disclosure is likely to be. If it were to happen in, say, 2015, it would bring dramatic upheavals of the kind I have been describing. If it were to happen in 2025, the changes would still be dramatic, but probably less so. By 2050 or 2060, Disclosure will probably be minimally dramatic and disruptive. This is because human society is already going through tremendous, rapid change.

Can it be that there will be no official, government-sanctioned Disclosure? Personally, I think the truth will surface, come what may. Our own path as a society will open that door, regardless of what the political powers have to say about it. That acknowledgement, whenever it comes, whether now or fifty years from now, will still come as a shock.

There is a statement from an American Zen practitioner named Adyashanti. "Enlightenment is a destructive process," he wrote. "It's not about becoming better or happier. Enlightenment is the crumbling away of truth. It's seeing through the façade of pretense. It's the eradication of everything we imagined to be true."[372]

I like this statement and believe it is relevant here. To assume that the truth will make us happy is something that children might believe, but we know better. It is said that the truth will set us free, and the stripping away of illusions can do that. Freedom, however, is difficult. It is not for the timid or weak. Whether any of us desire the kinds of change we are seeing in our world, it is happening nonetheless. Our world will continue to become very different from the world of our grandparents. Indeed, it is already radically different from that of our own childhood. We had better get used to constant change.

Humanity's Destiny

For thousands of years, people have muddled their way through long periods of suffering and small-minded thinking. Occasionally, we made great, sudden strides, followed by long periods of suffering and more small-minded thinking. Yet, there was always something special about us, something undoubtedly that other observant beings noticed. Looking at all the other life forms on Planet Earth, how could they not? Here was a species that, primitive though we were, had potential. The question they have probably been asking ever since is: what kind of potential? *Potential* in a wonderful, fulfilling sense? Or in a threatening, dangerous sense?

Throughout our time on this world, most people have focused their lives on basic survival needs—understandable given the conditions they were born into. Nevertheless, in all times and places, there have always been a few people who shone light into the darkness, who offered a glimpse of our true potential, and hope for what we may become.

---

[372] Adyashanti. *The End of Your World: Uncensored Straight Talk on the Nature of Enlightenment.* Sounds True Audio Learning Course, 2008.

It is worth asking whether or not, in the next century and beyond, the human race will make strides toward achieving such a vision. For no matter who and what the other beings are who inhabit other parts of this galaxy, universe, and multiverse, it remains true that whenever we do encounter them, it will be with the consciousness we bring to the event. We must ask ourselves, what will that be? Ultimately, all of us must live within ourselves, within our mind and thoughts. We are born alone, and alone do we shed our mortal coils. The journey we must make on this ride we call life must be made by each of us, in our own way.

All of which is to say that if we are ever to achieve a relationship of any sort with beings from elsewhere, we will certainly need to raise our mental activity to a degree much higher than we have today. The beings that appear to be here on Earth, interacting with us as they do, have the ability to reach inside our minds in some way. They are telepathic, they are extremely intelligent, they know things far beyond the limits of our small-minded reality. In other words, most of us are not ready for them.

Looking at our society today, at our shallow and toxic mass culture, the gross inadequacy of our formal education institutions, the childish discourse of our politics and culture, I see no major trends that are moving us toward a true higher consciousness on a mass scale. But Disclosure could be the shock that awakens us. After Disclosure, we will see great numbers of people take stock of their lives. They will ask themselves why they have wasted so much of their lives on pointless, petty pursuits. They will set about to make real changes. In other words, Disclosure offers an opportunity for humanity to take charge of its destiny.

That remains the hope. Whereas the final reality may be different, we should always allow ourselves something good to strive for. Emerson understood that "we aim above the mark to hit the mark." The advent of UFO secrecy has twisted and distorted human civilization far away from its natural course. The ending of that secrecy will not guarantee us a perfect result. We may not fix all of our many inequities and problems. But we may at least take the chance to hit nearer the mark.

Conclusion

When assessing the full range of the UFO subject, one is struck by a richness, depth, and profundity that is nothing short of astonishing. Whether we examine it as detectives, philosophers, historians, political analysts, psychologists, intelligence experts, aviation geeks, biologists. astronomers, physicists, cynics, or utopians, we find that the subject simply gets deeper and deeper the further along we go. Two decades ago, I thought I would be able to satisfy my curiosity and "figure things out" after two or three months of checking into it. The next thing I knew, I was pulled in to the most fascinating subject I have ever encountered in my life.

Fascinating, but also frustrating. The field can attract unseemly characters. Some of these are troubled souls, whether from a genuinely anomalous experience or simply the random hauntings of their mind. Others are attention-seekers. Still others are self-appointed referees whose mission appears to be to stand at the sidelines and criticize every researcher who doesn't subscribe to a certain pet theory or fit an idealized vision of what a researcher should be. Yet others are narcissists claiming some amazing gift (meeting with Andromedans, channeling Pleiadians, traveling through time, being a genius, being a super soldier, being an astral ambassador, being chosen by black budget insiders to reveal the truth, *ad infinitum*) who are essentially trying to establish themselves at the head of their own church. It takes a strong stomach to deal with them.

More to the point, however, is the bare fact that so many of our questions cannot be answered easily, or at all. It is due to the inherent difficulty of the topic combined with the obfuscation surrounding it. In other words, the subject of UFOs by itself is hard, and the secrecy doesn't help any.

However, the rewards are plentiful, at least if you put in the effort and ask the right questions. There are a number of subjects in this world that are like crowbars—they help us to pry open the barriers of deception and illusion that encase our minds and our lives. Ufology is an excellent one. By delving into its myriad aspects, we open ourselves up to a new understanding of nearly every aspect of our world. It causes us to ask the obvious existential question: *are we alone in the universe?* It's an important question, but barely scratches the surface of what lies below. As I have tried to show in this book, a proper study of ufology opens up vistas of thought in our politics, science, culture, technology, and more. It forces us to reconsider many of the truisms that underlie our worldview. That is exciting and unsettling. Small wonder that it has always been such a pariah of a topic, despite its deadly seriousness.

Of course, you might reasonably ask, what is the reward in having your worldview shattered? Why endanger your job and community standing? The answer depends on what kind of person you are. Some people are happy with the truths they grew up with. They don't want to be heroes or solve the problems of their world. They want a simple life with a home, job, and family.

Others are driven to dig deeper. They are not satisfied with simplistic answers to important questions, and they believe they have a right to know more. For such people with a deep-seated need for truth, nothing else can satisfy them. Even if they haven't yet realized it, they feel it in their bones. They know by instinct, if not always through books, the great dictum of Socrates: "the unexamined life is not worth living."

Over the years, such people learn that truth is never simple, and never reveals herself without a struggle. They also discover that learning important truths separates them from most of their friends and family. Eventually, they understand this is the price of leadership, and if they are lucky, they grow into their new persona and role. They become leaders who inspire others to find their own paths.

That is what a study of ufology can do for you. It may not answer every question you have, and there will always be unexplored mysteries about it. But that is part of its beauty. The late UFO skeptic, Philip J. Klass, used to talk of the "UFO curse." The curse was that every UFO believer would go to their grave just as mystified about UFOs as they are today. Typical of Klass, the statement betrays a complete misunderstanding of the importance of UFOs. Aside from being factually wrong (researchers have learned a great deal about UFOs in the past many decades), his implication is that studying the greatest mystery of our time offers nothing of value. Such an attitude is shortsighted and foolish.

As we move forward into the 21st century, we may well find that answers continue to elude us, even after a possible Disclosure event. Most likely, there will be things about the nature of reality that will forever be beyond us. This is no reason for despair. We are fortunate indeed who have the opportunity to embark into the seas of the Great Unknown. If given the chance, why shouldn't we make that journey?

Index

3-D printing, 401, 438, 457, 458
9/11, 1, 3, 366, 450, 461
A.D. After Disclosure, iv, xvi, 440, 451, 507
abduction, xv, xvi, 73, 99-100, 218, 263, 291-318, 327, 328, 373-378, 384, 387, 443, 455
abovetopsecret.com, 364
Acuff, Jack, 331, 336
Adak, Alaska, 85
Adamski, George, 321, 322, 388
Adyashanti, 467
Aerial Phenomena Research Organization (APRO), 143, 175, 301, 331-335
Affa, 324-327
Africa, 33, 35, 57, 60, 61, 69, 108, 248, 266, 358
Adobe AfterEffects, 12
Adobe PhotoShop, 12
Air Defense Command, 93
Air Force, 13, 21, 88-90, 93, 94, 97, 111-113, 120, 122, 124, 125, 127-129, 131, 132, 136-142, 144-146, 149-155, 157, 159, 160, 164, 166, 167, 169, 174, 176-179, 182-186, 194, 199, 211, 215, 218, 220, 221, 223-228, 233, 238, 241, 242, 246, 273, 274, 276, 279, 281, 284, 286, 288, 297, 300, 301, 326, 330-333, 335, 336, 342, 349, 357, 359, 374, 386, 411, 412, 450, 464
Air Force Intelligence, 178, 184, 335, 374
Air Force Manual 55-11, 159
Air Force Office of Special Investigation (AFOSI), 335
Air Intelligence Estimates Division, 141
airships, 72-77, 79, 86, 96
Akhenaten, 53
Alaska, 79, 85, 237, 238, 271
Albany, New York, 282
Alcubierre, Miguel, 418-420
Aleutian Islands, 85
Alien Reproduction Vehicle (ARV), 193, 242, 446
alien, xv, 7, 10, 14, 22, 24, 25, 28, 30, 36, 62, 73, 75, 76, 79, 99, 100, 106, 116, 131, 157, 163-165, 169, 170, 180-187, 193, 200, 202, 216, 218, 225, 226, 242, 253, 261-263, 265, 267, 275, 291-295, 297, 299, 300, 302, 305-312, 315-318, 328, 339, 342, 345, 348, 349, 361, 363, 373-377, 384, 388, 392, 423, 434, 443, 446, 454, 456, 460-462, 465
alienscientist.com, 364
Allingham, Cedric, 322
Altshuler, John, 115
Alvarez, Luis, 143
Ancient Aliens, xvi, 28, 44, 47, 68
ancient "nuclear devastation," 50
ancient "wooden bird model," 47
Andreasson, Betty, 305, 306, 378, 391
Andrews, John, 189, 190, 192, 193
Andrus, Walter, 237, 238, 332, 333
Angelucci, Orfeo, 322
Annunaki, 56-59
Anonymous, 441
Antarctica, 38, 39, 196, 200, 201
Antelope Valley, 195, 241
antigravity, xv, 42, 85, 174, 193, 195-197, 205, 407, 408, 411-413, 415
Arab Spring, 439
Arctic Ocean, 287
Area 51, 174, 186, 188, 189, 195, 241, 242, 248, 348, 349, 415, 450
Argentina, 116, 179, 196, 198, 199, 281
Arizona, 86, 132, 152, 170, 172, 173, 273-276, 302, 325, 331
Armed Forces Special Weapons Project, 136
Army Intelligence, 89, 106
Arnold, Kenneth, 69, 87, 89
artificial intelligence, 29, 382, 401, 437, 456, 458, 466
Ascended Masters, 319, 320
Ashtar Command, 294, 395
Associated Press, 120
Astrophysical Journal, 68
Air Technical Intelligence Center (ATIC), 123, 124, 131, 140
Atlantic Ocean, 69, 72, 108, 209, 222
Atlantis, 437
Atrevida, 222
Aurora, Texas, 74
Australia, 36-38, 41, 84, 226, 227, 255, 262-264, 283, 349
australopithecus afarensis, 35

Austrian Air Force, 228
alien autopsy, 182, 183, 268
Avatar, 381
Aviano Air Base, 224
Aviation Week and Space Technology, 188
ayahuasca, 451
Aylmer Lake, 79
Azores Islands, 97
Aztec, 170-172
B-2 stealth bomber, 188, 413
Baalbek, 46
Bacon, Francis, 437
Bailey, Alice, 320, 368
Banner, F.W. 69
Barnes, Harry, 92
Barrier Canyon, 37
Barwood, Francis, 275
Bashar, 294
Basterfield, Keith, 84
Battle of Los Angeles, 80, 83, 123
Bearden, Tom, 416
Bedell Smith, Walter, 142
Belgium, 95, 246, 247, 362
Belgian Congo, 91
Bergier, Jacques, 51
Berkner, Lloyd, 144
Bernstein, Carl, 203
Bethurum, Truman, 322
Biefeld, Paul, 409
Biefeld-Brown effect, 410-411
Big Black Delta, 277
Bigelow, Robert, 336
Bilderberg Group, 152, 345, 348, 450
Bing, 351
biowarfare, 454
black budget, 14, 19, 25, 189, 203, 204, 206, 207, 209, 280, 314, 392, 442, 445, 446, 454, 456, 459, 460, 465, 470
black helicopters, 217, 300
Black Manta, TR-3A/B, 277
Blanchard, William, 166, 168
Blavatsky, Helena 318, 328, 368
Blumrich, Josef, 54-55
Boas, Antonio Villas, 99, 100, 295
Boeing, 113, 238, 239, 259, 260, 276, 277
Bohemian Grove, 345
Bolender, Carroll, 159
Bolivia, 44, 179, 180, 196, 208, 226
Bragalia, Anthony, 110

Brazel, Mac, 165, 166
Brazil, 94, 100, 174, 224, 225, 237, 248, 267
breakaway civilization, 19, 121, 162, 202, 204-207, 247, 280, 315, 388, 442, 456, 459
Brickner, Stephen, 84
Briggs, Katharine, 63
British intelligence, 85, 120
Brown, Harold, 152
Brown, Thomas Townsend 202, 409-411
Brussino, Franco, 52
Bryan, Joseph, 331, 336
Buddha, 453
Buddhism, 28, 452
Buffalo, New York 180
Bulebush, Bill, 178
Burroughs, John, 230
Bush, George H. W., 223, 349
Bush, George W., 286
Bush, Vannevar, 185
Bustinza, Adrian, 231
Byrd, Richard, 200
Cahill, Kelly, 264, 265, 270
Cahn, J. P. 170, 172
California, 72, 83, 88, 89, 110, 138, 179, 187, 195, 241, 261, 321
Callahan, John, 238
Cameron, Grant, 185
Canada, 94, 114, 177, 178, 219, 271-273, 296
Canadian Navy, 114
Canary Islands, 108, 222
Carey, Tom, 168
Cash, Betty, 232
Clamar, Aphrodite, 307
Carter, Jimmy, 135, 343
Cash-Landrum Incident, 231-232
Casimir, Hendrick, 420
Cassidy, Kerry, 355
Cavitt, Sheridan, 166
CBS, 151, 354
Canadian Forces Base (CFB) Kingston
Canadian Forces Station (CFS) Alert, 287-288
cellular phones, 370, 408
Central Intelligence Agency (CIA), 91, 94, 120, 132, 133, 141-144, 146, 148, 149, 153, 160, 198, 203, 223, 227, 238, 335, 336, 338, 347, 374, 445, 461,

Index

Chadwell, H. Marshall, 142, 144
Chalker, Bill, 263, 264
Challender, Jeff, 258
channeling, xvi, 49, 64, 292, 318, 320, 324, 327, 376, 393-396, 470
chemtrails, 1, 450
Cheyenne Mountain, 464
Chicago Tribune, 285
Chile, 200, 227, 228, 254
China, 11, 33, 41, 78, 227, 242, 248, 263, 353, 439, 459
Christianity, 28, 62, 63, 319, 324, 362, 452, 453
Clark, Jerome, 117, 325, 332
clean energy (see free energy)
Counter Intelligence Corps (CIC), 182, 332
Civilian Saucer Investigations (CSI), 143-144
Close Encounters of the Third Kind, 225
CNI, 350
coal, 27, 446, 448
Cocklin, Howard, 92-93, 140
Cointelpro, 337
cold fusion, 29
Cold War, 2, 86, 121, 133, 163, 165, 195, 338, 349
Collins, Robert, 350
Colovito, Jason, 51
Comcast, 354
Comet Elenin, 356
Comet ISON, 132, 169, 326, 356
Committee for the Scientific Investigation of Claims of the Paranormal (CSICOP), 238
Communion, 375
Condon, Edward U. 154-157, 330
Condon Committee, 21, 150, 152, 154-158, 211, 330, 334, 339
Congress, 25, 147, 148, 152, 156, 165, 168, 169, 203, 207, 331
Congress for Cultural Freedom, 338
Connecticut, 233
consciousness, xv, 4, 30, 225, 262, 294, 309, 310, 316, 317, 319, 320, 323, 327-329, 377, 394, 397, 399, 402-404, 427, 429, 432-434, 454-456, 468
Constantine, 62, 63
Contact: The Phoenix Project, 362
contactee, 323, 390, 394

Cook, Nick, 85, 195-197, 201
Cooper, William, 346-348
Copernicus, 33, 57
cover-up, iv, xvi, 3, 24-26, 31, 87, 119, 123, 146, 147, 153, 155, 160, 175, 202, 209, 210, 218, 222, 227, 229, 240, 290, 336, 337, 342, 345, 347, 348, 412, 413, 444, 450, 459
Coyne, Lawrence, 215, 216
Craig, Roger, 155
Crain, T. Scott, 185
crash, 24, 88, 89, 101-105, 126-128, 165, 170-182, 184, 185, 187, 190, 204, 226, 341, 342, 344
Crawford, Robert, 85
creatures, 22, 34, 47, 54, 64, 95, 182, 231, 265, 268, 304, 306, 314, 339, 381-384, 449, 456
Cronkite, Walter, 151
crop circles, 399
Crowley, Aleister, 318, 369
Cruiser Tromp, 84
Cruttwell, Norman, 98, 99
culture, 2, 4, 8, 22, 30, 31, 33, 46, 87, 118, 122, 164, 319, 320, 323, 331, 352, 366, 377, 439, 444, 452, 468, 471
Curtin, Major, 168
Dalnegorsk, Russia, 181, 243
Darwin, Charles, 33
Davenport, Peter, 269
Davies, Paul, 425
debunker, 10, 19, 204
December 21, 2012, 320, 368, 369
Defense Intelligence Agency (DIA), 223
Defense Satellite Program (DSP), 236
Delarof, 85, 86
Delphos, Kansas, 211-214
Department of Homeland Security (DHS), 439
Descartes, Rene, 437
Deuley, Thomas, 332
Dewilde, Marius, 95
Dibitonto, Giorgio, 323
Dickinson, Rod, 253
Dilletoso, James, 275
dimensions, xv, xvii, 4, 30, 292, 308, 340, 395, 396, 420-423, 426, 451
dinosaurs, 34, 426
Disclosure, iv, xvi, 5, 24, 28, 29, 32, 138, 151, 164, 181, 194, 226, 238,

349, 350, 356, 436, 440-442, 444-449, 451-454, 456, 458-460, 462-466, 468, 472, 507
Disney, 30, 143, 354
DMT, 451
DNA, 263, 264, 380, 383, 396, 398, 454
Doolittle, James, 120, 122, 123
Doty, Richard, 335, 342, 343
double slit experiment, 430, 432
Drioton, Étienne, 52
drones, xvi, 10, 11, 14, 440, 457
Druffel, Ann, 110
Dunning, Brian, 45
Easter Island, 55, 56
EBE, 174
Ecker, Donald, 347
Ecuador, 208
Edison, Thomas, 75
Eglin Air Force Base, 221
Egypt, 33, 41, 42, 47, 51, 53, 54, 66, 340
Einstein, Albert, 366, 410, 417, 419, 422, 424, 427, 428
Eisenhower, Dwight, 326, 346
El Mercurio, 200, 201
electrogravitics, 205, 408-413, 416, 455
electronic stimulation of the brain (ESB), 374
Element 115, 415
Elohim, 61, 62
Emerson, Ralph Waldo, 468
England, 63, 66, 77, 253
English, Bill, 346
entanglement, xvii, 3, 366, 427, 428, 432, 433
Estimate of the Situation, 131, 133, 232, 279
ETH, 123, 132, 318, 322, 338-341, 374
Evans, Hilary, 340
Exempt from Disclosure, 350
Exodus, 54
Exon, Arthur, 124
Extraterrestrial Hypothesis (ETH), 123, 132, 144, 318, 338
Ezekiel, 28, 54, 55, 62
Facebook, 3, 4, 41, 352, 353, 356, 360, 437
Fahrney, Delmar, 146, 147
false flag, 460-462
Farrell, Joseph, 120, 121, 195, 197, 199, 201
fascism, 32, 459, 460, 463
Federal Bureau of Investigation (FBI), 106, 123, 135, 136, 144, 167, 168, 171, 282
Federal Aviation Administration (FAA), 235, 238, 285, 286
Federal Reserve Bank, 450
Figel, Walter, 113
Filer, George, 225, 226, 350
Filer's Files, 350
financial, 1, 27, 75, 160, 164, 199, 208-210, 336, 398, 413, 446, 450, 461, 463
Fire in the Sky, 218, 302, 305
Fitts, Catherine Austin, 207, 209
Florida, 221, 239, 241, 251
flying saucers, 10, 88, 90, 100, 101, 109, 117, 124, 145, 146, 164, 166, 167, 175, 185, 193, 196, 197, 199, 200, 224, 228, 232, 244, 245, 253, 298, 299, 414
Fontes, Olavo, 100, 175
foo fighters, 71, 80, 85, 120-123, 196
Ford, Gerald R., 151, 223
Forrestal, James, 24, 133-135
Fort, Charles, 67, 144
Fort Dix, 225
Fort Ritchie, 221
Fortean Times, 340
Fourth Army, 136
Fowler, Raymond, 172, 173, 306, 391
Fox Lake, Yukon, 271
France, 86, 94-96, 107, 116, 259, 340
free energy, 29, 164, 198, 409, 416, 445, 447-449, 457
Freedom of Information Act (FOIA), 91, 135, 171, 216, 224, 218, 285, 341, 342
Freedom Ridge, 242
French Academy of Sciences, 116
Friedman, Stanton, 88, 166, 168, 184, 342, 416
Friend, Robert, 326
Friendship Case, 389-391
fringe science, 405, 406
Frye, Daniel, 322
Fuller, John, 298
F-117A stealth fighter, 130, 189
Galactic Federation, 30, 320
Galileo, 34, 437
Gardiner, Alan, 52

Index

Hall, Alan, 336
General Accounting Office (GAO), 168, 169
Gatto, John Taylor, 19, 20
General Electric (GE), 354
GeBauer, Leo, 170-172
Gehlen, Reinhard, 198
GEIPAN, 277
genetics, 34, 438, 454
Geophysical Institute at Bergen, 108
Germany, 64, 84-86, 94, 120-122, 127, 195, 197, 200, 243, 247, 259
Gervase of Tilbury, 63
Ghana Air Force, 238
ghost rockets, 87
Gibson, Chris, 276
Gill, William Booth, 97-99
Glaser, Hans, 64
Glimpses of Other Realities, 381
Globalization, 463
Gobekli Tepe, 43
Goddard Air Force Base, 128
Gödel, Kurt, 424, 428
Goethe, Wolfgang, 463
Goldwater, Barry, 186
Goodall, James, 188, 192
Google, 4, 138, 348, 351, 361, 363
Google Earth, 348
Gorbachev, Mikhail, 242
Gordon, Stan, 177, 178, 232, 282
Grays, 22, 270, 308, 318, 377, 379-384, 388, 391, 392
Great Firewall, 439
Great Pyramid, 40-43, 55, 56
Greece, 33, 86, 87
Green Fireballs, 89
Greene, Brian, 421, 422
Greenland, 287
Greer, Steven, 181
Greer, William, 347
Groom Lake, 188, 189, 195, 242, 415
Guadalcanal, 84
Guam, 89
Gulf Breeze, Florida, 239-241, 251, 252
Haines, Richard, 232
Haisch, Bernard, 412
Hall, Richard, 225, 336
Halt, Charles, 119, 229, 230
Hancock, Graham, 38
Hanford Atomic Energy Commission, 90, 136

Hapgood, Charles, 39
Hard Copy, 242
Harmon Field, 89
Harzan, Jan, 191, 359
Hastings, Robert, 113
Hatshepsut, 53
Hawaii, 102, 138
Hawkins, Mike, 251
Heflin, Rex, 110, 111
Heine, Johan, 60
Heisenberg Uncertainty Principle, 433
Heiser, Michael, 59, 62
helicopter, 93, 94, 215, 216, 219, 220, 232, 254, 288, 289
Hessdalen, Norway, 236, 237
Hickson, Charles, 214, 215
Hill, Betty and Barney, xiv, 101, 106, 295-299, 302
Hill, Paul, 406-408
Hillenkoetter, Roscoe, 146-149, 335
Hind, Cynthia, 266
Hinduism, 452
Holloman Air Force Base, 300
homo erectus, 35, 57
Hoopes, John, 46
Hopkins, Budd, 294, 307, 308, 311, 312, 315, 345, 384, 387
Houston, British Columbia, 280
Hudson Valley, New York, 232-236, 275, 280
humanoid, 23, 94, 101, 106, 114, 172, 182, 183, 225, 262, 298, 301, 339, 383
Hungary, 252
hybrid, 22, 100, 309, 310, 379, 380, 443
Hynek, J. Allen, 99, 129, 149-153, 156, 215, 332, 333
hypnosis, 265, 299, 301, 310-312, 318
Icke, David, 392
Institute for Defense Analyses, (IDA), 185
Illinois, 74, 278
Illuminati, 345, 348
implants, 291, 309-316, 328, 378, 380, 382
Indian Point Nuclear Facility, 234, 235
Indian Springs AFB, 173
Indonesia, 41, 208
insectoid, 23, 383
Institute of Noetic Sciences, 432
intelligence community, 3, 21, 142,

477

144, 145, 191, 204, 210, 332, 333, 335-337, 349, 360, 367, 442-444, 459, 461, 462
Interavia, 188, 410, 411
Internet, 52, 228, 305, 344-346, 350, 351, 360, 361, 368, 370, 395, 413, 437, 439, 456
Internet Search by Date, 362-363
Islam, 452, 453
Israelites, 28
Italy, 41, 94, 224, 389
J. Allen Hynek Center for UFO Studies (CUFOS), 332, 333, 337
J-Rod, 174
Jacobs, David, 308-311, 315, 379, 387, 443
JANAP-146, 159
Jane's Defense Weekly, 188
Jasek, Martin, 272
Jasons, 348
Jawesta, 108
Jessup, Morris, 54
Jesus Christ, 28, 62, 306, 361, 453
Jet Propulsion Laboratory, 191, 235
Jinn, 452
Johnson, Kelly, 193
Johnson, Ronald, 211
Johnston Island Atoll, 102
Joint Chiefs of Staff, 94, 229, 247
Journal of Scientific Exploration, 110
journalism, 73, 138, 145, 158, 170-172, 174 188, 189, 203, 244, 298, 348, 353, 354, 445, 461
Judaism, 452, 453
Kaku, Michio, 414, 421, 422, 425, 427, 428, 432
Kammler, Hans, 196, 201
Kasputin Yar, 243, 244
Kecksburg, Pennsylvania, 176-179
Keel, John, 339, 340
Keller, Tom, 191
Kellerman, Roy, 347
Kelson, Eric, 110
Kennedy, John, xiii, 152, 261, 347
Keyhoe, Donald, 131, 139, 146-148, 160, 297, 331, 336
KGB, 243-245, 374
Khoury, Peter, 262-264, 270, 295
Kimball, Dan, 138
Kingman, Arizona, 172-174
Kirtland Air Force Base, 90, 136
Kissinger, Henry, 223

Klarer, Elizabeth. 322
Klass, Philip, 99, 238, 472
Knapp, George, 189, 348, 349
Knight, J. Z., 396
Knowles, Herbert, 325, 462
Knox, Frank, 82
Kosina, Lajos, 252
Kucinich, Dennis, 444
Kurzweil, Ray, 438, 456
Kuwait, 227
La Très Sainte Trinosophie, 390
Lake Ontario, 180
Landry, Robert, 132, 133
large stone spheres, 45
Larsen, Junius, 326-327
Larsen, Sherman, 182, 332
Las Vegas, 175, 176, 189, 348, 386
LaViolette, Paul, 409, 412, 413
Lazar, Robert, 189, 348, 349, 355, 414, 415, 419
Lear, John, 346, 347
Ledger, Don, 114
Leir, Roger, 268, 289, 312-314
LeMay, Curtis, 186-188
Leonard, R. Cedric, 52, 53
Life Magazine, 109, 124, 137, 138
LaPaz, Lincoln, 89
Lima, Otávio Moreira, 237
Lindbergh, Charles, 146
Lockheed, 192, 193
Lorenzen, 100, 107, 175, 301, 302, 331, 333
Lorenzen, Coral, 301, 331, 333
Loring Air Force Base, 218, 221
Los Alamos, New Mexico, 89, 135, 136, 141, 312
Lovelock, James, 18
Low, Robert, 155
Luftwaffe, 121
Luke Air Force Base, 176, 273, 274
Lundahl, Arthur, 326
Maccabee, Bruce, 83, 274, 282
Mack, John, 266, 267, 307, 315-317
Magonia, 63
Magonia Magazine, 340
Passport to Magonia, 63
Maine, 114, 218, 325
Majestic Documents (see MJ-12)
Majic Eyes Only, 165
Malmstrom Air Force Base, 112, 113, 220, 221, 246
Maltsev, Igor, 245

Index

Manhattan Project, 87
Manning, Bradley, 441
Mansfield, Ohio, 215, 216
Mantell, Thomas, 128, 129
Marcel, Jesse, 88, 166, 167
Marciniak, Barbara, 395, 396
Marines, 80, 174, 183, 287, 289, 414
Marshall, George, 81
Maryland, 9, 221
Maryland Air National Guard, 274
Masse, Maurice, 107, 108
Maxwell Air Force Base, 93
Mayan, 49, 56, 250, 320
McCandlish, Mark, 193, 194
McDonald, Bill, 192
McDonald, James 86, 152, 153, 155, 156, 160
McGuire Air Force Base, 225
McMinnville, Oregon, 90, 157
McRoberts, Hannah, 232-233
media, 82, 122, 124, 134, 143, 145, 150, 158, 167, 169, 178, 194, 203, 210, 229, 271, 273-275, 279, 284, 285, 296, 321, 337, 338, 351, 354, 359, 443, 444, 461
Mediterranean Sea, 68
Meiwald, Fred, 112, 113
Menger, Howard and Connie, 322
Menzel, Donald, 10-12, 99, 204
Methorst, William, 84
Mexican Air Force, 284
Mexico, 88, 89, 106, 109. 124, 131, 136, 166, 168-171, 184, 221, 250, 251, 281, 282, 284, 300, 312, 342, 349
Michigan, 150, 151, 177, 220
Middle East, 94, 248, 358, 446
military, 2, 3, 8-11, 18, 21, 24, 26, 62, 81, 82, 84, 88, 89, 91, 93, 94, 111, 112, 114, 118, 119, 123-125, 128-130, 133, 135-137, 142-147, 153, 160, 162-165, 169, 170, 174, 175, 178, 180, 181, 183, 186, 195, 199, 200, 202, 217, 218, 220, 222, 225-229, 231, 236-238, 241-243, 245, 247, 250, 267, 268, 271, 274, 279-281, 284-287, 297, 314, 325, 331-333, 335, 341, 342, 374, 375, 392, 413, 460, 461
Minot Air Force Base, 111, 112
Missing Time, 294, 307
Mitchell, Edgar, 194, 432

MJ-12, 185, 335, 343, 348, 454
Mohammed, 453
Monast, Serge, 361, 362, 462
Moody, Charles, 300-302
Moore, William, 168, 199, 335, 342, 343
Mormonism, 452
Moses, 28, 54, 453
Mosier, Alex, 313, 314
Mothman, 339
Moulton Howe, Linda, 171, 343
MSNBC, 354
multiverse, 421, 422, 468
Muroc Army Airfield, 88
Murphy, John, 177-179
Museum of Natural History, 34
mutilation, 115, 300
Mutual UFO Network (MUFON), 14, 75, 191, 283, 286, 332-334, 336, 337, 357-360, 370
Naga, 61
nanotechnology, 29, 401, 438, 456
National Aviation Reporting Center on Anomalous Phenomena (NARCAP), 285
National Aeronautics and Space Administration (NASA), 54, 121, 178, 191, 232, 255, 256, 258, 276, 343, 406, 413, 462
National Academy of Sciences, 158
National Guard, 219, 235, 274
National Investigations Committee on Aerial Phenomena (NICAP), 144, 147, 148, 152, 159, 160, 297, 331-333, 335-337
National Photographic Interpretation Center (NPIC), 326
National Press Club, 113, 312, 313
National Public Radio, 443
National Security Agency (NSA), 94, 204-206 208, 332, 343, 349
National UFO Reporting Center, 9, 249, 260, 269, 273, 280, 281, 285, 351, 356
natural gas, 27, 446, 448
Navy, 76, 82-84, 101, 103-105, 114, 129, 138, 146, 183, 200, 222, 325, 326, 332, 335, 336, 347
Nazca, 55, 56
Nazi, 121, 123, 127, 195-201
NBC Universal, 354
near-miss, 259, 260

Neasham, Robert, 326
Nebraska, 299
Nellis Air Force Base, 176
Nellis bombing range, 348
Nephilim, 58
Neumann, John von, 185
Nevada, 102, 175, 176, 188, 195, 241, 273, 348
Nevada Test Site, 102, 195
new age, 28, 293, 318-320, 324, 366, 368, 394-396, 452, 454
New Guinea, 97-99
New Hampshire, 101, 295, 296
New Jersey, 137, 184, 225, 233, 261
New Mexico, 88, 89, 106, 124, 131, 136, 166, 168-171, 184, 221, 281, 282, 300, 312, 342, 349
New World Order, xv, 361
New York, 34, 49, 67, 74, 77, 85, 116, 120, 124, 137, 140, 145, 147, 155, 175, 180, 233, 236, 243, 261, 282, 366, 409, 507
New York Times, xiv, 77, 85, 116, 120, 124, 137, 140, 145, 147
Newfoundland, Canada, 94
News Corporation, 354
newspapers, 72, 110, 119, 122, 145, 149, 203, 216, 354
Newton, Isaac, 34, 417, 424, 437
Newton, Silas, 170, 172
Nibiru, 57, 58, 368
Ning Li, 412
Nixon, Richard, 192, 336
Nixon, Stuart, 336
non-locality, 3, 366, 368, 398
nordic aliens, 22, 376, 392
North American Air Defense (NORAD), 110, 220, 267
North Atlantic Treaty Organization (NATO), 224, 246
North Dakota, 111, 112
Northrop Grumman, 11
Northwest Territories, Canada, 79-80, 341
Norton, Lord Hill, 231
Nova Scotia, Canada, 114
nuclear technology, 29, 50, 51, 89, 90, 92, 101, 102, 105, 113, 126, 163, 183, 218, 230, 234, 235, 287, 289, 321, 323, 380, 383, 395, 414-416, 446, 460
National UFO Reporting Center (NUFORC), 260, 269, 356, 357
O'Hare Airport, 284, 285
Oak Ridge, Tennessee, 93, 141
Oberg, James, 178, 222, 257
Occupy Movement, 449
Odom, Charles, 84
Office of Naval Intelligence (ONI), 325-326
Office of Strategic Services (OSS), 120
Ohio, 41, 112, 123, 170, 177, 215, 216
oil (see petroleum)
Okinawa, Japan, 374
Omni, 178, 222
Ontario, 180, 279
Operation Dominic, 101-106
Operation Highjump, 200-201
Operation Windmill, 201
Oz Factor, 403
Pacific Ocean, 77, 82, 85, 89, 101, 102, 104, 105, 122, 210
Pakal, 56
Pauwels, Louis, 51
Project Blue Beam, 98, 108, 305, 356, 361, 362, 461, 462
Project Blue Book, 13, 97, 107, 125, 137-139, 144-146, 149, 150, 152-154, 157, 159, 160, 164, 176, 178, 183, 211, 326, 330, 332, 333, 357, 359
Project Mogul, 124, 169
Project Moon Dust, 178, 180
Project Paperclip, 196, 198
Papoose Lake, Nevada, 348
Papua, New Guinea, 97-99
Paranet, 345, 346
Parker, Calvin, 214-215
Pascagoula Incident, 214-215
Pech Merle, France, 35, 36
Penniston, James, 230
Pennsylvania, 176, 177, 232, 282, 385, 387
Pentagon, 107, 125, 137-139, 141, 168, 169, 185
Perkins, John, 207-208
Peron, Juan, 199
Peruvian Air Force, 228
petroleum, 26, 27, 29, 74, 163-165, 170, 205, 276, 299, 437, 445-448, 463
Pflock, Karl, 336
Phillips, Ted, 212
Philosophical Transactions, 66, 67

Index

Phoenix Lights, 273-274
Pine Gap, Australia, 349
Piri Reis map, 38, 39, 55
Pleiadians, 294, 395, 396, 470
Podkletnov, Yevgeny 409, 412
police, 97, 106, 108, 150, 171, 174, 177, 179, 212, 214, 216, 217, 221, 226, 233, 234, 246, 254, 273, 278, 281, 299, 303, 312, 347, 366, 440, 450, 457, 461, 462
Prague flying saucer, 197
pre-Columbian gold trinket, 47
Proceedings of the London Royal Society, 67
Project Aquarius, 174
Project Camelot, 355
Project Grudge, 137
Project Sign, 127, 128, 131, 132, 137
propulsion, xvi, 126, 163, 174, 191, 197, 235, 259, 348, 403, 406-408, 411-413, 434, 446
pseudoscience, 405-406
Pumapunku, Bolivia, 44-45
Puthoff, Harold, 407, 408, 412
pyramids, 40, 41, 43, 55, 56, 306, 448
Qabala, 452
quantum computing, 29, 401, 438, 457, 459
quantum mechanics, 3, 34, 433
Quintanilla, Hector, 107, 152
Rachewiltz, Boris de, 52
Radford, Arthur, 138
Radin, Dean, 432
Raechel's Eyes, 380
RAF Bentwaters, 229-232
RAF Lakenheath, 157
Ramey, Roger, 140, 141, 167, 168
Ramsey, Scott and Suzanne, 171
Ramtha, 396, 397
RAND Corporation, 332
Randle, Kevin, 131, 168, 176
Rational Wiki, 361
RB-47, 94
Regehr, Ron, 235-236
regression, 215, 295, 297, 299, 307, 308, 310, 311, 373
religion, 2, 8, 27, 324, 365, 451-453
remote viewing, 367, 394, 432, 433, 455, 456
Rendlesham Forest, UK, 229-230
Reptilians, 23, 383, 392, 396
Reverse Image Search, 363

Rich, Ben, 189-193
Rickett, Lewis, 166
Riedel, Walther, 144
Robbins, Peter, 229, 230
Robertson, H. P., 143
Robertson Panel, 143, 146, 151, 153, 160, 333, 335
Roboziero, Russia, 65
Rochefort, Nicolas de, 335
Roddenberry, Gene, 361
Roerich, Helena Ivanovna, 328
Roerich, Nicholas, 77-78, 328
Romansky, Jim, 177, 178
Rone, Finn, 201
Roosevelt, Franklin, 81
Roswell, New Mexico, 24, 74, 88, 89, 119, 121, 123, 124, 127, 128, 131, 141, 165-171, 173, 176, 181, 187, 195, 199, 204, 205, 243, 268, 342, 343
Roswell Daily Record, 166, 167
Rowlands, Sharon, 258
Ruppelt, Edward, 124, 131, 137-139, 142, 144, 146, 148, 149, 164
Russell, Bertrand, 19
Russia, 65, 66, 122, 124, 137, 146, 196, 201, 243, 244, 272, 341, 386, 459
Ruwa, Zimbabwe, 266
Ryan, Bill, 355
Sagan, Carl, 156
Salas, Robert, 112, 113
Samford, John, 139, 140
San Luis Valley, Colorado, 115
Sanderson, Ivan, 15-17, 384
Santorini, Paul, 87, 123
Sarbacher, Robert, 184, 185
Saunders, David, 154
Schauberger, Viktor, 196, 197
Schiff, Steven, 168, 169
Schirmer, Herbert, 299, 300
Schmitt, Donald, 168, 173
Schoch, Robert, 42
Schofield, Frank, 77
Schulgen, George, 125-127, 199
Schweinfurt, Germany, 120
Scientific Study of Unidentified Flying Objects, 330
scientific ufology, 334, 344, 345, 358, 370
Scott Air Force Base, 279
Scully, Frank, 170, 172

Searl, John, 416
Seattle, Washington, 85, 277
Second World War, 18, 80, 86, 108, 127, 143, 162, 195, 196, 203
Secret Life, 308-310
Sego Canyon, Utah, 38
Selfridge Air Force Base, 150
Shag Harbor, Canada, 114, 115
Sheldrake, Rupert, 433, 434
Shining Ones, 61, 62
Sight Unseen, 312, 384
Simon, Benjamin, 101, 295, 297, 298
singularity, 424, 456, 458
Sitchin, Zecharia, 56-61
Situation Red: The UFO Siege, 181
skeptics, 14, 23, 60, 84, 91, 99, 100, 126, 132, 168, 177, 222, 238, 240, 244, 265, 273, 284, 290, 295, 304, 311, 316, 326, 331, 333, 341, 346, 361, 364, 365, 369, 373, 374, 388, 393, 394, 408, 437, 445, 452, 454, 462, 472
Skunk Works, 189, 190, 192, 193
Skyhook balloons, 129, 137, 142
Smith, Wilbert, 184
Snowden, Edward, 207, 441
Sorensen, Brad, 193
South America, 47, 69, 94, 114, 115, 196, 224, 377
Soviet Union, 86, 87, 102, 114, 123, 125, 136, 143, 163, 178, 181, 195, 200, 242-245, 248
spacetime, 392, 394, 403, 404, 408, 415, 417, 419, 420, 425
Spain, 73, 109, 216
Sphinx, 42, 43
Spielberg, Steven, 225
Sprinkle, Leo, 299, 300
SR-71 Blackbird, 186
St. Germain, Count, 389-391
Star Trek, 30, 100, 188, 270, 361, 419, 462
Star Wars, 30, 188
stealth bomber, 188, 246
stealth fighter, 130, 189, 190, 246
Steinman, William, 184-186
Stephenville, Texas, 285-287
Stewart Air Force Base, 234
Stiglitz, Joseph, 207-209
Strategic Air Command (SAC), 111, 220
Strieber, Whitley, 375

String theory, 421-423
Stringfield, Leonard, 173, 181-184, 225, 226, 332, 342
Stuart, Mark, 260
Styles, Chris, 114
submarine, 102, 114
Swan, Frances, 325-326
Sweden, 86, 122, 318
Swedenborg, Immanuel, 318
Swords, Michael, 131, 144
Symington, Fife, 275
S-4, 174, 189, 348, 349, 415
Tehran, Iran, 223, 224
telepathy, 240, 290, 292, 298, 299, 301, 305, 306, 309, 316, 318, 321, 323, 324, 326-328, 367, 368, 376, 378, 385, 387, 388, 395, 398, 404, 432, 455, 468
Tellinger, Michael, 60
Terauchi, Kenju, 238
Tesla, Nikola, 202, 409, 410, 413
Tether Incident, 255, 257, 258
Texas, 74, 75, 166, 167, 231, 260, 280, 285-287, 332
The Addams Family, 386
The Bell, 121, 195, 197
The Black Vault, 351
The Matrix, 5, 370
The Men Who Stare at Goats, 367
The Mothman Prophecies, 339
The Pirate Bay, 458
The Pope, 321, 322
The Threat, 275, 293, 310, 462, 463
theosophy, 318-321, 323, 327, 328, 368
Thompson, Richard, 61
Thule Air Base, 287
Thutmose III, 52, 53, 66
Tibet, 61, 77, 78, 320, 328
Tikaboo Peak, Nevada, 242
time travel, xv, 197, 424-427
Time Warner, 354
Timor Sea, 84
TinEye, 363
Trainor, Joseph, 281, 350
Trans-en-Provence, France, 232
Trent UFO Photo, 90-91
Tretyak, Ivan, 245
triangular UFOs, 188, 232, 234, 246, 247, 260, 275-282, 462
Truman, Harry, 24, 132, 133, 142, 144, 162, 164, 202

Index

Tuella, 395
Tulagi, Solomon Islands, 84
Tulli Papyrus, 52-53
Tulsa, Oklahoma, 109
Turkey, 43, 289-290
Tutankhamun, 53
Twining, Nathan, 125-127, 199
Ubatuba, Brazil, 174
UFO Hunters, 75
UFO Roundup, 350
ufology, xii, 2, 3, 5, 19, 20, 264, 330-334, 337, 341, 342, 344, 345, 348, 349, 358, 365-370, 372, 373, 376, 386, 395, 418, 426, 434, 471, 472
UFOs and the National Security State, xvi, 124
Uhouse, Bill, 174
Unconventional Flying Objects: A Scientific Study, 406
United Airlines, 284
United Kingdom, 19, 33, 63, 85, 94, 120, 157, 201, 229, 231, 257, 259-261, 283, 321, 340, 392
United Nations, 163, 216
United Press International (UPI), 110
University of Colorado, 21, 150, 154, 155, 211, 330
University of Wales, 419
Unidentified Submersible Objects (USO), 103, 104
USS Finch, 101
USS Supply, 76
VA-243, 57-59
Vaimanika Shastra, 49, 50
Valensole, France, 107
Valentich, Frederick, 116, 226, 227
Valleé, Jacques, 95, 232, 243-245, 339
Valley, Alabama, 252
Valone, Thomas, 409, 412, 413, 416
Van Tassell, George, 322, 395
Vandenberg, Hoyt, 131
Varginha, Brazil, 180, 267, 268, 270
Vatican, 52, 321, 322, 452
Venezuela, 94, 108
Venus, 11, 12, 99, 128, 129, 274, 321
Vesco, Renato, 196
Viacom, 354
video, 11, 12, 58, 99, 102, 188, 192, 195, 235, 241, 242, 250-253, 256-258, 264, 266, 274, 275, 281-284, 289, 290, 347, 352, 364, 370, 409, 414, 421, 425, 428, 432, 434, 441, 463
vimanas, 48-50
Voice of America, 335, 338
Voltaire, 389, 390
von Daniken, Erich, 54-56
Voronezh, Russia, 244
Walker, Eric, 184-186
Walt Disney, 143
Webb, Walter, 260
Walters, Ed, 239-241, 251, 252
Walton, Travis, 218, 302-305
Wandjina, 36, 37
War of the Worlds, 145
Warren, Larry, 229-231
Washington Post, 281
Washington, D.C., 92, 113, 133, 281, 312, 331, 336
Washington (State), 87, 268
Watchers, 61
Weaver, Bill, 178
Wendell Stevens, 301
Werner, Fritz, 173
West, John Anthony, 42
Weygandt, John, 181
whistleblower, 355
White Sands, New Mexico, 243
Wicca, 28
Wikileaks, 441, 442
Wilcox, George, 166
Wilhelm, Charles, 173, 182
Williams, Gordon, 231
Williamson, George Hunt, 325, 327
Wills, Roger, 260
Wood, Robert, 110, 454
Wood, Ryan, 165
World Bank, 208
World Trade Organization, 209
World War Two, 80, 119, 121, 207, 218, 332
wormhole, 425
Wright Field, 123, 124, 167, 168, 170
Wright-Patterson Air Force Base, 112, 124, 127, 152, 153, 174, 179, 182-186, 226, 450
Wurtsmith Air Force Base, 220, 221
X-47, 10, 11
Yahoo, 351
YouTube, 267, 289, 352, 353, 360, 361, 363, 370, 399, 427, 437, 441
Yukon, Canada, 271-273
Zabel, Bryce, 451

Zaire, 362
Zamora, Lonnie, 106, 107
Zapruder Film, 347
Zero Point Energy (ZPE), 29, 415, 416
Zeus, 453

About the Author

Richard Dolan has researched UFOs and related phenomena since the early 1990s. He is the author of the historical series, *UFOs and the National Security State* (volumes one and two), as well as an analysis of the future, *A.D. After Disclosure: When the Government Finally Reveals the Truth About Alien Contact.*

He has appeared widely on radio and television, including *Coast-to-Coast AM*, CNN, The History Channel, SyFy, BBC, and elsewhere. Since 2012, Richard has hosted "The Richard Dolan Show," airing on KGRA Radio.

In his writings and interviews, Richard has analyzed the destruction of our political liberties as a result of the UFO cover-up, the possible nature of the non-humans themselves, what their presence means for our civilization, why he believes the cover-up will end within our lifetime, and what is likely to happen after that.

With the completion of *UFOs for the 21st Century Mind*, Richard plans to complete the third volume of *UFOs and the National Security State*, which will take the history of the UFO reality and cover-up to the present day.

In earlier years, Richard had been a Rhodes Scholar finalist, earned a Bachelor's and Master's degree in History, and received a Certificate in Political Theory at Oxford University. Born in Brooklyn, raised on Long Island, he continues to live in Rochester, New York, where he spent many years raising his family.

Visit his website at *richarddolanpress.com*.

Also by Richard Dolan Press

Grant Cameron and T. Scott Crain, Jr. *UFOs, Area 51, and Government Informants: A Report on Government Involvement in UFO Crash Retrievals.*

Richard M. Dolan, *UFOs and the National Security State: The Cover-Up Exposed, 1973-1991.*

Chase Kloetkze with Richard M. Dolan. *Admissible: The Field Manual for Investigating UFOs, Paranormal Activity, and Strange Creatures.*

Eve Lorgen. *The Dark Side of Cupid: Love Affairs, the Supernatural and Energy Vampirism.*

Philip Mantle. *Once Upon A Missing Time: A Novel of Abduction.*

David Marler. *Triangular UFOs: An Estimate of the Situation.*

Richard Sauder, Ph.D. *Hidden in Plain Sight: Beyond the X-Files.*

Robert M. Wood, Ph.D. *Alien Viruses: Crashed UFOs, MJ-12, & Biowarfare.*

http://richarddolanpress.com

Made in the USA
Lexington, KY
25 February 2014